POLICE: ORGANISATION AND COMMAND

POLICE STUDIES

Police: Organisation and Command

R. S. Bunyard
D.M.S., M.B.I.M., M.I.P.M.
Chief Constable of Essex

MACDONALD AND EVANS

Macdonald and Evans Ltd.,
Estover, Plymouth PL6 7PZ

First published 1978

© R. S. Bunyard 1978

ISBN 0 7121 1671 0

Printed in Great Britain by
Latimer Trend & Company Ltd Plymouth

Foreword

For years it has been true and, to some extent, it is still the case that the student seeking information about the police service would discover that, while much had been written in America about law agencies in the United States, there was not a great deal available in the United Kingdom.

In recent years, however, the opportunities presented by enlightened police authorities, the Home Office and the Police College to serving police officers to widen their educational experience, are bringing about a change in the situation. Further, polytechnics and colleges of further education are increasingly arranging educational courses of value to both police officers and others concerned with the study of crime and criminals.

In an attempt to encourage these developments, it is the intention of Macdonald and Evans to produce a series of books on various aspects of police work under the general title of *Police Studies*. All will be written by experts in their own field, many by experienced serving or retired police officers. The series will prove useful not only to senior and junior police officers who wish to improve their academic status, but also to the practical police officer and to those whose work is in any way connected with criminology.

The police service in the United Kingdom has recently experienced a revolution by way of re-organisation, training methods and use of technical equipment. These changes, involving, for example, a reduction of over 75 per cent in the numbers of independent mainland regular forces to the current figure of 50, have called for a reappraisal of attitudes to organisation and, more particularly, to the principles of command.

Growth and increasing complexity of organisation are presenting a severe challenge to senior police officers to make the best use of the limited resources at their disposal, especially in a period of economic limitation. While scientific and technical equipment are vital to police efficiency, a much more important element is that understanding use should be made of the talents and good will of the men and women in the service.

Mr Bunyard's book helps to crystallise thought on these problems and suggests practical ways of meeting them.

1978   Sir John McKay

Preface

All civilised countries employ a body of people to maintain the rule of law, but a glance at the police forces of other countries quickly reveals widely differing relationships with the society in which they exist. In some countries, the police are military or para-military or may be responsible for functions that would be undertaken here by the judiciary or public control departments of local or national government. In a democratic country, the system of policing is closely linked to national history, the needs of society and the nature and temperament of the people. The study of the way in which the British police service has been shaped by social forces in the past not only helps to explain its present form but also indicates how it may be expected to develop in the face of continuing social change. At the same time, though the exact nature of the British police is peculiar to this country, it is also well worth while making comparisons with police forces in other parts of the world.

Social change not only affects the relationship between police and public, it also influences the attitudes of police personnel towards their work. To cater for the needs of the people within the police and at the same time provide the level of service required by the public, makes heavy demands on police organisations and the men and women who command them. Within one generation of police supervisors there has been a marked decrease in the extent to which supervisors can rely solely on the authority of their rank; the result has been that command by leadership has become more important than ever.

A service that relies on its members using such qualities as initiative, discretion, humanity and common sense requires supervisors who can practise command in such a way that they obtain the full commitment of their subordinates to the aims of the police. At the same time, increased expectations of people in terms of consideration for their welfare needs the active involvement by all supervisory officers in the personnel management of the people under their command. The growth in size and complexity of police forces adds to the need for operational commanders to appreciate the importance of ensuring that all police personnel are given the opportunity to enjoy a worthwhile career and make their best contribution to the police service.

There are, therefore, two areas of professional concern to the modern police officer; the way in which police personnel are commanded within police organisations and the way in which those organisations meet the needs of society. These are the two areas explored by this book.

1978   R. S. Bunyard

Acknowledgments

The preparation of this book would have been impossible without a considerable amount of help and encouragement from many people. That the project was feasible at all was due to the support of Mr Alan Goodson, O.B.E., Q.P.M., LL.B., Chief Constable of Leicestershire, who also kindly permitted the use of material relating to the Leicestershire Constabulary. I am also indebted to Mr C. James Anderton, Q.P.M., F.B.I.M., Chief Constable of Greater Manchester for his part in the initial planning of the book, and to Sir John McKay, C.B.E., Q.P.M., M.A., formerly Her Majesty's Chief Inspector of Constabulary, for supplying the invaluable advice, criticism and experience that helped to shape the final product.

In the preparation of the sections on overseas police forces, my thanks are especially due to Mr Kenneth B. Burnside, O.B.E., Commissioner of the New Zealand National Police, Mr Edward M. Davis, Chief of Police of Los Angeles Police Department, Mr A. A. Russell Q.C., Deputy Solicitor General, Ontario, Miss Jacqueline Blythe of Paris, Herr Herbert Wisniewski formerly of the Berlin Police and Frau Marie Luise Kros of the Bereitschaftspolizei, Bochum, Germany.

On the subject of police research, ready help was forthcoming from Mr R. R. Dewar, Editor of the Home Office *Police Research Bulletin* and Mr Thomas V. Brady, Director of Communications, Police Foundation, Washington D.C. Expert advice on helicopters was provided by Inspector John Saville, Metropolitan Police Helicopter Unit and Air Commodore M. J. Ridgway, Royal Australian Air Force.

I am indebted to the Director of Publishing, H.M. Stationery Office for permission to reproduce extracts from H.M.S.O. publications and to the Commissioner of Police of the Metropolis for permission to draw on material originally written for Metropolitan Police training purposes. Willing assistance was given by Mr Denis Brett, F.L.A., Librarian of the Police College, Bramshill and by many members of the Leicestershire Constabulary, particularly Miss Joyce Tickner who undertook the daunting task of preparing the manuscript for publication and who carried it through with indomitable patience and thoroughness.

To all these people I tender my gratitude for the part they have played in producing this book but at the same time I absolve them from any responsibility for any errors or omissions or for the opinions expressed in the text—these are mine alone.

Contents

Foreword   v
Preface   vii
Acknowledgments   ix
List of illustrations   xii

1. The development of the British police   1
2. Police and government   36
3. Police organisations   62
4. Police objectives   84
5. Manpower requirements   105
6. Policing methods   126
7. Specialist departments   159
8. Making the best use of manpower   171
9. Personnel administration   189
10. Recruiting   196
11. Training   209
12. Personal assessment   226
13. Personnel interviews   247
14. Promotion   277
15. Welfare   289
16. Decision-making   308
17. Leadership   334
18. Delegation   354
19. Personal communication   364

Bibliography   379
Index   383

List of illustrations

1. Proportion of crimes known to the police   29
2. Control   42
3. Metropolitan Police, 1830   63
4. Organisational chart of a British police force   66
5. Headquarters structure of a county force   67
6. Organisation of a police division   71
7. Alternative organisational chart   72
8. Office of Operations Management Team, Los Angeles Police Department   80
9. Measurement of police activity   109
10. Self-reporting cards   112
11. Kansas City Preventive Patrol Experiment   119
12. Organisation of police services   153
13. Specialist departments   161
14. Paper flow chart   180
15. Characteristic chart   243
16. Rank-structure pyramid   279
17. Promotion rate of progress   280
18. Cyclic process of decision-making   309
19. Sources of information   318
20. Communication and control system   328
21. Pattern of delegation   356
22. Communication chain   365
23. Formal committee discussions   374
24. General discussion group   375

Chapter One

The development of the British police

The lessons of police history

The present form of the police service in Britain has been shaped by developments over the past thousand years. Many beliefs that govern policing today have their origins in the past, when the "police" adapted to the demands of society in those times. Only by understanding the nature of these demands and the reaction to them can we understand the relevance of the resultant thinking to modern conditions. The very nature of a police service must be fashioned by the role that it plays in society.

Police history cannot, therefore, be looked at in isolation; it is not enough to know what happened, we must know *why* it happened, in order to relate the response to the needs of the time. The brief account of police history that follows is concerned with the "whys" rather than details of "what" and "when" that may be readily found elsewhere. The principal objective is to relate police history to the social development of the country.

Early policing

The Statute of Winchester 1285 laid down a policing system—much of it borrowed from Saxon times—in which:

1. the responsibility for law and order rested with each citizen, who had to have arms available according to his means;
2. in each town, the citizens had to be prepared to act as watchmen at night to ensure that the gates of the town were closed, to detect and question strangers, and to hand over wrong-doers to the constable in the morning (watch and ward);
3. the constable for the year would be responsible for detaining

wrongdoers and bringing them before a court. He would also be expected to report unlawful activities in his domain —usually on a quarterly basis;

4. felons who escaped capture by the watchmen would be pursued by all the able-bodied men in a "hue and cry" led by the sheriff or other responsible officer;

5. failure to take part on watch, or in a hue and cry, was punishable as a criminal offence;

6. every citizen had not only the right to arrest wrongdoers, but a duty to do so.

Despite its many weaknesses, this system survived with only minor variations until the formation of "modern" police forces in the nineteenth century. One problem which became apparent, almost from the outset, was that of travelling criminals— the forerunners of the villains whose activities necessitated regional crime squads several centuries later. To cope with these, justices of the peace were given the job of overseeing local police arrangements and providing a form of co-ordination.

One factor upon which the success of the early policing system depended was the lack of mobility of the people. Many efforts were made to limit migration, principally to enable the system of poor relief to work; each parish was responsible for the relief of its own poor and a parish would not wish to receive anyone who was likely to become dependent on the rates.

Travel was in any case difficult, for the roads of Britain were poor; in winter, mud made them unusable in many places, whilst in summer, the dried-out ruts made travel uncomfortable, slow and expensive.

One further factor in the survival of the early police system was the nature of employment. Children were employed as soon as they were physically able and the daily period of work for everyone was likely to be over twelve hours, for a minimum of six days a week, leaving little time or energy for mischief. There was no unemployment benefit: people relied on "outdoor" relief, payments from the poor rates that were distributed at the discretion of the justices—an incentive to conform to the law.

These factors enabled the "watch and ward" in towns and the "hue and cry" for catching criminals to work quite effectively, since the system was geared to the type of society of those times.

It would be wrong to suppose that there was no unrest in the country but it was of a local nature and was quelled by the use of the militia or its mounted equivalent, the yeomanry. This part-time army, organised on a local basis by the lord lieutenant of the county, was the principal means of preventing uprisings in Britain and defending the country against invasion in the absence of a standing army. Even when a standing army came into existence following the 1688 revolution, the militia was retained.

England and Wales, 1759–1829
Social conditions
This brief outline of the relation between the social conditions of the period and the ways of keeping the peace indicate some of the types of social change that could create difficulties for such methods of policing. The first significant change was in the growth and distribution of the population.

In 1600, the population of England and Wales was estimated at about four millions; by 1750 it was probably about six-and-a-half millions, and in 1801 (when the first census was taken), it was just under nine millions. Even more significant was the rise in the population of cities during this period. In 1760 there was only one really large city, London, with about three-quarters of a million people. Bristol was second with about sixty thousand. By the end of the century, London had grown, but so too had a number of industrial towns. Liverpool grew very rapidly from a small town of 6,000 people in 1700 to a large one of 202,000 by 1831.

London—crime and riots
As London was by far the largest city, it was there that the inadequacies of policing first became most obvious.

In his speech to the House of Commons in 1751, King George II urged Parliament "to consider seriously of some effectual Provisions to suppress those audacious Crimes of Robbery and Violence, which are now become so frequent, especially about this great Capital . . .".

As well as crime, the people of London had to contend with riots, a feature of life throughout Britain during the eighteenth century. Riots occurred as a result of differences of opinion about religion, food prices, elections and politics. The most devastating of those in London were the Gordon Riots of 1780, sparked off by Lord George Gordon as a protest against liberalising the law so as to enable Roman Catholics to enjoy equal rights with other citizens. The result was a week of riots in which 458 people died; prisons, houses and distilleries were burned. Some of the deaths were caused by people drinking raw spirit, while others were burnt alive as the spirit caught alight. The Gordon Riots were eventually quelled by a combination of the regular army and militia.

Attempts to improve policing in London
Some attempts were made to improve the policing of London. Henry Fielding, the novelist, became Chief Magistrate in 1748 at Bow Street and produced a forerunner of the *Police Gazette* by publishing details of wanted criminals. He also, later with his half-brother John, who took over the office on the death of Henry in 1754, instituted patrols (to become celebrated as the Bow Street Runners) to catch criminals. The practical work the Fieldings did was probably less important than the ideas they promulgated during years of active campaigning. These ideas eventually contributed to an attempt by William Pitt, Prime Minister in 1785, to set up a police force in London. The combined opposition of the press, the justices (whose powers would have been reduced) and the City of London (he had ventured to include the City in his proposals) caused Pitt's Bill to be withdrawn, although it re-emerged in Dublin, a year later, to found the police force that became the Royal Irish Constabulary.

In 1792, the Middlesex Justices Act provided seven centres for magistrates, with six constables at each. These constables were paid and so represented the first official recognition that the concept of the unpaid, amateur constable was not appropriate for modern conditions in London.

So, with the exception of the Bow Street Runners and the constables appointed under the 1792 Act, policing in London in London in 1800 was much as it had been since 1668 when, during the reign of Charles II, paid night watchmen were introduced in London (promptly nicknamed "Charlies"). Although, since 1737, some watchmen had been employed during the day as well as night, they were very poorly paid, with the result that they were usually recruited from elderly or infirm men, totally incapable of exercising a policing function. The only measure taken to combat crime on a national scale was the introduction of the death penalty for more and more offences. New capital offences were created at a rate of about one a year until, at the beginning of the nineteenth century, there were 223 offences carrying the death penalty. They included sheep stealing, theft from the person of goods of any value, and shoplifting to the value of five shillings (25 pence) or more. But, while punishments became more and more savage, the chances of being caught and hanged diminished. Policing was inadequate and the cumbersome machinery of the courts facilitated acquittals on technical grounds.

In 1798, a London Magistrate, Patrick Colquhoun, who had been actively campaigning for police reform, helped to set up a full-time police force to patrol the Thames. This private police force became in 1800, by virtue of the Thames River Police Act, the first "modern" professional police force in London. Bow Street became the centre of a revised patrol system in 1805, aimed at highwaymen on the outskirts of London and this was extended to the suburbs in 1821. Other partial measures were adopted in subsequent years, up to 1829, but the scene was now set for a major change.

The murder of two families living in the Ratcliffe Highway area in the East End of London, in 1811, had caused a Parliamentary committee to be set up in 1812, but it produced very little of any moment; it was followed by further committees in 1816, 1818 and 1822. They were all emphatic that there could be no "continental" style police force in Britain, because it would be incompatible with liberty. In the words of the 1822 committee: "It is difficult to reconcile an effective system of police, with that perfect freedom of action and exemption from interference, which are the great privileges and blessings of society in this country."

What was it about the idea of a police force based on the "continental" model that led to this view? To gain some idea, we need to take a brief glance at the French police system of the time.

The French police system around 1800
There had been an organised police system in France since
Roman times. Prior to the French Revolution it was a centralised, militaristic system of professional police, with power
centred on the Throne. In Paris at the time of the Revolution in
1789, there were over 1,000 police and this body survived the
Revolution more or less intact by the simple expedient of not
opposing it. Thus, there was the basis of an established police
system available to the revolutionary government.

The power of a centrally-controlled body to execute the
"law" by having the total command of "police" and "courts"
can be seen from the events from July 1793 to July 1794, when
Robespierre reigned as head of the Committee of Public
Safety. In that one year some 2,600 people were arrested and
guillotined in Paris alone. In 1796, a Ministry of Police was
established to suppress violent political factions; then, in 1800,
civil police *préfectures* were formed to set a pattern that is still the
essence of French policing today. The prefects (in French,
préfets) were controlled by the mayors of the communes of
France but, as the mayors were appointed by the government,
the system was basically centralised and the Prefect of Paris
was directly under the control of the government.

The prefects had many functions that would not be thought
police matters in Britain. For example, the Prefect of Paris was
responsible for passports, residents' permits, identity cards,
public health, the maintenance of supplies to the city, the fire
service and many other administrative duties. He also controlled the ordinary law-enforcing police and para-military
gendarmes, who were available to provide armed intervention
when required.

Napoleon was quick to see how a police force could aid him
in maintaining his position as Emperor, and the police were
used as agents of repression. A code of criminal procedure of
1808 gave wide powers of arrest and interrogation which
brought about a state of affairs resembling an Inquisition.

This, then, was the model available in the early years of the
nineteenth century and it is hardly surprising that many people
in Britain were fearful of what a police force could do. Paris had
shown just how a centrally-controlled body can aid a govern-

ment to suppress opposition in a ruthless way and there was a determination that no police in Britain should be able to emulate the French. Despite these fears, there were aspects of the French system that had some appeal. Travellers, who had seen the effectiveness of the Paris police in keeping the streets free of violent crime, could see the merits of an organised police force, when watching helplessly as riots raged and robbery was an everyday hazard of walking in London streets. This was the attractive feature of a police force which censorship, spies, informers, secret dossiers and interrogative methods made generally unacceptable to the British.

England and Wales, 1759–1829

As mentioned above, the principal change from 1350 to 1759 was in the size and distribution of the population, but there were additional factors that placed strains on the old system of policing. The eighteenth century was a time of great industrial innovation and large enterprises were built on the combined resources of coal, iron and textiles.

There were still many people working on the land, although a policy of "enclosing" land into large farming-units and the introduction of agricultural machinery drastically reduced their number. The result was a steady flow of people from rural areas into the towns.

This flow was aided by rapid improvements in travel following the development of toll roads. In 1750, it would have taken a fast coach some four or five days to travel from Manchester to London but, by 1800, the journey could be done in something like 30 hours.

Basically, the rule of law survived in rural areas under the old police methods but not in the towns where, as we have seen, the conditions were not appropriate for a part-time, amateur policing system, supported by a few paid watchmen in some, but not all, of the towns. Local government in Britain at that time was also haphazard and made reforms difficult.

Government in England and Wales

Justices of the peace had become the most important single class of people in rural areas and towns that did not possess a charter. Their functions went beyond the administration of justice; they were also the principal agents of local government administration, even though they had no staff to fulfil their responsibilities for roads, bridges, poor relief and the maintenance of public buildings. These tasks were therefore done in the same way as the policing—by the local people, on the basis that if they did not do it they could be punished. The effectiveness of the justices' administration depended on the men appointed and they varied widely from the downright corrupt to the relatively enlightened and forward-thinking but, in general, they seem to have done a reasonable job in maintaining law and order where social conditions remained unchanged. They were, however, hard-pressed by the increasing administrative demands made on them and the prevalence of riots stemming from such unpopular matters as the price of food, tolls, the introduction of machinery, elections, trade disputes and attempts to obtain political reforms.

Of the towns that possessed charters, less than a quarter had a democratically elected council and even then the vote was restricted to property owners. Very few towns in which rapid growth was taking place introduced sufficient measures to cope with the needs of their increased population, although most obtained authority to levy rates to provide for street improvements and paid watchmen. Once again, the quality of watchmen tended to be low because of poor wages and such supervision as there was was done by unpaid citizens who might be "constables" or "inspectors" or even "superintendents of the watch". Inevitably, most such systems worked badly and did not meet the real needs of the towns; nor did they cope with the rising number of riots and demonstrations.

The only means of dealing with any outbreak of disorder was still the militia and its use could cause bloodshed. When demonstrations were broken up, the ringleaders were given savage sentences, not least because they appeared before justices of the peace whose principles and interests were often the targets of the demonstrators.

In such matters as public order and crime prevention, government involvement was negligible. There was a new government department called the Home Office set up in 1782 but it had little authority and acted principally as a means of collecting and disseminating information. It employed agents to seek information about possible unrest or sedition but, as they were paid by results, it is hardly surprising that much of their information was inaccurate or that some acted as *agents provocateurs*.

England and Wales therefore depended on the local government systems, which could be moderately successful or thoroughly inadequate, depending on the calibre of the local leaders and the complexity of the problems they faced.

Scotland, 1603–1800

The office of constable appears to have emerged in Scotland after the Union of Crowns in 1603, when James VI of Scotland became King also of England and Wales. Basically, an attempt was made to graft the English system on to the local government system of Scotland; constables were supposed to be appointed at a rate of two per parish, to serve for six months at a time, in much the same way as in England and Wales.

An Act of 1617 setting up these arrangements seems to have been largely ignored and Cromwell's Parliament issued edicts in 1649 and 1655 ordering that they be fulfilled throughout Scotland. When the monarchy was restored, the system fell into disuse but was subsequently revived when Scotland, Wales and England united in 1707.

During the eighteenth century, crime increased in much the same way as in England. Several burghs formed "town guards", apparently a refurbished version of the watch-and-ward system that suffered from the same defect as the earlier models —the employment of inferior, paid substitutes. The result was that in 1800, Glasgow, quickly followed by other burghs, introduced paid police in small numbers, with duties ranging from crime detection to street cleansing. The nature of these arrangements can be gauged from the system in Glasgow, where the police were employed under the command of a Master of Police assisted by three sergeants, with an active strength of nine "day-officers" and sixty-eight watchmen. Their duties were to sweep the streets as well as patrol them, fight fires and call the hours.

This can be seen as the existing British tradition with a touch of a European model and so formed a halfway position between the old police system of unpaid constables and watchmen and the "new police", inaugurated first in London and later throughout Britain.

The "new police"
The formation of Metropolitan Police

The two threads of constable and a paid police force were finally pulled together by Robert Peel, the Home Secretary, in 1829. He had done some political spadework to ensure the passage of his "Bill for Improving the Police in and near the Metropolis", mainly by using the exclusion of the City of London as a bargaining tool.

The Metropolitan Police Act 1829 duly became law, and Peel set about finding the two commissioners that the Act provided for. The curious thing about this Act was its vagueness as to what sort of police force was to be set up. It seems probable that Peel knew that a police force was wanted but had little idea as to how it would be constituted. To work out the details he relied upon the first two commissioners, Colonel Charles Rowan and Richard Mayne—a soldier and a lawyer respectively. The actual mechanics of the organisation fell to Rowan and he chose to organise the Metropolitan Police on military lines, while emphasising the fact that the police were not soldiers.

The objectives that Rowan laid down for his organisation were set out in the instructions that were issued to everyone when they started duty as policemen: "the object to be attained is the Prevention of Crime", Rowan wrote. To this, Peel added the word "principal" so that it now read: "the principal object to be obtained is the Prevention of Crime". Why Peel added this is not known, but it seems likely that he was merely acting as a good politician and keeping his options open. Certainly the role of the Metropolitan Police was not just the prevention of crime; it had a social and public-order involvement from the outset and developed wider objectives as time went on, including the detection of criminals, which was not included by Rowan, other than as a poor alternative to crime prevention.

In many ways, the actual deployment of men into companies (one per division) and sergeant's parties (one sergeant and nine men) with inspector's parties consisting of four sergeants' parties (one-fourth part of a company), was not particularly

original, based as it clearly was on an army model; nor was the
idea of beats—this was an adaptation of coverage by armed
sentry. What was both original and profound was the underlying awareness of the need to establish a good relationship with
the public. From the outset, it was recognised that, without the
co-operation of the people, the police could accomplish very
little. For this reason, the whole tenor of the instructions to the
first policemen was to maintain what would be termed today a
"low profile". The emphasis on the quality of behaviour of a
policeman, the limited powers of arrest, the exhortations to
refrain from interfering in legitimate activities, all contributed
to the idea of the police as a body of people geared to respond
to the legitimate needs of society rather than to act as a source
of repression.

Public order in London, 1833
The first major demonstration that the Metropolitan Police
dealt with was bound to be a trial of strength. The occasion
came on 13th May 1833, when a meeting was held in Cold
Bath Fields, Clerkenwell, by the National Union of the Working Classes. There was ample evidence, well in advance, that a
number of the movement's leaders would be armed with knives,
coshes and a variety of other weapons but not firearms. Rowan
decided to deal with the situation by using divisions of 100 of
his police, each under a superintendent, with himself in overall
command. A mistrustful government had the military in reserve lest the police should fail. The object of the exercise was
to break up the meeting before it could form into a mob and go
on the rampage, as had happened at Spa Fields in 1816, when
a similar mob broke into a gunsmith's shop and tried to take the
Tower of London.

The result, in 1833, was a successful operation; the meeting
was dispersed and a number of arrests were made. However, the
costs were high, as three policemen were stabbed and one of
them, Constable Robert Culley, was killed.

Much has been made of the verdict that the jury pronounced
at the inquest on Constable Culley's death: "justifiable homicide". This, admittedly, throws some light on the view that this
section of the public held about the police but, four years after
its formation, there were still many misunderstandings about

its role. The seventeen-man jury at the inquest was a collection of bakers, grocers and other small tradesmen who had no understanding of the situation at Cold Bath Fields, no knowledge of the law or sympathy with the government. This would not be the last time that, to their detriment, the police would be identified with the government.

The true importance of the Cold Bath Fields incident was that it showed how a properly constituted police force could deal with a hostile crowd without the need for arms or for the military to help them. The methods used in 1833 were basically those that have been used ever since in Britain.

New police in the towns

The lack of any organised body to prevent serious disorder in some of the larger towns became apparent in 1831 when riots occurred in Bristol, Coventry, Derby and a number of other towns. The initial response was a Special Constables Act 1831, which was based on a slightly updated version of a seventeenth-century idea. In 1833 the Royal Commission on Municipal Corporations was appointed, and the Municipal Corporations Act 1835, established a form of democratic local government in 178 chartered boroughs, providing for police forces in these reformed boroughs.

The relationship between the Commissioners of the Metropolitan Police and the government at this time was not at its best; there had been a change of government and the Whigs who were now in power failed to build on the experience of the Metropolitan Police, even though it was becoming more and more acceptable to the people of London as time went on.

Instead, they chose to introduce a hybrid type of policing that was not much more than a rationalisation of the old watch-and-ward system on a paid basis. Initially, it was optional and did not become compulsory until 1856. The 1835 Act provided for a town council from which a "watch committee" could be appointed—the very title "watch committee" clearly indicates its relation to the old night-watchman system that was being "replaced". The watch committee appointed constables to preserve the peace and prevent robberies. Such matters as to who was to be in charge of them, the regulations under which they were to be employed, pay and conditions were all left to the watch committee. Thus began a system of borough police forces which from the outset had a number of weaknesses. There were no national rates of pay or conditions of service, some of the police forces were so small that they were little better than the early watchmen systems and, most important of all, the relationship between the watch committee and the police was not defined.

New police in the counties
In contrast to the hurried provisions that were made for policing the boroughs in 1835, the problems of the counties were examined by a Royal Commission consisting of Charles Rowan, Sir Charles Shaw Lefevre (a county magistrate) and Edwin Chadwick (Secretary of the Poor Law Commissioners and a prolific writer on the subject of police reform). The evidence they produced revealed a startling lack of law and order in the country and their solution was, in effect, a national police force for England and Wales, with the Metropolitan Police Commissioners directing its deployment according to the needs of each county. Considerable emphasis was placed on the need to sever the relationship between the justices and the police— a recommendation hardly likely to commend itself to the justices, who were still at that time a powerful group of people.

Predictably, the report of this Royal Commission (it was supposed to be an interim report but in fact was the only one) was not acted upon but, as a new wave of disorder was spreading through the country, something had to be done. A "People's Charter" was published in 1838 seeking votes for all adult males, secret ballots and the payment of Members of Parliament. The Chartist movement began to hold meetings at which the need for violent action was advocated and there was a real fear on the part of the government that there was to be an armed rebellion. The result was yet another piece of hasty legislation, which ignored the recommendations made by Rowan and Chadwick. The County Police Act 1839, merely enabled counties to form police forces but did not compel them; the result was that less than half did so.

In three important respects, the new county forces were different from those in boroughs. The county forces were under the control of justices; the Home Secretary was given the power to make rules for their government and pay and he was given the right to approve the choice of chief constables.

To have achieved more than this would have been politically impossible, for even these proposals were given a stormy passage through Parliament. *The Times* of 26th July 1839, took the view that the arrangements would be ". . . very injurious to public and general liberty and the free expression of opinion". In the event, the fact that so few police forces were set up under the Act of 1839 was not due to the problem of retaining free speech, but to the cost of running them.

The situation in 1853

When a select committee was set up in 1853 to review the state of policing in the country, it found that it ranged from the very good to the non-existent. In towns, Birmingham and Manchester had Metropolitan-type forces that had been originally under Home Office control, but were now run by watch committees. Liverpool, one of the most progressively-administered of all provincial towns, had a large and well-run police force but thirteen municipal boroughs still had no police.

Of the counties, just over half had a police force covering either the whole or part of a county, while the remainder still relied on the rural system of policing.

After much controversy and two abortive police bills, the recommendations of the select committee were eventually reflected in the County and Borough Police Act 1856. It compelled all counties to have rural police forces, it appointed three "Inspectors of Constabulary" appointed by the Crown to assess the efficiency of all police forces and all chief officers were ordered to submit annual reports. The government undertook to provide a quarter of the cost of the pay and clothing of all forces serving populations of over 5,000 people—a move to discourage the smaller forces from staying in existence.

The control of the police

By the last quarter of the nineteenth century, there were in England and Wales three main types of police force—the Metropolitan which was headed by a commissioner and controlled by the Home Secretary, who was in turn answerable to Parliament; borough forces headed by "head constables", "chief constables" or "superintendents" (depending on local preference) and controlled by watch committees who were answerable to the borough council; and county constabularies, headed and largely controlled by chief constables, who were answerable to magistrates sitting at quarter sessions.

In Scotland, by an Act of 1857, the county chief constables were required to "obey all lawful Orders and Warrants of the Sheriff and Justices in the Execution of his duty".

The subject of control of the police has always been a source of controversy and was certainly so in 1888, when local government reforms were being discussed. The government wished to have a greater say in the affairs of the borough forces, a move resisted by the politically-strong boroughs. There was also the question of the relationship between the newly-created county councils and the county constabularies. The outcome was that the watch committees retained control over the borough forces (unfettered by interference from Home Office) while the county constabularies were administered by joint committees composed of justices and county-council members. Obliquely, the power of the Home Office was slightly increased through the raising of the Exchequer grant to one-half, thus offering a greater inducement to counties and boroughs alike to obtain the necessary certificate from H.M. Inspector of Constabulary.

This pattern survived unchanged until the Police Act 1919 gave the Home Secretary power to make regulations governing the pay and conditions of service of *all* police forces in England and Wales. Unlike the previous measures already discussed, which had originated from causes outside the police service, the 1919 Act was a direct result of pressures from within. To see how these pressures developed, it is necessary to look at the life of a police officer in the early part of the twentieth century.

Policemen
Peel's recruiting "policy"
Returning briefly to the formation of the Metropolitan Police in 1829, it is possible to see the start of a pattern that hampered the police for many years—the calibre of the men who were recruited because of police pay and conditions. For this Robert Peel must take full responsibility for, when the low amount that was to be paid to "his" policemen was queried (three shillings

a day, at a time when the wage of a skilled worker was five shillings) he replied in this way:

> I have refused to employ gentlemen—commissioned officers, for instance —as superintendents or inspectors, because I am certain they would be above their work. . . . A sergeant of the Guards at 200C. a year is a better man for my purpose than a captain of high military reputation. . . . For somewhat similar reasons, a three shillings a day man is better than a five shillings a day man.
>
> (Letter to John Wilson Crocker dated 10th December 1829.)

It is impossible to be certain why Peel was so determined to keep the pay and status of the police so low, but there are several possibilities. For example, he may have had reservations about the amount of power that the police might have in the hands of senior officers drawn from the "ruling classes"; it may have been simple economising, or that he wanted his police to be "of the people". Whatever the reason, the result was unfortunate, for it meant that the quality of the men who were recruited at 21s. (£1.05) a week, less 2s. (10p) deductions. was not of the best and the wastage rate (often for drunkenness) was very high. The long-term effect of the standards that Peel set lasted into the twentieth century for, as forces throughout the country copied other aspects of the Metropolitan Police, so they followed in the wages offered—at about the level of farm labourers. The county constabularies paid between 15s. and 21s. a week (75p to £1.05) but boroughs, in the absence of national rules, could pay less. To add to their financial problems, the early policemen were severely restricted in their private lives. For example, uniform was compulsory at all times in the Metropolitan Police for many years and an armlet was necessary to show whether they were on or off duty. They had no regular rest day. They were likely to find themselves the target of abuse from public and magistracy alike, for the new police system had separated the close ties between justices and police in towns. The hostility of courts in London resulted in cases of policemen being sent to prison, for nothing more than failing to obtain a conviction. In the absence of solicitors to defend them, constables were easily found guilty of wrongful arrest—for three shillings a day there were few skilled legal advocates amongst them!

Police conditions, 1872–1919

In 1872 the first police strike occurred. The tragic nature of this can best be seen from the stark recital of dates from a contemporary publication:

Large meeting of police to agitate for an increase in pay;	17–24 October 1872
Request granted; meeting of some constables through misapprehension;	16 November 1872
Some constables prosecuted;	18 November 1872
109 dismissed; 65 reduced in rank;	20 November 1872

(Dictionary of Dates, Benjamin Vincent, 1873.)

A further strike in 1890 was no more successful. Apart from pay, other demands were for at least one rest day in seven, a guaranteed pension and the ability to form a union. This last demand reflects the times and the way in which what was happening in society affected the police. Trade unions outside the police had been made legal in 1825 when the Combination Act was repealed but, in 1867, a case brought against the Boilermakers' Union resulted in the Lord Chief Justice declaring that unions, because they were "in restraint of trade", were illegal. The result was legislation in 1871 allowing unions the right to exist and laying down reasonable terms on which they could do so. Thereafter, trade unions flourished and policemen wanted a union to obtain improvements in their working conditions.

In the absence of any official means of conferring together, men resorted to unofficial methods and, from 1892, they were aided by a new magazine, *The Police Review*, set up by John Dempster who, as a journalist, had realised that there were just grievances that the policemen could not air. At a time when there was no way in which policemen could confer nationally, the provision of a means of communication like *The Police Review* was invaluable to the police cause.

The much-needed one rest day a week arrived in 1910 but the remainder of the police demands were as far off as ever when war broke out in 1914. Meanwhile, industrial unrest was widespread and the military were called in to assist in quelling riots at Tonypandy in the Rhondda Valley (1910), when large contingents of the Metropolitan Police were sent as aid to the Glamorgan Constabulary, and in Liverpool (1911) when a number of forces acted in aid. Such militancy on the part of trade unions was bound to rub off on the police, who could clearly relate their own conditions to those of the industrial workers with whom they were brought—often violently—into contact.

Police strikes, 1918–1919

Towards the end of the 1914–1918 war, police pay was at poverty level and, despite some tentative moves on the part of the Home Office to improve matters, the unrecognised "Police Union" was gaining support and becoming more militant, even though to be identified as a member meant dismissal. This sort of situation produces informal leaders who are willing and able to defy the official heads and the likelihood of martyrs is great. In August 1918, a London policeman was dismissed for his work in the union and his case became a focal point that resulted in a threat to strike unless he was reinstated; a pay rise was given and the union was recognised.

The strike took place on 30th August 1918, in which 6,000 Metropolitan Police were supported by the City of London Police.

Once again, as a hundred years previously, the politicians were looking over their shoulders—then it was to the French Revolution, now it was to the Russian Revolution of 1917. The government attempted to settle the issue by the Prime Minister, Lloyd George, meeting the strike leaders, giving them their rise in pay and reinstating the sacked policeman, but deferring the subject of the Police Union until the war was over.

This agreement brought peace for a few months but, when the war ended, the demand for a union was renewed. In 1918, a form of consultation between representatives of the constables, sergeants and inspectors and the Commissioner had been instituted but it did not work and, in May 1919, policemen were holding protest marches. Against this background, a committee of inquiry under Lord Desborough was sitting to review the police and, at the end of May, the Home Secretary announced that police constables would be given a 233 per cent rise—from £1 10s. (£1.50) to £3 10s. (£3.50) a week. He also announced the formation of what was to be the Police Federation, but no union. It was at this point that the Police Union leaders decided to press for recognition and they called for a national strike. Only seven forces responded and the total number of men involved was only 2,364, most of whom were dismissed and never reinstated. In contrast to the strike of 1918 in which, although London was almost totally unpoliced, there was little disorder, the 1919 strike did illustrate what *can* happen in the absence of police. In Liverpool, where a substantial proportion of the policemen went on strike, the result was an orgy of rioting, looting and damage with one rioter shot dead by a soldier. It was quelled by a combination of troops, criminal investigation department men, non-striking police—and rain.

The Police Act 1919

The Desborough Committee produced recommendations that were put into effect in the Police Act 1919. The principal results were as follows:

1. The status of the police constable for pay purposes was raised above the manual labourer level. The skills and attributes that a policeman needs were recognised in a tangible way for the first time.
2. A federation (later named the Police Federation) was set up, the cost to be borne from public funds.
3. Representatives from the Federation (plus those from the Superintendents' Association formed the following year) were to meet with members of Home Office, local authorities and chief police officers to advise the Home Office on general questions affecting the police.
4. A standard discipline code was introduced.
5. No one should be appointed chief constable without previous police experience, unless he had exceptional qualifications or experience.

Some of the Desborough Committee recommendations were not carried out, notably those affecting the borough and city forces. It was recommended that all the non-county borough forces in England and Wales should be amalgamated with the county constabularies and all powers of watch committees to appoint, promote and discipline policemen be transferred to chief constables. As had happened in the previous century, this produced a storm of protests from the boroughs with the result that these recommendations were not implemented.

Britain, 1920–1945

The Depression

Social conditions during the period 1920–1939 were governed to a large extent by the economic climate. These were times of depression when the number of people unemployed was the most obvious statistic—two million in June 1921 and 2·7 million ten years later. By 1939, the depression had not receded, but the war came and attention was diverted elsewhere, as the need for men in the armed services quickly absorbed the unemployed.

Motor transport

The arrival of the motor vehicle in increasing numbers created new problems. Large towns had always had traffic problems (people in London were complaining of the volume of traffic before 1666) but the motor car extended traffic problems to most parts of the country and thus created the need for traffic patrols. A new race of law-breakers was created; hitherto, the middle classes had encountered the police only as complainants or witnesses, but now they provided the bulk of the defendants accused of speeding and other traffic offences. This, in turn, changed the relationship between this section of society and the police.

Public order

By 1900, groups of people marching through London and holding meetings on Sundays were already a part of the accepted way of life.

> London police are taught and trained to avoid any interference likely to provoke hostilities. Their instructions are to preserve order, not to provoke disorder. If an anarchist who had denounced them as miscreants were attacked by the bystanders, they would protect the anarchist and call upon the bystanders to disperse.
>
> (*Some Familiar Things in London*, George R. Sims, 1903.)

The reference in this quotation to the police protecting an anarchist from the crowd is the clue to future developments. It is one thing to protect an individual who expresses unpopular beliefs but what happens when two opposing groups of people meet, often with the deliberate intention of causing violence that will bring publicity to their cause? This was the problem of the 1920s and 1930s. During the General Strike of May 1926, the police were able to steer just the right line of impartiality between sides but, as more and more political capital was seen to be obtainable from disorder, the position the police were forced to adopt to protect property and prevent disorder made them a target for criticism. The problem is simply stated: if people seek some change by the use of public disorder and damage and the police try to prevent disorder and damage, they must seem to be opponents of that change; therefore they must seem to be the opponents of the people seeking the change. Thus they find themselves at the mercy of political extremists, who can use the peace-keeping efforts of the police as raw material for publicity. This tactic came into prominence in the 1930s, when political extremists sought publicity by the use of provocation and violence, the police often being between them in an attempt to maintain the rule of law and prevent mob battling with mob. In an editorial, *The Times* of 5th October 1936 neatly summed up the situation:

> The activities of both the Fascists and Communists in this country seem to most people to be a tedious burlesque; but the law rightly allows them, like other people, to express their opinions and to testify to their beliefs by the methods of procession and of public meetings, even though, as the Home Secretary has said, these methods are a great nuisance to large numbers of police officers deprived of their usual period off duty and involved some charge on the rate payers.

One further development during this period deserves mention, for it focused attention on the role of the National Council for Civil Liberties. Formed in 1934 to provide observers to monitor police behaviour at the scene of the hunger marches of that year, on that occasion it found little to report but, in 1935, it set up an unofficial inquiry into an incident, in respect of which the Home Secretary had declined to do so.

> . . . a serious riot might easily have been caused by the action of police who would have been solely to blame. . . .
> *(Report of National Council for Civil Liberties, 1936.)*

To the police at the time this must have seemed an odd way to sum up an incident in which 2,000–3,000 people met near the Albert Hall in contravention of a Commissioner's Direction, and groups of 200 tried to force their way through a police

B

cordon to break up a meeting that was being held by fascists inside the Hall.

These aspects of the 1930s have been dealt with in some detail because of the obvious parallels with events in the post-1945 period, one example of which led to an inquiry into disorder at Red Lion Square on 15th June 1974, when once again right and left-wing extremists were at loggerheads and the police were between them. As then, the principal objective of some of the combatants appears to have been to make capital from violent confrontation.

The 1939–1945 war

The war brought a temporary halt to some problems for the police but new ones took their place. Recruiting was stopped and, after an initial pause, many policemen went into the armed services. They were replaced and the service was augmented by a reserve drawn from ex-policemen, the Special Constabulary (many served on a full-time paid basis) and the Police War Reserve (people recruited for the duration of the war).

In December 1941, 4,000 miners in Kent decided to strike after rejecting an arbitration award. This was illegal and the government decided that they should be prosecuted. A decision was made to prosecute the 1,000 who had first gone on strike. Summonses were served by extra police brought in for the purpose, courts were organised and all the miners turned up, pleaded guilty (by prior arrangement with the unions) and most were fined £1. Unfortunately, the magistrates sentenced the union leaders to imprisonment for short periods and so the people who should have called off the strike were in prison. A compromise was reached and the union leaders were let out again. And the £1 fines? Only nine were paid and the prospect of crowding over nine-hundred men into Maidstone gaol on commitment warrants brought common sense—the fines were never collected.

This bizarre but true story has been recounted because it so clearly illustrates the limitations of the criminal law in a free society. There are definite limits to what a democratic government can achieve. It cannot force people to go to work and it cannot enforce a law which is rejected by the bulk of the population. Thus, a democratic government, and the police as part of the executive, are limited in potential. The senior officers in charge of police must sometimes make a decision as to whether they should try to achieve something that might require the use of excessive force outside the scope of the present British police. Violent scenes in connection with strikes, where police have tried to maintain freedom of access to picket-bound premises, provide many examples of this.

Police 1920–1945
The period immediately following the Desborough Committee report was one during which the police enjoyed a higher status and better pay, but the conditions of service were still hard, with the disciplinary code often being applied harshly. One objective of the Desborough Committee had been to encourage the appointment of police officers to the highest posts in the service, but ex-military men were often appointed to these positions, causing inevitable differences of viewpoint between policemen and their leaders.

In 1929, a Royal Commission was sparked off by a trivial matter that happened to involve a man who made for good headlines in the press. The way in which male police officers questioned a woman came in for criticism and led to recommendations about the wider use of women police for police work.

Technological advances in radio and forensic science led to the Home Office wireless depots and forensic laboratories in the 1930s and the motor car provided both a policing problem and a method of dealing with it.

On the whole, there was little real development of policing methods as such, because the traditional beat and patrol system was fully manned and conditions had not changed sufficiently to discredit it.

Britain since 1945
Changes in society
The nature of the changes that have taken place in society since 1945 will be much easier to place in perspective in the year 2100 than now for, by then, ephemeral issues will be seen as such. The changes that are discussed here are therefore no more than

a tentative selection of those that have affected the police service. Many of them are not new, parallels will often be found between the events of recent years and those of the past. One such is the increase in the mobility of people, for this has been a continuous process since feudal times. It is easier to keep track of local villains who are confined to their own village or town than it is to catch criminals who can use fast cars and motorways to commit crime hundreds of miles from home.

Similarly, the policing problems of urban areas are not new. Where residential property has been demolished in slum-clearance schemes, established communities have been dispersed and, in some areas, high-rise flats have created a society which the police cannot easily join—it is one thing to walk along a street of small houses to meet and talk with people and learn what is happening, but it is quite different if those same people are distributed up sixteen floors of a block of flats. Such dwellings also provide less supervision for children playing a long way below their mother's kitchen window.

Supervision of children is also affected by both parents working, very much a post-1945 phenomenon. Before 1939, there was a prejudice against married women working that seems to have been vanquished by the work that women did during the war. The number of houses that became empty during the working day therefore increased, while the amount of parental supervision for children decreased. The school leaving-age being raised increased the number of children who disliked school, with consequent effects on truancy and crime.

There also appears to have been rejection of some of the standards that governed behaviour in the pre-war era. This again is nothing new; the standards of society have fluctuated over the years. For example, overt sexual permissiveness was high in the eighteenth century, low during the reign of Queen Victoria and higher again in the twentieth century. Nevertheless, the rejection of previously held standards does cause problems for society and many of these affect the police. During the nineteenth century and into the twentieth, the churches and schools, by teaching a set of ethics, gave everyone a standard by which behaviour could be judged. During the decline of that standard, people, especially young people, became uncertain as to the extent to which non-conformity may be taken.

Clashes of ideals between parents and children have not helped. Immigration produces a challenge for the police:

Most of them have something written on a piece of paper which they produce creased and soiled from a pocket. It is the address of a friend or relative. . . . Others have no idea where they are going. Many, asked what money they have, confess to twenty or thirty shillings as their entire fortune. . . . For most of them have friends "somewhere". It may be a brother, it may only be a fellow townsman or fellow villager, who came to London years ago.

What could easily be an account of West Indians arriving in the 1950s or 1960s is, in fact, a description of Russian Jews arriving in London in 1903. Britain was no better prepared for them then than it was during the height of immigration from Asia, Africa and the West Indies, between 1950 and 1970. The address that each man or woman has on the "piece of paper" takes him into an area where he forms part of a community separated from the rest of society by language, custom or religion, or combinations of all three. Conflict with the native population during transitional periods occurs and the police are called upon to arbitrate. An arbitrator rarely pleases both sides and seldom even one; hence, the basis for conflict is already there. Add to this the attempts by the police to enforce laws of behaviour which are not acceptable to certain members of the immigrant community and confrontation is inevitable. All that is needed is some form of real or apparent discrimination by society against the immigrant and the stage is set for the police to bear the brunt of hostility on behalf of the whole of society.

Another continuing aspect of change has been the evolution of the trade unions and the balance of power between employers and employees. The power that certain groups of workers have been able to wield has caused violent disputes during which the police have been sandwiched between rival interests.

Despite a decrease in the value of money over the years, there has been an increase in prosperity and the number and value of items owned by people. Motor cars became commonplace and therefore a target for thieves; as car-radios became more common, so the thefts of them rose. The more goods there are in circulation, the more opportunity there is for theft.

In the 1930s, radio was in its infancy; not until the 1950s did television become able to focus attention on the detailed events of policemen at work and present edited versions within hours to an audience of millions. The police have had to learn to live with the television camera and the press. Obtaining balanced cover from either is difficult, because both press and television have different priorities from the police who do not, and would not wish to, exercise control over the finished article.

These changes are by no means all that might be listed. Others that could be mentioned include the increased intervention of central government in local and industrial affairs; the change in retail trade from shop-service to self-service; the effects of a welfare state on self-sufficiency; an increase in leisure activities and a consequent reduction in the time that people have for voluntary unpaid service to the community. All of these factors and others have a bearing on the needs of society as they affect the police, but enough has probably been said to indicate the rapid rate of change facing the police from 1945 onwards. The next subject must be how the police changed.

Change within the police, 1945–1960
For many years, recommendations had been made that the number of British police forces should be reduced. Local opposition prevented much action being taken but in 1940 the government insisted that a number of smaller forces amalgamated for the duration of the war. Then, rather than allow them to regain their independence, the Police Act 1946 increased the number of amalgamations which had already taken place under wartime emergency legislation and provided a framework for further compulsory and voluntary amalgamations. The effect was a reduction in the number of police forces in England and Wales from 183 in 1939 to 125 twenty years later.

At the same time, the opportunity was taken to regionalise training with nine (later eight) training schools serving most of England and Wales, with two additional schools for the Metropolitan Police and one for the Scottish police. The Police College was also set up to undertake higher police training.

Thus moves were being made to improve the organisation and training of the police but conditions for the men within the service were less satisfactory. After the 1919 Desborough Committee, the police were well paid, enjoyed a high status and consequently attracted ample numbers of good recruits (doubtless aided by the unemployment levels). By 1945, police pay relative to industry had declined, jobs were easier to find than before the war and for the first time there was a shortage of recruits for the police. It particularly affected large cities and towns, as they had ample opportunities for well-paid employment elsewhere.

In 1949, two reports were produced by a committee under the chairmanship of Lord Oaksey which had been given similar problems to solve as the Desborough Committee. They did much to improve conditions of service, but did not recommend the same level of monetary reward relative to other forms of employment as Desborough had done. The Oaksey Committee wrote: ". . . we are convinced that police responsibilities are more exacting now than they were when the Desborough Committee reported in 1919 and are not likely to become less and we have had this at the forefront of our minds in all our inquiries into police emoluments" (para. 19, Part I of the report, 6th April 1949), but it seems probable that the government's policies of wage restraint at that time were slightly more to the forefront of the Committee's minds than the role of the police. The subjects of pay, status and recruitment continued to occupy the thoughts and efforts of the Police Federation until the Royal Commission of 1960. The means that the Federation had to use to gain improvements was the Police Council of Great Britain, set up following a recommendation of the Oaksey Committee. However, at times when the government was attempting to curb public spending, negotiations often failed and recourse was had to independent arbitration.

It was during this period that the traditional methods of policing became the subject of scrutiny. In towns, the old "beat" system relied on having enough manpower to be able to give a policeman a small area that he could walk round and provide a "presence" in each street. In country districts, the village policeman was a man who was never really off duty. Nor was his wife, who acted as a telephone-answering service and "deputy" for her husband. By 1950, both town and country conditions had changed.

The problem for police in towns was mainly that of maintaining a presence that would serve to prevent crime and disorder. In 1903, there were 16,000 men in the Metropolitan

Police, they worked eight hours (there was no meal break) for six and a half days a week (two days off per month) and had one week of annual leave. In 1959 there were 2,000 less men, the working week was shorter and annual leave longer. Furthermore, specialisation was beginning to take its toll—the increased size of the Criminal Investigation Department and traffic patrols was at the expense of men on the beat. As a result, two new concepts emerged: "civilianisation" and mobile policing.

There had always been "civilian" employees in the Metropolitan Police (the "civil staff" in that force had grown up alongside the "police staff"), but a new move, prompted by a Parliamentary Select Committee on Estimates, sparked off a drive to replace policemen with civilians in "non-constabulary" positions. By 1966, a working party set up by the Home Office was able to report that: "Considerable progress has been made in recent years in extending the range of civilian employment in support of the police and there are now over 16,000 civilians so employed" (*Police Manpower, Equipment and Efficiency, Reports of Three Working Parties*, 1967, p. 28). The figure of 16,000 excluded the staff employed by the Receiver for the Metropolitan Police District.

The first attempt to revise the beat system fundamentally was the "Aberdeen method" (1948) pioneered by that city and, from then onwards, a variety of discretionary beat systems, team-policing, "saturation" policy, "commando" squads and other methods were tried by various forces, with one of the most notable being "unit beat policing" first introduced in Lancashire in 1966.

Most stemmed from a desire to satisfy the competing needs of a quick response to emergency calls, for contact with the public and for a police "presence". The strength of the old system had been due to the omnipresence of uniformed policemen; to maintain that system would have cost more than the country was able or willing to pay, although it must be a matter of speculation as to whether a fully-staffed beat system on the old pattern would have coped with the rapid increase in crime that has occurred since 1945, since crime only began to rise steeply between 1930 to 1939, when the beat system was in full swing (*see* Fig. 1).

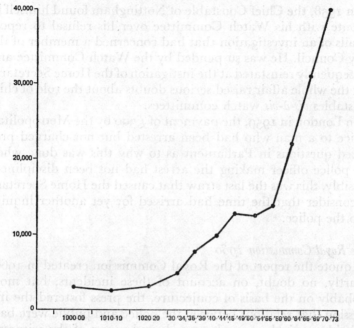

Fig. 1—Proportion of crimes known to police per million of population.
(Source: *Criminal Statistics, England and Wales*, H.M.S.O.)

The problems facing the police, 1945–1960

The total number of indictable offences hovered around the half million mark for most of the period from the end of the war to 1958, when it rose above 600,000. Traffic offences rose as the numbers of motor vehicles on the roads increased and the social factors mentioned above all contributed to a period of intensive police activity.

From 1956 onwards, a series of unconnected incidents gave rise to sensational headlines in the press about the police. These included disciplinary action against a Welsh chief constable and the conviction for fraud of an English one. In Brighton, two senior officers were convicted on charges of corruption and criticism was levelled at the Chief Constable of the borough. In Scotland in 1957, following an inquiry into allegations of assault by police on a boy, a tribunal diagnosed weaknesses in the way with which complaints against the police were dealt.

In 1958, the Chief Constable of Nottingham found himself in dispute with his Watch Committee over his refusal to report details of an investigation that had concerned a member of the City Council. He was suspended by the Watch Committee and subsequently reinstated at the instigation of the Home Secretary. But the whole affair raised serious doubts about the role of chief constables *vis-à-vis* watch committees.

In London in 1959, the payment of £300 by the Metropolitan Police to a man who had been arrested but not charged produced questions in Parliament as to why this was done when the police officer making the arrest had not been disciplined. Possibly, this was the last straw that caused the Home Secretary to consider that the time had arrived for yet another inquiry into the police.

The Royal Commission 1960
To quote the report of the Royal Commission created in 1960: "Partly, no doubt, on account of these incidents, but more probably on the basis of conjecture, the press fostered the impression that relations between the police and public were bad. This idea quickly gained ground, and many of the witnesses who appeared before us, both representative of the police and the public, took its truth for granted." In fact, according to the Royal Commission, the relations between the police and public were, in general, very good, but the need to tell everyone this does seem to have been necessary, even to policemen themselves.

In the event, the Royal Commission produced a curious result, for it contained a minority report that was more widely acclaimed than much of the report itself, yet it was the main report that was followed in subsequent legislation. The Commission considered, in particular, whether the police should be a national organisation, or a local one with more central government involved. The majority of the Commission decided on the latter, whilst the principal dissenter (there were a number of small dissensions in other matters from individual members of the Commission), Dr Arthur Goodhart, a distinguished legal scholar, preferred a national police force administered regionally.

The argument centred around a number of points but one of the most basic was whether a national police force could be a danger to democracy if misused as was done in Germany in the 1930s. The majority view could best be described as "we don't think so, but don't let us risk it", while Dr Goodhart argued that the danger to democracy was not in strong centrally-controlled police forces but in local police forces so weak that they cannot control extremist organisations (see Chapter 2, p. 52).

The decision as to what should happen after the report was presented was taken by the Home Secretary, Mr R. A. Butler, who firmly opted for the majority view at the Annual Conference of the Association of Chief Police Officers held in Torquay when he said: "I am quite convinced that it would be quite wrong for one man or one government to be in charge directly of the whole police of this country. Our constitution is based on checks and balances. This has kept our liberty throughout the generations" (*The Times*, 27th June 1962). The Police Act 1964, which adopted many Commission proposals, became law with very little controversy.

Apart from the Police Act, the Commission also affected the police service in the same way as had its 1919 predecessor: it improved the basis for police pay in an interim report; and it tried to assess the unusual factors that need to be taken into account when assessing this, recommending an immediate increase of 40 per cent—a verdict that did a great deal to help police recruiting at that time.

The Police Act 1964

The Police Act 1964 consolidated most of the existing legislation concerning the police and removed a number of anomalies. The differences between the roles of chief constables in boroughs and counties were removed and the relationship between central government, local government and chief constables was defined, up to a point.

It set up Police Advisory Boards, one for England and Wales and one for Scotland and the Police Council of Great Britain was made the negotiating body (see Chapter 2, p. 48).

The jurisdiction of constables was extended and, for the first time, the chief constable became liable in respect of torts committed by members of his force (costs to be paid from the police fund).

The system for investigation of complaints against the police was closely prescribed and provision made for an officer from another force to be called in when necessary. Liaison between forces was made easier by provisions for collaborative agreements and the arrangements for central service were put on an established basis.

Sections 22 and 23 were devoted to the subject of amalgamations aimed at reducing the number of police forces. A long programme of amalgamations was begun and, in some cases, the newly-amalgamated forces had barely been established when further amalgamations were brought about by local government reorganisation, caused by the Local Government Act 1972, an Act which had the dubious distinction of creating some smaller police forces from larger ones in the interests of making local government areas and police force areas co-terminous.

The Police Act 1976

The Police Act 1976 created a Police Complaints Board to monitor the action taken by chief officers of police in dealing with complaints made by members of the public against police officers. The object of the Act was to make the police more accountable for their actions by ensuring that allegations of improper behaviour were thoroughly investigated with disciplinary action being taken against offending police officers. Additional procedures were grafted on to those prescribed by the 1964 Act, which had already provided for an independent element when dealing with complaints alleging that police officers had committed offences against the law. The independent element for these, more serious, cases continued to be the Director of Public Prosecutions whilst the Police Complaints Board concentrated on reviewing the steps taken to resolve non-criminal complaints.

One notable feature of the Police Act 1976 the way in which it reduced the autonomy of chief officers of police, is discussed in Chapter 2, p. 46.

Local government revisions

The growth of local government in England and Wales was a haphazard affair. Even after the reforms of the nineteenth century there were a great many anomalies left over from earlier times, and although during the first half of the twentieth century there were many developments in the services provided by local government, the means whereby they were financed and organised did not keep pace. There was an ever increasing involvement of national government into what had been locally-administered functions, not only to provide an element of standardisation but also because of the enormous sums of money needed to finance public services, money that could no longer be found from the traditional source of local authority income—the rates levied on the occupiers of premises.

In 1963, the London Government Act created a two-tier system with the Greater London Council and thirty-two London boroughs, but the police were kept apart from this, the 1829 pattern of having the Home Secretary as the police authority being retained.

In 1974, the Local Government Act 1972 completely revised the structure of local government outside London and had a marked effect on most police forces, either by re-organising them or by changing their relationship with the local authority in their area. It is against the background of this local government system that the organisation of police forces will be viewed in Chapter 2.

Recent trends
Social violence
It is clear from the history of Britain that social violence is nothing new. Aspects of modern life now accepted as important parts of democracy, like universal suffrage and trade unions, were the causes of social violence in the past by Chartists, suffragettes and trade unionists. In every society there will always be militant minorities who seek to impose their views on the majority. The aim of the police in a free society must be to allow people to express their views, of whatever nature, within the bounds of free speech, yet to prevent minorities imposing their wishes upon other people by force or by the use of threat of violence.

The use of terrorist tactics has a long history but the modern terrorist is aided by two things:

The first is the greater sophistication and striking power of the violence inspired by political motives. The second is the certainty that it will attract public attention on a scale undreamed of by earlier generations. Newspapers, radio and, above all, television have made violence a cause for concern by millions irrespective of the country in which it occurs.
(*Policing a Perplexed Society*, Sir Robert Mark, George Allen and Unwin, 1977.)

International terrorism has become big business and every country can expect its share of hijackings, armed groups seizing hostages, bomb incidents and political murders. The probability of incidents will, in part, depend on the success of previous terrorist activities. It is therefore essential that the police should prepare themselves to deal with a wide range of terrorist situations firmly, but without over-reacting.

The emergence of rival political groups using violence to attract attention to themselves is a familiar feature of British life. Conflicts between the National Front and left-wing extremists are reminiscent of the fascist/communist clashes of the 1930s (see p. 21). The aims of the British fascists of 1930 were directed against Jews. The National Front uses coloured immigrants in much the same way and in doing so places the police in the familiar position of having to intervene to prevent riots. Once again there is the danger that the police may be associated with extremist views since they must protect those who hold them from attack by those who oppose them. The reputation of the police for complete impartiality is its greatest asset at such times.

Finally, a most disturbing trend towards violence has been in relation to industrial disputes where the police have been confronted by large numbers of "pickets" using mass violence as a means of putting pressure on the government. The limitations of legal action in dealing with industrial confrontations were mentioned on p. 22 and there are extremists who are willing to exploit these limitations for political advantage. The role of the police is to ensure that intimidation and violence cannot be used by extremists to subvert democracy. Occasionally this will mean thousands of police officers upholding the law against even more thousands of militant pickets but within our society there is no alternative. If militant minorities are allowed to break the law in order to intimidate the government then democracy itself is in danger. An occasion on which this occurred in Germany is discussed in Chapter 2, p. 52.

Police developments

The police service has made considerable advances during recent years both in terms of organisation and technology. The need for the police to provide a response to terrorism and mass intimidation has led to unprecedented co-operation between police forces, not only in supplying aid in terms of men and equipment, but also in exchanging information and training facilities. Faced with a need for massive assistance, any police force can request its neighbours to supply a number of "police-support units" of thirty constables with their own supervisory officers, an inspector and three sergeants. Such aid can be summoned quickly and a steady build-up of men can be arranged for lengthy problems.

Local government has also developed its response to emergencies; contingency plans in which the police have participated are now generally available for serious floods, fires or other disasters.

The police use of advancing technology has been greatest in the field of communications, one of the key requirements of good policing. The development of the Police National Computer has greatly aided the operational police officer, and command and control systems being installed one by one throughout the police forces of the country are improving their response to emergency calls and providing a valuable source of management information.

Changes are also taking place in policing systems as police forces try to use their limited resources to deal with the demands imposed upon them by rising crime rates and increased violence and social tensions, particularly in large cities. The subject of policing systems will be dealt with in some detail in subsequent chapters, but trends that may be noted here are increasing specialisation as policing problems become more complex, the increasing involvement of police within communities in order to prevent violence and the increasing recognition that the police must come to terms with the public media.

Chapter Two

Police and government

Police and central government
Basic responsibilities

The events outlined in Chapter 1 have produced a police system in Britain that is locally administered but subject to strong central government influence. Each of the forty-three separate police forces in England and Wales, eight in Scotland and one in Northern Ireland has a local police authority, its own chief constable who is an independent officer of the Crown, but the English and Welsh forces are part of the responsibilities of the Secretary of State for the Home Department while the Scottish police forces and Royal Ulster Constabulary are part of the responsibilities of the Secretaries of State for Scotland and Northern Ireland respectively.

The relationship between police authorities, Secretaries of State and chief constables is a crucial part of the British police system and may be summarised by reference to three key sections of the Police Act 1964:

> It shall be the duty of the police authority for every police area . . . to secure the maintenance of an adequate and efficient police force for the area. (Section 4.)
> The police force maintained for a police area . . . shall be under the direction and control of the chief constable. (Section 5.)
> The Secretary of State shall exercise his powers under the Act in such manner and to such extent as appears to him to be best calculated to promote the efficiency of the police. (Section 28.)

Thus it can be seen that the police authority is responsible for the *maintenance* of a police force, a chief constable is responsible for its *direction and control* and the Secretary of State is responsible for exercising a wide range of powers to ensure that the police service is efficient. In the analysis that follows, the

English and Welsh system will be described but it is closely paralleled in Scotland and Northern Ireland.

The Home Secretary

The Home Office, presided over by the Secretary of State for the Home Department (usually referred to as the Home Secretary) is concerned principally with the administration of matters concerning the internal security of the nation. The Police Department of the Home Office and Her Majesty's Chief Inspector of Constabulary advise the Home Secretary on all police matters.

The following are some of the more important of the Home Secretary's powers in respect of the police; the numbers in brackets indicate the relevant section of the Police Act 1964:

1. He may require a police authority to call upon the chief constable to retire in the interests of efficiency (s. 29).
2. He may require any chief constable to submit to him a report on matters connected with the policing of his area (s. 30).
3. He may make grants in respect of expenses incurred for police purposes (s. 31).
4. He may cause a local inquiry into any matter connected with the policing of the area (s. 32).
5. He may make regulations as to the government, administration and condition of service of police forces, special constables and cadets (ss. 33, 34, 35).
6. He hears appeals from police officers who have been dealt with for an offence against discipline (s. 37).
7. He provides and maintains central services such as the Police College, police training centres, forensic-science laboratories and wireless depots (s. 41).
8. He may set up bodies to undertake research (s. 42).
9. He must approve the decision of police authorities in respect of: (i) the appointment of chief constables, deputy and assistant chief constables; and (ii) buildings, structures and premises (s. 38).
10. He determines the number of "Her Majesty's Inspectors of Constabulary" who: (i) inspect and report to the Secretary of State on the efficiency of all police forces (other than the

Metropolitan Police); and (*ii*) carry out such other duties for the purpose of furthering police efficiency as the Secretary of State may from time to time direct (s. 38).

It is clear from this list that the Home Secretary has considerable powers to enable him to ensure that the police service is efficient. Using them, successive Home Secretaries have seen to it that there is a substantial degree of uniformity of practice and conditions of service throughout the country and that resources that cannot be maintained by individual forces are provided on a national basis as central services. To aid the Home Secretary, Inspectors of Constabulary inspect each police force (except the Metropolitan Police, where internal arrangements for inspection are made) and report as to its efficiency, advise him about local conditions and proposals and, with the Chief Inspector of Constabulary, provide an experienced source of advice on police matters. Intervention in police matters may be through regulation, advice or finance. As at least half the cost of police forces is borne by central government, the Home Secretary is in a strong position to influence decisions and enforce standards. Although, in practice, the threat to withhold government monies from a police force has not been made in recent times, there can be little doubt but that it is a strong card to have in reserve.

The Home Secretary plays a key role in the appointment of chief constables, their deputies and assistants and may order the removal of an inefficient chief constable. But he does not have *operational* control over chief constables. Even in the one force where the Home Secretary has a dual role (in that he is also its police authority), the Metropolitan Police, he does not have operational control over the chief officer, the Commissioner. The Commissioners of the Metropolitan Police and the City of London have similar autonomy, in so far as the direction and control of their forces are concerned, as the chief constables of provincial police forces.

The role of the chief constable
The position of a chief constable (or commissioner in the case of the two London forces) is well established in British law. In addition to s. 5, Police Act 1964, quoted above, the courts have

emphasised that a chief constable is independent of the executive:

> No minister of the Crown can tell him he must or must not keep observation on this place or that, he must or must not prosecute this man or that —nor can any police authority tell him so. The responsibility is on him. He is answerable to the law and the law alone.
>
> (*R.* v. *Commissioner of Police of the Metropolis, ex p. Blackburn* [1968] 2 Q. B. 118.)

But, whilst he may not be subject to operational control, every chief constable is, of course, accountable for what he does. There is a line of accountability running right through the police service. Every police officer, by virtue of his holding the office of constable, is "an officer whose authority is original, not delegated, and is exercised at his own discretion by virtue of his office: he is neither a crown servant nor a servant of the police authority" (*Royal Commission on the Police, Final Report,* 1962). For the exercise of that authority, a constable is answerable to the courts, civil and criminal. Additionally, the chief constable is accountable for the actions of himself and members of his force, not only to the law but also to his police authority, central government and the public. By s. 12 of the Police Act 1964, he may be required to submit to the police authority "a report in writing on such matters as may be specified in that requirement, being matters connected with the policing of the area". There is a right to refuse to submit such a report if it would contain information which "in the public interest ought not to be disclosed, or is not needed for the discharge of the functions of the police authority" (s. 12 (3)). Where there is disagreement between the police authority and the chief constable, the request for information can be referred to the Home Secretary, who must decide whether or not it should be given. Section 11 of the Police Act provides for arrangements to make the police authority accountable to the county council through a member of the council who is also a member of the police authority and is nominated by that authority for the purpose.

As has been indicated earlier, the Secretary of State also has the right to require a chief constable to submit to him a report on any matter connected with the policing of his area (s. 30 (1)). Here then is another continuation of the line of accountability for, as the chief constable is accountable to the Secretary of

State, so is the latter accountable to Parliament for police matters and many of the Secretary of State's requests for reports from chief constables are to enable answers to be given to questions from Members of Parliament.

The role of local government
Local government

England (excluding London) and Wales are divided into administrative counties, six of them being metropolitan counties centred on large conurbations like Manchester and Liverpool, and the rest containing a mixture of urban and rural areas.

Although counties have police responsibilities, some of them are linked together for police purposes to form joint authorities, the remainder having police forces covering an area coterminous with county boundaries.

The second tier of local government below the counties is formed by districts, some of which are called boroughs. Districts have specific responsibilities, one of which is the collection of the rates for local government, since counties do not collect monies for themselves but make an annual demand from the districts within each county for money to finance county operations (including police) in the forthcoming year.

Other than in the larger urban areas, there is a third tier of local government based on parishes, towns or communities. These parish councils have limited responsibilities aimed at providing the smaller urban areas with amenities that are not forthcoming from the larger units of districts and counties.

Each county and district appoints paid officials to administer the policies and decisions arrived at by the unpaid, elected council members. The scope of such officials varies from council to council according to the extent of the delegated authority given to them.

The main functions of county and district councils are usually exercised through a series of committees and sub-committees, which allow decisions to be based on detailed discussion that would not be possible in a full council meeting. Each committee has specific responsibilities and this may result in certain decisions having to be referred from one committee to another. For example, certain financial decisions that are made by the police committee may be referred to the finance committee of the county council. Police building-programmes are usually submitted to a county council committee that is responsible for the preparation of capital programmes for the county.

The police committee of a county is unique in that it is not entirely composed of elected councillors: "two thirds shall be members of the council of the county appointed by that council; one third shall be magistrates for the county appointed by the court of quarter sessions for the county" (s. 2 (2), Police Act 1964).

The police committee is the police authority for the purpose of the Police Act. It may appoint special sub-committees for particular purposes and commonly has a permanent sub-committee that acts as a steering group for the main committee.

Where one police force serves more than one county, a combined police authority exists, consisting of two-thirds of county councillors from the constituent county councils and one-third of magistrates from the constituent areas. The principal difference between a police committee of a single county and a combined police authority is one of finance. A combined authority has a separate police fund and precepts on the constituent areas for its money. The police committee of a single county has no police fund separate and distinct from that of the county council.

The police authority

The Police Act 1964 lays down a list of duties for the police authority:

1. To secure the maintenance of an adequate and efficient police force (s. 4).
2. To appoint the chief constable and determine the number of persons in each rank in the force (s. 4).
3. To provide and maintain buildings, premises and structures for police purposes (s. 4).
4. To provide and maintain vehicles, apparatus, clothing and other equipment required for police purposes (s. 4).
5. To appoint chief constables, deputy chief constables and assistant chief constables and, when necessary, require them to retire in the interests of efficiency (s. 5).

All of these provisions are subject to some measure of overall control by the Secretary of State.

The police authority, therefore, supplies the people, buildings and equipment necessary for policing. But the role of the police authority does not end with the provision of resources; it holds the ultimate sanction over the chief constable for, with the approval of the Secretary of State, it can call upon him to retire in the interests of efficiency. As we have seen, the police authority can call for reports from the chief constable and it must also be supplied with an annual report as to the policing of the area (s. 12).

The provisions of the Police Act give a police authority wide powers in respect of its police force but its role is much wider than providing a regulatory mechanism. The central position of the police authority can be seen from the diagram in Fig. 2, in which the arrows show the direction of controls.

The controls by the Home Secretary and the role of Her Majesty's Inspectorate of Constabulary have already been discussed. The controls exercised by the latter are shown in Fig. 2 as dotted lines, since they do not exercise direct control but may offer advice and criticism and influence the Home Secretary in issuing firm controls, either financial or regulatory. The position of the police authority between the chief constable and the county council shows the county council exercising control over the police authority, a control that is almost entirely financial but given additional significance because of the position of the chief constable *vis-à-vis* the county council.

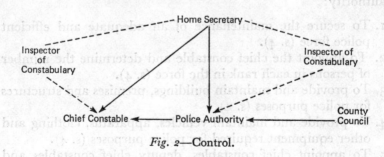

Fig. 2—Control.

At officer level, the county councils have a chief executive and a series of chief officers, each responsible for a department —social services, education, public protection, etc. Collectively, all or some of these make up a management board to administer the decisions taken by the elected members of the county council. The chief constable is not a chief officer of the county council, for he is appointed by, and is accountable to, the police authority. Thus the relationship between the police authority and the county council is of considerable importance to the police.

The police authority and local government
In practice, because the finances of the police committee are firmly linked with those of other council committees, for financial purposes, the police committee is often treated in the same way as any other county council committee which is composed entirely of county councillors. The odd effect of this can be seen when considering such matters as police manpower establishments. These are set by the police authority subject to the approval of the Secretary of State and the agreement of the county council is not required. Yet, when the time comes to find the money to pay the people to fill the places in that establishment, the decisions of the police authority *are* subject to county council approval, for the county council (or county councils in joint authorities) controls the purse strings.

The interweaving of police authorities and county councils can be seen in the employment of civilian police staff. With the exception of traffic wardens, who must be employed by the police authority, all civilian police staff *can* be employed either by the police authority *or* the county council. Thus, the direction and control of a police force by its chief constable may be limited when it comes to the civilian police staff who work alongside the police officers (who definitely work under his direction and control). Even where a county police authority employs members of the civilian police staff, their conditions of service are likely to be closely linked to those of the parent county council, and so there may be overlapping responsibilities between police administrators and county council administrators (*see* Chapter 7).

Such problems can be, and usually are, avoided by goodwill on all sides—chief constables, police authority members, county councillors, county council officers, trades unions, Superintendents' Association and Police Federation representatives—but the system can go awry if that goodwill is absent.

The independence of the police authority

A police authority has been described as having four main duties:

> The first is to provide an adequate police force for its area, properly paid, equipped, housed and administered.
>
> The second is to constitute a body of citizens concerned with the local standing and well being of the police, interested in the maintenance of law and order, and able to give advice and guidance to a chief constable about local problems.
>
> The third is to appoint and if necessary discipline or remove, the senior officers of the force.
>
> The fourth is to play an active role in fostering good relations between the police and the public.
>
> (*Royal Commission on the Police, Final Report,* Cmnd. 1728, para. 154, H.M.S.O., 1962.)

In these capacities, it can provide an enormous amount of support for a local police force and ensure that the police in that area are aware of local feelings and problems. If it is basically non-party political, then it can aid the police to retain the politically-neutral role that has been the strength of the British police for so long. Unfortunately, such neutrality on the part of a police authority may be in danger due to the growth of party politics in local government. The significance of this was foreshadowed in the evidence given by some county councils to the 1960 Royal Commission but the effects were underestimated by that body. The view of Essex County Council was:

> In a county such as Essex, where political persuasions are of some considerable consequence in the county council, it is of the utmost importance that there should be no opportunity for allegations to be made that the administration of the force is subject to political influence. It is not enough that such allegations could easily be refuted; it is in the public interest that the very opportunity for their being made should not be available and this can only be achieved by the maintenance of the *status quo ante* whereby the administration of the police not merely is, but can be seen to be, in control independent of the county council.

The Royal Commission dismissed this with: "We understand these misgivings, but experience in Scotland and in the English and Welsh boroughs suggest they are groundless." This view failed to allow for the pressures upon a county councillor member of the police committee who is also a prominent member of a political party; he must inevitably be swayed to some extent by the national policies of that party. The balance of two-thirds county councillors and one-third magistrates may provide an effectively non-political police authority but, if one political party is in office with a large majority in the county council, the effect is to produce a police authority which has the same political leanings. Decisions may then be taken following the policies of that party rather than in the interests of the efficiency of the police.

What has so far been said may seem to suggest that there are fundamental weaknesses in the system of police authority/ Secretary of State/chief constable but these have to be seen in context. The system works very well in most places for a number of varied reasons:

1. In many areas party-political balances are quite even and so the one-third of magistrates in police committees makes them fairly independent of party-political considerations.
2. Even where there may not be an even balance, national party-political considerations are often diluted by local considerations.
3. Many local councillors become adept at wearing more than one hat, dependent on whether they are sitting in full council or as a member of a police or other committee.
4. Law and order is usually of considerable local concern and therefore neglect of police interests may alienate the voters.
5. The independence of the chief constable to direct and control the police ensures that operational police activities are under professional police control.
6. The roles of the Home Office and of Her Majesty's Inspector of Constabulary ensure that standards do not fall below an acceptable minimum.

The function of the police authority has been dwelt upon at some length because of the unique part it plays in producing a police service that gains many benefits from centralised co-ordination and control, yet remains local in character. The continued existence of the system depends on the maintenance of a workable balance and this means that there must be agreement on the limits of the responsibilities of the three participants and willingness not to attempt to upset the balance.

The general trend has been for the powers of central government to increase at the expense of those of the chief constables and police authorities. One example will suffice to illustrate this process. When, in 1973, the Home Secretary announced his government's intention to monitor complaints against the police through an *ex post facto* review system, this could have been linked with the provisions of s. 50 of the Police Act 1964, which laid down that police authorities "shall keep themselves informed as to the manner in which complaints . . . are dealt with by the chief officer of police". Instead, the government chose to add to its own powers by creating a Police Complaints Board, with members selected by the Prime Minister and accountable to the Secretary of State.

The Police Act 1976, which created the Police Complaints Board, not only emphasised the role of central government at the expense of local government, but also lessened the autonomy of chief constables as disciplinary authorities. The Board can make recommendations as to the discipline charges which they consider should be preferred and, should a chief constable demur, "they may direct him to prefer such charges as they may specify" (s. 3 (2)). To ensure that a chief constable cannot assert his independence when he hears discipline cases of this kind, he must sit as a member of a tribunal with two members of the Police Complaints Board who can out-vote him when a decision as to the guilt of the accused is made. Only in respect of punishment does the chief constable retain his former powers and even here he must consult his fellow members of the tribunal before making a decision.

The autonomy of chief officers of police has also been the subject of attacks by some local authorities who wish chief constables to take up a position in the county council hierarchy that would make them operationally accountable to county councils. This is nothing new for, in 1960, local authority representatives were seeking the power to issue instructions to a chief constable "to take steps to enforce the law more vigorously or as to his methods in dealing with a political demonstration" (*Royal Commission on the Police, Final Report,* 1962, para. 76).

In endorsing the existing legal status of the chief constable as "defined by the courts, and not that of a Crown or a local authority servant" (ibid., para. 151), the Royal Commission concluded that:

The basic soundness of our present police system is not due merely to the fact that responsible people operate it successfully—though that is certainly true. Nor, again, is the system sound merely because it follows a tradition of local policing which is traceable back for many centuries though that also is true. In our opinion the present police system is sound because it is based upon, and reflects, a political idea of immense practical value which has gained wide acceptance in this country, namely the idea of partnership between central and local government in the administration of public services. This idea, working itself out in a variety of ways in our education, health, housing and other services, admirably suits the British temperament. It gives free rein to discussion and ample scope for compromise, thus promoting the growth of an enlightened and mature public opinion. It provides for the central pooling of knowledge and experience gathered from the whole country, but for the local application of this knowledge and experience to suit the needs of each particular community. By bringing into the administration of public services large numbers of men and women of goodwill it encourages the development throughout our society of a sense of civic responsibility. These are imponderable but very real gains. They ought not to be lightly surrendered. (Ibid., p. 142.)

The test for the future will be whether "men and women of goodwill" will be able to maintain that sense of civic responsibility in the face of the pressures that will certainly occur.

Police representative organisations

It is impossible to consider the relationship between police and government without taking account of the role of the representative organisations of police officers. The Association of Chief Police Officers (ACPO) fulfils two functions: it acts as a representative organisation for ranks above chief superintendent and also serves as a means of their meeting to consider professional topics of common interests, to formulate common policies and to make representations on behalf of the service on policing matters. Regional conferences are held four times a year in each region and resolutions and recommendations are forwarded to the Secretariat at New Scotland Yard for consideration by the Standing Committees of the ACPO Council on Traffic, Communications, Crime, Computer Development, Training, and General Purposes, who may then refer them to the Council which consists of the Commissioners of Police for the Metropolis and for the City of London, the officers of the Association and all chief constables in England, Wales and Northern Ireland.

In Chapter 1 mention was made of the formation of the

Superintendents' Association and the Police Federation but their influence upon the police service has increased considerably since they were set up, following the Police Act 1919. The Superintendents' Association represents superintendents and chief superintendents, the Police Federation all other ranks from constable to chief inspector. Although ACPO and the Superintendents' Association are an important part of the police service, it is the Police Federation, representing the bulk of the police officers in the country and the nearest to a trade union, that is of prime concern here because of the ambiguities in its position.

The Police Federation is ". . . for the purpose of representing members of police forces in England and Wales . . . in all matters affecting their welfare and efficiency, other than questions of discipline or promotion affecting individuals" (s. 14, Police Act 1964). As to what constitutes "welfare and efficiency", the Act is silent, but they cover a wide range of topics. The prescribed channels of influence for the Federation are through the Police Council and Police Advisory Board.

A Police Council was established in 1953 but in its present form it was created by s. 45 of the Police Act 1964 to consider questions of leave, pay, hours of duty, allowances, pensions, clothing and equipment. It is composed of an Official Side and a Staff Side, the former consisting of representatives of central and local government and the latter of representatives of ACPO, the Superintendents' Association and the Police Federation. Before making regulations in matters within its purview, the Secretary of State is required to take account of any recommendations made by the Council, and to furnish it with a draft of the regulations.

The Police Advisory Board advises the Secretary of State, who is its chairman, on general questions affecting the police, and is made up of representatives of central and local government and the three police representative organisations. The various conferences held by the representative organisations, the Police Council and the Police Advisory Board, provide an opportunity for the police to influence government on a wide range of matters of interest to them and, on the whole, the system works well. There is, however, one controversial area that is of great concern to the Police Federation and to the police service generally, namely, the bargaining powers of the Federation relative to those of trade unions. In 1976, the representatives of the Police Federation of England and Wales expressed disquiet at the attitude of the Official Side of the Police Council to a pay claim, by leaving the Council and demanding direct negotiations with the Home Secretary. Not for the first time, suggestions were made by some police officers that the police should press for a trade union and the freedom of action afforded other work people, including the right to strike.

In some other countries, police officers are civil servants and, therefore, generally have the same rights as other government servants. In the U.S.A. there has been a growth of police unionism accompanied, in some places, by militant action (*see*, for example, New York (p. 58)). The Police Federation is a hybrid organisation which fulfils some of the functions of a trade union, but is not one. Its powers are limited by law and, in particular, it may not be affiliated to the Trade Union Congress: ". . . every branch [of the Federation] shall be entirely independent of, and unassociated with, any body or person outside the police service except if authorised by the Secretary of State . . ." (s. 44, Police Act 1964).

There are three main reasons why police representation poses problems for the government and the police themselves: the first is the obvious harm that can result from a police strike (*see* Chapter 1, p. 19 (the Liverpool strike of 1919)); the second is the need for police to be neutral at times of violent confrontation involving trade union members; and the third is the necessity to keep the police free of political involvement, particularly in view of the increasing use of trade union power to achieve political ends. The second and third factors are linked by the very important concept of police neutrality and it will be necessary to deal with this in more detail later after the specific subject of police and politics has been considered.

Apart from being allowed to vote in elections, police officers are debarred by police regulations from taking any active part in politics. Some indications as to the reasons for this can be gained by considering quotations from two very different sources:

I would like to see the Police Federation say to the Government that their members are no longer prepared to work in areas like Notting Hill unless they step in and improve the housing conditions.

(National Union of Students representative at a Police Federation Seminar on *The Developing Role of the Police in a Changing Society*, June 1971.)

Right now we're organised . . . so that if the Mayor does not do what we want him to do, we defeat him at the polls. And someday we'll have that nationally.

(Policeman attending the 1969 Omaha National Union Organisational Convention, cited by J. H. Burpo and J. J. Irwin in *The Police Labor Movement*, Charles C. Thomas, 1971.)

The implication of both statements is that the police should use their power to force national/local government to act. As John C. Alderson, then Commandant of the Police College, replied to the first statement: "That is the sort of naive view that is expressed from time to time. What political postures are the police to adopt?" Clearly, the answer he expected was "none" for, as this chapter has attempted to show, the police are accountable to central and local government and should not try to usurp their functions. The problem for Police Federation members is that, by not being able to use their full political weight in the way that a trade union may, they have difficulty in maintaining parity in pay and conditions with other, less inhibited, sections of the national work force. The result has tended to be a continuation of the nineteenth- and early twentieth-century pattern, in which police conditions fell behind those of more powerfully-organised workers until they reached a critical point when action would be taken to improve them.

The labour organisations guarding the interests of workers in other fields would be unlikely to accept the idea of rules restraining, in any way, the private lives of their members, but it is important to recognise the unique position of a constable.

(*Police Training Manual*, J. English and R. Houghton, McGraw Hill, 1975.)

This unique position depends to a very large extent on the fact that the British police are *not* involved in politics and the dilemma for the Police Federation is that while it would be advantageous in terms of pay and material benefits to be able to use trade union methods, the whole nature of the service and the manner in which its members carry out their work would change if the police moved significantly from a position of neutrality.

Police and democracy

All countries have to arrive at a balance between allowing total freedom for the individual and restricting that freedom in order to preserve law and order. They then have to fit the police into the framework of their legal and social systems and provide safeguards to ensure that the police act within that balance. In a much simplified form, this process has provided a plot for countless western films: a small town is terrorised by a gang of outlaws; the senior citizens of the town hire a gunfighter to kill the outlaws and restore law and order; the town may then find itself being ruled by the gunfighter and so one oppressive regime has been replaced by another.

In totalitarian countries where the police are an instrument of the state dedicated to the preservation of the dictatorship, their role is clear cut and they can operate with few inhibitions. In a democratic society, the police need to be constrained so that their powers are balanced against the freedom of the individual. The means that different countries use in order to achieve this balance vary considerably, as does the amount of power given to the police.

The Royal Commission on the Police gave serious consideration to the question as to whether a national police force should replace the existing local organisation. Despite a formidable array of arguments favouring a unified police service, the Commission concluded that "the police forces of this country should not be brought under the direct central control of the Government. In our view the improvements which the advocates of such a change wish to see can be achieved without seriously disturbing the local basis on which the present police system rests, and thus sacrificing much that is valuable" (*Final Report*, 1962, p. 49).

Among the arguments against a national police force, "It was put to us that, so long as the police in Great Britain are not controlled by the Government, tyranny will be impossible in this country; but that, if the present system of local forces were to be abolished in favour of a unified police service, any future Government would have ready to hand the means of establishing a police state. We find this argument unconvincing, for it rests, in our view on fallacious assumptions. British liberty does not depend, and never has depended, upon a dispersal of police power. It has never depended upon any particular form of police organisation. It depends on the supremacy of Parliament and on the rule of law" (ibid., p. 45).

In his Memorandum of Dissent to this Report, Dr A. L. Goodhart was more positive about the role of police in preserving freedom in a democracy: "The danger in a democracy does not lie in a central police that is too strong, but in local police forces that are too weak. It was the private gangs of the Fascists and of the Nazis that enabled Mussolini and Hitler to establish their dictatorships when the legitimate police proved impotent."

The Nazi Germany example is one that is often cited to illustrate what can happen when ruthless politicians set out to take control of a country and a brief account will be given below. Further, it can be useful to compare the police arrangements in other countries, for example, the U.S.A. with its local system and France, which, as was seen in Chapter 1, has a long tradition of centrally-controlled police.

Police in Germany, 1930–1945

The causes that would set up a dictatorship in Great Britain would far transcend the means at the disposal of the dictator to impose his will. They would be of a kind that would sweep an extremist party into power with a policy so radical as to change the forms of government itself and not merely its instruments.

The validity of this quotation from the 1960 Royal Commission report is exemplified in the experience of Germany from 1930 onwards.

At that time, there was an international economic crisis that hit Germany very hard. The two main symptoms of the country's problems were unemployment and inflation, both of which were completely out of control. In such a climate, extremist political organisations could flourish and there were violent pitched battles between members of the Fascist Nazi party and communists. The Nazis were particularly effective in such confrontations. They had built up a formidable paramilitary organisation, complete with uniforms, that could be used with frightening efficiency against their less organised opponents.

In the elections of 1932, the National Socialists (Nazis) emerged as the strongest party. Their leader, Adolf Hitler, promised to rescue the country, restore public order, cure unemployment and regain economic stability. In 1933, he became Chancellor of the Reich.

The burning of the Reichstag (Parliament) building in February 1933 was used as a pretext for the new government to issue an emergency decree which restricted basic rights under the existing constitution. In March 1933, an "Enabling Act" gave Hitler unrestricted power.

One of the first acts of this government was to infiltrate the police with Nazi party members. A prominent Nazi, Hermann Göring, was made Minister President, Minister of the Interior and Head of Police in Prussia, the largest and most important state of Germany. On 10th March 1933, a proclamation introduced the Hilfspolizei (Auxiliary Police), uniformed "police" wearing the emblem of the Nazi party, a swastika, and recruited from National Socialist Units. Their main tasks were to guard public buildings, the offices of the Nazi party and to patrol the streets to prevent public disorder.

Although the Hilfspolizei were disbanded in August 1933, many transferred into the regular police. To facilitate this, two things were done: in September 1933, 295 senior police officers and about 2,460 junior ranks were dismissed on political grounds and, in December 1933, the police union was disbanded after an intensive propaganda campaign aimed at discrediting it.

Thus in one year, the Nazi party had effectively removed all opposition to their take-over of the police. In 1934, a large national police force was created and the following year, part of it was merged into the army. Following the 1914–1918 war, Germany had been limited to an army of 100,000 professional soldiers who had to serve for 12 years but, in 1935, conscription was introduced. The existence of some police units trained to act as task forces, enabled them to be converted into soldiers with very little effort and so they and the men at police-training centres were merged with the army.

Despite these dramatic changes in police organisation, the vast majority of police officers went about their normal police work. The purges carried out in 1933 had virtually silenced all

C

opposition and, from that year onwards, a new and very deadly organisation was being built up under Göring and another prominent Nazi official, Heinrich Himmler. This organisation, the Geheime Staatspolizei (Secret State Police), or Gestapo as it became known, was developed first in Prussia by Göring and in Bavaria by Himmler. It was then extended to the whole of Germany under Himmler, who became Chief of the German Police in 1936.

With a Nazi party member occupying all key positions in the police, it became simple to round up millions of people and place them in concentration camps. Later, many of these people were exterminated in gas chambers, everything being done under the cloak of normal police activities and, apparently, within the law.

Even from this brief summary of the collapse of a country into totalitarianism, it is possible to see that the main cause was the disintegration of the government system under the pressures of the economic situation, rather than the nature of the police organisation. One clear lesson, however, is that the failure on the part of the German police forces to control the growth and activities of the organised private armies of the National Socialists was an important factor. Yet even here they lacked the necessary governmental support. As has been seen elsewhere in the world, the ineffectiveness of police is not always due to practical considerations but rather to political expediency or indecision.

The conversion of a number of state police forces into a national one by the Nazis does suggest that a centralised police service is of more value to a totalitarian regime than separate police forces under local control. It is noticeable in other, non-democratic, countries that a nationally organised police force is the norm.

Also common to totalitarian countries is some form of highly organised secret police, accountable to no one but the leaders of the ruling party. It is this body that executes the orders to eliminate opposition under the cloak of legality.

The question of legality is a key issue. The strength of the British system is the independence of the legislature, the executive and the judiciary. In some countries, for example France, this separation is not so distinct. In pre-1945 Germany, the normal rule of law was eliminated by the Nazis and since imprisonment or execution without trial became commonplace, what was happening was that the same people were acting as law-makers, police chiefs, judges and executioners.

The evils carried out by the Gestapo were made possible by a strong central government in sole command of the police, courts and prisons, but it is not necessary for a police force to be a national one for it to act unconstitutionally. The U.S.A. has provided many examples of purely local police forces which have been used to limit democracy.

The United States of America
General characteristics
The U.S. police service is divided into about 40,000 separate agencies with no national governmental control, support or inspection and often with more than one agency having jurisdiction in one place.

In addition to the local police, there are federal government agencies of which the Federal Bureau of Investigation is the nearest to being a police force in the British sense of the word. The F.B.I. is not, however, a national police force, but is rather a support agency, as it concentrates on providing a service of scientific aids and information (it has the largest fingerprint collection in the world). Additionally, it acts as a security organisation and detection agency for those crimes such as kidnapping, extortion and bank robberies which have been specially placed under its jurisdiction by legislation.

The normal police functions are carried out by a mixture of police forces based on states, counties, townships, towns and villages. Police officers can be sheriffs, marshals or constables and it is possible to have in any one town, members of the F.B.I., the state police, the county sheriff's office and the city police department, all with some form of jurisdiction. In some cases the state police may have two branches, a general police force and a highway patrol and, in addition, there are occasionally police forces based on "special protection districts". It can be seen that the scope for individuality is wide and it is not really possible to identify a "typical" U.S. police force—a large number of which consist of one man.

The police forces of the larger cities of the U.S.A. are probably the most similar to the British models. The New York City Police Department was founded in 1844 and originally resembled the early Metropolitan Police of London, which was, in part, used as a model. Unlike the Metropolitan Police, however, the New York City Police Department is still entirely a local force, for the excuse used to bring the London force under the Home Secretary in 1829 was that London was the capital of the country and therefore had special problems, but of course New York is not a capital city. There are differences, too, in the nature of the Commissioners of the two: the New York Commissioner is a political appointment and is answerable to the Mayor, an office holding a great deal more power than in Britain.

Police and politicians
The relationship between local politicians and the police has always been a problem in the U.S.A. because of the way in which the heads of police departments are dependent upon local government elections for their continuance in office. Many ingenious schemes have been devised in the past whereby the police have assisted the local party machine to maintain control over the votes that will keep the party in office. One of the cities with the most notorious problems of this kind has been Chicago, a report on the policing of which, in 1931, cited the case of a mayor who appointed his tailor as chief of police, apparently working on the basis that a good tailor will make a good chief of police. (*National Commission on Law Observance and Enforcement*, No. 14: "Report on Police" (U.S. Government, 1931).)

The absence of central governmental involvement in U.S. local affairs results in powerful local government. Such "control" as there is tends to be administered by courts and the press rather than by national government. Thus, although it is possible to see some of the problems associated with purely local control of police, the difference between local government in the U.S.A. and elsewhere must be borne in mind when trying to make generalisations from the U.S. experience. In the same way that the laws of the U.S.A., particularly gun laws and rules of evidence, affect the working of the police, so do the relationships between the national government, local government and the courts. U.S. courts are much more closely involved in the regulation of everyday affairs than the British, and recourse is had to law in matters which would be dealt with by government in Britain.

To obtain an indication of the way in which the local government of some U.S. cities may influence the police, Chicago may again be cited. The extent to which this particular police force was controlled by the Mayor can be illustrated by the example of an order given in 1968 by the Mayor, Richard J. Daly. At the time of the assassination of a popular black leader—Martin Luther King—the police chief gave instructions to his men that they were to use discretion in dealing with the subsequent hysteria and violence. These instructions were immediately revoked by the Mayor who insisted that an order be published to command the police to "shoot to kill" arsonists and to "shoot to maim or cripple" people looting stores, instructions that were duly given to the police but subsequently amended in the face of public protests at their severity (*see* "The Mayor and the Police" in *Police Forces in History*, ed. George L. Mosse, Sage, 1975, p. 277).

Problems in U.S. police forces
That total local control is not a guarantee of success is clear from the problems of U.S. police forces, even apart from Chicago. The New York City Police Department was the subject of a comprehensive two-and-a-half-year investigation which revealed the scale of the problems that can beset a large modern police force. The *Knapp Commission Report on Police Corruption* (published by G. Braziller, 1972) divided corrupt policemen into "meat eaters" (actively corrupt but few in number) and "grass eaters" (passively corrupt but large in numbers). The "grass eaters" were seen as "the heart of the problem. Their great numbers tend to make corruption 'respectable'. They also tend to encourage the code of silence that brands anyone who exposes corruption as a traitor". The Knapp Commission suggested that the answer to the problem of the "grass eater" was leadership and support.

Certainly, where good leadership has been provided, there have been some examples of individual police forces making enormous strides forward. One example, Los Angeles, will be discussed in a later chapter; another is Chicago. In 1960, following allegations that police officers had "hired" a burglar to steal property for them, a new commissioner, Professor O. W. Wilson, was appointed. He undertook a programme of modernisation and reforms over a period of seven years during which, by his personal authority and diplomacy, he was able to achieve at least a measure of separation of the police from the workings of the political party machine.

Returning to New York, it is salutary to note the extent to which the professional police (as distinct from political appointees) have formed themselves into a strong police union. Whilst some of the union/commissioner disputes have concerned welfare and operational matters, many have been as a result of the precarious finances of the city. Like many long-established cities, New York has lost much of its income due to the decline of its centre, as the people with money have moved out to the suburbs and left parts of the city to become ghettos. In such circumstances, there is an increase in social problems and less money to finance solutions. In New York City, this reached the stage where, against a background of rising crime, 2,500 policemen were made redundant because there was no money to pay them. Herein lies one limitation of looking at policing as a purely local matter instead of as a national one. In the absence of a national contribution to the upkeep of a police force, an area may find itself the centre of attraction for people who create a policing problem but do not contribute to the cost of dealing with it. This may be on a temporary basis such as a pop festival or tourist attraction. Or it may be a permanent problem, caused by immigration or the drift of moneyless people into the area.

France

For administrative purposes, France is divided into *départements*, each with its own budget, rather like a British county. Unlike counties, however, *départements* are managed by a high-ranking civil servant, the *préfet*, appointed by the central government in Paris. *Préfets* are also responsible for law and order as representatives of the Ministry of the Interior.

There are two national organisations that carry out most of the policing: the Police Nationale has jurisdiction over the whole of France but is principally responsible for towns with more than 10,000 inhabitants; towns with less than 10,000 people and rural areas are policed by the Gendarmerie Nationale. The Police Nationale consists of two main sections, the Police Urbaine (Town Police) which, as its name implies, carries out the day to day policing of towns and the Compagnies Republicaine de Sûreté (C.R.S.) which is concerned with public order. The C.R.S. consists of units of over 200 men who train to deal with public disorder on the task-force principle and use a wide range of riot gear.

The Police Nationale is under the direct control of the Ministry of the Interior, whilst the Gendarmerie Nationale is a special military corps with a public-order role as well as responsibility for policing rural areas, and is controlled by the Ministère des Armées (Defence Ministry). Although the mayors of towns may exercise some direction over their local police, the control of public order is solely the responsibility of the *préfet*, who has at his permanent disposal the Police Urbaine and local units of the *gendarmerie*. If these are inadequate, he can ask the Ministry of the Interior for the aid of one or more companies of the C.R.S. and, in serious emergencies, the Defence Ministry for the help of the mobile *gendarmerie* and the army. With the exception of the last two sources of assistance, the *préfet* is in overall command. Only the mobile *gendarmerie* and army officers retain the right to direct the methods that will be used to deal with the situation. It can be seen, therefore, that policing is, in a very real sense, a function of central government since, as was stated earlier, the *préfet* is a local representative of the Ministry of the Interior.

The co-existence of the two large police organisations is due to historical accident rather than deliberate design, but suggestions that they should be amalgamated have always been resisted, since the dual system prevents the whole of the country's national police being under one operational command. It is argued that this provides a safeguard against the police being used unconstitutionally but, since members of both organisations are civil servants and the Ministries of the Interior and Defence are clearly instruments of one government, it seems possible that the safeguard is purely notional. Nevertheless, it serves to illustrate the strength of feeling that exists in many democratic countries that the police must be kept under control, to ensure that they are not used by a ruthless political group to subvert the democratic processes of government.

Police independence

In Germany from 1934 to 1945, the police were an instrument of the ruling party, the Nazis; in the U.S.A. the police officer is often seen as part of the local political party in office at the time; in France, the police are civil servants ruled from Paris and therefore tend to be seen as an arm of the central government of the time and an enforcer of its policies. In contrast, the British police are not under the operational command of anyone other than their own senior officers. As John C. Alderson has pointed out, "In England, the police are associated with the law of the land rather than politics. They are neither civil servants nor local government officers. Their commissioners and chief constables have an independence which their counterparts in France and America do not possess. The policeman here is thus seen as a servant of the public, a general, impartial guardian of life, liberty and property" (*The Police We Deserve*, Wolfe, 1973, p. 41).

If their present independence is to be preserved, the police themselves must ensure that they cannot be justly accused of showing favour to any one section of the community. Where there is social unrest it is difficult to maintain a neutral image, particularly if society is divided along racial or religious lines. Even when the divisions are political, it is difficult to balance free speech and peaceful protest with the need to prevent violence. There are frequent demands from one faction to ban the activities of its opponents. From a policing point of view, it would be easier to accede to such demands but to do so would be to step onto a slippery slope. Prohibiting one group from demonstrating may tend to unite other minorities against the police and raise the vital question as to what criteria should be used to differentiate between those groups that may demonstrate and those that may not. As it stands at the moment, the police apply an impartial test; people may protest provided that they do so in a lawful way and provided that any disorder that may result from the demonstration can be controlled by traditional police methods. These methods are a crucial part of the role of the police as part of society, and not as a body imposed upon society and obeying the dictates of central or local government. As the Commissioner of Police for the Metropolis wrote following a year of almost non-stop demonstrations in London:

> . . . the man in the front row of a police cordon may be working a foot patrol at Wimbledon on the day before and the day after he is called up for this special duty, . . . we do not wear protective clothing, and do not make use of tear gas, water cannon, barbed-wire barriers or any equipment that could be said to give rise to provocation to the demonstrators. In order to keep the temperature cool, and prevent the battle from escalating, the men have to show a tremendous restraint, for they are pushed, kicked, abused and insulted. . . .
>
> (*Annual Report 1968*, H.M.S.O. 1969.)

The principle of non-provocation, neutrality and passivity, applies not only to the policing of demonstrations but to every aspect of police work. It is part of the tradition of the British police whose success to date is largely due, according to T. A. Critchley, to "three principal factors: their mild demeanour, the willingness, in consequence of this, of the public to accept them (and the body of the law they enforced) on their own terms; and widespread satisfaction with arrangements for controlling the police that made them amenable to democratic processes and answerable, for their wrongful acts, to the ordinary courts" (*The Police We Deserve*, Wolfe, 1973, p. 36).

The continued existence of the three-part control system for the British police will depend on a number of factors, many of which are outside police control. For example, it is not possible to predict whether British society will remain amenable to policing by consent or whether it will become so violent as to need "a tougher, more authoritarian institution, in which the traditional concept of 'service' gradually gave way to that of 'force' " (T. A. Critchley, ibid., p. 36). Such possibilities are speculative and are, in any case, outside the scope of this book. As far as the police themselves are concerned, the retention of the present system will depend on two things: first, the willingness of all members of the service to fight to keep their neutrality, for which a prerequisite is that they continue to accept restrictions on their private lives; and second, the ability of police leaders, at all levels, to adapt police organisations and methods to meet the changing demands of the community.

Chapter Three

Police organisations

The nature of organisations

An organisation is a structure that enables people to work together to achieve a common aim. In a well-run organisation, the work that has to be done is allocated, responsibilities are defined and authority is delegated so that the work that everyone does is properly co-ordinated. Wasted effort caused by duplication or lack of discretion is avoided by correctly specifying each individual's job and by supervisors ensuring that these jobs are done.

There are many types of organisations, the structure depending on its objectives, for some require much more flexibility than others. At one extreme, a research laboratory may consist of a series of small groups each working independently but with their efforts loosely co-ordinated to enable them to benefit from one another's results and to stop unnecessary duplication of effort. This type of organisation may be used in the police service when it is necessary to give a roving commission to squads of men to deal with a specific type of police work, for example, crime squads. At the other extreme, there are rigid hierarchical structures in which there is a line of authority according to rank from the top of the organisation to the bottom, and departmentalisation in terms of what has to be done, where and when. Examples of this type of organisation are to be found in the civil service, the armed services and police forces.

Early police organisations

The Metropolitan Police in 1830 had a simple structure that is shown diagramatically in Fig. 3. The Metropolitan Police District was divided into seventeen divisions each under the

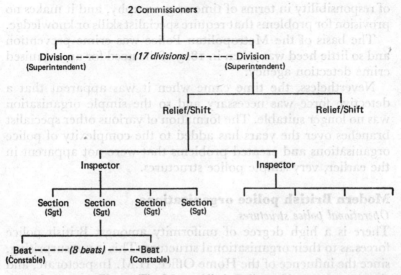

Fig. 3—The Metropolitan Police, 1830.

command of a superintendent. Each division was divided into eight sections and each section into eight beats. To police these, each superintendent was given a "company" consisting of sixteen "parties". Each party consisted of one serjeant [*sic*] and nine men. Four serjeant's parties formed one inspector's party. To patrol the 64 beats on each division there were about 144 men. They worked in shifts of six or seven hours without a break and there were no regular leave days. It can be seen that the work was divided by place (divisions) then by time (shifts) and place (beats and sections). This classical model, with suitable adaptions to take account of reduced working hours, has formed the basis of many police systems ever since. The provincial police forces that were set up after 1829 certainly followed similar lines in the cities and towns of Britain.

This simple hierarchical system has strengths and weaknesses. The main strength is the degree to which each man knows the limits of his job—it is clearly delineated in time and space—and the corollary that each man can easily be held accountable for what happens within his area of responsibility. The principal weaknesses are that such a simple structure makes no allowance for problems which cross the boundaries of areas of responsibility in terms of time or geography, and it makes no provision for problems that require specialist skills or knowledge.

The basis of the Metropolitan Police was crime prevention and so little heed was taken in 1829 of the need for an organised crime detection agency.

Nevertheless, the time came when it was apparent that a detective force was necessary and so the simple organisation was no longer suitable. The formation of various other specialist branches over the years has added to the complexity of police organisations and created problems that were not apparent in the earlier, very simple police structures.

Modern British police organisations
Operational police structures

There is a high degree of uniformity amongst British police forces as to their organisational structure. This is not surprising, since the influence of the Home Office, H.M. Inspectorate, and the representative organisations, is bound to produce a standardised approach to the ranks and functions of police officers in particular posts. For example, Home Department circulars authorised specific rank structures in Scotland (1967) and England and Wales (1968) and, in 1972, a joint working party set up by the Police Advisory Boards of England, Wales and Scotland carried out an extensive review of police ranks from constable to chief superintendent. By basing their recommendations on a job evaluation exercise, the working party was able to make objective statements as to the level of responsibility that should be attached to each of the six ranks considered necessary. Some of the recommendations of the working party were as follows:

Rank	Post
Chief superintendent	Officer in charge of a division normally with between 150 and 450 personnel.
Superintendent	Deputy to officer in charge of a division. Officer in charge of a sub-division with more than 100 personnel.
Chief inspector	Deputy to officer in charge of a sub-division with more than 100 personnel.

	Officer in charge of a sub-division with between 25 and 99 personnel.
Inspector	Deputy to officer in charge of a sub-division with 25–99 personnel. Officer in charge of a sub-division with between one and 24 personnel. Officer in charge of a relief.
Sergeant	Foot-patrol sergeant. Section sergeant (detached section).
Constable	Beat constable. Motor patrol officer. Resident constable.

Recommendations were also made as to the appropriate ranks for the officers in charge of the criminal investigation department, traffic department and administration at force and divisional levels. That is not to say that there are not different ways of doing things in different forces, but it does mean that the basic skeletons are usually the same, suitably adapted for the size of the force. For convenience, the organisation of a middle-sized police force will be discussed here but the same principles can be applied to larger or smaller forces.

At the top of the pyramid, the chief constable (or commissioner in the two London forces) has the responsibilities that were discussed in Chapter 2. The main line of command for operational purposes then goes from the chief constable through an assistant chief constable who is usually designated as Assistant Chief Constable (Operations). From him, it goes to the divisional commander, who normally holds the rank of chief superintendent and from there to the sub-divisional commander, usually a superintendent but it may be a chief inspector. Up to this point, the distribution has been by operational responsibility and geographical area, but now the question of time also comes into the scheme. A sub-division must operate continuously day and night and therefore it needs shifts and the organisational structure split into shifts (responsibility by time) and sections (responsibility by area). At the bottom of the pyramid are the constables who actually perform the primary

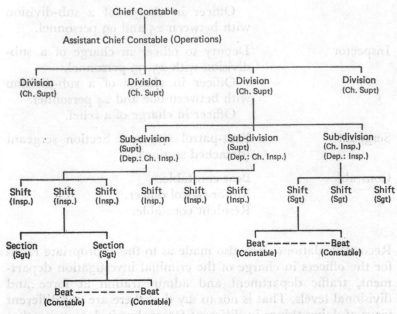

Fig. 4—Part organisational chart of a typical British police force.

functions of the organisation and work in terms of shifts and beats, the same mixture of time and area as their immediate supervisors, the sergeants and (usually) inspectors. The form of this part of a police organisation is shown in Fig. 4, where, for clarity, only one division and two shifts have been shown. It can be seen that this chart is very similar in principle to Fig. 3, which showed the early Metropolitan Police. A chart of the present Metropolitan Police structure would be similar in principle to Fig. 4 except that it is headed by a commissioner and the ranks of divisional personnel reflect the much larger units that make up the force, but basically the pattern is much the same as in Fig. 4, with local variations to allow for the different circumstances that can arise in a very large police force.

Whereas Fig. 3 represents almost the whole structure of the Metropolitan Police at that time (only the Receiver responsible for the finances of the force and clerical staff are not shown), Fig. 4 represents only a part of a modern police force. The actual structure at the top of a typical county force, for example,

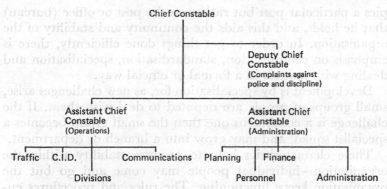

Fig. 5—Simplified headquarters structure of a typical county force.

looks something like Fig. 5 which, although much simplified, begins to show the way in which modern organisations have become more complex.

The type of organisation that has resulted from the need for police forces to keep pace with the increasing complexities of life is known as a bureaucracy. Although often loosely used as a term of abuse, the word "bureaucracy" has a definite meaning and to refer to an organisation as a bureaucracy is to define its nature. It is possible to have good and bad bureaucracies, depending on the quality of leadership within them. In order to understand something of police organisations, it is useful to look at the nature of bureaucracies, their strengths and weaknesses.

Police bureaucracies
Bureaucracies have a number of features that make them the natural form of organisation for stable institutions. There is a hierarchy of authority and responsibility, and positions in that hierarchy are designated by such factors as rank, status and pay. The organisation is governed by a series of impersonal rules and procedures that cover all the activities within the organisation, so that there is always a set and proper way of doing things. These rules permit decisions to be made according to a standard pattern or "policy" and so help to prevent arbitrary judgments based on personal prejudices. From this it can be seen that, in a bureaucracy, the emphasis is not on the individual who occu-

pies a particular post but rather on the post or office (bureau) that he holds, and this aids the continuity and stability of the organisation. In order to get things done efficiently, there is emphasis on centralisation, standardisation, specialisation and dealing with matters in a formal or official way.

Development is by specialisation for, as new challenges arise, small groups of people are deputed to deal with them. If the challenge is a continuous one then the small group becomes a specialist squad, and may grow into a branch or department.

These characteristics help to produce stability within the organisation—individual people may come and go but the organisation keeps functioning. The rules and procedures encourage a basic integrity and conformity to the approved pattern of behaviour. There are, however, in-built disadvantages that need to be recognised and disadvantages which are invariably present in all bureaucracies, not only police forces, and to which there is no general answer other than the constant vigilance of the leaders of the organisation.

The effects of specialisation

The growth of specialisation within the police has increased in recent years. To take just one force, the London Metropolitan Police, the process can be seen to work in the number of specialist sections that have been created in Scotland Yard between 1965 and 1975, a total of eleven in A, B, C and D Departments alone.

The advantages of the use of specialists are fairly obvious, but are perhaps worth summarising:

1. Training and experience can be concentrated to produce a high level of expertise.
2. A team can be developed and with it a team spirit, which encourages an interchange of ideas and expertise, support and co-operation.
3. Work can easily be delegated by type; it is easy to ensure that action has been taken by monitoring the output of the specialist group.
4. A good specialist group develops an interest in its subject and voluntarily monitors the activities of the organisation that bear on its specialisation.

5. Specialists can maintain a closer working relationship with outside organisations operating in the same field as themselves.
6. By concentrating on one type of work, a specialist is better able to perform lengthy time-consuming tasks without distraction or being side-tracked.
7. It is often easier to obtain agreement to an increase in a police establishment for a specialist than it is to acquire additional general-duties personnel. This is simply because the need can be pointed to, measured and expressed in a way that can be easily understood.

Against these advantages, it is easy to under-estimate the problems that specialisation can cause. Some of these will be dealt with in detail in Chapter 7 but one example is organisational and must be considered here. The presence of a complex system of specialists in an organisation greatly adds to the demands made upon supervisors to co-ordinate and control the activities of the force. It is often very difficult to avoid an overlap of duties between different groups of workers and this can cause confusion and duplication of effort. Nor can the opposite effect be entirely avoided, the creation of grey areas between groups, that not one of them will own. Similar effects may occur between specialists and general duty police officers.

The effects of specialisation: an example. In one force, there was a genuine lack of agreement as to who should deal with routine traffic accidents. Some years earlier there had been a policy that, because traffic patrol cars were few in number, if a traffic patrol car was first at the scene of a routine traffic accident, the crew would take the initial action until a beat constable arrived and then he would take over and thus free the traffic car. As traffic cars became more numerous, it was decided that they should deal with the bulk of traffic accidents and the original policy was changed. For years afterwards there were frequent disputes between beat constables and traffic constables as to who should do what at the scene of accidents, despite frequent attempts in force orders to clarify the position.

At the root of this problem was not only the difficulty of defining the role of the traffic men but also the mutual antipathy between two groups of men—specialists and general duty

—that tends to grow if one group is seen to be favoured at the expense of the other.

There are general rules that should apply to all hierarchical organisations and help to provide an understanding of what is happening when conflicts occur.

Organisational theory
Study of the nature of the organisation has revealed the existence of a number of general principles for the smooth running of all hierarchical organisations, of which a police force is a typical example.

When separate units are created their functions must be clearly delineated, for example by *time* (e.g. shifts, rotating duties), *place* (e.g. beats, sections, divisions), *purpose* (e.g. fraud squads, traffic patrols), *method* (e.g. plain-clothes patrols, crime prevention departments, dog-handlers), or *people dealt with* (e.g. school-liaison schemes, aliens department). Unless such delineations can be made, there is a high probability that the aims of the unit will become diffuse and cause problems of overlapping responsibilities.

Attention must be paid to co-ordinating the activities of different units and to providing a means of resolving difficulties. In general, co-ordination is the responsibility of the supervisory officer who commands more than one section, but in some forces it is not uncommon to find that there is no formal way in which the various activities of specialist units are drawn together, often because the supervisor has too wide a range of duties.

The span of control of a supervisor must not be too great. The actual number of subordinates a supervisor should be responsible for depends on the variety of work covered by their activities, the complexity of this work and the amount and quality of supporting staff he has at his disposal to aid him in his co-ordinating role. At one extreme, a supervisor may be unable to grasp the essential features of his subordinates' work and have insufficient time to give them for discussion and guidance. At the other extreme, a supervisor may have insufficient to occupy him and consequently do most of the decision-making for his subordinates.

An individual should have only one boss. Every person is

entitled to know to whom he should look for orders and to whom he is accountable. As we shall see later, this apparently elementary point is not as straightforward as it seems, for many specialists in the police have more than one boss. The reason is that within any organisation there exists two sets of functions—staff and line. Line functions are those which are aimed directly at achieving the objectives of the organisation. Staff functions are those that reinforce the line function by providing support, advice and expert services. The theory is that the direction to be taken by the organisation is the responsibility of the "line" supervisors whilst the "staff" personnel provide the necessary expert advice and guidance to aid the decision-making process. In practice, life is not quite so simple and nowhere can the difficulty be seen more clearly than in the relationships at divisional level between the ordinary duty personnel and the specialists in traffic duty and criminal investigation.

Organisational practice
The organisation of a police division is shown in a simplified form in Fig. 6. This shows that the Chief Superintendent of Z

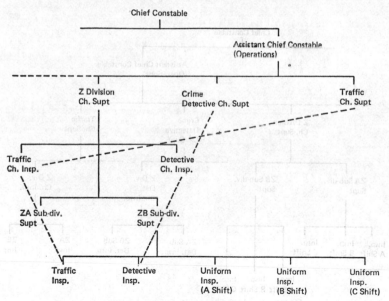

Fig. 6—Organisation of a police division.

Division is in command of all the divisional personnel including traffic and C.I.D., but that there is a "staff" relationship between the various ranks of detectives and a similar one between traffic personnel. In other words, according to this diagram, one would anticipate that the Divisional Chief Superintendent would have the services of the two specialist Chief Inspectors at his disposal and the Sub-Divisional Superintendents would have the specialist Inspectors. In both cases, the specialists would be free to seek and receive technical advice and instructions from their specialist supervisors. The Detective Chief Superintendent and Traffic Chief Superintendent would be responsible for the technical quality of the work done by their subordinates whose efforts would be directed towards divisional objectives set by the Divisional Chief Superintendent.

An alternative organisational chart might be as shown in Fig. 7. Here, C.I.D. and Traffic are shown as separate functions of their own, although the areas of responsibility of the Chief Inspectors (Traffic) and Detective Chief Inspectors are geographically the same as the territorial divisions. What happens in many forces is that the theory is represented by Fig. 6 but

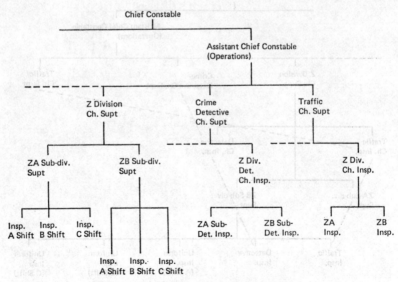

Fig. 7—Alternative organisational chart.

reality is represented by Fig. 7. In practice, many operational detectives see their boss as the detective chief superintendent who makes decisions as to their professional competence, controls such matters as transfers, promotions and even retention in the department, rather than the uniformed chief superintendent who heads the division on which they happen to be working. The more a specialist department becomes isolated from the main "line" of the organisation, the more difficult it becomes for the specialist to identify with his "territorial division" rather than his "department".

For the divisional "ordinary duty" senior officers, the second chart is untenable principally because, although they have the responsibility for the policing of a territorial area, they are denied the full command of the resources needed to carry out that responsibility. Apart from this, there are a number of by-products of Fig. 7 that can create tensions between specialist and non-specialist. One of these is the way in which information travels to and from headquarters via specialist departments and bypasses the senior officers of the division. Occasionally, such information may amount to instructions passed to the divisional specialist officer, who then may have to carry out actions without the knowledge of the divisional personnel. It is also not unknown for specialists to use their own chain of command to seek a reversal of a decision that has already been made by a non-specialist senior officer; there are two sides to this problem for, even accepting Fig. 6, the range of instructions that the non-specialist can give to a specialist subordinate must be limited and cannot include matters that require the very expertise that the specialist is there to provide.

On balance, the pattern illustrated by Fig. 6 is the normal working method but clearly it requires a good deal of understanding on the part of everyone to make it work, for it means that the specialist has, in effect, two bosses—one technical and one functional. There are a number of points that need to be observed if it is to work harmoniously. One rule for a line supervisor to remember is that although the specialist is part of his "team", and therefore should normally take his objectives from the line supervisor, the means taken to pursue those objectives must be left to him to work out; after all that is why he *is* a specialist. The next is that, although he should deploy his resources towards his own objectives, the time will come when it will be necessary for headquarters to re-deploy force resources to meet force objectives. Finally, he should remember that the specialist is invariably conscious of the fact that his specialist capabilities are being assessed by the senior officers of his own department who may use different criteria from the divisional line supervisors.

After this analysis of inter-organisational problems, it is worth restating the objective: the whole purpose of the organisation is to obtain results to which all the people in it have contributed their skills.

Rules and procedures

Specialisation is not the only aspect of police organisation that causes problems. The need for set procedures and rules is essential, but they require frequent attention to prevent them from strangling the organisation.

The rules of most police organisations have not usually been designed but have accumulated over the years or have been adapted from another set of rules that have accumulated in another force. It is no accident that sets of orders tend to become larger and need pruning at intervals to keep them to a reasonable size. As something goes wrong, the question is asked, "How did it happen?" closely followed by, "How can we stop it happening again?" The result is a new order laying down another rule or procedure. The set of rules becomes "bitty" and difficult to remember and, because they are so difficult to comprehend, people give up trying, they make more mistakes and so more rules are made—a spiral that ends in confusion unless a decision is made to re-write the orders. Many orders, particularly at the lower levels of the organisation, are difficult to trace because they were issued some time in the past and may be lost from sight until they are needed for evidence in a discipline case! Consolidation and weeding are essential.

Too many rules stifle initiative, too few create anarchy; a balance needs to be struck to ensure that they are just enough to guide people along the right lines towards the objectives of the organisation. Care must be taken that rules do not become an end unto themselves—the common enemy of all bureaucracies, "red tape" (*see also* Chapter 8, p. 179).

Organisation charts

Examples of partial organisation charts have been given to illustrate the structure of police forces. Provided that some of their limitations are recognised, it is often of value to prepare such a chart for a police unit, as it can help to analyse the structure of the organisation and reveal weaknesses or inconsistencies. For example, it can show whether the basic law "one man, one boss" is being observed. Not that this law is absolute (as has already been seen in relation to specialists) but it is useful to know when one individual has more than one boss, to show the pressures that are upon him.

Organisation charts: an example. In one force, when an organisation chart was being prepared, one individual in the headquarters was found in three places. Three senior officers had been asked to show the people primarily accountable to them and this individual appeared on all three lists. None of the three senior officers was aware of the extent of the commitment that he had to the other two. Little wonder the man seemed unduly harassed.

Organisation charts can also enable people to see at a glance where they fit in the organisation, who they report to and who reports to them. It is particularly useful to prepare a chart when changes are being made in the organisation, for a change in one place often causes changes elsewhere. Failure to identify these consequential changes can result in stresses that can be avoided by making things clear from the outset.

Unfortunately, some people try to do too much on an organisation chart; if they are too complex, they defeat their purpose of making things clear. In general, they should emphasise the *work* of each post, reflecting the office rather than the individual who happens to hold it at that time. They must also be up to date and realistic—so many are neither.

What organisation charts cannot do, is to show the actual lines of communication within the organisation. No organisation, police or otherwise, sticks only to the vertical or horizontal lines of a chart, there are many links between departments and between individuals in departments that help to keep things moving smoothly, yet are not part of the "official" machinery as shown on an organisation chart. Finally, an organisation chart must reflect the organisation, not the other way round. One of the main problems for a bureaucratic organisation is to be able to change to meet new conditions; this is difficult enough to overcome without trying to tie the organisation to a structure that it had at some time in the past. The principal challenge for police supervisors is to be able to recognise the need for change within the organisation, a structure which is more noted for stability than flexibility.

Other organisations for policing
From what has been said of the bureaucratic model that most police, civil service and other large units have developed, it may be wondered why, if it has such manifest disadvantages, no better organisational structure has been found.

In certain specialised areas other such structures have been successfully introduced. The use of task forces under their own commanders, with their own transport and equipment, has proved effective for dealing with localised problems of a short duration. Similarly, crime squads, each operating in a basically unstructured way under a co-ordinator, also provide indications that a less rigid organisational framework can meet some policing needs. At a more fundamental level, many of the variations on unit-beat policing have attempted to introduce an element of discretion and freedom of action into the deployment of police personnel. These methods will be discussed in more detail in Chapter 6.

The use of team policing has also achieved some success in avoiding the excessive centralisation that bureaucracies encourage. It is necessary to distinguish between the U.S. use of the expression "team policing" referred to here and the British "team policing" discussed in Chapter 6. The team system that was used experimentally by a number of British police forces but is no longer in general use, is best described as the "Aberdeen system" after the city in which it was invented. It was not so much an organisational development as a method of deploying foot-patrol officers so as to gain the maximum flexibility. The U.S. "team policing" is more of an organisational concept and represents a marked change of direction for U.S. police forces away from highly centralised and often over-specialised

organisational structures. The outline that follows is based upon
the orders, reports and manuals of the Los Angeles Police
Department, and is reproduced by kind permission of the Chief
of Police.

Los Angeles Police Department
Re-organisation
The re-organisation of the Los Angeles Police Department
shares a characteristic with that of the New Zealand Police
which will be discussed in Chapter 6. Both were based on the
conscious application of organisational principles to the problems of the police service.

The Los Angeles re-organisation sought to produce a joint
commitment between the police and the public to make the
city a safer place to live in. Over the period 1970–1975, when
repressible crime rose by about 35 per cent throughout the
U.S.A., the Los Angeles police were able to hold crime below
the level of 1970.

The introduction of a team-policing system in 1971 followed
an inquiry and report by a task force that obtained the views
and opinions of all the chief officers and scores of police officers
and civilian police staff. The task force report highlighted two
main problems: "The co-ordination of the many large and
diverse organizational entities had become difficult and the top
command structure had become geographically and administra-
tively remote from the people in the field and from the public."

These are typical problems that beset all large and highly-
centralised organisations, but it is seldom that their effects are
sufficiently appreciated to spark off a major re-organisation
programme. Most organisations tend to treat the symptoms
rather than diagnose the disease, for example, by introducing
yet more specialist groups to co-ordinate the activities of those
already in existence.

The objectives of reform
The principal objectives of the re-organisation can be stated as
follows:

1. To decentralise operational activities towards a "territorial
   imperative" concept of one community, one police team.

2. To preserve the functional expertise that supervisors in all operational units possess and which enables them to provide effective supervision over the operational people below them. A supervisor in patrol, detective or traffic work needs to have some expertise in his specialism to be able to direct and control his subordinates effectively. Such expertise must not be lost in a re-organisation and, if anything, should be enhanced.

3. Decentralisation of functional responsibilities had to be accompanied by an effective system of inspection and control from Headquarters in order to ensure:

   (a) achievement of the goals of the whole Police Department;
   (b) attainment of uniformity in enforcement policies;
   (c) maintenance of high standards of efficiency and quality in systems and procedures;
   (d) accumulation of adequate data to enhance police development.

Organisational precepts
A number of practical considerations had to be borne in mind; for example, it was sometimes necessary to sacrifice a certain amount of efficiency in one department in order to improve the efficiency of the total organisation. Thus, whilst it was recognised that a centralised traffic division might be the most effective way of providing a traffic service, for some areas, decentralised traffic personnel with added supervisory specialisation made better sense when viewing the overall objectives of the whole police force. It was also recognised that the conditions in different parts of the police force required a different approach, so that complete homogeneity was neither possible nor desirable. Operational police officers needed to be kept as free as possible of secondary functions and so a separate support structure was created to relieve operational personnel of administrative work.

The new organisational structure
The operational resources of the Los Angeles Police Department were divided into four territorial bureaux and one head-

quarters bureau. The territorial bureaux were then broken down into a total of seventeen areas. Two territorial bureaux retained centralised responsibility for traffic, whilst the other two areas did not. Each of the seventeen territorial areas was composed of two parts, an operational division and a support division each, usually, under a captain of police. An operations division was composed of district teams, responsible for uniformed and investigative activities for their assigned districts. The support divisions consisted of a headquarters team and a special investigation team. The headquarters team was staffed on a twenty-four hours basis to provide technical and auxiliary support to the district teams; it usually included facilities for dealing with prisoners, inquiries, records and station security. The special investigation team could include homicide, juvenile, narcotics and robbery units. Personnel assigned to the special investigation team were also expected to advise and assist members of district teams with specialised investigative activities.

The district team was considered to be the primary-line operations unit. In 1975 there were 65 district teams, each composed of uniformed and investigative personnel and commanded by a lieutenant. The basic patrol unit of each was the basic car unit, a team of nine police officers assigned to one car to maintain a twenty-four hours service. This patrol system will be discussed in more detail in Chapter 6.

The team nature of the organisation could be seen in the emphasis placed upon the dual role that each supervisor plays. It was made very explicit that the leader of a district team was also a participant in the division management team. This consisted of all the lieutenants within the division and the divisional commanding officer. Similarly, the commanding officer of a division had a further role as a member of the area management team, upon which he and his colleagues served with the area commanding officer. This dual management role was extended throughout the various levels of the organisation so that each level worked as a team and tied the many parts of the organisation together.

The team concept can be seen in the management team chart for the Los Angeles Police Department. Figure 8 shows a much simplified version of the chart as at 1976 where, for

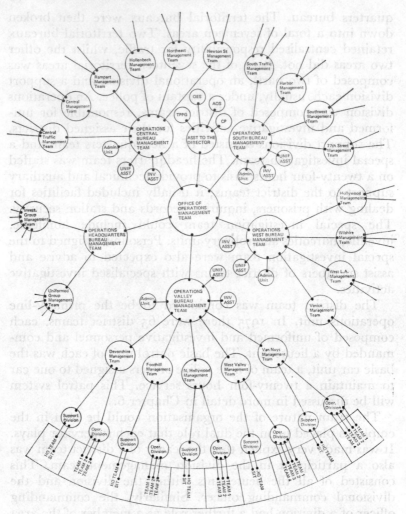

Fig. 8—Part of the Office of Operations Management Team, Los Angeles
Police Department. (By courtesy of Los Angeles P.D.)

clarity, only one of the four geographical-area bureaux has
been shown in detail. The scale of the operation can be assessed
from the uniformed manpower required by the bureau shown
—26 lieutenants (approximately equivalent to the British
inspectors), 115 sergeants and 600 police officers (equivalent to
British constables).

Team policing in practice

The Los Angeles Police Department provides a good example of a conscious attempt to bring a police department into line with the changes that have taken place in its environment and give it a structure that will enable it to keep pace with further changes. The team-policing system as applied in the Los Angeles Police Department sought to obtain the benefits of the very small police department that serves a small community plus the uniformity of practice and quality of technical support that can only be achieved by a large organisation.

The basis of the system is the district team which gives the effect of a small police agency of about 50 police officers serving a community of about 40,000 people. The lieutenant who commands each team has a degree of autonomy to deploy his uniformed patrol and traffic personnel, and his detectives. He is expected to become involved with "his" community and to gear his efforts to its needs.

The system, at this level, has some similarities with unit-beat policing (*see* Chapter 6, p. 143), and has one of the problems traditionally associated with decentralised small units, that of providing supervisory cover over the twenty-four hours. Within each team, supervision at sergeant level is probably feasible at all times, but this means that the most senior officer on duty during the night over the whole of the uniform operations, is a sergeant. To provide a higher level of cover, the Los Angeles Police Department adopted a compromise solution by employing an Area Deputy Officer, either an *ad hoc* position staffed on a rotating basis by all the lieutenants assigned to the area, or by arranging the hours worked by all the team leaders in the area so that there was always one on duty. To avoid clashes of personality that can come from one supervisor being involved in a colleague's district when he is off duty, it was made clear that the on-duty lieutenant would only exercise line command over all the teams in the event of an unusual occurrence or the emergence of a special problem requiring area-wide co-ordination.

One further aspect of the Los Angeles Police Department re-organisation is worthy of note, that is the amount of flexibility that was exercised in formulating the new structure. Due allowances were made for local problems, geographical and organisational, that made it desirable to have exceptions to the general rule. The use of a centralised traffic department for part of the force area and decentralised traffic personnel for other parts has already been mentioned, but there were many other cases in which some adaption of the basic scheme was necessary. In general, the criterion applied was that, whenever possible, activities should be decentralised to the district teams unless there was a very good case for doing otherwise. The adoption of this approach meant that the team leader was given the maximum amount of freedom to relate his policing to the needs of the district for which he was responsible.

Management principles
The philosophy of the Los Angeles Police Department was expressed in a series of principles. Some of these were derived from those of Rowan and Mayne in the early years of the Metropolitan Police, but others were developed from modern management concepts. Two of the latter were "management by objectives" and "management by participation":

MANAGEMENT BY OBJECTIVES
In order to effectively deal with the most important problems, objectives must be established. The establishment of objectives and the means used to ensure that they are reached must include the participation of those involved in the task. The setting of an objective has very little meaning without the participation of those involved.

MANAGEMENT BY PARTICIPATION
Since employees are greatly influenced by decisions that are made and objectives that are established, it is important for them to be able to provide input into the methods utilized. To reach these decisions, employees should be encouraged to make recommendations which might lead to an improvement in the delivery of police services and assist in the furtherance of the department meeting its objective.
(*Management Principles of the Los Angeles Police Department*, E. M. Davis, Chief of Police, 12th February 1975.)

The way in which these two principles were applied in practice can be illustrated by the way in which goals were set. Each year, a critical analysis would be made of the performance of the police department during the preceding year. From this analysis, the Director set out recommended goals in general terms which he then forwarded to all operational bureaux. Each bureau commanding officer would review each goal to determine the extent to which it related to his command and added any necessary administrative comments. This process was then repeated at area and divisional-command level, before forwarding the recommended objectives to the team or unit leaders. The team leaders were then encouraged to put forward their own goals/objectives and to formulate programmes to attain them. These would be discussed with the divisional commander, who would collate the efforts of his teams and then discuss them with the area commander. The area commander would then evaluate the information supplied to him, formulate area goals and discuss these with the bureau commanding officer, and so on, until the Director of Operations was able to set the annual Office of Operations goals and objectives. Wherever possible, objectives would be expressed in terms of quantifiable data, for example, numbers of repressible crimes, rather than subjective statements such as "reduce crime".

The emphasis placed by the Los Angeles Police Department on explicit objectives serves to focus attention on the need for all police supervisors to be conscious of the objectives that they are seeking to achieve through their work.

Chapter Four

Police objectives

Nineteenth-century objectives

The objectives of the Metropolitan Police at its inception as stated by Rowan and amended by Peel (*see* Chapter 1, p. 10) were primarily the prevention of crime. Rowan envisaged that the employment of policemen as mobile "sentries" would effectively prevent crime. As, at that time, much of the crime that led to the formation of the force consisted of "street crime" —thefts from the person and robbery—committed by criminals on foot, clearly the primary objective was a realistic one and the method of attaining that objective was appropriate. In addition to providing a "presence" in the streets and so discouraging thieves from operating, foot patrols produced a quick response to emergency calls, for there were sufficient policemen on duty with such small areas to patrol that, although they were on foot, they could get to the scene of a theft or robbery quite quickly. Furthermore, the method of patrolling by walking at a set pace along a set route made it relatively easy to know where to find the local policeman to direct him to the emergency.

Thus, from the outset, the Metropolitan Police provided a preventive patrol plus a response to emergency calls that under nineteenth-century conditions (no telephones, little transport, relatively static population) was effective.

When other city and borough forces were set up later in the century, they were modelled on the Metropolitan Police and, provided sufficient men were employed, they also fulfilled the needs of the time.

In the case of the rural police, the existence of a village policeman provided a twenty-four-hour response to calls and the very nature of village life enabled detections to be made without too much difficulty.

When Constables are not employed upon duty, they must either be at
home or within reach of summons; therefore, when they absent themselves
from their quarters, they will leave word where they are to be found and
the probable time of their absence.

They are not to absent themselves from their beats without leave, except-
ing when the quick pursuit of an offender is necessary. . . .

(*Regulations and Instructions*, Cumberland and
Westmorland County Police, 1857.)

With regulations like this, the rural constable was constantly
available to provide the same preventive presence and response
to calls as his borough contemporary.

Superimposed upon their preventive and response roles were
several other responsibilities. The most important of these was
public order and it is here that the military structure adopted
by Rowan proved extremely valuable, as it was simple to muster
the Metropolitan Police into companies and divisions, and to
act in concert under their inspectors and superintendents. It is
noticeable that the only training initially given to policemen
was military-style drill instruction; not until much later was it
considered necessary to have formal courses in such subjects as
law and procedures. These were expected to be learned from
handbooks and written instructions, aided by periods during
which superintendents would "drill and instruct the officers
and constables so assembled for one hour from the time of
meeting, and read and fully explain to them the General
Orders, together with the principal Rules and Regulations for
their government and guidance" (ibid.).

In addition to their roles in crime prevention, public order
and responsibilities in courts, the police had a social role to
play. For example, in the instructions previously quoted, there
are orders relating to police acting as "assistant" Relieving
Officers for Vagrants under the auspices of the Poor Law
Guardians. The same instructions also contain the following
amongst the general duties expected of the police: ". . . to do
everything which seems to him to be necessary for the security
of life and property . . .".

In the absence of any other social agency, the police became
responsible for a number of tasks that had no direct relevance
to crime prevention, including in London (and probably other
towns) such unlikely jobs as giving workmen an early-morning
call (the going rate at the turn of the century seems to have

D

been twopence a morning or sixpence a week!) for, in days before cheap alarm-clocks and watches, providing the time on request was a useful service and "if you want to know the time, ask a policeman" was part of the image of the nineteenth-and early twentieth-century policeman that helped to "humanise" him.

Two other tasks undertaken by police were traffic ("to notice . . . obstructions of the highway dangerous to the public, and offences by drivers of carriages or other vehicles") and crime detection ("to effect the immediate arrest of persons who have committed offences, for which they are likely to be taken into custody and of persons who, upon sufficient grounds, are suspected of felony" (ibid.)).

The objectives of the early police forces can be summarised as follows:

1. To prevent crime.
2. To detect offenders when the law had been broken and take appropriate action.
3. To prevent breaches of the peace.
4. To execute warrants and to serve summonses issued by magistrates.
5. To ensure a danger-free flow of traffic.
6. To preserve security of life and property.

To these the public added a variety of tasks ranging from aiding the homeless to dealing with missing children, an objective that might be termed as follows:

7. To provide an immediate response to certain social problems.

The methods adopted by policemen to deal with these objectives were, principally, patrolling the streets and making themselves familiar with the detailed way of life of the area for which they were responsible. Police stations, scattered widely through most towns and cities, provided a place to which people could go for assistance if a local patrolling constable could not be found. The training of policemen in drill and the use of authoritarian methods of supervision quickly converted the police into a formal, disciplined body when necessary for large public-order events, small incidents being dealt with by the man on the beat.

From the outset, one vital principle was paramount: the need for the acceptance of the police by the public. Early orders given to the Metropolitan Police (and subsequently copied by other forces) emphasised the need to gain the co-operation of the public. The qualities that were required by those early policemen were tolerance, civility, good temper and discretion, mildness of behaviour and language, good humour, calmness and propriety—a formidable list for three shillings a day! There can be little doubt but that this deliberate policy of adopting a conciliatory image, combined with the "of-the-people" approach that inevitably came from employing people who would, otherwise, have been unskilled labourers, contributed to the success of the nineteenth-century British police. In essence, they preserved the peace amongst people of their own class and provided them with a certain amount of support. In a highly-structured society based on social classes, their role was clear and widely understood. Such contact as the early police would have with people higher up the social scale would cast the police in a favourable role as protectors, and seekers after lower-class criminals.

A Royal Commission view
The Royal Commission on the Police, 1960
In 1960, the Royal Commission on the Police spent some effort on identifying the role of the police (*Final Report*, 1962, pp. 21–22) and started with the basic concept of "the maintenance of the Queen's Peace—that is, the preservation of law and order".

After considering the duties of the police in Scotland as stated in the Police (Scotland) Act 1956, which are basically "to guard, patrol and watch so as:

(*i*) to prevent the commission of offences against the law;
(*ii*) to preserve order; and
(*iii*) to protect life and property",

the Royal Commission attempted its own definition thus:

1. the police have a duty to maintain law and order and to protect persons and property;
2. they have a duty to prevent crime;
3. they are responsible for the detection of criminals and in the course of interrogating suspected persons, they have a part to play in the early stages of the judicial process, acting under judicial restraint;

4. the police in England and Wales (but not in Scotland) have the responsibility of deciding whether or not to prosecute persons suspected of criminal offences*;
5. in England and Wales (but not in Scotland) the police themselves conduct many prosecutions for the less serious offences;
6. the police have the duty of controlling road traffic and advising local authorities on traffic questions;
7. the police carry out certain duties on behalf of Government Departments—for example, they conduct enquiries into applications made by persons who wish to be granted British nationality;
8. they have by long tradition a duty to befriend anyone who needs their help, and they may at any time be called upon to cope with minor or major emergencies.

Little need be said of some items on this list since they are straightforward and unambiguous. The role of the police in the prosecution of offenders, including an element of discretion as to whether a prosecution should be taken or not, is one of the characteristics of the English and Welsh police and, to a lesser extent, of the Scottish police. It starts with the police officer who first sees someone committing an offence, when he may decide to ignore it, administer a caution or take the first steps towards legal action.

The duties of the police in making inquiries for government departments is an administrative function that is not significant in determining police objectives. The elimination of these and other "fringe" activities from consideration leaves the police with the responsibility for the:

1. maintenance of law and order and the protection of persons and property;
2. prevention of crime;
3. detection of criminals;
4. controlling of road traffic; and
5. befriending of anyone who needs help and their being available at any time to cope with minor or major emergencies.

Closer inspection of these reveals some of their limitations as objectives for practical policing.

Law and order
It is difficult to define what exactly is meant by "law and

---

* The decision in certain cases rests with the Director of Public Prosecutions.

order". The 1960 Royal Commission put it like this: "The police in this country are the instrument for enforcing the rule of law; they are the means by which civilised society maintains order, that people may live safely in their houses and go freely about their lawful business. Basically their task is the maintenance of the Queen's Peace—that is, the preservation of law and order. Without this there would be anarchy" (*Royal Commission on the Police, Final Report*, 1962, p. 21).

Such a statement is useful for giving a general picture of the role of the police in a civilised country, but it lacks definition. For instance, the police alone cannot enforce a rule of law; it requires basic acceptance on the part of the population (who outnumber the police by about 500 to 1) that they will abide by the laws of the country. As has already been seen in Chapter 1 and will be emphasised later, there are definite limits to the action that the police in a democratic society can take to enforce laws against the will of large sectors of the community.

The "rule of law" can only operate in a country if there are a number of factors at work:

1. There must be a government that makes practicable laws, abides by those laws and endorses the need for acceptance of them by all sections of the community.
2. An independent judiciary must apply the laws in such a way that respect for the law is maintained and people are induced to obey.
3. The police must enforce the law to an acceptable degree, relative to the nature of the offence. We will return to this concept later but suffice it to say here that a higher level of enforcement is expected for an offence like murder than speeding in a car.
4. There must be a general acceptance on the part of the population that the laws are necessary, that they should be obeyed, and that sanctions should be applied against people who break them.

Police, law and order

The police can be seen to be but part of the system for maintaining law and order, albeit an important part.

The enforcement of the law to the extent that no crimes are

committed is not possible; there will always be crime. The extent of that crime and its nature will affect the ability of people to "live safely in their homes and go freely about their lawful business" and *feel able to do so in safety.*

The police must enforce the law to ensure that there is a high degree of obedience to it. The people of the country must also feel free from the fear of criminals. It is perfectly possible to have a period during which the probability of any citizen being the victim of crime is no higher than at any other time, yet people *feel* less safe. This can be because of the publicity surrounding a specific series of crimes such as murder or rape, or because of the emphasis placed by politicians and news media on crime or one type of crime. A classic example of the latter occurred during the early 1970s, when the term "mugging" was imported into Britain to describe a street robbery. Although the level of robberies remained static in most of the country, the publicity given to this "new" crime created a great deal of unease amongst the community and increased the level of fear in many people who were afraid that they might be "mugged".

Policing must provide an aura of security—people must not only actually *be* safe from attack but they must also *feel* safe from attack and the two things are not the same. It is perfectly feasible to be safe but feel threatened and to be threatened yet feel safe, it depends on awareness of the true facts.

If the police are to do their job, they must not only enforce the law but they must also create a general awareness that the law is enforced. These closely inter-linked concepts will be discussed further later, for they are at the very heart of the problem that the police must try to solve.

Protection of persons and property

The Royal Commission reference to the police duty "to protect persons and property" relates, *inter alia,* to disasters like flood and fire, for police have an important part to play in most emergencies of this nature. There is also the matter of protecting people from themselves; the police have statutory powers to deal with certain classes of people suffering from mental illness and also children who are in need of care or control.

Discussion of this kind serves to indicate that the first of the Royal Commission "functions" can be considered only as a general statement of police responsibilities rather than as a specific set of objectives.

Crime prevention

If we compare the work of the police in 1829 with that of today, it is clear that to say (as did the Royal Commission), "the purpose of the police is unchanging" conceals an enormous area of development in the actual functioning of the police. The nineteenth-century concept of crime prevention was essentially one of providing sentries, who guarded the property adjacent to the streets that they patrolled, arresting suspicious characters found loitering in the vicinity.

Police activity in respect of crime prevention is no longer restricted to acting as watchmen and detectives but includes, for example, the prevention of crime by teaching people how to safeguard their own property and helping to educate young people in the rule of law, and so divert them from committing crime.

The proportion of limited police resources that should be allotted to these means of preventing crime is often the subject of fierce debate. The allocation of resources for crime-prevention measures is complicated by the lack of any measure whereby crime prevention can be gauged. Even the traditional crime prevention activity of foot patrol cannot be directly linked with firm results in terms of crimes prevented. Just occasionally, it is possible to say that a quick police response to an emergency call, a good piece of work by an observant policeman, or the installation of a police alarm-system, has resulted in the prevention of crime and the arrest of the criminal, but the mass of routine work which a police force does in the name of crime prevention goes unmeasured.

The factors contributing to the growth of crime are complex and are rooted in society itself. The extent to which the police can influence the level of crime in a country is not fully understood. A number of things that the police do, like arresting criminals, patrolling to reduce the opportunity to commit crime, helping to fit better locks and alarms, all contribute to crime prevention, but the actual extent to which they do so in return for the amount of effort expended is unknown.

Detection of criminals

The probability of detection deters people from committing crime and the act of detection provides society with the opportunity to deal with the criminal as it sees fit. Detection can also be necessary to exonerate innocent people, recover stolen property and satisfy a desire for revenge. When it comes to the deployment of police in order to detect crime, a number of factors must be considered. To take one of the most straightforward motives for seeking the identity of a criminal—revenge on the part of the victim—there must clearly be a limit to the extent to which an individual is entitled to expect that a community-financed organisation like the police should go in order to satisfy his wish for retribution.

The effectiveness of detection in preventing an individual from committing further crimes depends on the methods that society uses to deal with the people caught by police. The attitudes of courts and the remedial measures at their disposal will largely determine this. So too will society's attitude towards the people who have been caught. Social disgrace can be an incentive not to be caught committing crime but the effectiveness of this will be determined by society's attitude to the crime in question at the time. Some forms of "fiddling" have become almost socially acceptable at various times, whilst other crimes have remained steadfastly repugnant and therefore bring social disgrace upon the perpetrator. The whole question of what to do with criminals who have been caught has been one of society's biggest problems since the retreat from the harsh penalties of the nineteenth century. This uncertainty creates problems for the police and frequently raises the question as to what police effort is justified to catch a criminal whom society either does not know what to do with or regards with disinterest.

The recovery of property or its value should, probably, be linked to revenge were it not for the intervention of insurance, which has dulled the edge of people's desire to report some crimes to police and go to the trouble of prosecuting the criminal if he is caught. Many people report crimes merely to satisfy what they regard as a whim on the part of their insurance company. Thus, quite often, the police find themselves acting as an agent for an insurer rather than for an aggrieved citizen.

Of course insurance companies are part of society but this aspect of modern life can distort the view of police objectives, certainly from the vantage point of a detective who may sense that he is being asked by the insurance company to verify the bona fides of the owner who reported the theft, rather than catch the thief.

The need to exonerate innocent people by catching the real criminal is probably rare in practice, but when it does occur it is, perhaps, sometimes under-rated by operational police officers who may not see it as a justification for expending very much police effort. In fact, it is a valuable contribution to society, for suspicion can cause many social tensions.

The detection of crime as a deterrent to other people has been left until last because it is, in some ways, the most difficult of all of the items in the above list to evaluate, and deserves some detailed consideration.

Detection as a deterrent

The value of detection as a deterrent is limited by a number of factors. Detection alone is not sufficient, since there must be a high probability of guilty people being convicted by the courts and effective action taken. There are a vast number of crimes that never come to the notice of police. Thefts from employers and stores, and assaults and frauds occur much more frequently than police statistics would suggest. The police cannot therefore directly influence the extent of this type of crime through detection. In any case, detection can never be guaranteed. As we know from murder cases, even when huge police resources are employed to solve the crime, success is not assured. Many crimes that are reported are not solved, nor could they be, however many policemen were employed on the investigation.

The art of deploying men on detection is to choose the crime on which to concentrate effort. There are two main factors that usually determine the amount of effort that police apply to a given crime: the probability of solving it and its seriousness.

The first of these requires professional judgment to determine the amount of effort that should be expended on a particular crime to provide a given probability of solving it. However, some crimes are insoluble however much time and effort are put into the investigation and it then becomes necessary to decide at what point any active efforts to solve them should cease. Such decisions are complicated by the seriousness of the case and the fact that the public expect action from the police when crime has been committed.

Measuring crime

The interpretation of crime statistics has always been rather unrewarding because of the difficulty of giving proper weight to the different crimes summarised by the figures. For example, one police force found that its statistics for one year showed a large increase in robberies. At a time when street robberies were the subject of nationwide comment, this seemed a serious matter until the figures were analysed. It was found that the entire increase was due to the activities of a small gang of schoolboys who had robbed their fellow pupils of small amounts of money. Technically, the statistics were correct but the message that they conveyed was not clear.

In order to give a better measure of crime, a number of studies have been carried out in many countries over a period of many years. A popular approach has been to ask a large number of people to arrange a given list of crimes (armed robbery, burglary of a store, simple theft, etc.) in an order of seriousness but, to date, no universally-accepted scale has been devised and it is not too difficult to see why. Many researchers have tended to assume that there is only one variable determining the seriousness with which a crime will be viewed, whereas there are a number of factors including the following:

1. The nature of the crime. Murder is obviously more serious than a minor assault, and burglary is more serious than theft. Yet, the theft of a large amount of property will not necessarily be regarded as being more serious than a theft of a small amount.
2. The nature of the victim. For example, the theft of property from an elderly pensioner will usually be seen by society as more serious than from a large company.
3. The method of committing the crime. Crime by force is usually considered more serious than crime by deception. The physical theft of a small amount of property is often regarded as socially more significant than quite large swindles.

4. Whether the crime is one of a series. An isolated case of a woman being attacked may soon be forgotten by the general public whereas, in a series of such attacks, the weight given to each one increases with each successive attack.
5. The perception of the person making the judgment. Some crimes are regarded as being more serious by one section of the community.
6. The potential of the criminal to commit further acts. Having a violently-insane man at large creates a large amount of public disquiet and so police direct huge amounts of resources towards finding him.

Controlling road traffic
This is one aspect of police work that distinguishes the British police from some other countries, where a separate organisation deals with traffic matters. The actual arguments for and against police dealing with *moving* traffic are fairly evenly balanced, but with a slight edge in favour of the police continuing to deal with it. The early role of police, physically directing traffic and maintaining traffic flow by enforcing parking laws, has greatly diminished as traffic signals and traffic wardens have taken over these functions.

The actual level of involvement that police should have in what may be termed "road safety" in its widest sense—the enforcement of traffic laws, encouraging better driver behaviour and guiding local authorities on traffic matters, for example—is difficult to determine. The proportion of police resources devoted to it varies from force to force. As with crime, one of the reasons for variation is the inadequacy of available measures of police activity. Traffic accidents account for a very large proportion of unnatural deaths and injuries, many of which could be prevented by the police, in much the same way that crime could be prevented. But, like crime, some accidents could *not* be prevented by police—the number that actually happen while the police are watching must surely indicate this! Furthermore, the relation between the amount of police activity and accidents is not known, any more than the relation between policing and crime. Once again, as with crime, there are too many variables at work. There is every indication that the number of accidents is related to such features as the nature of the population (some countries have higher rates than others under similar conditions), the number of vehicles on the roads, the price of fuel and the weather, rather than the number of policemen. Yet police activity does produce some benefit—the problem is how much benefit relative to how much police effort.

The high level of human suffering acceptable on our roads seems to arise from a low level of social concern compared with, say, the attitude to the numbers of people murdered or even killed in any other type of incident. This is an aspect of society that, once again, affects the police and yet is little understood. It seems to be linked to what society is willing to accept in return for freedom of travel. It certainly makes it difficult for senior police officers to gauge their objectives in terms of competing demands for manpower. Fortunately, many police activities can be directed towards minimising the evil effects of both crime and traffic and so the need for accurate assessment of priorities can be disguised to some extent.

Befriending people who need help
The job of the police in responding to calls from the public can best be described by reference to the other emergency services. For example, the police tend to deal with those emergency calls that do not fall within the terms of reference of the ambulance and fire services. The police deal with people who cannot be aided by the social services. The police provide a support service to alleviate the effects of many minor and major disasters, a service that has nothing to do with the law but is entirely dictated by the history and traditions of the British police in society. It is here that the differences between the police in different countries is at its most obvious. As law-enforcement agencies, police forces the world over greatly resemble one another and the main differences are those stemming from the different laws and legal systems in different countries. When it comes to the extent to which the police "help and befriend" the public, the true nature of individual police forces becomes evident.

Yet even here, the actual *amount* of police effort that may legitimately be expended on performing this role is not clear and it frequently depends on the common sense and humanity of individual officers and the amount of discretion they are given.

Police priorities

The amount of police effort that should be directed at different objectives should depend on how the various objectives are rated against one another. Since police resources are limited, what is spent on one activity must be at the cost of another. A difficulty of allocating police resources has already been suggested above—many police activities fulfil more than one objective so that it often becomes a matter, not of allocating resources to specific objectives but rather ensuring that each objective receives some share of attention consistent with the pressures upon the police.

Nevertheless, it *is* worth considering the value of different police activities if only to re-assess some time-honoured beliefs that may or may not be true. A good example of a re-thinking of the functions of police can be seen in a review that was carried out in Ontario in 1972.

A Canadian approach

In 1972, the Solicitor General of the Province of Ontario set up a task force composed of representatives of the government, municipalities and general public to examine the policing of the province. Faced with the problems associated with rapidly-growing urban areas and the escalating cost of traditional police methods, the task force examined the state of policing in Ontario; it analysed present and future needs and studied alternative approaches related to those needs. (*Task Force on Policing in Ontario*, Report to the Solicitor General, February 1974.)

At this time, the population of the province was 7½ million, over 80 per cent of the people living in the larger cities and towns. Policing was in the hands of 179 municipalities each with a police force ranging in size from 4,000 in Metropolitan Toronto to 103 forces with fewer than 10 men. Outside the municipalities, the Ontario Provincial Police provided cover with just under 4,000 men. The Royal Canadian Mounted Police, with its national coverage for specific Federal duties, but only providing normal policing in the country areas outside Ontario and Quebec, was excluded from the terms of reference of the task force.

The police role in Ontario was identified as having six principal functions:

1. *Response.* The service that police give in response to emergency calls and which cover a wide variety of needs, only a few of which involve crime.
2. *Referral.* Incidents in which police are called initially but are referred by them to other social agencies. Special note was taken of the needs for some of these social agencies to provide an out-of-office-hours service to which the police could refer people.
3. *Prevention.* Crime prevention through:

   (a) alleviating social conditions closely associated with crime;
   (b) detecting and apprehending criminals and subsequently reintegrating offenders into communities;
   (c) making it difficult for people to commit crime.

4. *Public education.* Educating the public about the law, its application and about criminal activity through public relations and schools programmes.
5. *Crime solving.*
6. *Law enforcement.*

Of the priorities that the police should allocate to these six functions, the task force said: "Popularly, the latter two [crime solving and law enforcement] have been seen to be the main components of the police role. To a large degree, this perspective is shared by the police tradition and the other functions are seen to be largely peripheral to 'real police work'. We are of the view, however, that a far better balance among the six functions must be sought if the province's needs for crime control, protection of life and property, and peace and order are to be met" (ibid., p. 17).

Comparing the list of functions produced by the Ontario task force with the Royal Commission list, the most obvious differences are the suggestions that police should be responsible for such activities as preventing crime by social methods and educating the public about the law and its application. Many police forces in Canada, Britain and elsewhere already have moved some way towards recognition that these are perfectly legitimate activities. The main question facing the officers of such forces is not whether police should apply themselves to social methods of policing but rather the extent to which they should do so. The Ontario study highlights the difficulty by referring to the question of priorities that the police have traditionally observed. The "main" tasks have been seen as patrolling the streets and detecting criminals. Other activities have been considered as "fringe activities" which can only be justified when there is spare effort that can be spared from the "main" tasks.

A modern approach to policing

There has long been a school of thought that the police role should be confined to the traditional activities and that progress should be made through increasing the numbers of police employed and the sophistication of their equipment. Yet there are valid reasons for at least questioning this philosophy, not the least of which must be that traditional police methods have failed to control the rise of crime over the past fifty years. Various means of improving on the original Victorian model have been tried and some of these have proved effective, although often only in the short term.

As has already been argued, the police in Britain have always had a wider role to fill than crime prevention and detection: "they have by long tradition a duty to befriend anyone who needs their help, and they may at any time be called upon to cope with minor or major emergencies", is how the 1960 Royal Commission put it. But apart from this social aspect of their work, the police have become more and more involved in what can only be called social activities, not so much as a response to cries for help from the public but rather as an extension of the methods that they deploy to achieve their primary aim of preventing crime. It has become clear that there are more ways of preventing crime than by patrolling the streets to make it difficult for thieves, and catching them when they have committed theft.

In a country where more and more people are prepared to commit crime, there are several broad approaches that might be taken. One is to educate the potential victim on self-protection, another is to educate the potential criminal on the

undesirability of committing crime and a third is to try to reduce tension in the community by social means. The British
police have taken up these methods to supplement their traditional patrol and detection roles.

Of these approaches, that of aiding potential victims is the
oldest. At one time this would be done by checking shop doors
and padlocks to ensure that they were secure; more recently it
has included offering free guidance on locks and bolts, burglar
alarms and other devices to make property more secure.

The other approaches, the education of the potential
criminal and the easing of tensions in society, are more controversial and less uniformly applied; yet the concept underlying both is surprisingly clear and straightforward. In essence
it is this: if it is the job of the police to prevent crime and preserve public order, then they should use any legal and acceptable way of doing this.

The problem seems to be that it is even more difficult to
assess the results of such activities than more conventional
policing, and they are likely to be long-term results. The use of
police manpower on such activities as school-liaison schemes
and community-relations activities is often seen as a fringe
activity that diverts police effort away from its rightful place,
patrolling the streets. In terms of crimes prevented, it is impossible to compare directly the effect of the same number of
police man-hours spent patrolling, as against working with
children in a school. Such limited evidence as is available suggests that, given the right men doing the right things in the
right schools, it is possible to achieve direct results in terms of
crimes prevented. The key to success seems to be to involve the
same policemen in the day-to-day or week-to-week activities
of schools, so that the children can identify with them and what
they stand for. This is particularly true if the school serves the
local community, so that any child who commits a crime will
find himself facing "his" policeman from school.

The success of such schemes depends on many factors including the background of the children, the quality of the
policemen and the attitude of the school-teachers. A clear
understanding of the limited role of the police officer in the
school is required to avoid conflicting interests. The goodwill of
the teaching staff is so essential that it is worth while to en-

courage teachers to learn at first hand the work of the police, through attachments of short courses. It also has to be acknowledged that the home environment and parental attitudes will so affect some children as to put them beyond the reach of the concepts of law and society that can be put across by a police officer as an aid to school staff.

With all community-relations work, there are similar problems of assessing results against effort. The aim is to reduce friction within split communities, so that tensions do not develop into conflict. The tendency has been for this to be regarded as a specialist function but there are dangers here. A great deal of harm can be done if there is a difference in the attitude of operational officers from that of the specialist in the community. A specialist cannot convince a minority group that the police are not against them if, every time one of them meets a police officer, he finds that the police are hostile. Similarly, in trying to encourage self-help from communities in dealing with vandalism or street violence by asking them to telephone the police to report incidents, it is useless to assure them of police co-operation if, when people make such calls, they are treated with discourtesy by the police officers answering the telephone.

The gap between the community-relations specialist and "ordinary" police officers can be too wide to permit any real progress and, for this reason, better results are obtainable from schemes in which properly trained, ordinary duty police act as part of any community-relations scheme. If this is done, both police and public can benefit, the police from the support of the public and the public from the feeling of security.

Practical police objectives
The police role
The whole development of the police in free societies has been in response to the demands of society for relief from problems that cannot be solved in another way. If no-one committed crime and everyone behaved reasonably in public, observed the rules on the roads, and was prepared to help less fortunate fellow citizens at times of sudden emergencies, then there would be no need for a sophisticated police force. The police provide a service that, in effect, cements over some of the cracks in the

structure of society. All of its services are supplementary to others. For example, the prevention of crime by police is supplementary to the requirement that each citizen shall take reasonable precautions to safeguard his own property. No-one is expected to leave valuable property where it can be easily taken by a thief. Similarly, police normally only aid people who are faced with an emergency which is out of their ordinary experience and for which there is no other suitable remedy.

The lines of demarcation between what is a matter for police and what is not, are flexible and allow a police officer considerable discretion. They also change as society changes but the change is relatively superficial. As has been seen, the *basic* objectives of the police have not radically changed for 150 years, but what has changed is the way in which the police have responded to those objectives. As society changes, so the police are expected to take on new tasks and relinquish others, but most of these are fringe activities, the central core of police objectives remains. The changes in society do, however, dictate changes in how the police must do their work. For example, changes in the laws of evidence impose new rules within which the police must work, new legislation gives the police more power to detect drunken motorists, the modern pattern of both husband and wife working increases the work of the police and the introduction of telephones in more homes makes it easier for people to alert the police to anything suspicious. None of these affects the basic objectives of the police but they, and many more factors (*see* Chapter 1), do change the nature of the response that the police must make towards achievement of those objectives. It is therefore necessary to differentiate clearly between the *objectives* of the police and the *methods* which the police adopt to attain them.

Basic police objectives

The principal objectives of the police in Britain today can be stated as follows:

1. *The protection of life and property*. This covers a wide range of responsibilities and may indeed be a summary of many of the remaining objectives. It is worth stating, however, that one of the prime functions of police is to help to save life, to

minimise injury to people and to assist them to protect their property against attack by other persons or the effects of natural disasters.

2. *The prevention and detection of crime.* This objective, more than most, needs to be differentiated from the means that police use to achieve it. The basic responsibility has not changed greatly over the centuries but there have been considerable changes in the police approach to it. Whilst the basis of crime prevention may still be the presence of uniformed police officers patrolling the streets, police activity is no longer restricted to acting as watchdogs and detectives. Emphasis has moved towards the police preventing crime by teaching people how to safeguard their property, and by helping to educate people in the rule of law and so to discourage them from committing crime.

3. *The maintenance of public order.* The traditional method of keeping the peace by patrolling has been supplemented by the use of social methods to achieve the same ends. The involvement of the police in community relations is now an important way of preventing conflict within the community by helping to reduce the tensions that cause conflict.

4. *To respond to and deal with emergency calls.* The service provided by the police in answering "999" and other emergency calls goes beyond the basic police role. The definition of the police function in respect of emergency calls can best be related to the two other emergency services: the police deal with all calls which are not within the province of the fire or ambulance service; and the police also work with the other two services in dealing with many other emergencies, for example, accidents involving injury and certain fires.

5. *To provide a 24-hour, first-line social service.* This function of the police must again be seen in relation to other agencies, as it reflects a diverse role assumed by the police, in the absence of any other organisation, to provide advice, guidance and assistance to people who cannot obtain it elsewhere. This may be because of the time of day or because there is no other social agency which deals with the particular problem, e.g. tracing missing persons, informing relatives of accidents and illnesses, and dealing with domestic disputes.

6. *To prevent road-traffic accidents, to improve driver behaviour and to enforce traffic law.* This is an area of police responsibility which has grown steadily as the volume of traffic and the number of accidents has increased. Police involvement is not confined to enforcement alone but extends to road-safety activities, traffic-management advice and investigations into causes of accidents.

These then are the objectives that form the basis of subsequent discussion in this book, which is primarily concerned with the use of police resources to achieve them.

Chapter Five

Manpower requirements

Police establishments

> The Police Authority shall, subject to the approval of the Secretary of State . . . appoint the chief constable . . . and . . . determine the number of persons of each rank in that force which is to constitute the establishment of the force. (Section 4 (2), Police Act, 1964.)

This then is the "establishment" of a police force: the maximum number of men and women authorised by the police authority and the Home Secretary to be employed to form an "adequate and efficient police force" (s. 4 (1)).

The development of current establishments

The authorised establishments of many police forces have been arrived at as a result of compromises between what chief officers have considered necessary and what has been achievable within financial, political and recruitment constraints. From time to time over the years, individual forces have had their authorised establishments pegged to what they could be reasonably expected to recruit at that time. Thus police forces in areas of full employment, usually large cities, tend to have establishments that are unrelated to the policing problems of the area.

The absence of a quantitative method for calculating the optimum number of people required to police a given area is not for want of trying. In the 1930s attempts were made in the U.K. and the U.S.A. to gauge the optimum distribution of men by using objective data. In 1956, a Home Office working party under the chairmanship of Sir Arthur Dixon produced a formula to assess the strength required for ordinary street-duty in the Metropolitan Police.

In 1962, a committee of the Association of Chief Police Officers reported that it had been unable to derive a formula for urban policing but it did produce a formula for rural policing.

Urban policing

The ACPO committee that produced the rural formula gave up the search for its urban equivalent and the subject was handed over to the Home Office Research and Planning Branch.

"As its first task, the administrative unit of the Branch was given the job of producing a mathematical formula for accurately assessing police establishments" (*Police Research Bulletin*, No. 1, 1967, p. 6). This led to field surveys in some thirty city and borough forces using the concept of a "standard beat", the area that a single constable might be expected to cover on a single shift.

Two formulae were produced, one for the centre of towns and the second for suburbs which could be described as predominantly rural. For truly urban areas with a resident population (P), an area of A acres, a total road-length of M miles, and with a level of recorded crime C, the number of constables needed to produce a "standard" cover (N) was given by the following formula:

$$N = \frac{P}{2,000} + \frac{A}{355} + \frac{M}{6 \cdot 3} + \frac{C}{160}$$

In predominantly rural suburbs, the factor relating to area was omitted and the formula became:

$$N = \frac{P}{1,360} + \frac{M}{6 \cdot 3} + \frac{C}{160}$$

(*Problems of Standardisation: Police Establishments*, The Home Office, Police Research and Planning Branch, 1967.)

A U.S. study took a different tack. Studies of patrolmen in California led to the conclusion that they spent about 25 per cent of their available time handling cases and the average time spent on each was half an hour. This produced a formula for the number of officers required to handle all the cases in an area (N):

$$N = \frac{C \times 0 \cdot 5}{25 \times H} + K$$

$C =$ number of cases.
$H =$ hours worked per year by a patrolman, exclusive of overtime.
$K =$ a constant determined by the number of days an officer works per year. This factor was given as $1 \cdot 6$ for the area under study.
(*Police Administration*, John P. Kenny, Charles C. Thomas, 1972, p. 158.)

Note that this formula deals only with the number of cases that have to be dealt with, it does not include any other activity.

Rural policing
The formula produced in 1962 by the ACPO working party used as its variables the motor road mileage (M) and population of the area (P). From information supplied by chief constables as to the number of policemen that they thought appropriate to the rural areas in their counties, the working party derived two constants and came up with the formula:

$$\text{Number of constables required} = \frac{M + (P/40)}{75}$$

It should be noted that this formula was not based on work loads or any quantitative data but was rather a mathematical expression of a consensus of opinion amongst chief constables at that time and it was, of course, related to the methods of policing that were then being used.

The subject of rural policing to prevent crime was later analysed by the Home Office Research and Development Branch which produced a formula to give the number of beats required in a rural area. This used the variables: population (P), area in acres (A), road mileage (M) and crime (C):

$$\text{The number of beats} = \frac{P}{11,384} + \frac{A}{32,952} + \frac{M}{148} + \frac{C}{136\cdot4}$$

("A Study of Rural Beats", C. F. Payne, *Police Research Bulletin*, No. 12, 1969, p. 29.)

The National Survey Team in New Zealand (*see* Chapter 6) found that the only variables to show an acceptable level of significance were the sub-station population and total file-load (a measure of the total number of incidents and other matters dealt with by the officers at that sub-station). The head of the team was very close to the mark when he concluded that it would be difficult to produce a formula as "Changes in organizations and methods, introduction of new equipment such as computers, and more extensive employment of civilians—all have a profound effect on the numbers of police needed" (*National Survey—Distribution of Manpower*, K. B. Burnside, New Zealand Police, 1970, unpublished).

The heart of the problem lies in the complex nature of policing—it is not a single function but a combination of functions.

The search for a formula

The continued efforts to derive a formula for police establishments has some features in common with the alchemists' search for the philosophers' stone that would transmute lead into gold. Many people feel that there must be a formula if only it could be found. As in the study of alchemy, the main aim may not have been realised but much of value has been learned along the way.

If it could be proven how many policemen were needed in a given area, this would be of great value when seeking to obtain resources. The weakness of the present system can be illustrated by the comments made by a Home Secretary when he restricted the intake of recruits into the British police: "I cannot regard the existing level [of police manpower] as particularly realistic and because of the introduction of new methods it is not enough to say that a particular force is well below establishment. I want to know whether the establishment really fits modern policing" (The Right Hon. L. James Callaghan, M.P., in an interview with Anthony Judge, in the *Police Federation Newsletter*, Jan./Feb. 1968). No politician was ever in a better position to hoist a police service with this particular petard than Mr Callaghan, who had previously spent some years as parliamentary consultant to the Police Federation.

Another reason why a formula would be useful would be to provide a way of allocating resources within a police area and avoid some units having more men than they need while others are hard pressed. There is, however, no absolute measure of police effectiveness and therefore no way in which a simple formula can express the number of police officers required to police a given area. However, the studies that have been made of police deployment have provided useful guides that enable experienced police officers to design policing systems using an empirical approach.

The measurement of police activity
Men or method?

The operational supervisor is usually concerned with the problem of deploying his limited manpower to meet the needs of the area for which he is responsible. The divisional commander, the duty officer or section sergeant is therefore concerned mainly with the methods open to him to deploy the men under his command, the number of whom has been laid down by headquarters or senior officers.

In contrast, a research team that is concerned with trying to set a proper establishment of police for a given area needs to identify the number of personnel required and may accept that the method of policing that is in operation is correct for that area.

In assessing the resources needed in a given area, neither the methods of policing nor the objectives of the police in that area should be ignored. The three variables are linked, as is shown in Fig. 9.

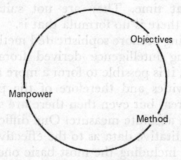

Fig. 9—Measurement of police activity—three variables.

The police objectives must be realistically set within the limitations imposed by the men available and the methods that can be used to deploy them. Whilst a sub-divisional commander may be limited, in the sense that he cannot obtain additional manpower easily because establishments are set at headquarters, he should be aware of what his true requirements are. Only then can he ensure that his needs are known to the headquarters staff responsible for setting establishments and allocating manpower, and be aware of the extent to which he must adjust the priorities of his objectives to match his resources. He must also be very conscious of the need to examine continuously the methods of policing that he uses, to ensure that he is obtaining the best use of what men and women he has to achieve his prime objectives.

Similarly, any attempt by headquarters staff to set the establishment of a police unit without looking at the objectives of the unit and at the methods being used to achieve them is to shirk the real issues.

The use of formulae

It follows that any attempt to use a set formula that does not acknowledge the differences in objectives between the police units in different areas, faced with different populations with different expectations and requirements of the police, will at best be superficial. The formulae outlined earlier should only be taken as being a very rough guide to the level of policing that was employed at the time they were prepared, using the methods of policing employed at that time, to meet the police problems of that time. They are not suitable for general application and there is no formula that is.

With the coming of more sophisticated methods of deploying manpower (using intelligence derived from command and control systems), it is possible to form a more accurate estimate of policing activities and therefore of the people needed to police a given area, but even then there are serious difficulties in the way of an absolute measure. One difficulty is caused by the lack of quantitative data as to the effectiveness of different police activities, including the most basic one—police preventive patrol.

Work-loads—uniform patrols

Work-load methods

A common way of measuring what policemen do is to issue them with a form on which they record their day's activities under a number of headings that can later be analysed statistically. This method has the advantage of providing the opportunity to divide activities into very fine graduations so that a detailed study is possible. It has some disadvantages; one

is that because it has to be filled in by an operational policeman, he has to co-operate by willingly giving his time and
thought to completing a return that he may see as a waste of
his time. Knowing that they are recording their activities, may
also make people act somewhat differently, or at least *record*
that they act differently from normal. This is where a study of
historical data scores. Using this method, the researcher
examines all the records for a period and so builds up a picture
of the police activity at that time—when the people concerned
are of course unaware that they will be the subject of a detailed
study. The operational methods of rural-beat officers, who were
supposed to use their vehicles to drive from village to village
and to patrol on foot, were the subject of two studies, one in
which they indicated the work that they did on cards, and the
other using historical data. The first method showed that they
spent 22·9 per cent of their time on foot patrol, whilst the
historical data study suggested that a figure of 5 per cent was
more realistic. Despite some reservations, the use of self-
recording may be useful for identifying activities that are part
of the policing system but do not contribute directly to the
police objectives (*see* Chapter 8). It can also provide a comparative measure of activity from division to division and so
provide a means of balancing resources to meet the needs of the
different parts of the force area.

Historical-data studies tend to be of value only if the police
unit in question keeps adequate records of what it does. Depending on how vehicle-logs, incident messages and pocket-
books are completed, there will either be a little or a lot of
detailed information. In some police forces, each police officer
keeps, in effect, a small diary which he fills in as the day progresses. Other forces do not require their men to make any
records at all and so there is little to study. One must be careful
about requiring too much time to be spent on unnecessary
paperwork but some records are useful, both as part of an
operational record system and to supply valuable management
information.

Some of this information, although usually excluding some
of the detail of self-initiated and non-incident work, may be
derived from command and control systems. Here there is the
added advantage of being able to process the information

quickly and so an up-to-date picture can be maintained. The problem here is that of obtaining useful information without being overwhelmed by a wealth of detail.

Self-reporting methods
Most self-reporting studies carried out in Britain have tended to be of similar type—the issuing of cards similar to that shown in Fig. 10. The card shown was used for a study of the Leicestershire Police by A. A. Mullett and M. J. Clow in 1973. It provided for 32 different activities with the time scale divided into 15-minute intervals. These are rather more activities than are usually employed. For example, the study carried out by M. D. Comrie and E. Kings into urban work-loads used only twelve classifications of activity (*Police Research Bulletin*, No. 23, 1971). The use of a large number of classifications provides rather more information on fringe activities but increases the time needed by the "guinea pigs" to fill in the form. As it was even with 32 separate classifications, there were still activities that were difficult to define; one officer inquired as to the

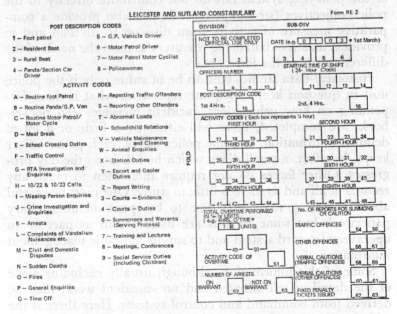

Fig. 10—Self-reporting cards.

proper classification for dealing with a stray circus elephant that was blocking a main road!

Preventive patrol

Most surveys of this kind concentrate on the amount of time that policemen spend on "preventive patrol", that is to say they are patrolling on foot or cycle or in motor vehicles as distinct from going to an incident or being engaged on some other activity.

The Comrie and Kings study of twelve towns gave an average value of 51·5 for patrol time as a percentage of total time (taken over 28 days). The highest value was 59 per cent and the lowest 46 per cent. The Mullett and Clow study gave similar values.

The level of patrol shown by these figures merely reflects the ratio of the time a policeman spends in patrolling as distinct from such activities as attending incidents, eating his meals and writing reports. The effect that this patrolling has on crime prevention, the number of traffic accidents prevented and the public confidence, is a different question altogether.

Measuring police effectiveness

The need for measurement

In deploying uniform-police patrols, the most resource-consuming of all police activities, there is a clear need to be able to assess the benefits being derived from the large numbers of police being used.

The problem for police supervisors is that there is no direct quantitative measure of police patrol effectiveness. It is just not possible to say how much crime a police patrol car prevents in one shift, for example.

There are a number of reasons why it is difficult to measure police effectiveness, some of which have already been mentioned. Probably the most fundamental is that standards of behaviour of society are determined within society itself and not by the police. The police merely respond to these changes; they seldom initiate them. Police patrols are generally regarded as the most basic and worthwhile necessities for all police forces but consideration as to what they actually achieve returns us to the problem of measurement.

Crime and accident statistics

The importance attached to crime and accident statistics might suggest these as a useful measure of police effectiveness but, as we have already observed, such statistics tend to measure changes in society and the environment rather than police effectiveness. Of course, local crime and accident figures do say something about a police force and may point to one that is more (or less) effective than others. Even here, caution is necessary, because the figures for any given police force may be inadvertently or deliberately distorted. For example, the number of crimes of violence may reflect the policies of a police force in categorising assaults rather than the amount of violence in that area. Similarly, a high number of driving offences recorded by a police force may mean either that the local population drive very badly or that the local police chief attaches great importance to the prevention of accidents through law enforcement and deploys a high proportion of his resources on traffic duty.

The basic weakness of crime statistics and the need to look behind the actual numbers at the nature of the crimes, has been discussed in some detail in Chapter 4. The seriousness of crime may not be reflected by its legal definition and therefore by the way in which it appears in the crime statistics.

Finally, there is the unknown element in all crime statistics: the crimes that are not recorded because the police do not know of them. Apart from crimes that have been so successful that no one knows of them (for example, murders that have been accepted as natural deaths), there are possibly millions of crimes each year that are not recorded because the victims have not reported them to the police. In some cases this is due to shame on the part of the victim (for example, in some sexual offences), to a belief that it is not worth reporting (cases of minor theft or damage) or simply that it is too much trouble to report the crime. It is even probable that, in some ways, a more effective police force can actually *increase* the number of crimes recorded. If the police make it easy for people to report crimes and encourage them to do this, then some crimes will be reported that might otherwise not have been. One example of this can be seen in a police force that encouraged the schools in its area to report cases of theft and damage occurring on school premises instead of dealing with them internally. This immediately increased the number of crimes recorded in the statistics of juvenile crime; yet, in reality, the crime pattern had not changed, only the statistics.

Other measures of police effectiveness
Police activities can be divided into two categories. There are those that seek to prevent crime, accidents and disorder. These may be termed *pro-active*. Then there are those police activities that are necessary to deal with crime, accidents and other incidents when they have occurred. These may be termed *reactive*.

A common measure of the effectiveness of reactive policing is the time taken for police units to attend the scene of emergency calls. Response times can provide a useful measure of the adequacy of police resources in a given area and can be supplemented by cross-over ratios—the percentage of calls in an area which arc answered by a unit from a neighbouring police area. One of the useful features of computerised command and control systems is the facility for providing this sort of data quickly and without the effort that is required in manual systems.

The use of response times to set policing levels means that only one dimension of the work of the police patrol car is being considered, its ability to provide a *reactive* police response. Typically, police patrol cars spend some forty to fifty per cent of their time on "preventive patrol" and every effort is usually made to keep this figure as high as possible (*see* p. 113 above) but apart from providing a source of cars to answer emergency calls, there is no direct measure of the pro-active effect. Because the most common pro-active activity is routine preventive patrol, there is an urgent need to consider its effects. This was the aim of the Kansas City Preventive Patrol Experiment of 1972/1973 and this will therefore be reviewed in some detail.

This study made use of a number of techniques to provide a measure of police effectiveness, including various surveys. Surveys had been used to measure police effectiveness by the President's Commission on Law Enforcement and Administration of Justice which was established in the U.S.A. in 1965. Using large random samples to assess the proportion of the population which had been the victim of crime, overcame some of the drawbacks of crime statistics, particularly the existence of large amounts of unrecorded crime. As a means of deriving management information, surveys of victims of crime are expensive and time consuming, but can be used as a periodic check to help test the value of police activities.

Another survey used in the Kansas City experiment also deserves special mention. Police have always had some difficulty in reconciling the hostility caused by preventive measures such as vehicle checks and stopping and questioning people, with the need to preserve public co-operation. This is a question which a follow-up survey can help to resolve. By measuring the attitudes of people who have previously had direct encounters with the police, it is possible to gauge the effects of such encounters on police/public relations. These surveys do not show whether pro-active methods of this kind are a worthwhile activity. But, what they can show, is the loss in goodwill from certain types of police strategy; it is then for the police commander to decide whether the results obtained from those strategies are worth that loss of goodwill. Alternatively, they may indicate that some additional measures, such as officer training or supervision, are needed to reduce the ill effects of a given strategy.

One further type of study, used in the Kansas experiment, is worth consideration as a tool for monitoring police effectiveness. This follows the lines discussed in Chapter 4 of surveying the level of security felt by members of the public and their confidence in the police. Once again, it is limited by the cost and difficulty of carrying out a proper survey but, as an audit measure rather than an on-going management tool, it may provide some measure of police effectiveness.

It should be noted that none of these survey methods provides information that can be taken as an absolute measure of police effectiveness. At most they can furnish the data for comparative purposes, for example, to see whether the people in an area feel more or less secure than previously and to measure any increases or decreases in public faith in the police.

Before considering the Kansas experiment in detail, there are two British studies that suggest that the results obtained in Kansas might have some validity in Britain.

Urban foot-patrols—Britain
As part of its programme to derive a formula for the establishment of an urban police area, the Home Office Research and Planning Branch undertook experiments in Manchester, Sheffield, Newcastle and Cardiff to study the effects of different levels of foot-patrol on crime. They selected experimental areas in which they increased the incidence of foot-patrols from zero to 4 and measured the results statistically with similar areas in which the patrol level was unchanged.

The results may be summed up in the words of the Deputy Director of the branch, when he reported on ". . . an investigation into the sensitivity of crime to different levels of the now-outmoded foot patrol". His report contained this conclusion: "Within the limitations of the experiment, we were able to measure the performance of these patrols in terms of crimes prevented. It was found that this performance was not significantly improved by quite large increases, three or four-fold, in patrol densities" (A. G. McDonald, *Police Research Bulletin*, No. 10, 1969, pp. 2–6).

Rural motor-patrols—Britain
The same branch undertook a study of policing in three rural areas. Comparisons were made of the reported crime figures for periods when the amounts of patrol were appreciably different. No significant differences in reported crime could be detected and from this it was concluded that patrol in rural areas does not significantly prevent crime, although the possible existence of a minimum threshold was acknowledged (A. Holt and M. J. Lee, *Police Research Bulletin*, No. 16, 1970, pp. 17–25).

The Kansas City preventive patrol experiment
The origins and nature of the experiment
The lack of a measure as to the value of routine police motor-patrols led to speculation as to whether they had *any* measurable effect on crime. It was to resolve this that the Police Foundation (a privately funded, independent and non-profit organisation, established by the Ford Foundation in 1970 to support innovation and improvement in policing) financed a
E

carefully prepared and executed study made by the Kansas City Police Department.

Kansas City Police Department in 1972 consisted of some 1,300 police officers in a city of just over half a million people. For the experiment, 15 car-patrol beats covering a 32-square-mile (79 km²) area of the city was selected:

> These 15 beats were computer matched on the basis of crime data, number of calls for service, ethnic composition, median income and transiency of population into five groups of three each. Within each group, one beat was designated reactive, one control and one pro-active. In the five reactive beats, there was no preventive patrol as such. Police vehicles assigned these beats entered them only in response to calls for service. Their noncommitted time (when not answering calls) was spent patrolling the boundaries of the reactive beats or patrolling in adjacent pro-active beats. While police availability was closely maintained, police visibility was, in effect, withdrawn (except when police vehicles were seen while answering calls for service).
>
> In five control beats, the usual level of patrol was maintained at one car per beat. In the five pro-active beats, the department increased police patrol visibility by two or three times its usual level both by the assignment of marked police vehicles to these beats and the presence of units from adjacent reactive beats.
>
> Other than the restrictions placed upon officers in reactive beats (response only to calls for service and patrol only the perimeter of the beat or in an adjacent pro-active beat), no special instructions were given to police officers in the experimental area. Officers in control and pro-active beats were to conduct preventive patrol as they normally would.
>
> (*The Kansas City Preventive Patrol Experiment—A Summary Report*, George L. Kelling, Tony Pate, Duane Diekman and Charles E. Brown, Police Foundation, 1974, pp. 8–9.)

The way in which these beats were distributed is shown in Fig. 11. After an initial trial period during which a number of administrative and training problems were identified and solved, the main experiment was conducted from 1st October 1972 to 30th September 1973.

Measuring the effect of patrol methods

As in Britain, the standard measure of police effectiveness in preventing crime had traditionally been the incidence of reported crime and the number of these "cleared up" by the police. As was seen on p. 114 above, crime statistics are not an accurate or reliable indicator of police activity. For this reason, the Kansas City study used a wide variety of means of gauging the effects of the experiment other than crime and accident statistics. In the main, the approach was to measure the degree

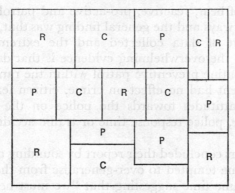

Fig. 11—Kansas City Preventive Patrol Experiment, schematic
representation of the 15-beat experimental area.
P = Pro-active
C = Control
R = Reactive

of confidence that various sections of the community had in the
police and to see how these were affected by the change in
policing.

The main methods of measuring the effects of using these
forms of policing were of three kinds. First there were a number
of different types of survey aimed at measuring the attitudes
and victimisation levels of private people and commercial
firms. Included amongst these surveys were follow-up ques-
tionnaires for people who had been involved in a direct encounter with police and for people who had called police, to
measure their attitude to the response time in answer to their
call. Secondly, there was a series of interviews and recorded
observations in which trained observers noted the nature of
police/public transactions. Thirdly, there were the usual range
of police statistics concerning reported crime, traffic accidents,
arrests and computer dispatch data.

Conclusions
The results of the experiment were published in summary form
by the Police Foundation in 1974 and immediately caused
controversy, because the findings seriously challenged some
long-held traditional beliefs. The experimental data for the

three kinds of beat, reactive, pro-active and patrol were compared in 648 ways and the general finding was that, "Given the large amount of data collected and the extremely diverse sources used, the overwhelming evidence is that decreasing or increasing routine preventive patrol within the range tested in this experiment had no effect on crime, citizen fear of crime, community attitudes towards the police on the delivery of police service, police response time or traffic accidents" (ibid., p. 39).

The authors concluded their report by sounding a cautionary note to anyone tempted to over-generalise from their findings, but at the same time suggesting that "we must begin revising our expectations as to the police role in society". The concluding sentences of the report are of special interest since they highlight the nature of the problems facing police organisations. Of the various police programmes such as team-policing and community relations, the authors say:

> These programs are attempting to deal with particular problems in the field of policing, including police and citizen alienation, the fragmented nature of police work, the inability to provide adequate supervision for police officers, the inability to coordinate the activities of officers in a variety of areas, the inability to adequately transmit information from officer to officer, from beat to beat, and from watch to watch, and the antiquated, quasi-military organizational structure in predominant use. These problems exist, but they were not the concern of this study.
>
> The relevance of this study is not that it solves or even attempts to address many of these issues which admittedly are interdependent and central to the ability of the police to deal with crime. Rather, the experiment has demonstrated that the time and staff resources do exist within police departments to test solutions to these problems. The next step, therefore, will be to use the time and these findings in the development of new approaches to both patrol and policing. (ibid., p. 49.)

To these strictures, some further reservations need to be added, for the experiments in Britain and the U.S.A. do not mean that foot- and motor-patrols in towns and motor-patrols in country areas are useless. But they do suggest this proposition: "When considered as an isolated variable, the value of random patrols whether on foot or in cars cannot be measured by their direct impact on crime." This means that, when introducing police preventive patrols in any given area, the police supervisor must be very clear in his mind just what he is aiming to achieve and must be prepared to evaluate the results not only in their possible effect on crime but also on other relevant factors to see if they justify the effort that is being expended.

Notice that throughout these experiments the subject has been *random* patrols—those in which the policeman is given an area to patrol with no *specific* direction as to his objectives. Note too that they have been measured in isolation as accident and crime prevention measures. There may be other reasons for having preventive patrols that form part of an overall strategy. Preventive patrolling is only one aspect of a policeman's work, it now remains to be seen what other activities he engages in and their relevance to police objectives.

Police deployment
Public demand

Other than when they are doing something wrong, members of the public like to see policemen about. Most communities like to have "their" police who are there to keep an eye on things. They like their police to be friendly and approachable; they may not wish to talk to them, but they like to feel that they could if they wished. Also, wherever they are and at whatever time, when there is an emergency, they want the police there—and quickly.

Most police commanders have come to recognise two conflicting pressures upon their resources: the need to provide an interface between the citizen and the police on a day-to-day basis and the need to provide a rapid response to emergency calls. These needs usually conflict, because the means of providing one will not provide the other and, with limited resources, there is competition between the two.

The policeman on foot, acknowledging greetings, available for informal advice or just to talk to, has been a part of Britain for 150 years. Although a slightly remote figure, he is clearly an ordinary mortal and, equally clearly, he is part of the community. The more modern phenomenon, the police officer in a motor car, has an entirely different image. Contact with the public is reduced to those occasions when there is something to be done and the police are less clearly part of the community but, rather, may seem imposed upon it.

However, the police officer on foot provides a poor response to emergency calls other than in crowded city-centres, or in some villages where he might beat a car to the scene. To obtain an effective response to emergency calls, radio patrol-cars are essential. They are also needed to deal with the modern criminal who is likely to be in a vehicle. Such tangible advantages led a number of police agencies to dispense with the foot-patrol and the locally-based police officer in favour of a totally mobile force, but under-estimated the importance of the loss of social contact which adversely affected the relationship between police and public.

It seems good sense to put the police into motor cars: they can continue to provide a crime prevention patrol and give a better response to emergency calls, but many police agencies have had to attempt to provide a means to maintain good police/community relations while retaining the efficiency that they can obtain from mobile patrols.

This example illustrates how little is really known about the effectiveness of some police activities, a conclusion that has been reinforced by the studies that have been discussed earlier in the chapter. The exact value of police preventive patrol is not known other than as a means of answering emergency calls. Hence, there is a tendency to concentrate on this aspect when setting levels of policing.

The limitation of research
Most of the studies of police work that have been carried out have concentrated on trying to relate police deployment to quantitative data such as crime and response time. What can be said, without reservation, is that rapid response to emergency calls is a valuable commodity, both in terms of arrests and public satisfaction. Elsewhere, the conclusions are less definite. There is no clear indication that the mere presence of police preventive patrols has any significant effect on crime or accidents. As has been indicated earlier, no absolute measure of policing needs has been established, nor has the extent to which police/public contact should be maintained.

All of this makes it difficult for a police commander to judge the way in which he should deploy his resources. It can be particularly difficult to gauge the various pressures upon him. An example of such pressures can be seen in the way in which rural villages have reacted where mobile policing has replaced village constables. In practical terms, it can be shown that the response time to incidents has improved, that more police time is actually allocated to each village by the patrolling mobiles. Against these arguments are ranged the feelings of the villagers who have been deprived of "their" police officer. They point to cases of theft and vandalism that would not have happened had they still "their" policeman. They claim that they never see a police officer to speak to, there is no-one to sign various forms, to give advice, to speak to the children when they are mischievous. Such arguments can be dismissed as being merely emotional and yet they are very difficult to refute. The fact is that the logically-thinking senior officer and the villagers have totally different concepts of policing. If policing is a public service then, clearly, the views of sections of the public cannot be ignored, since as they pay their share of the costs of the police, their wishes should be considered. However, this raises yet another practical problem: the concept of an always-available policeman in a village clashes with the wishes of many modern police officers to work in towns, where they can enjoy the same quality of life as other people. So what starts as a simple matter of police deployment may easily turn into an intractable problem of public relations, police effectiveness and welfare.

There is no simple answer to such problems, each one of which has to be treated according to its merits. The police commander tries to achieve the maximum effect with his resources and, at the same time, to gain public co-operation and support without which the most efficient police system is useless.

Supervisory ranks and specialists
Whilst it is not possible to set police establishments generally by formula, there are approved figures for supervisory officers and detectives. Supervisory officers are normally allocated to police forces on the basis of the number of people they must supervise. Therefore, once the level of constables has been agreed, the number of sergeants, inspectors and higher ranks can be calculated (*see* Chapter 3, p. 64).

The figure for detectives is normally by case load, calculated by dividing the number of reported crimes by the number of operational detectives. Within police forces, case loads can also be used to balance the allocation of detectives among units. In general, detectives in rural areas carry a lesser case load than their urban colleagues, because of the time that they spend in travelling when making inquiries, but there is no hard and fast rule about this and attention must be paid to the type of crime when evaluating case loads.

Practical considerations
Even if the results of scientific studies tend to be inconclusive, they should not be ignored when setting up police systems. They may not give the answers, but they can at least high-light some of the problems and potential problems. The difficulty with any scientific study is that it is usually necessary to measure one variable at a time and, with a complex organisation like the police, it is not easy to do this. For example, the value of a patrol car in terms of direct crime prevention may not be very high but the activities of a good car-crew can make an enormous contribution to police objectives. The stopping of suspected vehicles and people can lead to detections; the conspicuous presence of a police car at the right place and time can prevent disorder and reassure the public: a number of routine checks can be made on potential trouble spots. As with so much police work, the actual output per man depends on the ability and motivation of the individual police officer and the quality of supervision that he receives.

In setting up a police system, it is most unwise to ignore the possibility of public reaction. A badly-installed system may severely damage police/public relations and thus fail from lack of support. Wherever possible, the necessary police/public interface should be built into the system and not have to be imposed on it as a separate entity. Public-relations departments cannot replace the day-to-day contact between individual police officers and members of the community that they police.

The basic measurement of an effective police system may be its response time to emergencies but this must not be the sole criterion in designing the system. There is much more to policing than providing a fire-brigade-type response to emergency calls. Whilst there may be no quantitative measure of police effectiveness, there is a qualitative test that can be applied—how secure do the citizens of the area feel? This important question will be taken up again in Chapter 8, after some practical policing methods have been examined in the next two chapters.

Chapter Six

Policing methods

Foot-beats

The basic system of beats evolved in the early years of the
nineteenth century survived unchallenged for over a hundred
years. There were two main classes of beat systems, a shift
system providing 24-hour cover in towns and one man providing a 24-hour police presence by living on his rural beat in
country areas.

London beat system

A good indication of the original London beat system can be
obtained from this description of about 1900.

> Ordinary street duty is of two classes—either "beat" or "point" work.
> The former consists in patrolling a definite round of streets and squares
> at regular intervals; the latter, which is a modern invention, involves
> standing on sentry duty, as it were, for four hours at a time at certain
> appointed stations. To ensure the performance of their duty and to
> prevent shirking, both the pointsman and the man on the beat are visited
> at intervals by a patrol-sergeant to whom they must report any unusual
> occurrence or suspicious circumstance that has come to their knowledge
> meantime.   (*Living London*, ed. George Sims, 1903.)

The size of the beat was determined by the nature of the area
up to a maximum size which was such that the police constable
could walk around it at a regulation pace of two-and-a-half
miles an hour, during the eight-hour tour of duty. In vulnerable
areas like shopping centres, the beats would be small in area, to
enable the constable to pass along each street several times
during his tour of duty. In residential areas, the beats would be
longer so that the constable might pass along each street perhaps once or, more often, twice in each shift.

The basic town-beat system had one big advantage: it was
very predictable. It was not at all difficult to work out when a

police constable would be walking along a given street and how long it would be before he returned. One partial solution to this was to use a schedule of, say, four different starting points, routes and refreshment times. On parade at the beginning of each shift, the sergeant or inspector would tell the constables the schedule for the day. Schedule A would indicate a given starting point for each beat, the route to be followed, any points to be made, refreshment times and booking-off points. Schedule B would be a different set and so on through C and D. This at least added some unpredictability to beat duty as far as the criminal was concerned, but he could still bet that, once he had seen the constable in a street, he would not see him there again for some time.

Because of the predictability of police beats and the need to provide extra cover in vulnerable streets, more complex systems were evolved. Most of them consisted of similar elements although the names of each function varied from force to force.

The basic cover in the inner and semi-inner areas of London until 1939 was provided by a mixture of the following:

1. *Foot-beats*. Areas to be patrolled along set routes from a given starting point to a given finishing point. Refreshment to be taken either at a police telephone-box or at a police station. Two "rings" to the police station from police boxes were made, one before and one after the refreshment period, at the times provided for by the schedule being worked.
2. *Beat patrols*. These were fixed routes that criss-crossed two or more beats and gave additional cover to the more vulnerable streets. Once again, there were usually two "rings" to be made from police telephone-boxes or posts.
3. *Patrols*. Often just one street or part of one street, or perhaps a busy junction that needed a constant police presence.

The times of parade of some of the beat patrols and patrols would often be one hour later than the beats, to provide cover during the change-over of shifts.

Local variations on these themes included different arrangement for supervision. In some forces, it was the practice to have "points"—places at which a constable should be at a given time so that he could be met by his sergeant or inspector. These points were often at public telephone-boxes where a constable could be contacted. The shortest time between points appears to have been about twenty minutes, thus pacing the constable's progress around his beat with some precision. They also provided a measure of security for the constable since, if he failed to arrive at a point, a search would be made to find him, aided of course by the fact that, as he had a set route, this could be quickly checked. Many constables who had been attacked or accidentally injured were saved from further harm in this way. Some beats were often called "discretionary" to distinguish them from fixed-route beats, but the amount of discretion was limited by the number and frequency of points that had to be made.

Rural beats
The rural-beat constable was very much a part of the community he served. He lived in his village, knew and was known by all the residents in his area and was available to perform duty when required throughout the day and night.

He would be expected to patrol on foot or on a pedal cycle for at least eight hours a day and, when he was out on his beat, his wife would be expected to act as his unpaid locum or message-taker.

Because the area that he could patrol on foot or bicycle was fairly small by rural standards, it was necessary to have a policeman in every sizeable village unless two or more villages were close to one another. The ratio of policemen to population in some rural areas could therefore be quite high and it was to the rural policeman that attention was turned when motor vehicles first became available for beat work. The theory was that the rural constable should travel from village to village by motor cycle or car and then patrol on foot. It was thus seen not as a motorised patrol but rather as a way of linking parts of one foot-beat.

Foot-beats reviewed
In its second report (1947), the Police Post-War Committee considered that in towns "as a general principle the working of some beats wholly on foot must remain, in view of the foot men's special value in maintaining public confidence and obtaining information".

A proviso was added that the beat system should be flexible and initiative should not be too severely limited by prescribing routes or too many fixed points.

Notice was also taken of the need for a system of cars fitted with two-way radio to patrol the area covered by several beats. The use of wireless cars greatly improved the police response to emergencies and if the crews of these cars could be persuaded to stop and talk to foot-beat men, it was possible to pass on urgent information to them and receive useful intelligence in return. For rural beats, the introduction of the motor vehicle was welcomed by the committee and recommended for consideration for semi-urban areas.

The period following the publication of the report was one during which the pattern of police recruitment was set for the following decades. As was seen in Chapter 1, a great chance to build up the depleted strength of the police in the large towns was lost and the subsequent emphasis on police methods was towards making more effectual use of very limited resources.

By 1966, when three working parties were set up by the Home Office to look at police manpower, equipment and efficiency, the situation was that, although nationally the number of policemen had increased relative to the population from 1:660 in 1939 to 1:549 in 1965, there were fewer policemen in, say, London than twenty-six years previously. The Metropolitan Police and City of London Police had a strength of 19,650 in 1939 but only 18,987 in 1965, a drop of about 3·4 per cent as against the overall figure of 32·9 per cent increase for the whole of England and Wales.

The Working Party on Operational Efficiency and Management in its report (1967) concluded that:

> We are in no doubt that the system of policing large areas of the country,
> which still adheres to the principles of the beat system instituted over one
> hundred years ago, ought to be reviewed as a matter of urgency. (p. 115.)

On the credit side, the working party found:

> That the system has been of value in the past and still possesses marked
> advantages is beyond dispute. When it is properly worked (that is, when
> enough men are available to work it), it is possible to arrange for every
> street in an urban area to be visited by a uniformed policeman at least
> once in every twenty-four hours, and in many instances more frequently.
> By his mere presence the uniformed policeman undoubtedly prevents
> some crime and affords a degree of protection to life and property. He

contributes to the maintenance of order and is available to control traffic, prevent accidents and establish close relations with the people living in his area. By these means mutual confidence and respect can be fostered, and the concept of the policeman as a citizen in uniform gains reality. Moreover, the "beat" policeman is able to feed information to his colleagues in the specialist branches of the force, since he knows the movements of people in the locality and is in a position to report irregularities in the routine of day to day living. Thus he knows when people are on holiday and houses are shut up, has a keen eye for open windows and gates, and knows in advance the man who is likely to make trouble at closing time on Saturday nights—or rather, he would know these things where the same beat is worked regularly.   (ibid., p. 115–16.)

On the debit side, it was considered that the traditional beat system:

. . . embodies an idealisation from the past which, in the conditions of modern society, and given the chronic shortage of police manpower, is unfortunately no longer attainable.

. . .

There are probably many young policemen who find it difficult to derive much interest or satisfaction from working their beats in the traditional manner in urban areas . . . many intelligent young men, fresh from a police training centre, are unlikely to be convinced that their mere presence on a street deters potential wrong-doers; and they are therefore liable, particularly on beats where little occurs, to suffer from boredom and frustration. The work might be more readily tolerated if the conditions of service provided some measure of atonement for the boredom, but they do not. The liability to night work, weekend work and split shifts merely underlines the drawbacks of a job performed in a manner which is innately frustrating and which may seem old-fashioned.

(ibid., p. 116.)

The working party pinned its faith on more flexible systems of policing using the "modern resources of mobility and electronic equipment".

Nevertheless, despite such criticisms of the foot-beat system as "its lack of appeal to the young man of today and the inefficient use of manpower which it involves" and that it "fails to exploit to the full the advantages of modern equipment", the foot-beat was still considered the best method of policing "densely populated areas such as the centre of cities".

As far as rural areas were concerned, the working party concluded: "Here it is not the principle of policing that needs to be reviewed, but the size and distribution of the beats and the equipment, in particular the transport, required to work them effectively." As an example of the flexible police systems that were advocated, the working party pointed to unit-beat policing, which had just been introduced in Accrington, Lancashire. The report also painstakingly listed a large number of local experiments in basic police coverage.

Before considering some of these schemes in detail, it is salutary to go back to the very fundamentals of policing to look at the activities from which policing systems must be composed.

Basic methods

There have been many attempts at producing police systems that provide the best service to the public at the most economic cost. Analysis shows that the actual number of basic police methods used is very limited, there being only a few ways in which a uniformed police officer can work.

He can remain stationary, walk or travel by vehicle. For each activity there are variations, with advantages and disadvantages, so that devising a policing system is a matter of assembling the best package to fit the circumstances. As was seen in Chapter 5, the only effective way of determining the policing needs of an area is to look at the problems of each individual part of that area and to relate the method of policing to those problems. It is therefore preferable to start from basic principles and apply them to an area than to adopt a ready-made system from elsewhere. Ready-made systems have a habit of not fitting the new surroundings and many mistakes have been made in the past through failure to appreciate this point.

The requirements of a police force are much too complex to be satisfied by any one type of activity. It is therefore necessary to use the various methods of policing to produce a balance which satisfies as many of the requirements as possible. Sometimes an activity which satisfies one need also satisfies others. Sometimes there is a pull between methods. Foot-patrols do not usually give a rapid response to emergency calls but provide good contact with the public. Motor-patrols provide poor contact with the public but a good response to emergency calls. Given limited resources, if the police supervisor wishes to provide a quick reaction to emergencies and good contact with the public, then it is clear that he has to make a compromise. To make this sort of judgment, it is necessary to know the strengths and weaknesses of each activity and how to take advantage of the former.

Why uniformed police?
The main aims of having uniformed police officers on the streets are related to the objectives of policing discussed in Chapter 4: first, to provide a visible police presence to deter people from breaking the law and to reassure law-abiding members of the public; secondly, to detect offences against the law and take action against the law breakers; and thirdly, to befriend anyone who needs their help and provide a response to calls for assistance in cases of minor or major emergencies.

With these aims in mind, the effect of each police activity can be seen even if it is not possible to ascribe a quantitative value.

Fixed points
Derived as it clearly is from the army sentry, the fixed point or post is often used as a means of providing protection for items, people or premises which are particularly vulnerable to attack by criminals.

As a means of policing, it is very unpopular with the people who work the fixed posts and is not much better regarded by most supervisors. It is tedious to be confined to one spot and duty of this kind causes fatigue and difficulty in maintaining concentration.

Fixed points are also of limited value relative to the cost. Only to a limited extent does the presence of one man reassure the potential victim and act as a deterrent. With a well-trained police dog or the use of electronic aids, the range of the man may be extended, but the fact that he can be easily diverted or overwhelmed by determined criminals will always detract from the value of police sentries.

A wider use of the fixed point to provide a police presence at a particularly busy place was common in large cities during the first half of the century (*see* the quotation on p. 126 above). The presence of a police officer at a strategic point prevented disorder and enabled the local people to be sure where they could find a policeman in cases of emergency.

A modern extension of the static policeman might well be achieved through the use of electronic surveillance equipment. A number of experiments have been conducted on the use of television for watching city streets, car parks and the like. The results have not been completely successful. In part, this has been due to limitations of the medium, lack of sufficient definition to be able to identify criminals, vulnerability of the system to bad weather conditions and operator fatigue. Another feature of such systems is the need to have the resources on hand to take action when the operator sees something suspicious; they are not as economical in their use of manpower as might be thought. The main developments of television for police purposes have therefore been for traffic systems, to aid the security of buildings and for monitoring public-order events.

Foot-patrols
The comments of the 1967 Working Party on Operational Efficiency quoted on p. 129 above, have to be read in their proper context. The criticisms were mainly directed at the continued use of the traditional beat and patrol system described at the beginning of this chapter. Deeper consideration is needed as to the possible uses to which foot-patrols can be put if they are to form part of a flexible policing system. There is value to be obtained from the ability of people on foot to hear suspicious sounds without the distractions of engine noise and see suspicious sights without having to focus most of their attention on the road ahead. They are quiet and so do not excessively advertise their presence at night, yet they are prominently visible as a deterrent during the day. They are available to anyone who wants to stop them to talk, or seek advice or help. At the social level, they are most obviously at one with the people they police. They can form relationships with the public as they walk amongst them. They become known as individual men and women, their personalities become known; the people are able to select the one police officer that they feel able to speak to about a given problem. In return, the police officers are given information that they can feed into the system or use to solve crimes or problems in their own areas.

Provided that they are equipped with effective radio-sets, they can call for aid to enable them to tackle problems that are too much for one person on foot and can carry out inquiries in their areas when directed by radio.

Given sufficient scope and support, plus an element of stability, a foot-patrol officer can know the area he polices at a depth impossible in any other system. His patrolling is not dictated by one-way streets or width of roads. For certain types of area, the police officer on foot-patrol is the most effective means of policing. Above all, he can stimulate social activities to prevent crime by working within the community. He can identify tensions before they erupt; he can remonstrate with children, advise families and diagnose welfare problems; work of this kind cannot be done from a motor vehicle.

Yet, foot-patrols are expensive in the sense that the area that a man or woman can cover on foot is limited. Such patrols are open to the elements and quickly become fatigued in very hot or very cold or wet weather.

Furthermore, the foot-patrol officer makes a very small contribution to the response of the police to emergency calls. Walking is the least efficient of the means of moving from one place to another and so much of an individual's physical energy is used just for this.

It is often said that foot-patrols are unpopular amongst police officers. This is an overstatement. Some police officers prefer to walk around a beat than to do duty in a motor vehicle, but there are provisos. The foot-patrol officer needs to be given the responsibility for policing an area at his own discretion and not according to a set route. The area must also be suitable for foot-policing in that it has people in it to whom the police can talk. Dormitory areas and factory estates do not provide interesting beats because there is no one to whom the police officer can relate. Densely-populated city areas containing small shops, houses and flats are ideal, yet even here there may be problems if the population contains violent elements. For this reason, it may be necessary to use policemen in pairs rather than put individuals at risk. The foot-patrol police officer is always vulnerable even in relatively passive areas and may need very urgent assistance to save him from injury if he is involved in a skirmish. A foot-patrol system needs a mobile support system that can give a quick response to calls for help.

The police officer needs to be given the time in which to build up his relationship with the people of the area and this precludes too many changes. In order that people can know him or her, the police officer has to be in the area often enough and long enough to become recognisable as an individual. Many foot-beat schemes fail because this essential feature of the method is not recognised. To change a foot-patrol officer frequently from one area to another on a rotation system is to destroy one of the main advantages of the system.

Motor cycles and scooters
When the foot-patrol system came in for criticism on grounds of manpower costs, the motor cycle was introduced as a labour-saving device. The theory was that the motor cycle would enable a patrolman to cover a much larger area in eight hours than if he was on foot. He would ride the motor cycle to a place of special police interest then get off his machine and patrol on foot. After checking one area, he would travel to the next and patrol that on foot and so on. In practice, the system was not a success due to the limitations of the motor cycle and the fact that policemen, once on or in a vehicle, are reluctant to quit it and parked motor cycles were vulnerable to vandalism. Furthermore, the increased areas allotted to each police officer meant an increased number of routine inquiry calls that tended to take up much of his time.

The motor cycle has a number of disadvantages:

1. They are dangerous for the rider, particularly in inclement weather and are virtually unusable in snow or heavy frost.
2. The rider is open to the elements and cannot operate at his very best in cold or wet weather.
3. Motor cycles are noisy, consequently they can be heard coming but the rider cannot hear what is happening around him.
4. Great concentration is needed on the road ahead and so there is relatively little possibility of looking around to see matters worth investigating.
5. It takes valuable time to get off a motor cycle and put it on its stand, when about to question a suspect or give chase on foot.
6. A motor cycle cannot convey prisoners or bulky property.
7. Reception of messages requires the motor-cyclist to stop his machine to be able to make a written note.

Against all these disadvantages, the solo motor cycle has two real advantages. First, it can be comparatively cheap, particularly if a low-powered motor scooter or a small motor cycle is used. Second, a motor cycle can get to the scene of incidents in crowded city streets by travelling on the outside of streams of vehicles in traffic jams.

Thus the only legitimate function of a motor cycle is for traffic work, or to provide a cheap means of transport for short journeys.

Pedal cycles

The use of a pedal cycle at once increases slightly the range of a patrolling officer but decreases his contact with the public. Whilst the pedal cycle does not suffer from all of the disadvantages of the motor cycle, it has enough of them to be of limited value.

The best use of a pedal cycle is probably as an optional aid for the foot-patrol officer to use at his discretion at times of the day or night when a slow, silent patrol is of value. Alternatively, it may be used for a beat of moderate size which contains areas needing the use of police foot-patrols separated by areas of little concern.

Motor cars

Given a motor car, a police officer can patrol large areas, carrying useful equipment, with very little physical effort. For areas where police patrolling is necessary but close contact with the public is not needed, the police car provides an effective way of spreading available manpower thinly over the ground.

Probably the most serious disadvantages of the motor car for police patrolling are, first, that the driver needs to concentrate on where he is going and, secondly, that the crew are isolated from the public by the metal and glass of their car. At one time, there was a tendency to under-estimate the effects of using police cars on the relations between police and public. As was said in relation to motor cycles, any system that relies for its contacts on the police officers getting out of their cars to walk around is adversely affected by the reluctance of police officers to do that. Checks on such systems have shown that as little as five per cent of the time will be spent on foot by the police officers who are supposed to be out meeting the public. This reluctance to patrol on foot has led to systems of policing in which a number of constables are conveyed in a vehicle under the supervision of a sergeant who directs them where and when to perform periods of foot-patrol. One such, the "Aberdeen system", will be reviewed in detail later.

Police vans

Closed motor vans are of value to transport property, prisoners and the like but have little value for patrolling purposes. Vision is usually restricted and noise is high, as is fuel consumption. Their use tends to produce a militaristic image and in some sensitive areas they can be regarded as provocative.

Police horses

In open areas, particularly to detect and prevent indecency offences in parks and woods, a mounted police officer can be used to good effect. The other main function of police horses is in crowd control and here their use, although controversial, is of great value.

> In my view mounted police are essential, if we are to avoid riot squads and riot equipment. . . . When used to suppress disorder, mounted police do cause apprehension: but, properly used they do not cause casualties.
> (*Report of Inquiry by Lord Justice Scarman into the Red Lion Square disorders of 15th June, 1974*, Cmnd. 5919, p. 40, H.M.S.O., 1975.)

Aircraft

Light fixed-wing machines and helicopters are part of the equipment of police agencies. Fixed-wing aeroplanes are usually found only where the area to be covered is very large, distances between operating centres great and the terrain difficult. Helicopters, on the other hand, are extensively used for a wide range of police duties.

Despite experiments with autogiros in the early 1930s, roto-craft were not deployed on a regular basis in Britain until 1970, when a trial helicopter scheme was introduced in London by the Metropolitan Police. Even seven years later, after the scheme had proved the potential value of helicopters, the service provided was still relatively small in scale compared with some police agencies in other parts of the world. The reasons for this are mainly economic but it should be noted that in some countries where aircraft are more extensively used, the police carry out a wider range of duties than in Britain and may perform para-military functions for which aircraft may be justified, even without the purely policing uses to which they can be put.

The virtues of helicopters are simple: they can fly at very slow speeds or hover in the air, they require only a small operating platform and they offer a wide field of vision which can be extended by the use of optical and electronic equipment.

One of their limitations can be stated as simply—they are expensive to purchase and maintain. It follows that there must be sufficient suitable work to justify using them.

In general, two modes of operation have evolved. In one, helicopters patrol cities in much the same way as police cars patrol on the ground. The speed of helicopters and their independence of traffic and roads enable them to arrive at the scene of incidents very quickly. An alternative and cheaper mode of operation is to have helicopters standing by on their landing bases awaiting emergency calls. In this case, the response time is much longer and limits their value. However, the cost can be further reduced by using helicopters on a joint basis with other agencies. The range of services that may be combined varies from area to area, but examples taken from different countries include emergency medical calls to remote areas, border patrols, bush and forest-fire detection, traffic management and the maintenance of water, electricity and telephone supplies. Clearly, the multi-use of machines restricts their availability for police purposes and tends to limit their use to long-term emergencies or foreseeable occurrences.

Where there is a high rate of incidents within a small territorial area, continuous helicopter patrols can be justified. A fleet of aircraft, deployed so that a very rapid response can be provided for emergency calls, is an effective weapon against certain crimes, notably those in which a helicopter crew can observe criminals leaving the scene of a crime and follow their vehicle until it can be intercepted by ground forces directed from above. Experiments using just one or two machines to patrol a large city may be inconclusive, simply because the area covered is too large to provide the rapid response needed. It is not always appreciated that most of the value of a helicopter patrolling a city comes from its response to calls rather than from actions initiated by the crew. Although an airborne observer may see something suspicious, he cannot readily intervene himself, since it is difficult and dangerous for a helicopter to land in a congested urban area.

Other restrictions on helicopter usage add to the problems of producing a viable scheme. The length of each continuous watch is governed by crew fatigue and the need to refuel the machine, something that must be done at frequent intervals to maintain a reserve of fuel so that the unit can deal safely with any incident that may arise. Regulations governing flying may also impose limitations, for example, on night flying, altitudes and the type of aircraft that must be used over built-up areas. Night patrols may present particular difficulties, not only from aviation laws but because of the additional hazards of flying at night in areas with high buildings. If patrols can be carried out safely at night, it has been shown that they can be remarkably effective although complaints about engine and rotor noise and the use of searchlights may be expected unless the scheme is properly introduced to the public. The prevailing climate of an area may also affect the extent to which a full-time service can be provided. Helicopters are susceptible to high winds, fog or mist, low cloud and freezing rain.

The limitations indicated above must be weighed against the advantages that can be gained from airborne patrols and clearly every area needs to be considered separately to determine whether its incident rate, terrain, climate, aviation regulations and financial resources justify either routine patrols or reserve machines. Where the provision of regular aircraft cannot be justified, commercial helicopters may be hired for special occasions but this course of action has its own limitations. Civil pilots may not be trained in the type of flying needed for police purposes and the range of equipment that can be fitted to the helicopter on a temporary basis will be necessarily limited.

As technology advances, helicopters can be expected to become increasingly valuable for police work. Already, using stabilised optical and electronic equipment, the type of intelligence obtainable from the air has increased far beyond what a human observer can see with his naked eyes. For example, image enhancement equipment can enable observers to see in the dark. It is possible to distinguish minute differences in temperature thus enabling people to be located by their body heat when they are not optically visible and recently-used engines or guns to be "seen". Buried bodies can sometimes be found through the heat generated by decomposition registering on infra-red photography. Television cameras can feed intelligence to ground operation rooms for command and control purposes and photographic cameras can make permanent records for debriefing and evidence. There is a whole range of technology developed for military purposes that can be applied to the fight against crime. This provides an added incentive to consider the use of rotorcraft where the conditions are otherwise favourable.

Some classic systems

There have been so many schemes using various combinations of the methods described above that it is only possible here to select a few examples that illustrate the way in which basic policing methods can be put together to form a system.

Foot-beats and area cars

A method used by many urban police forces is a mixture of foot-beats to provide a police presence on the streets to make contact with the public, carry out law-enforcement duties and obtain information. Superimposed on these is a fleet of cars, usually double-manned, to provide a quick response to emergency calls, to deal with suspicious motor vehicles, to pursue mobile criminals and to provide a visible police presence.

Provided that the rules for foot-patrols are observed and the number of area cars is sufficient to provide a guaranteed response, this system has considerable merit.

The foot-patrols and area cars are able to communicate with their base station by radio and they are thus able to aid one another, either physically or by providing information. The main aims of uniformed-police patrols are achieved in that the weaknesses of the foot-patrol are recompensed by the strengths of motor-patrols and vice versa.

The principal problems of this system are its cost in terms of manpower and the need for flexibility. It takes considerable ingenuity to be able to gear the number of men on duty at any given time to the policing needs at that time. Inadequate planning can result in police patrolling empty streets in which they are serving no useful purpose: it is possible to provide flexibility by using mobile crime-patrols in vulnerable areas during those times when foot-patrols are not effective.

Team-policing (Aberdeen system) and task forces
Care is needed in the use of the term "team-policing" because of the number of widely different schemes that have been called by this name. In the U.S.A., as has been pointed out, it is usually associated with decentralised systems of policing in which the control of a team of uniform patrol officers and criminal investigation officers is vested in one senior officer.

In Britain, the expression is usually synonymous with the Aberdeen system, the city in which a quite different notion of team-policing was first employed in 1948. This system aims at maximum flexibility in the deployment of foot-patrols. A given area is allocated to a sergeant and a team of constables, the number in the team depending on the nature of the area and the anticipated police requirement on each individual day during the hours to be covered by the shift.

Each team has a motor vehicle, car or van, which the sergeant uses to move his men around the area, directing their patrol towards the anticipated areas of need. When not being used for this purpose, the car patrols the area, driven either by the sergeant or a constable.

For its success, the system relies heavily on the initiative and common sense of the sergeant in charge of the team. It is difficult to generalise on the merits of the scheme, but it is probably fair to say that unless it is very skilfully administered, it cuts across a number of basic rules of foot-patrol, notably the need for foot-beat officers to be able to relate to the people on their beat and become known to them as an individual. It is also quite expensive in terms of manpower, although provision is made within the system for the numbers in each team to be varied according to need. The Aberdeen system has not proved to be a universally acceptable scheme, although it is of value for occasional use to combat particular outbreaks of vandalism or rowdyism.

Other team or task-force systems have also been used to combat surges in crime or disorder. The basic principle is usually semi-permanent squads of men, employed under their own supervisors and independent of the divisional structure, that can be deployed in any area in cases of sudden need. Such squads are ideal for large searches, outbreaks of violence and demonstrations, and can be trained in special techniques and provided with special vehicles and equipment. In a large force, the employment of a task force can usually be justified but there are drawbacks.

Special squads must be kept occupied either on active service or on training. The number of occasions when they are wanted for special tasks may not be enough to keep them occupied and there is then a problem of what to use them for. It is quite common for them to be imposed on part of a division to supplement the regular personnel, but this causes problems. First, the divisional personnel are likely to resent the presence of the "outsiders". Secondly, a task force forms no part of the relationship between the police and the local people and may easily upset the balance. The methods of a divisional police unit are likely to be geared towards maintaining a long-term balance with the public, while a task force has no long-term aims but merely needs to prove its effectiveness by producing results, whatever the long-term consequences. In its desire to produce results, a task force may easily create trouble which it then resolves.

In connexion with task forces or special squads generally, it is interesting to note the comments of Lord Justice Scarman on the role of the Metropolitan Police Special Patrol Group, for they give a clear indication of the strengths of such squads and the need for them not to be *too* special in this country to retain acceptability:

Since its establishment in 1965 the Special Patrol Group has been used as a reinforcement for any police job which is beyond the strength of the local police. Its members are volunteers, and are clothed and equipped in exactly the same way as other policemen. The police say that the Special Patrol Group is in no sense a riot squad. The extent of their use bears out the police contention. Since the beginning of 1972, Special Patrol Group units have been on duty in 13 per cent of the demonstrations taking place in the Metropolitan Police District. Only in a few of the demonstrations (5 per cent of the total) were they taken out of reserve and employed directly. But when they are used they are particularly valuable because of their mobility—Special Patrol Group units travel in their own personnel carriers—and because they are accustomed to teamwork.

(ibid., p. 21.)

Unit-beat policing

The idea of police officers living on their beat and being responsible for its management on a long-term basis is as old as the oldest county constabulary. This was the very basis of rural-policing but the extension of the concept to urban areas seems to have come into prominence in the post-1945 period, when "neighbourhood" beats were introduced into a number of urban or semi-urban areas. The names seem to vary but the principle appears to have been the same. A man (or sometimes two men) would be posted to an area, preferably one in which he actually lived, for an extended period. His duty would consist of patrolling his beat on foot, cycle or light-weight motor cycle or a combination of these, for eight hours that he was on duty. When he was not on duty, police cover would be provided by a car or motor-cycle patrol covering several "neighbourhood beats".

The basis of this method of policing was to capitalise on the close contact that the resident constable could maintain with "his" people in "his" area and the extent to which he could be held accountable for the policing of the area.

The idea of a resident constable was, in 1966, incorporated into a system known as unit-beat policing which, because it was initially introduced by the Lancashire Constabulary in conjunction with the Home Office Police Research and Planning Branch at Accrington, was also known as the Accrington system (*Police Research Bulletin*, No. 4, 1967, p. 22).

Unit-beat policing was an attempt to combine all the best features of the residential foot-beat patrolled by "area constables" with those of mobile-policing. It is useful to note the nature of the place in which the scheme was first introduced, an industrial town with a population of about 60,000; this is of significance when considering the application of the scheme to other areas. So is the fact that the centre of the town was still policed by normal foot-beats—for that seems to have been overlooked when the scheme was introduced in some other areas.

Excluding the town centre, the police area was divided into

four car-beats. The cars that they used were quite small, low-powered vehicles which were painted in a conspicuous blue and white patchwork pattern that earned them the name of "panda" cars, a name that has stuck, even where that particular combination of colours is not in use. The cars were operational around the clock, single-manned, the driver being equipped with personal radio. Each car-beat was divided into two foot-beats, each of which was the responsibility of an area constable who, if possible, lived on his beat and performed an eight-hour tour of duty each day, but was not replaced when he was off duty. Each unit car-beat had a detective constable assigned to it to liaise with the unit car-drivers and with the area constables. The idea was to create small teams of men who would be able to gain a thorough understanding of their area and be able to feed information into a central store at the divisional headquarters. To file the information and to provide a link between the various small teams, a constable was appointed as a collator and he maintained a variety of indices relating to local crimes, criminals and vulnerable premises. All of the people involved, including their supervisors, were linked by means of personal radio sets.

The role of the area constable was crucial to the success of the scheme. He was given a reasonable degree of autonomy in respect of his hours of duty, whether he wore uniform or plain clothes (although it was basically a uniformed role), where he patrolled and how he spent his day. It is interesting to note that the measure of his effectiveness was not, as might be expected, the level of crime in his area but the amount of information that he fed into the system.

Unit-beat adaptions

The unit-beat system had not been in use in Lancashire for very long before other police forces took it up and used it with varying degrees of success. The adaptions varied considerably from force to force as each one faced up to its different problems: lack of manpower, different type of area to be policed and limitations in equipment. What emerged was that the unit-beat scheme as applied to Accrington could not be universally implemented without some adjustments—often quite major.

The following analysis is not a criticism of the basic scheme but a summary of some of the problems that emerged when it was applied to different police forces. Not all forces encountered these problems and it is doubtful if any police force had to face all of them; nevertheless, it is worth looking at the type of problems involved because of the general lessons that can be learned.

The unit-beat scheme has very definite manpower requirements. In round numbers, five men are required per car-beat, plus two area constables. If a detective constable is added that makes eight men per beat. Many forces, particularly those that were seriously under strength, had to make a choice between beats too large or making do with less people per beat. The usual compromise was to increase the number of area constables covered by each car-beat; thus one unit-beat car would cover perhaps three or four area constables' beats.

The detective constable was often omitted from the unit beat, as it was more economical to have a central C.I.D. office in which all the C.I.D. officers would work together. This enabled case loads to be equalised and cover to be given for men on leave, courses and sickness.

Then there was the problem of emergency calls and inquiries. These tended to be given to the unit-beat cars, which thus became less and less able to work with the area constables and more and more tied up in answering calls received by radio. The situation was aggravated by the lack of reserve capacity in most police areas. Demonstrations, football matches, extensive inquiries, all required that large bodies of men be assembled: but where were they to come from? Not from the unit car-beats, for these were now providing the police response to calls from the public. The only other source was often the area constables. Thus gradually, the area constables came to be used as a reserve of manpower available for other jobs and their status and involvement in their area tended to decline. A symptom of this can be seen in the way in which many supervisors insisted on arranging the duties of area constables to provide a sectional "cover" at all times and thus reduced the autonomy of the area constables, who found themselves on duty at times when they could not do their job effectively.

One final point about the residential beat is also worth noting and that is the reaction of some supervisors to the concepts on which it was based. In order to form a useful working relationship with the people on his beat, a constable might argue that he needed to exercise considerable latitude in the enforcement of minor offences, including traffic offences. His supervisor, charged with the responsibility of law enforcement in his area, might well find himself at odds with the views of his constables. This sort of divergence of ideas needs to be avoided if any police system is to be successful.

Command structures
Alongside developments in unit-beat policing, experiments were being made in the size and command structures of small units. The problem was that, while in a large unit it was possible to ensure 24-hour coverage at a given rank, say inspector, with a small unit, to have sufficient officers of that rank to provide one on duty throughout the twenty-four hours would have upset the unit's rank structure. In some areas, this led to the amalgamation of small units into larger, whilst in other areas this was not possible or desirable. One solution was to use an "extended responsibility" system—an updated name for a very old concept. Basically, this meant that an officer in charge of a unit was given enough sergeants to be able to provide 24-hour coverage at that level, but he or his deputy had to be available to intervene should a serious incident arise that required the experience or rank of a more senior officer. In some cases, the unit commander was not even given a deputy and so was, more or less, on permanent call, unless he could hand over to a colleague on a neighbouring unit.

The advantage of the extended-responsibility scheme is the autonomy given to the unit commanders, many of whom respond by becoming thoroughly involved in the work of their unit, with which they are able to identify in much the same way as a residential-beat constable identifies with his area, but on a larger scale.

The scheme is sound for small towns which cannot be linked with others to form a large sub-division, since it encourages the formation of *rapport* between the police of the unit and the local townspeople. Care is needed to make the unit the right size, for there is a natural tendency to try to keep them as small as possible on economical grounds. There is a minimum workable size for any unit, based on the amount of policing required, and this size can be critical. Any attempts to run it even one or two men short can have serious results if one man represents between 7 and 10 per cent of the total manpower.

The extended-responsibility scheme has found rather less favour in urban areas where larger police units are possible. Larger units tend to be more economical in their use of manpower and 24-hour coverage at a more senior rank is possible. Nevertheless, in suburban areas particularly, the formation of smaller units with their own command structure and specialists has been found beneficial in terms of the relations between the police unit and the public it serves. Within the police itself, added co-operation is possible between the uniform-patrol officers and the detectives forming the unit. It is noticeable that this experience has not been confined to Britain; in the U.S.A. it has also been found that a number of small, semi-autonomous units can produce a better relationship with the public and be more effective in terms of crime prevention than one large unit.

Los Angeles Police Department
The organisation of the Los Angeles Police Department with its concept of small, semi-autonomous district teams linked to communities, was discussed in Chapter 3 (*see* p. 77).

The basic-car plan
The district teams, led by a police lieutenant, are composed of uniformed personnel and detectives. Within each district team, the primary unit of policing is the "basic car". Each district team consists of one or two basic cars, but may contain three basic cars under exceptional circumstances. Each basic car is manned by nine police officers who cover one beat over a 24-hour period. Not only must the basic-car teams maintain a 24-hour watch, but they are expected to cultivate a constructive working relationship with the people living on their beats. Each team must hold at least one meeting a month at which all residents on their beat are invited to attend. The objective is to create a joint commitment, between the nine police officers and the people living on their beat, to keep their community free from crime.

Each district team commander is also expected to "meet and interact with" the people living in his district in the pursuit of a concept that has been termed the "territorial imperative". The principle behind this is best explained in the words of E. M. Davis, Chief of Police, in a statement of principles dated 12th February 1975:

TERRITORIAL IMPERATIVE

Police work is one of the most personal of all personal services, it deals with human beings in life and death situations. The police officers and the people they serve must be as close as possible, and where possible must know one another. Such closeness can generate the police citizen co-operation necessary for the involvement of the whole community in community protection. Organization of assignments should ensure that the same police and the same citizens have an opportunity to continuously work for the protection of a specific community. Strength through interacting together and working together on common problems can be enhanced through officers and the people feeling at home with one another in an atmosphere of mutual cooperation. This may be described as a utilization of the "territorial imperative".

Each district leader has, in fact, taken over some of the duties formerly allocated to a headquarters Community Relations Officer who, under team-policing, is responsible for co-ordinating the efforts of the various teams in such activities as citizen support groups, youth services and the district team community-involvement programme.

The district team commander

The responsibilities of the district team commanders include the power to vary the cover provided by his basic cars to fit local conditions. For example, if he has two or three basic cars, he may choose to deploy only one during the a.m. hours, in much the same way that some unit-beat policing systems varied the number of panda cars at night. A measure of whether a district team commander is gearing his resources according to need, can be provided by monitoring the cross-over rate, the percentage of radio calls that have had to be handled by a team outside the team district.

It is interesting to note that the Los Angeles Police Department basic-car plan and team-policing system, was consciously based upon an updated version of the original concepts of Peel, Rowan and Mayne (*see* Chapter 1, p. 10). The same emphasis on crime prevention and the need for public acceptance, the close identification of the police as being part of the society they serve, and the need to obviate unnecessary force, in order to gain public co-operation, are all echoes from 1829. The aim has been to wed modern technology to established principles to obtain an effective public service.

New Zealand police

The police of New Zealand share common roots with British police forces and, in most respects, fulfil similar functions. The principal exception is that there is a separate organisation, part of the Ministry of Transport, that deals with traffic and has its own traffic officers. New Zealand police do not therefore fulfil the traffic function as in Britain.

Policing problems

Of similar numerical size to the Los Angeles Police Department and a larger British provincial police force, the New Zealand Police have the task of policing extensive areas of sparsely-populated territory and some sizeable urban areas. In 1966, it became apparent that a major review of police activities was needed to cope with the problems that became more pressing each year. That these problems were similar to those facing police agencies throughout the civilised world can be seen from the following statement:

> Law enforcement has always been a difficult task. It is especially difficult in a society such as ours that has a mobile population; that has so prosperous an economy; that is reaching a high degree of urbanization with its accompanying congestion and anonymity; and that places so high a value on individual freedom and upon equality under the law; and with changing moral and social standards.
> (*The New System of Policing*, New Zealand Government, 1970, p. 7.)

Reviewing police activities

The response the New Zealand Police made to their problems was to undertake a lengthy and thorough review of all their activities. The results of this review were related to the basic principles of policing and combined with the classical principles of organisation and management. The philosophy behind the review can be seen in a statement made by the man responsible for carrying it out after he had been appointed Commissioner of Police: "The police look to the future to ensure not only that

F

trends in crime and in public attitudes can be anticipated but also, and more importantly, that the men and equipment are ready and properly trained for that time" (Police Commissioner K. B. Burnside, *Report of the New Zealand Police*, 1975, p. 3).

In a circular to the force in July 1966, the objectives of what was termed the National Survey were set out. These were to examine:

1. the existing deployment of staff;
2. the present staff requirements, and those of the future;
3. existing procedures;
4. building requirements;
5. any other matter considered necessary.

Each police unit in New Zealand was to be visited but, prior to commencing the main survey, a pilot study was carried out to ascertain exactly what information would be required—an essential feature of any survey. A good deal of effort was also put into making certain that all members of the force knew of the survey, its purpose, aims and methods.

From the pilot study, it was possible to prepare forms that could be distributed in advance of survey visits so that there would be information for the team to work on and discuss with the police unit personnel when they arrived. This need, for information to be collected at the right time, is another crucial feature of a review. In the case of the New Zealand survey, the information supplied on the forms could be processed quickly using factor-analysis charts and was supplemented by such aids as detailed maps of the area and relevant newspaper cuttings over the past six months.

Field activities

When the team moved into the area to be studied, the first step was always to gather together as many as possible of the police staff to explain to them the nature and purpose of the survey, to seek their co-operation, to overcome suspicion and to invite their active participation.

This meeting would then be followed by a preliminary visit to each station within the police district to distribute and explain forms that should be filled in, to gain some first-hand knowledge of the topography of the area and establish *rapport* between members of the survey team and the policemen, and often with policemen's families, particularly in remoter areas. About four weeks later, the survey team would return to follow up the preliminary visit. Forms would be checked, the information processed, discussions held with key personnel and notes made of points that were to be kept for future reference.

It quickly became clear that the credibility of the survey team depended on action being taken to improve obvious faults in the existing system. It was therefore necessary to formulate conclusions at the scene, to put forward proposals that could be tested for viability and accepted or rejected.

In order to gain acceptance of these proposals, the local supervisors were always involved and the survey team spent some days in discussions with official representatives of local government, who were often able to add useful additional information. The last step in each district was to acquaint the district commander with the impressions and ideas which had been formulated by the team.

Recommendations could then be made and the schemes which had been devised could be implemented, initially as a pilot scheme, in the case of radical departures from existing practice.

The results of the survey
The survey identified grossly unequal work levels, unnecessary police stations, out-dated concepts (including that of the village constable and his wife), and inadequate urban methods. In contrast to the Los Angeles Police Department, which had become too centralised and had to be broken down into community-related teams, the New Zealand Police had become too fragmented and needed to be drawn into more functional units.

Predictably, many changes were unpopular, notably the closure of police stations and the re-allocation of police personnel. The use of good public-relations methods, involving local citizens in the discussions and encouraging the participation of local community leaders (for example, the Mayor of one town performed a small ceremony to mark the closure of one station) avoided any resistance to these closures in the majority of cases. Nevertheless, some animosity was caused, particularly amongst policemen who had long enjoyed an easy job, but this was counterbalanced by the improved morale of policemen who had been overworked for equally long periods and who now received help from re-allocated staff.

One change that caused a public reaction in an exactly similar way to similar changes in Britain, concerned the removal of rural police officers from small communities. In the words of the New Zealand 1970 report:

> It is significant to note that where the staff affected (and this is most of them) have been in agreement to the change there has been little or no opposition from the public. The only exception to this is in some rural areas where the local constable originally placed there, literally in the horse and buggy days, is regarded with respect and affection and the logic of his removal is clouded by understandable emotion.
>
> (ibid., p. 13.)

As we saw earlier, this is a problem that is often encountered whenever it is proposed to make policing changes that are seen to be reducing the status of a community, or taking from it *tangible* evidence of policing, in the shape of the community's own policeman. The depth of such feeling must not be under-estimated, for it can endure for a long time and cause bad public relations out of all proportion to the actual scale of the problem, measured in terms of crime and incidents (*see* also Chapter 5).

Policing by function
The various activities of the police were divided into three functions, pro-active, reactive and support. The first two functions are similar in concept to those used in the Kansas City study (*see* Chapter 5) but their use in the New Zealand re-organisation is somewhat wider.

1. *Pro-active services* are the positive steps taken to prevent crime and disorder.
2. *Reactive services* are those deployed when a crime or incident has occurred.
3. *Support services* are those needed to maintain the other two.

The way in which these functions are applied in practice can be seen in Fig. 12.

The types of patrol shown in Fig. 12 are as follows:

1. *E (enquiry) Patrols.* Groups of three men issued with one car to provide 7 a.m. to 11 p.m. cover, with the prime respon-

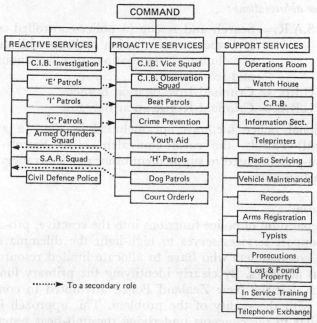

```
                        ┌──────────────┐
                        │   COMMAND    │
                        └──────────────┘
```

REACTIVE SERVICES	PROACTIVE SERVICES	SUPPORT SERVICES
C.I.B. Investigation	C.I.B. Vice Squad	Operations Room
'E' Patrols	C.I.B. Observation Squad	Watch House
'I' Patrols	Beat Patrols	C.R.B.
'C' Patrols	Crime Prevention	Information Sect.
Armed Offenders Squad	Youth Aid	Teleprinters
S.A.R. Squad	'H' Patrols	Radio Servicing
Civil Defence Police	Dog Patrols	Vehicle Maintenance
	Court Orderly	Records
		Arms Registration
		Typists
		Prosecutions
		Lost & Found Property
		In Service Training
		Telephone Exchange

·········► To a secondary role

Fig. 12—Organisation of police services according to broad functions. (Produced by G. E. Twentyman and reproduced by courtesy of the Commissioner, New Zealand Police.)

sibility of getting to know the people in their area. They are not normally expected to respond to incident calls.

2. *I (incident) Patrols.* Radio cars, manned by two constables operating in shifts to provide 24-hour coverage to deal with any call for police services.

When not engaged on incidents, they have the secondary role of patrolling.

3. *C (crime) Patrols.* Crewed by two detectives, these plain, unmarked, cars provide 24-hour coverage to attend to crime calls and when not attending to crime, they engage in preventive work.

4. *H (highway) Patrols.* Crewed by two constables, they specialise in night patrol on highways to check on the movement of criminals, intercept stolen cars and give protection to commercial and residential areas that do not have other 24-hour police coverage.

5. *Other abbreviations:*

    (*a*) S.A.R. = Search and rescue (a police-controlled search and rescue system which operates with the aid of voluntary organisations to effect mountain and sea rescues).

    (*b*) C.I.B. = Criminal Investigation Branch.

    (*c*) C.R.B. = Criminal Registration Bureau.

Additional police methods not included in Fig. 12 are R (rural) Patrols—the rural equivalent of E Patrols—and team-policing used to supplement other police arrangements in urban areas.

Conclusions

The separation of police functions into the reactive, pro-active and support services serves to high-light the dilemma of all police commanders who have to allocate limited resources to various activities. By clearly identifying the primary function of each unit the New Zealand Police attempted to come to terms with the reality of the problem. This approach is not dissimilar to the concepts underlying the unit-beat system, in which there was a definite attempt to distinguish between the police who patrolled in a pro-active sense and those who answered emergency calls.

The rejection of the use of a set formula in favour of an analysis of the needs of each individual community and then relating these to the needs of the total population was not, originally, intentional. The survey team had hoped to find a suitable formula but they concluded that there was none that would serve their purpose. This tends to reinforce the conclusion reached elsewhere that there is no formula that will give an absolute measure of policing needs. The approach finally used by the survey team had a number of advantages over simpler and less time-consuming methods:

1. It reached every person in the police and involved them in the new organisation of their force.

2. Each small part of the force area obtained a police unit individually tailored to its needs.

3. The use of a survey team enabled a proper balance of resources to be made between different areas.

4. Balancing work loads between police units prevented some people being overworked and others being under-employed.
5. The survey document provided a basis for long-term planning and will be updated periodically to provide an on-going review of police deployment.
6. The interest surrounding the re-organisation brought benefits in terms of police/public relations and political support for improvements.

The New Zealand survey showed the value of a police force thoroughly examining every part of its work so as to bring it into line with demands. The survey team went to some lengths to ensure participation of police officers in decisions that affected them in achieving practical and acceptable policing methods; their involvement being encouraged by ensuring that action was taken in respect of decisions in which they had participated. The participation of local people also was seen to aid the process of acceptance, particularly where a police station was to be closed or a police presence removed.

Relating police methods to needs
From what has already been said, it should be clear that there is no universal policing method that can be applied to every country, or even to every part of one country. Each area must be considered separately to identify its policing needs and suitable methods adopted to meet those needs. In general, the more detailed the examination, the more likelihood there is of the police system fitting its true needs. When the optimum policing method has been established in each small area (the "micro" approach), an overall view should be taken of the whole system to ensure that it meets all the contrasting services required from an efficient police (the "macro" approach).

The micro approach
To plan an effective police system, it is necessary to know all the policing problems of the area. This can be done by building up a picture from as many sources as possible. The use of statistics (population, crime, incidents, calls for police assistance, traffic accidents and densities, complaints) can give a preliminary indication of the work load to be expected but it must

be remembered that as an area changes, so will its policing problems. In many cities there is a continuous process of building, decay, clearance and re-building going on. As an area passes from one phase to another, dramatic changes can occur over a short time. For example, an area of solid suburban houses can become a twilight zone in which the suburban citizens are replaced by a transient population with quite different policing needs.

Statistics must not be taken at face value, they need to be interpreted to provide information about people of the area and their problems. The picture can be filled out by talking to the police officers working in the area and to people who live there. Local newspapers, local organisations and community leaders can all help to identify the problems as perceived by them. Naturally there will be vested interests, slants caused by the particular philosophy of the speaker but, by adding everything together, it is possible to form a balanced view. This will give some indication of the range of police needs and therefore the methods appropriate to the area. A densely-populated area, with a large number of social problems and frequent calls to the police for assistance, might require a form of neighbourhood beats to enable the police officers to work within the community as distinct from merely providing a rapid response to calls. The needs of dormitory suburb, where the prevalent crime is daylight housebreaking, may suggest a system of mobile crime-prevention patrols. In some areas, the range of problems will be so wide that a number of policing methods may have to be superimposed to provide the right level of service; in others, cost-effectiveness will have to be balanced against the expectations of the people in the community.

At this stage of the exercise, planning should be in terms of the policing "cover" that is needed, rather than the numbers of police personnel required. It is a simple matter to compute the personnel needed once it has been determined how many posts should be filled on a 24-hour, 7-days-a-week basis and how many are needed for perhaps 8, 12 or 16 hours a day. Thus, to crew a double-manned car around the clock requires about 11 men, the actual number being determined by the hours worked per week, the amount of leave and training per year and the allowance that must be made for sickness.

The macro approach

The results of a micro-survey are likely to be something of a patchwork of different requirements: neighbourhood beats, 24-hour foot-beats, mobile beats and patrols. To knit these into a viable policing system often requires compromise but the result should be a bespoke system tailored to the area. Even then it is unlikely to satisfy all of the needs of the area viewed as a whole. The most common missing feature is rapid response to emergency calls. If the area is extensively patrolled by police officers in cars, they may be able to provide this response but doing so may detract from their prime objective of preventing crime. For this reason, mobile patrols are often considered at two levels. At the level of police officers patrolling to prevent crime, to watch for suspicious behaviour and to maintain contact with the public by leaving their vehicle to patrol on foot for part of their tour of duty, a small car or motor scooter can be used successfully. At a higher level of motor-vehicle performance and a wider area to be covered, reliable, fast cars provide quick response to emergency calls, the number of such cars being geared to the incidence of calls and the response time required.

Once the level of police patrols and the emergency response to routine police calls have been established, there remain two further steps. First, to determine the needs for specialist support staff and secondly, to establish a command structure that will hold the whole system together. Statistics can be used to estimate the need for traffic patrols, detectives and other specialists required, as discussed in Chapter 5, and the command structure will tend to be governed by the type of organisational structure used. Where a police area can be seen to contain distinct communities that have a corporate identity, then the police will achieve greater identification with the people if police units can be linked to those communities. One or two policemen may be able to identity themselves with a village or urban estate. A small, semi-autonomous unit may be able to identify itself with a small town or a sector of a city. Such identification between police and community produces a far more co-operative relationship than any system imposed without consideration for community feelings.

In some cities, such communities are rare or may not exist in anything but name. Where there are no definable communities, the police command structure is less critical and a large, centralised organisation may be the most effective way of policing the area, compensation for the lack of police/public identification being sought in other ways.

Two assumptions have been implicit in this section so far: the first is that policing can be considered entirely in terms of localised priorities; the second is that the resources will be available to provide the optimum level of policing in each area. In practice, neither of these assumptions may be warranted. All police forces have to cope with problems that transcend divisional boundaries and therefore local arrangements sometimes have to be modified to meet force needs. One example that can be overlooked by unit commanders is the need for enough personnel to be on duty at all times to provide an immediate response to very serious emergencies. Thus, although a unit may need only a few people on duty in the early hours of the morning to fulfil its local commitments, force headquarters may have to insist on a larger number being available as that unit's contribution to the reserves needed to deal with a major incident.

The lack of resources to provide the personnel and equipment required for optimum policing of each area means that a central decision must be made as to how available resources should be distributed. If the review methods described above have been used to assess the problems of each area then much of the data needed to make a balanced decision is available. The needs of individual areas can be balanced against one another and their needs set against those of specialist departments. Inevitably, this means making compromises and some units will not be able to provide an ideal level of service. The fact that there is a difference between a system of policing which meets adequately the needs of the community and that which can actually be provided, gives a basis for a review of police resources by the police authority.

Chapter Seven

Specialist departments

The growth of specialist departments

Most bureaucratic organisations adapt to change by introducing new specialist departments which tend to be self-perpetuating, self-enlarging, engendering sub-groups with an even greater degree of specialisation and which may develop sub-objectives unrelated to the objectives of the parent organisation. Senior officers, therefore, need to be on their guard to minimise the ill-effects that can ensue.

Self-perpetuation

Specialist groups are usually first set up on an experimental basis or for a limited period. By the end of that time, it is often found that the group has proved of value and is made permanent because it is easier to continue the existing system than to re-allocate the work being done by the group.

The members of a specialist squad will usually justify their existence by finding enough work to use the time and resources available. With an "experimental" group, the feeling of being innovators has a short-term effect of obtaining the maximum effort from the people in the group. Once the initial novelty has worn off, the group will normally settle into a steady state and it is the achievements at this stage that indicate whether there is a genuine need for a specialist department. A group can appear to be successful and yet produce little of real value towards the aims of the organisation. To take a simple example, many towns have rowdyism problems and to counter this, special rowdyism squads may be set up. There is a tendency to measure the effectiveness of such squads in terms of their arrests for public-order offences and, provided they maintain a given level of "productivity" in this way, to consider the retention of the squad as justifiable. But the number of arrests is *not* the true measure of performance. The original objective of the senior police officer setting up the squad was to reduce rowdyism and it is against that objective that the performance of the anti-rowdyism squad must be measured. To have been aware of the problem of rowdyism, the police commander must have had some indications, either from his own observations or, more likely, from complaints by members of the public. The criterion for measurement of performance is, whether the original problem has been solved or not. Of course the number of arrests may indicate that the police are doing something about the problem and this may be the way to solve it, but it does not follow that a consistently high number of arrests is a valid measure of the extent to which the original objective is being attained. After all, if the objective was obtained, the number of arrests would fall because there would be no rowdyism for which people could be arrested!

Self-enlargement

Once a specialist group has been created there will be a tendency for it to grow in size. This is a continuation of the process of self-perpetuation for, as the group takes on more and more work to justify its existence, it will become overworked and so demand more men.

This is a perfectly natural process and although occasionally there may be additional factors at work, even without them, most specialist sections tend to grow if not checked.

The additional factors that aid this process include the tendency for other people in the organisation to hand jobs over to the specialist section when they could as effectively be done by the general-purpose personnel. Growth may also sometimes be caused by the ambitions of the man in charge of the group. In order to "prove" himself, he will tend to take on more and more work; then, to demonstrate how much he and his men are doing, he will claim to be overloaded and in need of more men. In some cases, he may seek to gain promotion by enlarging his section so that, under the normal rules of hierarchical organisations, he is entitled to a higher rank. This may not be a conscious process; it is part of man's normal desire for achievement and recognition.

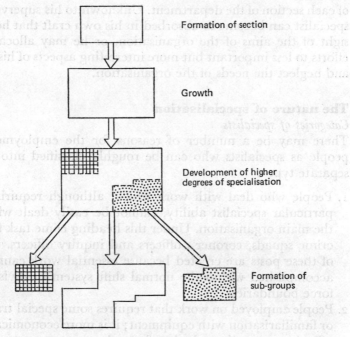

Formation of section

Growth

Development of higher
degrees of specialisation

Formation of
sub-groups

Fig. 13 Specialist departments—process of growth.

Sub-groups

As a specialist department grows, so does the range of skills of
the people within it. It soon becomes easier for certain people
within the group to specialise on some aspects of the work
rather than others and so even greater degrees of specialisation
are created. This process is shown diagrammatically in Fig. 13.
Each sub-group will tend to expand until it, too, begins to
develop separate sub-groups and so the cycle is continued. In
this way organisations grow in complexity and adapt to meet
new challenges but care is needed to ensure that the right
challenges are being met.

Sub-objectives

Supervisors need to ensure that the aims of the people under
their command are focused on the overall objectives of the force.
In the case of a specialist department, this may present problems because of their lack of detailed knowledge of the working

of each section of the department. Unknown to his supervisor, a specialist can become so absorbed in his own craft that he loses sight of the aims of the organisation, or he may allocate his efforts to less important but more interesting aspects of his work and neglect the needs of the organisation.

The nature of specialisation
Categories of specialists
There may be a number of reasons for the employment of people as specialists who can be roughly classified into three separate types:

1. People who deal with work which, although requiring no particular specialist ability, cannot be easily dealt with by the main organisation. Under this heading come task forces, crime squads, coroner's officers and inquiry officers. Many of these posts are created because essential work cannot be accomplished within the normal shift system or divisional/force boundaries.
2. People employed on work that requires some special training or familiarisation with equipment; it is more economical and effective to retain a body of people to carry out certain aspects of police work than to arrange the necessary training or familiarisation for everyone. Dog handlers, training staff, traffic patrols and criminal investigation department personnel provide examples of this group.
3. Those whose jobs require a high degree of training, formal qualifications or lengthy experience. Fingerprint officers, legal advisers, radio and laboratory technicians all come into this group.

The effects of specialisation
The deployment of personnel in any of these categories tends to remove them from the main stream of the organisation but there is a greater problem of reversibility as one moves from category 1 to 3. Few problems are encountered in transferring personnel from ordinary duty to a specialist job in category 1 and back again. All that may be needed is a period of attachment to familiarise each man with the particular aspects of the specialist group or task and, provided the man has the necessary

aptitude, he will be able to perform his new duties quite well.

There is a tendency not to disturb persons in category 2 because it takes time and money to replace them and returning them to ordinary duty "wastes" the experience and training that they have received. Nevertheless, within limits, interchange between ordinary duty and specialist work is feasible. With category 3, interchange is very difficult indeed because the skills required cannot be learned quickly by ordinary duty personnel and there is a reluctance to employ skilled people on work that makes no use of their skills.

Manpower planning

In terms of manpower planning, it can be seen that category 1 presents few problems, decisions can be made and implemented quickly with little effect on the organisation. People in category 3 tend to be few in number and are often recruited as specialists from outside the police. Where policemen are employed in category 3, succession must be planned, because the loss of one or two men in key posts can be a serious matter. Career prospects for such people also need careful consideration (because of their relatively low numbers), as it is often not possible to recognise their degree of expertise in salaries or rank. The British police rank-structure is based predominantly on supervision and many experts do not supervise anyone. It has tended to become common for a supervisory rank to be allotted to a specialist post, as an acknowledgment of its status, even though the level of supervision involved does not justify the rank in itself. In some ways this adds to the irreversibility of the specialist's career—he may be acceptable in a given rank as a specialist only and not in any other capacity.

The problem of promotion can also arise with people employed in category 2 and, as there are numerically far more people in this category, definite policies governing the employment of people in this class of specialism are required if the organisation is to avoid problems. Promotion can occur within a specialism or by interchange between specialist and general-purpose personnel, or some combination of both. The choice is not always easy for there are often advantages and disadvantages to be weighed. As these are often related to specific branches of specialisation, they are perhaps better discussed in that context.

Traffic departments

Of all the specialist departments in the British police, traffic departments occupy the most anomalous positions. In some countries, traffic-policing is performed by a corps specialising in traffic only, which may or may not be a police force.

Operational traffic duty

Despite implications that traffic policing can be hived off to another organisation or dealt with as a separate function, the British police tend to deal with traffic duty as a somewhat less specialised subject than might be thought. In many police forces it is difficult to distinguish the responsibilities of the traffic police from those of the general duty police (*see* Chapter 3, p. 69 for an example of this).

In general, it may be said that two factors appear to determine the relationship between the traffic police and other police units. These are, first, the pattern of organisation adopted and, secondly, the system of radio communication.

Two types of organisation charts describing the relationship between the main body of the force and its specialists are shown in Figs. 6 and 7 on p. 71 and p. 72 respectively. If the type of organisation (Fig. 6) places the traffic personnel under the direct command of divisional supervision, there is likely to be less formal distinction between traffic units and other radio patrol cars. If the organisation is of the form (Fig. 7) in which traffic personnel are accountable directly to their own traffic division supervisors, they are likely to be more readily distinguishable as a specialist body.

Where traffic personnel share a radio channel with divisional units, it is likely that they will serve as a first-line response to all calls and not simply traffic. To some extent this will depend on the policies governing the allocation of calls by the control room, but where traffic units are on a separate frequency, they tend to be regarded as more specialised.

If traffic units deal with non-traffic emergency calls, certainly non-traffic cars deal with traffic cases, including accidents. The demarcation between traffic personnel and other policemen is therefore not as clear cut as with some other specialisations and it is probably true to say that the number of true specialists needed in operational traffic work is quite small, as most of the skills for traffic duty are also needed for general police duty.

The level of traffic patrols that should be maintained in a given area is not easy to determine, although some guidelines have been provided by the Home Office Research and Planning Branch which, in 1967, advocated the following scales of policing (with two officers to each patrol car at all times):

1. *Motorways*

    (a) *Day* (8 a.m. to midnight) 1 car to each 10 miles (16 km) of route (= 20 miles (32 km) of carriageway).

    (b) *Night* (midnight to 8 a.m.) 1 car to each 20 miles (32 km) of route (= 40 miles (64 km) of carriageway).

2. *Selected primary routes.*

    (a) *Day* 1 car and 1 motor cycle to every 20 miles (32 km) of route.

    (b) *Night* 1 car to every 40 miles (64 km) of route.

The "selected" primary routes amounted to 5,624 miles (9,049 km) of the total primary-route mileage in England and Wales of some 14,000 miles (22,500 km) at that time.

The level of policing should be at least enough to cover the number of accidents that require the specialist knowledge of traffic officers and the equipment carried in their vehicles, and to deal with traffic offences requiring mechanical expertise.

The interchangeability of traffic and ordinary duty personnel tends to be higher than for some other specialisms and interchange on promotion is common. At higher levels of supervision, the mechanical skills required by good traffic constables must be replaced by a knowledge of resource deployment, interpretation of statistics and a good understanding of the role of police in relation to traffic.

In passing, these are pointers towards an argument for the retention of traffic duties by the police. If the relatively restricted need for specially trained traffic officers is accepted, then the "off-peak" traffic function can be handled by the general police; this is a much more economical proposition than maintaining traffic police when there is not a clearly-established need in terms of a high traffic density. It should perhaps be added that this argument for relating traffic police to vehicle density is not normally held to apply to motorways, where the potential need for specialised knowledge and equipment is usually high even at times when traffic density is low.

Other traffic duties
Police have tended to extend their involvement in traffic management where their principal contributions are:

1. to help identify traffic hazards requiring action, either through engineering or legislation;
2. to advise law-makers on the enforceability of proposed laws and to highlight contradictory pressures.

The extent to which police should become involved in road engineering is debatable and the role of the police should probably be confined to advising on potential hazards. The expertise that police can bring to such discussions is based on a wide experience of watching motorists and building up an understanding of just how a motorist can cause an accident if given half a chance, or indeed none at all! In the same way, police can contribute to road-safety work although once again, the relationship between police and local government is not always clear.

The enforceability of laws is of particular importance when laws are proposed on other than safety grounds. A number of legal provisions have been made to differentiate between road users—for example, bus lanes and limited access to certain roads on environmental grounds—that pose considerable problems for police if it is the intention of the legislators that the law shall be enforced. Selective traffic legislation—for example, allowing buses, taxis and certain other vehicles to go along roads that are prohibited to other traffic—are extremely difficult and costly to enforce at a realistic level. It is usually accepted that such schemes will be sufficiently effective at a low level of enforcement but this requires clear understanding on the part of all concerned in making the relevant law. It sometimes happens that the very people who help to pass unenforceable laws then protest publicly about the lack of police action in enforcing them. Police involvement at the planning stages might at least minimise this potential area of difficulty.

Criminal investigation departments

The alternative structures for criminal investigation departments were shown in Chapter 3. The principal problem, as with all other specialist departments, is to keep the C.I.D. and uniform branch working together to achieve the same objectives.

The relationship between C.I.D. and the uniform branch

Most instances of lack of co-operation between detectives and uniformed personnel seem to stem from failure to understand one another's point of view and this is less likely when there is free interchange between uniform and C.I.D. It is almost inevitable that there should be some misgivings on the part of the ordinary duty personnel about specialists, particularly the C.I.D. As early as the beginning of the century, a stereotype of a detective had formed:

> The detective—a famous branch, quite distinct from the "uniform staff" (from which, however, it is recruited) and receiving higher rates of pay. These plain-clothes officers have less regular and more responsible work than their comrades in uniform; they are occupied chiefly in "shadowing" suspects, tracing men who are "wanted", collecting evidence against offenders, . . . and other duties specially requiring shrewdness, caution and readiness of resource.
>
> (*Police Life in London*, E. Buxton Conway, 1903.)

The uniform constable sees the apparent freedom of his C.I.D. opposite number and may also feel the restriction on his scope at having to hand over to a C.I.D. officer inquiries in a case that he has initiated. The awareness that an unsuccessful C.I.D. officer is "returned" to ordinary duty creates an impress of second-class citizenship for the ordinary duty man.

The C.I.D. officer may envy the more regular hours worked by the uniform branch, the less frequent changes of duty and, in many cases, a lesser clerical involvement: many C.I.D. officers tend to have to spend excessive time on processing papers for courts.

The effects of interchange

Free interchange between C.I.D. and uniform personnel reduces the likelihood of friction by lessening their difference in status and by emphasising the common roots of the two groups of people. This gain is not achieved without some loss, but the actual extent of that loss is not clear and may well depend on the quality of the methods of selection, assessment and supervision, rather than the principle of interchange itself.

Many of the skills and attributes needed by a detective are not markedly different from those needed by a successful uniform policeman; the difference between the two jobs is often marginal. In many areas, more crimes are investigated by uniform officers than by the C.I.D. Usually, the more serious and involved crimes are investigated by C.I.D. officers and so it must be accepted that whilst the basic skills and attributes are the same, the level of those skills and their balance with other skills and attributes is likely to be different in a successful and experienced C.I.D. officer.

It can therefore be argued that, ideally, the people who possess the best balance for C.I.D. work should be the permanent C.I.D. officers. This cannot be so if there is free interchange and therefore the optimum performance might not be achieved. As so often in personnel matters, the key to the solution lies in good personnel management: interchange must be sensibly applied so that people who are patently unsuited to C.I.D. work are not employed on it simply to maintain a system. Exceptions must be possible to allow first-class detectives to be retained rather than to insist that they become second- or third-rate uniform officers; for it is not only the case that some good uniform men make indifferent detectives, but some good detectives lack the necessary skills and attributes to make good uniform officers.

Some mention must also be made of the need to preserve experience in a department and this is not only applicable to criminal investigation. Rapid interchange of personnel can create inefficiency because there is no continuity of experience. It is possibly most obvious in relation to the C.I.D. because of the emphasis placed by detectives on knowledge of local criminals, their methods and associates and on informants. There is sometimes a tendency for non-C.I.D. officers to underrate the importance of this type of experience which can be a vital ingredient for success in some areas and good personnel management is needed to preserve it.

Highly specialised personnel
The more specialised areas of C.I.D. work pose considerable

problems in terms of career planning for here we enter category 3 of p. 162 above. The effects of this on individual careers will be considered again in Chapter 12; a balance must be struck between career development for each individual and the need for constant availability of people able and willing to fill specialist posts. Once again, it tends to be a matter of striking a compromise between the optimum cost-effectiveness that comes with training only the minimum number of people needed, and training enough people to be able to provide a reserve capacity to allow individuals to develop a wider range of experience in the interests of their careers. Some people prefer to remain specialists because of job satisfaction and such people often form the central core of their department. The important point is that they should knowingly determine for themselves the course of their career rather than remain as specialists because of bad manpower planning.

Civilian police staff

A review of duties undertaken by police that might be "handed over to suitably qualified and trained civilians" was undertaken by a Home Office Working Party on Manpower in 1966. The working party concluded that there were duties which must be discharged only by police, based on special qualifications, personal qualities, particular training and the exercise of police powers.

The working party also concluded that there were many aspects of police work that could be dealt with by non-policemen but found some difficulty in deciding on the way in which a career structure could be developed within the police service.

In so far as administration and clerical work is concerned, the working party suggested interchange of personnel between police and local-authority departments, a practice that was facilitated for many forces by the changes produced by local government reorganisation in 1974. At that time, county councils had to choose whether they or the police committee would be employers of police civilian staff. In the event, some decided one way and some the other, depending on how the relative merits of the rather evenly-balanced alternatives were seen. Even where the police committee remains as the employing authority, the conditions of service of police civilian staff are usually identical with the staff employed by the county council and so interchange of staff on promotion presents no problem.

The matter is more difficult for specialists, including finger-print experts, photographers and scenes-of-crime examiners. Any career structure for such people will have to be created within the police service, in which case manpower planning must be employed to provide the structure and regulate pro-gression within it (*see* also Chapter 8, p. 175).

Traffic wardens

In 1960, legal provision was made for police authorities to appoint persons to discharge, in aid of the police, certain func-tions normally undertaken by the police in connection with the control and regulation of road traffic and the enforcement of road-traffic law—traffic wardens.

Originally restricted to enforcing the law in respect of ob-struction, no-waiting orders and lights on stationary vehicles, and acting as school crossing patrols, the powers of traffic wardens were extended in 1965 to regulate and control traffic. In 1970 their powers were further enlarged to enable them to carry out inquiries and to deal with a wider range of traffic offences.

Traffic wardens come under the direction of chief constables in the same way as police officers, although they are not con-stables (indeed, they are prohibited from being even special constables).

A career structure has tended to form within the police forces, its scope being determined by the size of the traffic-warden unit.

A relatively recent part of the police civilian staff, the traffic wardens have established a definite role in society that has effectively removed much of the friction that existed between the police and members of the public who own, and therefore park, cars. Because their terms of reference are more closely prescribed than those of a police constable, it is possible to set more specific objectives for traffic wardens and to measure their performance, provided that it is the absence of stationary vehicles improperly parked that is the measure and *not* the number of tickets issued!

Chapter Eight

Making the best use of manpower

Wasted effort

Since there is no absolute way of deciding a force establishment, as we have seen, it is necessary to adopt an analytical approach such as that outlined in Chapter 5. Establishments arrived at in this way need to be closely allied to the needs of each area and can be balanced with other areas as described on p. 110, using some form of work-load study. Such studies not only provide an indication of the relative manning levels in the force but help to identify non-productive effort. "Non-productive" activities include some which, whilst they are necessary to keep the organisation running, must be kept to the minimum.

A once-and-for-all review will not achieve the desired result of maintaining a high standard of effectiveness because the problems facing the police change and what may have been a useful activity at one time becomes valueless a few months, or even days, later.

There are three main areas in which it is necessary to look for wasted effort: the first is a failure to adapt deployment to changing circumstances, the second is the use of manpower on non-productive activities and the third is to fail to make capital out of the work that is being done. One purpose of this chapter is to high-light some circumstances in which, often unwittingly, police effort is wasted on tasks that can be more effectively dealt with in other ways; another is to emphasise the need for police to improve their effectiveness by telling the public. A police force can only succeed if it has the confidence and support of the public; it is not enough to do a good job, the public must *know* that the police are doing a good job.

Causes of wasted effort

Changing conditions

There is one basic question that any supervisor should ask himself of any activity that is not directly related to achieving police aims: "why do we do that?" If the honest answer is "I don't know", then the next step is clearly to find out why it is done. This can reveal time spent on the preparation of reports that are never read again, the compilation of statistics that no one ever uses, procedures that were started long ago for reasons long since forgotten, beats and patrols retained long after the need for them has disappeared. "We are aware of areas where the beats have been unchanged for upwards of fifty years", reported the 1967 Home Office Working Party on Police Efficiency.

When beats and patrols are planned, there is usually a good reason for them. But things change: streets are pulled down and others built; populations change as rehousing takes place. The policing needs may increase or decrease, or just change in nature, and when any of these occur, the police arrangements need to be adapted.

One further example will show how procedures may also fail to be adapted to changes in conditions.

Wasted effort: an example. One large police force used a booklet in which constables filled in printed spaces to report traffic offenders, but minor non-vehicular street offences were dealt with quite differently. In non-traffic cases, the reporting officer had to complete a long-hand report in his pocket-book, an inefficient procedure since although the offence booklet for traffic offences could be handed in for processing, the non-traffic offences could not, because the police officers required their pocket-books back quickly.

This double system persisted until the 1960s when it was discovered that the dual system had been devised in 1940 when, as a wartime emergency measure, it was decided to eliminate the wastage of paper that resulted from not filling in the motor vehicle part of the booklet. The origins of the decision had been forgotten and so no one reversed the decision when the wartime shortages ended.

This example illustrates how a sensible decision made at one point in time can become obsolete once conditions have changed. Many other instances could be given: for example, weekly returns submitted by teleprinter long after the information has ceased to be required, entries required in occurrence logs at police stations after they have ceased to convey anything of significance to anyone, and long-hand entries copied from form to book, or vice versa.

Supervisory checks

It is very easy to react to a mistake by inventing a complicated and time-consuming procedure for trying to ensure that the error never happens again. Now clearly there are some mistakes that can have serious consequences and therefore justify extreme measures to prevent recurrence but most are due to human error and whatever steps are taken, they will never be completely eliminated. What can be done in order to prevent serious consequences is to institute a system of checks that prevents errors from passing unnoticed for too long, so that corrective action can be taken.

Such procedures are a normal part of supervision but they must not be carried to expensive extremes in terms of manpower. If an error will have serious consequences unless it is detected quickly and remedied, frequent checks are justified. Similarly, if the consequences are potentially harmful and to provide checks is simple and quick, then it does no harm to have frequent checks. On the other hand, if the consequences of error are not serious, the use of valuable resources on frequent checking becomes difficult to justify and a periodic "audit" approach may be appropriate. The times between audits can be adjusted according to the consequences of error.

What should be avoided is constant checking and re-checking of routine matters, irrespective of their importance. Many such checks are more a matter of tradition than necessity and can draw attention away from the important matters which *should* be thoroughly supervised.

There is a natural tendency to impose procedures on all subordinates because one of them has been guilty of idleness or disobedience but there is a likelihood that these may restrict or frustrate the good workers, whilst the lazy man will simply find

a way round them. The benefits gained must be weighed against
the time needed to enforce controls and their effect on the work
of the unit.

Civilianisation
Manual and clerical personnel
Traditionally, the non-police members of police forces have
been employed either on manual tasks—cleaning, catering,
motor-vehicle maintenance—or on clerical work. Despite a long
history of employing such people to do these tasks, much police
time is still taken up with work such as vehicle cleaning and
maintenance, ferrying transport to and from workshops and
waiting for repair or service, report writing and typing,
operating telephone switchboards, and collecting and delivering property. While it is seldom possible to eliminate many such
tasks entirely, the time spent on them by operational police
officers can be reduced by the use of civilian staff.

The first step is to identify the nature and amount of time
that police officers at a given unit are spending on non-productive activities. These can then be broken down into classes and
linked together to form the basis of a job description. This part
of the process is best undertaken by someone trained in job
evaluation so that the salary grading allotted to the post can be
set at the correct level relative to others. Local police guidance
may be necessary to ensure that the job description accurately
fits the requirements of the unit. Where it is not possible to
justify a full-time post, part-time employees may provide an
answer. Whichever kind of employee is appointed, there must
be exact terms of reference attached to the post. Failure to
attend to this can result in an employee creating his own job
and, in doing so, failing to fulfil the original purpose of releasing
operational police time. Such problems can be compounded by
the reluctance of police officers to use the services provided.

Each member of the civilian police staff should also know his
or her conditions of service, including civil-staff salary structures, superannuation conditions and grievance procedures. It
is also useful to give some grades of civilian police staff an induction course to help them to understand the structure and vocabulary of the police, since these can be very different from those
of their previous employer. Such considerations are important

if people are to feel part of the police and it is essential that they should have this feeling. No organisation is helped by a "them" and "us" atmosphere.

Skilled personnel
Many of the points outlined above in relation to manual and clerical workers apply with equal force to skilled employees. There is the same need to identify work that can be economically performed by non-police personnel and for a job description which has been properly evaluated for salary purposes.

With specialised personnel, however, career prospects become more significant and some thought must be given to the long-term effects of civilianisation. A common practice is to civilianise a post and fill it with a retiring police officer. Care needs to be exercised when doing this for, while it may seem a sensible course of action for the short term, it can create long-term problems.

Basically, the normal approach should be to civilianise posts only when they can be genuinely filled by non-police personnel, albeit after training. To create a post that can only be filled by an ex-police officer is to assume that it will always be possible to appoint a retiring police officer when the present incumbent leaves. Such a succession policy is very difficult to maintain and may be further complicated in the future by trade union controls.

Some thought must also be given to the different conditions of service of civilian police staff and police officers. In some countries, both police and civilians are civil servants and therefore have identical conditions of service; in others, all staff are sworn in as police officers to achieve the same result. In Britain, police officers are specifically excluded from union activity and so their right to take industrial action is limited. Such restrictions do not apply to civilian police staff members and so the extent to which key operational posts may be held by them must be a matter of judgment.

Mechanisation
A service as labour-intensive as the police must always be on the alert to take advantage of technology to provide a means of extending the range of police officers and cutting down the number of routine tasks they have to perform.

Although capital outlay may seem high, expenditure on such items as closed-circuit television, mechanical car-washers and centralised dictation systems can often quickly recoup their cost through saved man-hours.

Some labour-saving devices may require training and perseverance to be really effective. Dictation systems come within this category. In many cases, insufficient effort has been put into training people in the use of electronic note-books or centralised dictation systems, with the result that they are underused. The use of pro-formas and printed forms may require training to prevent people from wasting time in re-writing them or making notes on blank paper to be copied on to the appropriate form.

Introducing mechanisation

Any system aimed at saving police manpower must be carefully designed. It is perfectly possible for a "time-saving" device actually to waste time because the conditions of operation nullify any potential savings.

Equipment needs to be evaluated carefully to find out what actual benefit it produces. That care is needed can be illustrated by considering just one feature—time saving. It is often thought that to save the time of a worker by using a machine is enough in itself, but this is not so. It is only worth saving time, as such, if there is a useful alternative way of employing the time that has been saved.

The value of time saved can vary considerably and in some cases a few seconds can be well worth striving for. An example of this is in respect of response times to intruder alarm-calls. The arrest rate increases with a reduction in the time for the police to arrive at the scene and, if the average response time can be kept down to three or four minutes, every second saved pushes up the arrest rate. Steps to improve the rate of flow of information through the system can therefore be valuable in a rapid-response-time situation.

The installation of any equipment involves two sets of costs: the cost of the equipment and that of running it. There is a tendency to emphasise the capital cost and to forget the long-term expenditure involved. A good example of this can often be seen when office machinery is being considered. The initial cost of a photo-copier may be reasonable, because the manufacturers make their profits not from the sale or hire of machines, but from the paper the machine uses. In deciding on the value of such equipment, therefore, the cost of using it must be assessed with some accuracy.

Computers

Basically, computers are machines that store large quantities of information and perform lengthy series of calculations very quickly. Everything that is to be stored on a computer must be capable of conversion into numbers the machine can process. Much factual information can be easily expressed mathematically but some of it must be converted by the human brain, since there is no mechanical device that can do this. It is this problem that held up development of computerised fingerprints. The computer could easily store all the relevant data about fingerprints, provided that someone converted each print into a set of numbers for the machine. A computer can also only use such imagination as has been built into it, a difficult process that uses much of the computer's capacity. This made it difficult to produce an effective nominal index. A human using a card index could use some imagination in searching for a name; he could allow for possible different spellings or transposed forenames. The computer must be told to do this and how, a very complex operation.

A further limitation has been the high cost of computers and the need for everything to be on a large scale to justify the expenditure. A computer is not normally cost-effective for the storage of information which can be as readily stored and retrieved using a manual system. The labour involved in maintaining such an index tends to be much the same whether it is manual or computerised, since the records must be updated in much the same way. The advantages of the computer are that it can retrieve information much more quickly and can readily perform routine statistical selections and calculations.

A computer can be specially useful in situations where it can fulfil several functions at the same time. This is the basis of the command and control system. Here, the information used in the course of deploying police resources is fed into a police-dedicated computer, which not only stores it but can produce management information in the form of statistical analyses. The operational police who man the control have merely exchanged paper and pencil for an electronic display device. They receive, in return, a facility for immediate recall of messages, pre-packed emergency plans, summaries and location of resources and the knowledge that what they are "writing" can be read immediately elsewhere, where the information is needed.

Studies made of the total information storage and retrieval needs of police forces have suggested that there is much that can be achieved in the future. One notable study, carried out jointly by International Computers Limited and the Merseyside Police in 1975, has indicated the extent to which police can benefit from a comprehensive system where all information is stored in a computer, rather than in many separate files, for different applications. With a total information system, all police records are immediately available to operational police officers. Thus, a police officer going to an emergency call at an address can be forewarned if any known or suspected criminals live there and given a summary of their criminal intelligence file; whether there is a firearms certificate held by someone at that address; whether the police have been there recently and for what purpose; whether there are warrants in existence for anyone living there, and so on. Such information has always been present in police indices, but access to it has been a matter of having to obtain it from the different sources.

It should be noted that the reference to "police files" above was intended to distinguish between information that may be held and used by police and that which may not. There is a large amount of personal information stored in computers owned by local authorities, government departments, banks, credit houses and many other commercial organisations. One of the facilities that computers offer is for one computer to supply information to another and thus, in theory, many of the computers in the country could be linked together, so that all the information could be pooled. This possibility has led many countries to legislate to protect the privacy of the public and to guard them against secret files being maintained for unauthorised purposes. A Committee on Privacy, under the chairmanship of Sir Kenneth Younger, reported in 1972 that, "We cannot on the evidence before us conclude that the computer as used in private sector is at present a threat to privacy, but we recognise that there is a possibility of such a threat coming a reality in future." (Cmnd. 5012, para 619, H.M.S.O., 1972.) This was followed by two Government White Papers (Cmnd. 6353 and Cmnd. 6354, H.M.S.O., 1975) that were concerned with computers and privacy. The second of these White Papers, *Computers: Safeguards for Privacy*, emphasised the need for security and confidentiality of police records and that of personal information held by local authorities. The first White Paper, *Computers and Privacy*, made proposals to control the range and use of computerised information, based on the main tenet that an individual should know what information concerning him is held on a computer. However, it was acknowledged that there was a need for the police to hold some information unknown to the individual concerned and, subject to the approval of the Secretary of State, to maintain such types of computerised data.

On a more commonplace level, it is perhaps worth making an important point about computers and computerised information: what comes out of a computer is only as accurate and reliable as the information that is put into it. Care therefore needs to be taken in acting upon information which seems to be at odds with the circumstances and it should be checked in exactly the same way as information obtained from any other source. Sophisticated equipment tends to give verisimilitude to an otherwise unconvincing narrative, for it is easy to forget that the computer is only a machine that processes information fed into it by humans.

Streamlining procedures

Systematic studies can help to reduce paperwork and streamline office procedures, but care needs to be taken to ensure that the resulting administrative procedures fit the needs of the operational unit they support. One common area that affords scope for analysis of this kind is the submission of routine reports.

Figure 14 shows the stages in a procedure that was found on a rural division of an English police force. The actual example analysed here concerned a case of sheep-worrying by a dog, in which the identity of the dog was unknown. The report on this incident went through the procedure a total of three times: the first time it was endorsed by the superintendent, "Make further inquiries"; the second time it was endorsed, "Keep casual observation on the farm for two more weeks"; the third time it was marked "No further action, file". This one incident therefore involved something like thirty transactions. This is a lot of effort to allocate to supervision of a minor incident yet, until the procedure had been studied and written down in graphical form, what was happening was not obvious. A chart, even as simple as that in Fig. 14, high-lights the procedure and enables senior officers to see where delegation may obviate unnecessary paper work and allow supervisors to concentrate on more important tasks.

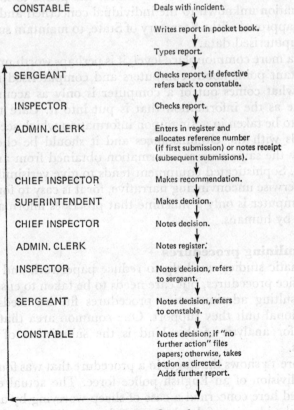

CONSTABLE	Deals with incident.
	↓
	Writes report in pocket book.
	↓
	Types report.
	↓
SERGEANT	Checks report, if defective refers back to constable.
	↓
INSPECTOR	Checks report.
	↓
ADMIN. CLERK	Enters in register and allocates reference number (if first submission) or notes receipt (subsequent submissions).
	↓
CHIEF INSPECTOR	Makes recommendation.
	↓
SUPERINTENDENT	Makes decision.
	↓
CHIEF INSPECTOR	Notes decision.
	↓
ADMIN. CLERK	Notes register.
	↓
INSPECTOR	Notes decision, refers to sergeant.
	↓
SERGEANT	Notes decision, refers to constable.
	↓
CONSTABLE	Notes decision; if "no further action" files papers; otherwise, takes action as directed. Adds further report.

Fig. 14—Paper flow chart.

A similar effect may sometimes be observed by noting the contents of "in-trays". Random checks will show the pattern of paper flow and may indicate the sort of paper that is passing through the organisation. The test to apply is always the same: why does this particular supervisor need this piece of paper? If the answer is (as it so often is) to keep him informed, then a supplementary question should be asked: "What benefit does the police gain from the fact that this particular supervisor knows of this particular incident?" A good rule to follow is that of passing up the organisation only those papers that are in some way exceptional or outside the limits of the delegated authority of the supervisors lower down in the hierarchy. This concept of management by exception can be written into the terms of reference of supervisors at all levels and can focus attention on those matters that really require the attention of senior officers.

Closely associated with the study of paper-flow is the design of books and forms. It is possible to seek trained help in their design; but some considerations are fairly straightforward. For example, forms should not require excessive lining up by a typist nor be taken out and put back in a typewriter; as much use as possible should be made of printed headings, boxes to be ticked and agreed abbreviated codes for routine statements.

A compromise is always needed between having too many types of forms and too few. A "too many" situation can result from having forms with too restricted a purpose with a consequent need for excessive storage space, forms becoming out of date because they are seldom used and difficulty for people in remembering which form is which. "Too few" means too many long reports or forms being used for so many purposes that they are confusing to fill in.

Wherever possible, if more than one copy of an entry is needed, it should only be necessary to write or type the data once. Copying information from one document to another can seldom be justified; not only is it a waste of effort but it introduces an additional source of error. While on the subject of copies, it is perhaps advisable to offer a cautionary word about the making and filing of unnecessary copies of documents. This has always been a problem but it has been aggravated by the introduction of copying machines—it is now almost too easy to

G

make copies. As far as possible, only one copy of a document should be used for action purposes; to use more than one invites duplication of action or confusion as to who is to do what. As far as filing copies is concerned, the guiding principle should be: "Who is going to look at the copies and for what purpose?"

In designing any paper system, book or form, it is essential that proper consultation should take place with the people who are going to use them. Despite what has been said earlier about unnecessarily complex systems, there are often good reasons why things are done in a particular way. To design a satisfactory system, it is necessary to know the "whys" as well as the "whats" of the existing procedure.

Given an objective approach, many police reporting systems can be greatly simplified but people must be willing to go back to basic essentials, including serious consideration of why things are done in a particular way, why certain information must be recorded and why the report must pass through several hands before a decision is reached. A good supervisor knows when to ask these questions and consequently to reduce waste of time or materials.

Building design

The specifications for police buildings are laid down nationally in a memorandum by the Home Office, *The Planning of Police Buildings* (1966, later revised), and the Home Office *Police Buildings Design Guide 2—Organisation, Activities and Relationships* (1970): "The object is to help police authorities and chief constables to decide what accommodation should be provided and architects to decide what will be the most satisfactory means of providing it" (Introduction to the memorandum by the Home Office, *The Planning of Police Buildings*, 1966).

The procedure for a typical county police force to obtain a new police building, such as a police station, follows this general pattern:

1. The chief constable identifies the need for a building.
2. He presents his arguments for the building to the police authority.
3. If the police authority agree that a building is needed, it is included as an item on the capital finance programme for

the force. Such programmes are normally based on a fore-cast for the next five years.

4. The building programme for the forthcoming five years is submitted annually to the Home Office.

5. Subject to the view of Her Majesty's Inspectorate of Constabulary and Home Office policies, the programme may be accepted in principle.

6. At about the same time, the programme will be considered by the county council. The police programme must be slotted into the whole building programme for the county.

7. If the Home Office and county council agree that the police building shall be scheduled for a particular year, preparation must begin well before, sometimes as much as three or four years, depending on the size of the project.

8. Using the Home Office guidelines, a brief will be drawn up by the police. At this stage it will merely indicate what offices, rooms and facilities are required and the floor area of each plus any special considerations like floor loadings, security and air-conditioning.

9. This will then be considered by the Home Office who will make adjustments in accordance with current policy.

10. The agreed brief now goes to the architect who will design the building, in consultation with the users—the police. The design must be approved by the police committee and, of course, comply with local planning conditions but the importance of police involvement cannot be over-stressed.

11. Once the plans have been accepted and permission has been obtained from the Home Office (who are governed by national constraints on money) and the county council (who are governed by national and local constraints on money), tenders are obtained.

Once a tender has been accepted and building has begun, the design cannot be changed without incurring additional, and usually prohibitive, costs. Even to change one aspect, once the plans have been drawn prior to the commencement of building, is difficult and so the importance of the original brief can be seen. The police must estimate what their requirements will be several years ahead, otherwise the building will be obsolescent before it is completed. Yet these estimates cannot be simple speculation or they will not be accepted as a basis for increasing the size and cost of the building. There is a clear need for all police forces to be aware of their objectives for the future and the resources that will be needed to attain them. The manpower establishment, resource deployment and building programme must be seen as an entity, each being linked to the objectives of the police in that area.

Public relations

It may seem strange that effort expended on public relations should be considered as a means of maximising police effectiveness and yet this is exactly why police forces must be conscious of the need to project a public image of the service.

For many years British police forces were content to adopt a "silent service" approach to the press and other media. Hampered by being unable to give details in answer to questions, either because of confidentiality or because the matter was *sub judice*, the line usually taken was to say as little as possible. The disadvantages of using this approach were that:

1. In the absence of "facts" released by the police the press would find their own. These might not be accurate and publication could harm the police effort;
2. valuable police manpower was required to control reporters who were using their own initiative to obtain news;
3. unofficial leakages were encouraged;
4. it was difficult to obtain press co-operation;
5. delay in answering criticism of police activity meant that any subsequent explanation lacked weight. The allegation, however unfounded, remained uppermost in people's minds;
6. people within the police felt that they were not being supported by senior officers, because no attempt was made to answer criticisms.

It is now accepted that all police agencies need a good working relationship with the news media and must be able to cope not only with the routine day-to-day matters of interest to local press and radio but must also be prepared to deal comprehensively with the national media when a newsworthy incident occurs.

As Sir Robert Mark, Commissioner of the Metropolitan Police, pointed out in a general memorandum to his force in 1973:

Most members of the public come into direct contact with policemen infrequently and it follows that their image of and attitude towards the force, when not dictated by hearsay, is largely governed by the approach adopted by the news media. It is therefore of the utmost importance that every effort should be made to develop and maintain good relations with news media representatives in order to render it more likely that their coverage of police activities will be full and fair. Furthermore, if the force as a public service is to be properly accountable for its actions, the public has the right to the fullest possible knowledge of its activities.

(*Policing a Perplexed Society*, Sir Robert Mark,
George Allen and Unwin, 1977.)

News

To the operational police officer attempting to deal with an incident, the press are often seen as yet another source of harassment to add to the rest of his troubles. To some extent this is understandable; the news reporter has a different frame of reference and needs information quickly, so that he seems to be trying to hurry, not to say harry, the police.

Most police organisations now accept that there is a need to designate to one individual the job of keeping the news media informed. Such an appointment may prevent contradictory official statements being issued, operational people being inconvenienced, and provide a channel through which all information flows.

It is essential that operational police officers should feed into this channel details of what is happening. They must be careful to distinguish between what is hard fact and what is not. The initial information about a disaster is often highly inaccurate, so that it may be better to await confirmation rather than to issue incorrect statements. It is also necessary that careful watch be kept to ensure that information is not released for publication that would hinder police operations or endanger lives as, for example, in a hostage or kidnapping case. A useful practice employed successfully, particularly in terrorist and kidnapping cases, has been to build up a working relationship with news editors who are provided with full details of an incident on an understanding that publication is delayed until it is safe to go ahead. Such arrangements require goodwill on both sides, but practice in Britain has shown that the press act responsibly, provided that the police are reasonable in their requests for silence and provide full facilities when the emergency is over.

In dealing with terrorist or subversive groups, the importance of the role of the media is vital. In a propaganda war, the police must be able to ensure that their voice is heard to good effect. Nothing must be released that is later found to be incorrect, otherwise ammunition is provided that can enable extremists to cause serious damage to the image of the police. In such cases, as in all other emergencies, the individual directing relations with the media must carefully balance the need for speed in releasing information with the need to ensure that it is accurate.

Public relations
The value of good relations with the press in terms of news coverage is clear but that of the wider aspects of public relations is perhaps less so. The Institute of Public Relations defines public relations as ". . . the deliberate, planned and sustained effort to establish and maintain mutual understanding between an organisation and its public." Many police forces actively practise public relations as a conscious policy, whilst others carry out many functions which are not operational policing but are recognised as being in the interests of good police/public relations.

The exact value of police press-publicity releases, "open days", exhibitions, demonstrations and talks cannot be calculated. They form part of the process of building up the faith of the public in *their* police, to create an image of the police as being composed of ordinary people who are aware of the problems of the public and are effective in dealing with them. Public relations exercises can help to paint the right picture but it must be recognised that there are limitations.

In the same way that publicity will not sell a bad product, public relations exercises will not disguise a bad police force. There is no point in presenting, through public relations exercises, an image of helpful, willing and courteous policemen, if whenever a member of the public meets a member of the force he is anything but helpful, willing and courteous. Selling the idea of the public using the "999" system to call for help is of no value unless the force provides an effective service to answer calls.

To a very large extent, the policeman on the beat fulfils a

public relations role. It was noticeable that it was personal contact that was missed by the public when policing became motorised. The relationship between the police and public is largely determined at this level.

Of critical importance in determining the image of a police force is the face that the ordinary members of the public see when they go to the police as witnesses, complainants or losers of property. There are many ways in which all the public relations work done on behalf of a force can be undone, as far as those people are concerned. One example is the manner in which people are spoken to over the telephone, the station-counter or in the street. Another is the way in which the organisation of a force is geared to deal with inquirers. Most police forces deal with emergency calls very efficiently, but some are less efficient when dealing with routine inquiries from members of the public. This is often due to the fact that a police station is run as an operational centre and the men who work from it are employed on shifts or on outside duties. No one should have to telephone a police station several times to try to speak to the officer who is dealing with his case, simply because there is no effective means of logging calls and passing on messages.

Police and public

The relationship between police and public is not simply a matter of convincing the public that the police are doing an effective job. The police need the active co-operation of the public. The emergency "999" call system depends on their being enough members of the public willing to call the police, not only to aid them but to draw police attention to incidents they have seen.

In a study carried out by Michael Chatterton (Manchester University), into the amount of public involvement in the arrests made by a police division, it was found that nearly half of the arrests for crime involved the co-operation of the public by detaining a suspect, giving information leading to the identification of the criminal or attending a parade. Vandalism of property, one of the most difficult offences for police to prevent, showed the greatest level of public involvement—85 per cent of arrests for damaging property were as a result of the public mobilising the police (*The Times*, 15th December 1975).

The effects of police/public relations can be seen as a circular system: if the public help the police, the police can be effective; if the police are effective the public feel secure; if the public feel secure, then they are willing to help the police. If one link is broken, the system fails. Once the situation is reached where members of the public no longer feel safe to tell the police when they see a crime committed, police effectiveness drops rapidly. This causes people to feel even less safe and so they are even less willing to risk calling the police and so on.

To survive, a commercial firm must sell its goods or services. To survive, the police must sell their services to the public and each police officer is part of the sales force. His job will be much harder if the reputation of the police is low. Therefore, everything that can be done to enhance the image of the police not only makes the police more effective by creating a public awareness of freedom from fear, but also makes the work of the police easier because of the co-operation that will be gained from the public.

Chapter Nine

Personnel administration

Police establishments and strengths
Establishment and strength
The authorised establishment of a police force (*see* Chapter 5) is distributed, according to need, into divisions, sub-divisions, sections and departments, but at any given time there will be vacancies caused by the fact that the actual *strength* is less than *authorised establishment*.

A force that is below strength distributes its vacancies amongst the various police units so that each one carries vacancies on its establishment. Each unit has an agreed establishment but this can be varied by the chief constable within the total numbers for the force to meet changes in need, for example, as the problems of one area increase and those of another decrease. But each unit may have to carry a number of vacancies, its share of the total number of vacancies in the force. Some units may have a temporary allocation of personnel above its establishment, in which case it is said to be "over-strength". A record must be kept of all such establishments, vacancies and over-strength personnel, if the manpower of the force is to be deployed properly. Increases in establishment can only be obtained if the police authority and Home Secretary can be satisfied that there is a genuine need and that existing resources are properly deployed.

Financial planning
Recruiting problems and retirements are not the only causes of police strengths being below establishment. A common cause is money or the lack of it and, to understand this, it is necessary to glance at the way in which police financial arrangements are made.

Although procedures may differ slightly, all police forces must estimate the amount of money that they will need in the coming year. This will consist of two main parts, the first the capital expenditure required for building new police stations, houses, other buildings and larger improvement schemes which cannot be financed out of the normal revenue for the year. The second estimates will be concerned with revenue required to run the force—pay and allowances, motor vehicles and equipment, uniform and many other incidental items. Capital expenditure may be part of a long-term programme, usually four or five years, because of the time span over which buildings, for example, are requested, approved, designed and completed, but each year the capital requirements for the following year must be approved by the police authority, the county council and finally the Home Office (*see* also Chapter 8, Building design, pp. 182–4).

Revenue estimates are prepared several months in advance of the year to which they apply and must be based on forecasts. For some items, forecasting is not too difficult; the need for cars and equipment, for example, is usually known well in advance, but the major resource—manpower—can present problems.

In a force of 2,000 police officers, the estimates for which are being prepared in September or October for the financial year commencing in the following April, typical figures might be:

Authorised establishment	2,000
Present strength (1st September)	1,800
Estimated strength at end of present financial year (31st March)	1,850

To calculate next year's wage, allowance and uniform bill, it is necessary to estimate the strength at the end of that year, i.e. in eighteen months' time. To obtain a *possible* figure, retirements on pension and premature wastage due to resignations, dismissals and illness all must be assessed and balanced against recruitment, which will depend, amongst other things, on the state of the labour market, pay and conditions and the amount of effort that can be put into recruiting. This type of forecasting is examined in a little more detail on p. 193 below, but the availability of money must also be taken into account.

It may be considered possible to recruit enough people to fill the 150 posts during the coming year as well as meet all wastage. In this case it would be feasible to set a target strength of 2,000 for the end of that year and make financial provision accordingly. This proposal would then be put to the police authority, but the question of availability of money will arise. The police committee will be under pressure to keep costs down. The committee might also consider the estimate too optimistic in terms of recruiting, or simply too speculative to justify asking for that amount of money. The decision might well be that the target figure for the end of the next financial year should only be 1,900, an increase of 50 over the estimate of 1,850 for the beginning of the year. In practical terms, this means that the force operates with an artificial establishment for that year, governed by the number of men and women (and cadets and civilian police staff) for which financial provision has been made.

The personnel department

In most modern organisations, there is a centralised headquarters personnel department. It is important that all supervisors should be aware of its exact functions and how what it does is related to the supervisor's role as a "personnel manager". In the police service, there is a long-established tradition that supervisors have a definite responsibility for the welfare and "man-management" of their subordinates. For this reason, most police personnel departments are quite small and have a collating rather than an operational function.

On behalf of the chief constable, a police personnel department duties include the following:

1. *Recruiting*. Recruiting police officers and cadets and supervising recruitment of police civilian staff.
2. *Personnel policies*. Setting and updating the conditions of service and personnel policies of all personnel, in accordance with national and local legislation and rules. Liaising with other local/national government departments.
3. *Allocation of personnel*. Assessing and distributing manpower according to the needs of each unit.
4. *Collating personal information*. Monitoring the performance of all personnel and identifying training needs, potential for

promotion or suitability for specialist work, collating such information and maintaining records in accordance with Police Regulations.

5. *Training.* Assessing and arranging training of personnel.
6. *Selection.* Establishing a centralised promotion-selection system utilising information supplied by operational supervisors.
7. *Sickness/injuries.* Supervising sickness/injuries to ensure that proper steps are taken respecting entitlements, welfare arrangements and ill-health retirements. Liaison with force medical officer.
8. *Manpower planning.* Forecasting future manpower needs to enable recruitment, training and financial policies to be formulated.
9. *Giving advice.* Providing advice and guidance on all personnel matters to all members of the force.
10. *Maintaining establishment records.* Monitoring established posts, identifying vacancies and anomalies, preparing job descriptions where appropriate.

There is a close relationship between many of these duties and those of divisional/departmental personnel and in subsequent chapters many of these subjects will be examined in depth to establish the role of the operational supervisor *vis-à-vis* the headquarters department.

Maintaining establishment records
Item 10 in the above list is one of the most fundamental personnel tasks required by police forces. So rapid are the changes that face the police service that there is frequently the need to re-allocate posts to meet new challenges.

Such changes can be made in one of two ways: either by creating a new post and deleting an obsolete one elsewhere or by seeking to establish a new post by obtaining the joint agreement of the police authority and Home Secretary to increase the force establishment. As the latter course involves lengthy procedures, the former method can be used either as a temporary measure or on a permanent basis. It is necessary to have some record of such adaptations to meet changing needs, so that the true disposition of resources is known and controlled. Temporary changes can easily become permanent by default if a close watch is not kept.

What is being discussed here is the post and not its occupier. It is quite common for a post to be adapted to meet the particular skills or failings of the individual concerned. There should therefore be a clear description of the true objectives of each post for reference purposes.

All police civilian posts should have a job description so that the exact terms of reference of the holder are known and his performance can be assessed in the light of the job description. Due to the inevitable changes that take place within all organisations, each job description needs to be updated periodically to ensure that the post is still necessary and that the rank or grade of person in it is correct.

Forecasting manpower needs

Chapter 5 (Manpower requirements) dealt with the assessment of a police establishment. Here we are concerned with estimating the number of recruits needed to fill vacant posts within that establishment.

The most significant causes of wastage are retirement on pension and premature resignations. It is more difficult to forecast the wastage in a police force in Britain than in many other countries. The reason is that there are many variables governing the retirement of British police officers. Unlike many organisations which have a set retirement age, so that wastage from this source can be forecast with reasonable accuracy, the police service has a complex system based on years of service and age. Some indication of the complexity of forecasting police retirements can be obtained by considering some of the variables that can affect a man's decision to retire.

Retirement can be made on half pay after 25-years' police service, but the probability of retirement may increase between 25 and 30 years of service, because the pension reaches its maximum proportion of salary at 30-years' service. Depending on the age at which a man joins the police, the question of age limit may be significant or not. The normal recruitment age enables people to complete 25-years' service but may bar them from completing 30 years. Even this is not an inviolable rule, as they may seek extensions to continue serving after they have reached the age limit and in any case, the age limit itself is linked to rank and so a promotion may extend the length of service that a man can perform. Apart from these factors, the rate of retirement is also affected by the economic climate. A large pay-rise tends to result in police officers, who might have retired, staying on for one year to obtain the benefit of averaging for that year to enhance their pension.

Premature wastage

Premature wastage will always occur in any organisation. Research has shown that the police have a good deal less than most commercial firms but it always needs to be monitored, as some of it can be caused by bad man-management.

Many resignations occur during the first two years of service when the recruit is attempting to adapt to a new way of life and may resign because he or she is unable to make the grade. Thereafter, the probability of a person resigning tends to remain fairly constant until after ten years' service when it starts to decrease.

Inquiries into causes of premature wastage seldom produce hard evidence and, unless carefully done, they may give a false picture because the people leaving the police do not necessarily state their true reason for leaving, even when they know it. A useful example of such a survey can be seen in Appendix 1 of the *Working Party Report on Manpower* (H.M.S.O., 1967), which showed the parts pay, transfers and domestic problems play in wastage at all stages in a man's service. It also showed that the effects of shift work was a prime cause of wastage in the first two years' service, a result that tends to reinforce the need to make quite clear to applicants the way in which shifts will affect their lives.

In spite of the difficulty of anticipating future wastage with accuracy, as was seen on p. 190 above, for financial planning purposes an intelligent estimate must be made. Further, where permitted, the need to recruit cadets, who provide a guaranteed source of recruitment, and the expenditure involved in recruitment drives and in provision of adequate training facilities for the future must be taken into account.

Personnel policies

The headquarters personnel department is responsible for advising the chief constable on personnel policies in general.

Police regulations prescribe some of these policies: for example, they lay down the nature of the basic personal records which shall be kept, but not the exact form. Apart from personal details such as previous service in the armed forces and police, a personal record must list promotions, postings, injuries received and disciplinary punishments other than cautions.

The statutory records are clearly inadequate for effective personnel administration. It is therefore admissible to keep supplementary records which include all the information needed to tailor a person's career to suit his capacity. Information from the individual is required to ensure that all his qualifications and personal details are up to date and supervisors must ensure that accurate reports are submitted as to his capabilities and potential.

To produce the necessary flow of information from supervisors, an appraisal system is necessary, one which has the full support of all the people in the organisation. In setting the policies for this (as in most personnel matters, because it is an emotive area), fully-consultative methods with representation from all levels must be adopted. Once the policies have been established, it becomes a matter for the personnel department to work with operational supervisors to ensure that the system is seen to be operating justly.

The same can also be said of selection systems. Whether the selection is for promotion or specialist work, it must be seen to be operated justly within established personnel policies.

Chapter Ten

Recruiting

Setting standards

Unlike police forces in many other countries, the British police recruit all police officers at one point of entry, at the rank of constable at the age of 18½ years or above. Selectors must, therefore, be aware of the full needs of the service when choosing police recruits. The range of careers that must be catered for in respect of just one variable—promotion—is considerable and, whilst it is necessary to obtain enough recruits who have the potential to become chief officers, it is almost more important to remember that people must be recruited who will be satisfied to remain in lower ranks.

Ideally, a police force should contain a representative cross-section of the population it serves, including a balanced proportion of all the ethnic groups within the police area.

Physical standards

From the outset, the British police have set height standards, although a standardised minimum height did not arrive until 1930, when 5 feet 8 inches (1·75 m) was adopted, although many forces had their own set standards above the minimum. The subject of minimum height was discussed by a Working Party on Manpower set up by the Police Advisory Board. In its report, published in 1967, it was made clear that the decision to retain a height standard was at the behest of the police representatives:

> The professional opinion supports the view that shorter men are unfitted to perform duty in the streets, since they lack the necessary air of authority and might find themselves in trouble in dealing with disorders.
>
> . . .
>
> . . . it is particularly desirable that [the policeman] should have the appearance and demeanour to command respect.   (ibid., p. 14.)

The same working party concluded that the medical standards of the time were satisfactory apart from eyesight, which precluded people who wore glasses from entering the police. As a result of the recommendation of the working party, eyesight standards were relaxed to allow entry to people who have a reasonable standard of eyesight without glasses and which is correctable to a high standard using spectacles.

Intellectual standards
Entrance tests
Standardised entrance tests were introduced in 1974 and replaced the individual written examinations that each force had previously employed but the pass-mark is not the same for all police forces. The standardised tests provide a measure of "trainability" of a recruit which, while it is not the same as the ability to do the actual work of a police officer, does provide a useful "cut-off" point. If a person scores badly on the test, he is unlikely to be able to absorb the basic knowledge that he will need to be acceptable. Above that level, success under training is as likely to be a product of the effort and concentration of the recruit as his innate intellectual capacity.

Educational qualifications
The educational standard of police recruits has been the subject of concern ever since changes in the education system made it more possible for any person to obtain educational qualifications commensurate with his ability.

The 1967 Working Party on Police Manpower drew attention to the 1962 report of the Royal Commission on the Police, which deplored the fact that the police should "for years have been failing to recruit anything like their proper share of able and well-educated young men" (1962 Report, para. 312). Recruiting publicity aimed at emphasising the promotion prospects open to well-educated entrants does not appear to have materially changed the picture. "Despite all efforts, far too many boys with grammar school education who enter the police do so with educational attainments so limited that they would not have access to a wide choice of occupations" (Dr J. H. Tobias, *Police Journal*, July 1974, p. 265).

As in the matter of height requirements, the working party

was split as to the nature of the remedies that should be applied. The representatives of the Police Federation, "while accepting the need for more highly qualified recruits . . . are anxious to avoid the injury that might be done to the morale of the service by any appearance of the creation of an 'officer class', with the disruptive effect on relations between ranks that this could entail" (*Working Party on Manpower Report*, H.M.S.O., 1967, pp. 17–18). This rejection of "officer class" referred back to the scheme introduced by Lord Trenchard into the Metropolitan Police in 1934 when the Metropolitan Police College at Hendon provided an avenue for accelerated promotion to "station-inspector" and allowed limited, direct entry to that rank. The scheme was brought to an end by the outbreak of war in 1939 and not reintroduced (*see* Chapter 11, p. 222).

Comparable with the concept of a system whereby people could join the police directly into a supervisory rank is the possibility of direct entry into the criminal investigation department. This was proposed by three members of the 1960 Royal Commission in a minority report on the grounds that better educated men "are more likely to be attracted into the detective establishments than as normal entrants into the police" (Cmnd. 1728, 1962, p. 154). This recommendation was made despite a number of arguments that suggested that such a course would:

1. segregate the detective establishment from the rest of the force;
2. prevent interchangeability between the two forces;
3. create a *corps d'élite*;
4. make administration of the establishment more difficult;
5. prevent co-operation between the uniformed and plain-clothes sections and create antagonisms;
6. cost too much.

Although the three signatories to the note of reservation rejected these arguments, the majority of the members of the Royal Commission evidently did not.

The effects of single-point entry

There are many arguments for and against direct entry into supervisory rank and the C.I.D., but one thing is certain, both "tiered" entry and single-point entry have difficult features that require good recruiting and personnel policies. As the British police service is committed to single-point entry, the associated problems will be discussed but this should not be taken to imply that there would be none if multipoint entry were to be adopted.

What single-point entry means is that all the police posts in the force must be filled from the people who are recruited as uniform constables, a self-evident statement that nevertheless conceals a number of less easily-appreciated features. It means that the intake of police recruits must contain people who have the ability and are prepared to:

1. serve as uniform constables for the whole of their service;
2. fill the middle and senior ranks of the service;
3. acquire specialist skills and knowledge to perform what are often highly-specialised duties;
4. become specialist supervisors, despite possible limitation in their careers due to the lesser opportunities open to them.

One intractable problem is that a man may not be a very good uniformed constable and, as a result, may be debarred from being made a specialist although he may be much better suited for such work. There is no firm evidence to suggest that the skills needed to be a member of a fraud squad have much in common with those needed to deal with a Saturday-night fight in a pub, yet the policemen doing both jobs will have been originally selected according to the same criteria.

From the recruiting point of view, it does mean that it may be necessary to accept a few people who, while they may not be particularly outstanding in physical attributes, have a good brain that can be used in solving problems that may not require physical prowess. Clearly, this concept should not be taken too far, because all recruits have to undertake the usual probationary period and so must have enough of *all* the necessary attributes to survive on the beat. Nevertheless, because a man is not an outstanding uniform constable, it should not follow that he would be passed over for other work for which he might be better equipped.

This principle also applies in reverse: to employ people who are *too* intelligent for their work, if it requires no depth of thought, can also cause problems. In the police service, it is often the type of supervision under which people work that determines the extent to which there is freedom to use individual initiative and skill. The subject of supervision will be dealt with in detail in later chapters.

In order to allow for the differences between human beings and to ensure that the right people are given the right posts, the personnel system must be able to identify and utilise the skills and attributes of each person.

Police cadets
Origins
The employment of young people between 16- and 18-years old as cadets as a means of recruiting policemen came into being in the late 1940s. Prior to that, there had been a small number of youngsters (about 500 in 1939) employed as "boy clerks", who were encouraged to become constables when they were 20-years old, but there was no formal organisation or training scheme. From the outset, there were reservations as to the extent to which cadets should be used to obtain police recruits:

> Our main objection to any considerable expansion of the cadet system is that policemen have to deal with people in all walks of life and should have had as much experience as possible of men and manners outside the police service.
> (*Report of the Committee on Police Conditions of Service*, Part II, Cmd. 7831, para. 201, 1949.)

Nevertheless, cadet schemes soon became a prime source of police recruits, particularly for the larger forces, and by 1959 provided about a quarter of the total recruits for the year. The seal of approval was placed upon them by the Royal Commission on the Police, 1960, who dismissed fears similar to those above, in the following terms:

> We think that these dangers can be exaggerated. It is a growing practice in industry to recruit boys from grammar schools and give them specialised training and facilities for education during their early years. The police service cannot afford to lag behind industry, and there is everything to be said for encouraging the young man who is keen on joining. The important thing, in our opinion, is to ensure that the cadet is never cut off from the normal stream of civilian life.
> (*Interim Report*, Cmd. 1222, para. 97.)

In 1963, the Home Secretary appointed a working party to consider the functions, qualifications, conditions of service, training and duties of police cadets. Some of its recommendations were later incorporated into legislation but others were left as guidance only.

In order to maintain the concept of a police force with members coming from a cross-section of the population, the working party suggested that, as a rough guide, not more than half of the police should come from the cadet system. Due to the lower wastage rates for police who were ex-cadets compared with those who were direct entrants meant "as a general working principle that ex-cadets should form not more than say 30 per cent to 40 per cent of the recruit intake to the regular force, but that this ratio should be readily subject to modification in the light of circumstances, with the general aim that the number of serving ex-cadets should not exceed 50 per cent of the total serving strength of the force" (*Report of a Working Party on Police Cadets*, 1965, p. 8).

The working party gave careful consideration to the proper objectives of a police-cadet system and identified the main object as being "to help recruitment by attracting young men who are likely to make good police officers". The way in which this was to be achieved was seen in this way: "One important function of the cadet system is to offer the school-leaver an opportunity to enter immediately upon a career in the police, thereby enabling the police to compete in a potential field of recruitment which would otherwise be monopolised by industry and the professions" (ibid., p. 6).

With regard to entry qualifications, the working party found itself in something of a dilemma. Having toyed with the idea that "provided that they were judged to have the requisite potential ability, candidates of a lower educational standard could legitimately be appointed on the basis that they would have time to bring themselves up to the required standard before seeking appointment as a constable", it was decided that "the standard must not be set so low as to diminish the status of cadets in the eyes of school-leavers, their parents or their career masters". The final recommendation was that "as a general rule . . . a cadet should normally be expected to have attained at least a good standard of education for his age and that, where recruiting presents few problems, it would not be unreasonable for chief officers to be selective and to impose higher standards;

but that intelligent boys with lower educational qualifications should not be excluded even in such cases if they are judged to have training potential" (ibid., p. 10).

The subject of girl cadets was considered separately by the working party in those pre-Sex Discrimination Act days. After concluding that the shortage of women police created a similar need for cadets, it went on to say: "But the wastage problem for the girls is different, being due primarily to marriage, and ex-cadets are as prone to get married as girls directly recruited. To the extent that the cost of training can be justified for boys on the ground of their very much lower wastage rate after joining the service, the case for girl cadets is less strong." In fact, only a minority of police forces had girl cadets at that time.

Nevertheless, the working party concluded that girl cadets were a useful means of attracting "the better qualified girls". Despite this, several forces, including the Metropolitan Police, fought shy of girl cadets for some years after this report. Gradually, however, the principle emerged of girl cadets being employed on the same terms and undergoing the same training as boys.

Organisation

The establishment of police cadets is prescribed by the police authority and Home Office in much the same way as for regular police but clearly the numbers actually recruited have to be related to the future needs of the force. Careful planning is required because cadets become eligible for appointment at any time up to two-and-a-half years from their appointment, i.e. the length of time between joining at sixteen and becoming constables at eighteen-and-a-half years of age. Vacancies in the force therefore have to be forecast as far ahead as that.

The input from cadets into the regular force can be varied either by adjusting the number of cadets recruited, or by varying the length of time of employment by regulating ages of recruitment.

Cadets are usually recruited during the year in which they sit for their General Certificate of Education examinations at the age of sixteen and over. As they are often selected before the results of their examinations are known, problems can be presented if scholastic achievement is one of the criteria for selection. To delay selection, or make acceptance "subject to passing *x* number of exams", makes planning difficult, particularly if local education establishments are used for cadet training in educational subjects.

Recruitment at seventeen and over has the advantage of being cheaper; more is known of the educational attainment of the candidate but recruitment at this stage is often confined to sixth-form "drop-outs", who may not be the best source of police material. The best of both worlds is possible by using a flexible system of recruitment.

Recruiting publicity

A great deal of effort and money is put into police recruiting publicity each year, much of it nationally and the remainder by individual forces. The police image that is reflected by such publicity is of great importance for a number of reasons.

The effects of recruiting publicity

Recruiting publicity, of course, advertises the police itself and, in the same way that an advertisement for a commercial product should emphasise the good features of that product, so police publicity should seek to give a positive image. Recruiting literature shows potential applicants how they could gain satisfaction from becoming members of the police. Properly-directed recruiting advertisements also affect the quality of the people who apply. The number of unsuitable people can be limited by stipulating conditions for acceptance—educational, height and age—but the effects of publicity can be wider than this. By portraying the positive attributes needed, either directly or by implication, people with particular attributes can be encouraged to join. Caution is needed when promoting any recruiting publicity because it can affect the morale of the people already in the service. Anything which appears to demean their job may cause people to become disenchanted, both with the organisation and the people responsible for the publicity. A subtle form of this can be observed in relation to advertisements which unduly emphasise the promotion prospects in an organisation. Such emphasis tends to lower the status of those members who have not been promoted—the bulk of the people in the organisation. Such advertising needs most careful handling, for not only does it lower the morale of members of the organisation but it also may discourage good people from joining, simply because it takes too long to be promoted from the lower ranks (which, by implication, have been devalued to the point where able people will not wish to serve in them other than as a penance prior to promotion).

Recruiting media
It is very difficult to evaluate the success of any recruiting activity and, the less direct it is, the more difficult it becomes. A team sent to recruit men leaving the armed forces can measure its success fairly accurately in terms of the number of ex-servicemen who later join the police, but the value of displays at public events and newspaper advertisements are much more difficult to assess. The reason why a person makes the decision that the police is a worthwhile career may not even be apparent to that person and it may not result in immediate action. Careers activities at schools are particularly difficult in this respect, for it is quite common for a young man or woman to leave school and start a non-police career, but then to apply to join the police when their first choice of career loses its attraction. Only when their first job fails to hold their interest is the visit of the police recruiting team to the school recalled. Many recruits who enter the police after trying a different job give a careers visit as the source of the inspiration that brought them to the police.

Apart from schools and the armed services, the audience reached by many public relations activities is often too diffuse to offer much in the way of direct recruiting value, although the effect of parents on the choice of young people's careers should not be under-estimated. The feelings that parents have about the police as a career will influence their children. It is not so important that parents should actively push their children towards the police than simply not oppose the choice of the police as a career when a son or daughter expresses an interest in it. Thus, police participation in exhibitions which are attended by people of a wide range of ages and interests may be useful, even though the direct result, as measured by the number of recruits obtained, may be disappointing.

The problem with such events as open days and police stands

at exhibitions is that they tend to attract people who are already interested in the police either positively or negatively and not those who are uncommitted. It is the people who have not really thought about the subject that one wishes to interest.

Selection methods

The subject of selection interviews is dealt with in detail in Chapter 13. It is essential for successful selection that the limitations of the interview as a selection technique be fully appreciated. It is for this reason that full use must be made of other methods to supplement the formal interview. A number of aids to selection are discussed below, most of which have some value but no one method is adequate on its own. Most forces use a mixture of checks and tests so that they tend to balance out faults. As yet, whatever the safeguards applied, it is impossible to make a choice with guaranteed success and, therefore, there must be a method of ensuring that full use is made of probationary periods to identify and correct selection errors. The selection process and the supervision of probationers must be seen as being complementary to one another. Confidence in the probationary system enables the selector to adopt a more realistic approach to his job. In the absence of a long-stop provision, he may become so intent on not making a mistake that he will reject many good applicants simply because he dare not "take a chance".

Interviews

The formal selection interview, conducted by a senior member of staff, suffers from the fact that the applicant may be tense and determined to try to present the image he thinks is required of him. A good interviewer can eliminate some of this tension and penetrate the role that the candidate is playing, but it is not easy within the constraints of the very formal interview. For this reason, additional, less formal interviews, with people who do not carry quite the same inhibiting status, can provide a useful insight into a candidate's motivation and ability to deal with people in more normal surroundings.

In the case of police applicants, one such interview can often be combined with a visit to his home where, as well as being able to carry out a more fruitful interview, there is also the opportunity for the interviewer to explain to the candidate and members of his family some of the facets of police life that often cause premature wastage due to family pressures.

Notes of all preliminary interviews should be made by the interviewer, so that views of as many people as possible are available to the selector, who can often find leads in such notes towards areas that need deeper exploration.

Inquiries

All police forces make thorough inquiries into the background of applicants for the police and demand details of all previous employment. The weight that should be given to the views of previous employers needs to be related to the nature of any criticism, the skills needed to perform the job in question and the length of time the candidate held that post. Patterns of behaviour can sometimes be observed in the reasons that a candidate gives for leaving previous jobs; for example a consistent attempt to seek "better" jobs may be in terms of money, responsibility, or favourable working conditions. Patterns of disagreement with employers, changing jobs for domestic reasons or boredom all provide cues for questions to probe deeply enough to get at the truth.

School reports are of particular interest if they are of recent origin, for they can be linked to academic success and intelligence-test scores to provide an indication of the extent to which the candidate used his innate ability while at school. Young people with poor academic records but high intelligence may claim that they have realised the error of their ways in not working hard at school, but the academic showing of such people, as cadets, rarely supports these claims. The guidance of a headmaster can be of great assistance in identifying those people who are worth a second chance.

Referees

It has long been the custom to insist that candidates for central and local government posts should provide the names of two or three referees who can vouch for the character of the applicant. The small number of referees who report anything unfavourable about a candidate suggests that, as a means of learning anything about the candidate, they are of questionable value.

Local inquiries by police in areas where candidates have lived are more likely to produce the truth than "testimonials" from people selected by the applicant.

Attitude tests

A critical factor for the police (and many other employers) is the basic set of attitudes a person brings to bear on his work and contact with other people. Such attitudes are very difficult to change once a person has reached adulthood and they can sometimes be extreme in form. It would be useful if there was a simple way of detecting, for example, excessively authoritarian or anti-authority attitudes, or marked biases and prejudices. Unfortunately, although a number of tests have been prepared, not one has yet been devised that can be universally applied without lengthy procedures requiring the candidate to undergo a traumatic form of self-revelation. Simple tests tend to be rather obvious and permit a candidate to predict the answers the examiner wants rather than those that reflect his true beliefs. It follows, therefore, that every attempt must be made by interviewers to try to detect any underlying attitudes or prejudices. This is no easy matter and, once again, resort may have to be made to the probationary period, to single out recruits who are dangerous in an organisation which invests its members with power over others.

Induction

A problem all organisations face is that of assimilating new people into the organisation and helping them to overcome the period of doubt and uncertainty that occurs because of the difference between the reality and their expectations. No one taking on a new job fully appreciates all the problems he will face and this is particularly true of a person joining the police. The problems that this creates will be dealt with in more detail in Chapter 12, but it is worth mentioning here that the amount of "shock" that occurs when a recruit faces the reality of the work of the police can be reduced by making sure that applicants are at least aware of some of the more obvious factors that will affect them.

Many people have formed their impression of the police from television fictional series and recruiting literature. The former give a false account of the work of a policeman, if for no other reason than they condense action so that all the routine patrolling, paperwork and frustration are omitted. Police recruiting literature emphasises the positive side of the police, its value to the community, the rewarding nature of the work; it seldom mentions such mundane aspects as shifts and weekend working, the complaints procedure and the punctiliousness associated with police reports. Essentially, the recruitment process is a two-way one: the selector takes a chance that he has chosen a suitable man or women, but the person selected is taking an even bigger chance that he or she has volunteered for the right job. It follows that while the service is entitled to know all about the applicant, there is an obligation to allow the applicant to find out about the police. The absence of proper steps to do this will be reflected in early wastage, the number of people who leave while at the training centre or in the first few months of operational service.

Similar problems arise for traffic wardens and all civilian police staff but it is particularly applicable to cadets. Cadet forces are usually "sold" on the basis of educational prospects, sport, learning about the work of the police and being involved in community activities. If the work he does reflects those expectations, the cadet still has to adapt from the level of discipline at school to that of the police cadet and, provided that this is reasonable, most will survive. Many will not if their work is markedly different from their expectations and therefore as much advance information as possible should be given of exactly what the cadet is in for. Once again, a lack of proper preparation will evidence itself in wastage.

Chapter Eleven

Training

Learning

The law of effect

All forms of learning are governed by the law of effect: people tend to repeat behaviour which seems to bring some reward and they do not normally repeat behaviour which seems either to bring no reward or to bring punishment. A child is taught by compliment or encouragement when it does something right, and by frowns or scolding when it does something wrong. What is true of children is also true of adults.

Unfortunately, in the police service there is sometimes a tendency not to show approval when a man does something right but to leave him in no doubt when he does something wrong. This attitude does not help the learning process to the extent that both positive and negative indications do. The positive side helps because it so clearly indicates that there is some reward in doing things the right way, that it brings an encouraging attitude on the part of the supervisor and recognition by him of the effort that has been made by the learner.

Willingness to learn

An aspect of learning that often requires more consideration in supervisory training than with recruits is the fact that learning involves personal change on the part of the learner. Many people who have become used to behaving in a certain way or doing a job in a particular way have great difficulty in accepting, first, that there is a need to be taught a new way of doing things and, second, that the new way is better. This may not be simply because the individual is deliberately being awkward, but because the prospect of change is unsettling and affects one's self-confidence. It must be proved to the trainee that he *needs* to learn for, if he does not accept this, he will not accept the teaching. In the case of a probationer constable, it should not be too difficult to convince him that he has a lot to learn. With experienced police officers, particularly those who have been supervisors for some time, a willingness to learn often has to be fought for by the trainer, who must prove that what he is teaching is of positive benefit to the learner and relates to his job.

Learning attitudes

Being willing to learn is a vital ingredient in the process of learning new attitudes and beliefs, for no change is possible unless the person who holds them is prepared to listen to other views and examine his own in the light of what he hears. A man's beliefs cannot be changed by simply talking to him. He may alter his outward behaviour to give the impression that he is conforming, but this change is superficial and his behaviour under pressure, or when he is not being observed will be governed by his original beliefs.

It should be noted that although the subject of changing attitudes is here discussed in terms of teaching a person to be a police officer or developing a supervisor, the same principles apply equally when trying to affect a member of the public's attitude towards the police, crime prevention, road safety or anything else. The steps are the same: create a willingness to receive new ideas; invite expression of existing attitudes; encourage an evaluation of these pre-conceived ideas against the new and assist in the formulation of a new pattern of beliefs and behaviour, if the change has been accepted as being desirable.

Developing skills

The learning of a skill depends on being shown how to do something and then being allowed to practise it, either in a realistic, simulated condition or in real life.

Whichever method is used, one factor is needed for success, as in all other forms of training—knowledge of results.

Imagine trying to learn how to shoot at a target without being able to see where your shots land and with no one to tell you. Progress would be impossible, you would not know whether you were doing well or badly. So it is with learning any skill. A police officer can only improve if someone tells him when he is doing well and when he is doing badly—and as soon as possible after the event. Telling a marksman that he has just fired a shot a centimetre too low lets him know how to improve. Telling a constable that he asked his questions too slowly in an interrogation will help him to do better next time. Merely telling him that he asked the *wrong* questions will not, for that is like telling the marksman only that he missed the target. Signalling when a bullet hits the centre of the target tells the marksman where to aim in future; similarly when a police officer is told that he has done something well, he learns more quickly how to do that part of his job. This process of feeding people knowledge of the results they are achieving is fundamental at all levels in the service.

Common police services
There has long been a recognition of the fact that individual police forces cannot be completely self-sufficient in such matters as training, research, criminal detection and communication. For this reason certain Common Police Services are financed jointly by the Exchequer and local government to provide such facilities as forensic-science laboratories, wireless depots, promotion examinations, standard entrance-tests, police representative and negotiating machinery, the police national computer, district police-training centres and the Police College. Contributions to their upkeep are made according to a cost per head of the establishment by all police forces except the Metropolitan Police, which contributes only to those services that it uses, mainly the Police College, representative and negotiating machinery and the central organisation of regional crime squads.

In this chapter we shall be concerned with the roles of two of the common services, district police-training centres and the Police College.

Probationer training
District training centres
Prior to 1939, initial training was carried out locally, but with many of the smaller forces sending their recruits on training courses run by larger ones. Regional training centres using a

common syllabus were introduced as a temporary measure after the 1939–1945 war, to cope with the needs of the large numbers of recruits entering the police service, after six years during which there had been no recruiting. The advantages of regional training soon led to its permanent adoption.

Although the district police-training centres are primarily the responsibility of the Home Secretary (s. 41, Police Act 1964), they each have two committees which are responsible for their administration. A local authority committee, made up of representatives of the police authorities of the district, is principally responsible for finance, and a chief constables' committee deals with technical matters and with the selection of instructional staff.

The Metropolitan Police do not make use of the district training centres but train their own personnel at Hendon Training School, using a syllabus that combines the first three phases of formal classroom recruit-training in the provinces. These phases are as follows:

1. A short introduction period with the trainee's own force, during which the recruit is sworn in as a constable, issued with uniform and equipment, and given some indication of the nature of the police force that he has joined.
2. The district training centre initial course.
3. A short course with the recruit's own force to teach him local law and procedures.

Initial training course
Co-ordination of training methods and subject matter throughout England and Wales is achieved through the work of the Central Planning and Instructors' Training Unit. Following a series of investigations into the needs of probationer constables, the unit used a system of "training by objectives" to produce the present short, but compact, initial training course.

The processes needed to produce such a course may be summarised thus:

1. Identify the needs of the people to be taught in terms of what they must learn.
2. Analyse those needs to isolate the knowledge and skills that are required.

3. Define that area of knowledge and skills that will be taught in the initial course.
4. Prepare a systematic programme that facilitates the process of learning.
5. Teach in a way that relates the knowledge and skills to the job that the student will do.
6. Check that the minimum level of learning has been achieved by all students.
7. Provide feed-back from the service to the training unit as to the relevance of the training to the actual work of the policeman.
8. Allow for updating as conditions change and for periodic checks to ensure that the mechanism of process 7 is functioning with sufficient speed and accuracy.

This is supplemented by a sequence of continuation training at a force training school, during the two-years' probationary period, a short continuation course at a district training centre and on-the-job training.

A short initial course has the advantage of cheapness and a rapid output of "trained" people for police duties, but it provides limited depth of knowledge or development of social and perceptual skills. So, whilst it is very functional, it does leave a lot to be learned by the probationer while actually doing the job. Considerable responsibility is thus laid upon the supervisors, who must build on the foundations laid by the training school.

On-the-job training
One of the responsibilities of any supervisor is to train his subordinates. This not only applies to probationer constables although the need is most clearly seen at this level.

The process of teaching people how to do their work while they are actually doing it is called "on-the-job" training, a term used to distinguish a practical "apprenticeship" from the training received in a classroom.

In the classroom, the student policeman learns the law and police procedures. He may also try his hand at applying these, together with what he has been taught about human behaviour, to simulated incidents. However, it is very difficult to simulate

H

the very wide range of human reactions that a policeman may encounter in reality. Therefore, the classroom training provides only a basis upon which the student can build from the experience that he gets at work.

What does a police officer need to know?
In order to be able to answer this question, the Home Office sponsored an extensive series of structured interviews with probationer constables and their supervisors in many forces, so as to form a firm basis for the syllabi that were to be prepared by the Central Planning Unit. Clearly, such sophisticated methods are not at the disposal of the operational supervisor but he must, nevertheless, have a clear idea of what he expects a probationer constable to be able to do at the end of his probationary period.

The list of jobs that a constable is expected to be able to do will vary from force to force, although there will be common elements in all forces. The list for one force specified that a constable should have the ability to:

deal courteously and efficiently with members of the public; use a telephone switchboard correctly and answer any telephone enquiries in an efficient and polite manner; identify the resources available in a headquarters communications room; identify the functions of the various departments of the force; call on resources available;

operate a personal radio and one fitted to a mobile patrol-unit; identify vulnerable premises; recognise well-known criminals active in the area; extract information from the collator's records and assess correctly the type of information that should be passed to the collator;

observe correct procedure when interrogating witnesses and persons arrested for crime; deal correctly with exhibits, witnesses and prisoner's property; formulate charges, know charging procedures and complete a file of evidence; pay expenses and deal with prosecution witnesses;

deal correctly with all forms of lost and found property including all documentation and disposal of found property after recording;

identify important routes, accident black-spots and traffic hazards; advise pedestrians and motorists on accident prevention; deal correctly with traffic offences and road accidents.

Such a list serves to emphasise the limitations of the classroom training given to police recruits, because so many items must be completely taught at work, while others can be only partly taught in a classroom.

Steps in training
There are four main steps to be taken in training:

1. Decide on the objectives of the training.
2. Set standards of performance for all aspects of the work to be learnt and ensure that the learners know these standards so that they understand what is expected of them. (Unless standards are set there is bound to be confusion on the part of the people being trained as to what they are trying to achieve. A common difficulty encountered by probationer constables is that of working under more than one sergeant and finding that what suits sergeant A will not do for sergeant B, and vice versa. This can apply at all levels in an organisation and is the cause of much re-typing of reports in order to conform to the individual standards of senior officers. It is particularly disturbing for people learning their job.)
3. Measure their performance against these standards.
4. Give them knowledge of their results so that they are aware of their progress (*see* p. 210 above).

These steps are applicable to on-the-job training and to classroom training. Because training is often superseded by operational needs, supervisors must take full advantage of opportunities for training that do present themselves. This does not mean that work and training are to be seen as separate functions—the whole idea of on-the-job training is that it should be done as the trainee goes about his work—but it is the structuring of that work and the method of supervision that should be adjusted to the needs of the trainee police officer.

The supervisor as trainer
From what has gone before, the role of the supervisor as a trainer of his subordinates can be seen to be one of working out what each subordinate needs to learn, providing him with the conditions under which he can learn it and keep a check on his progress, feeding back to him the essential knowledge of results.

Where possible, allowances should be made for particular individual abilities and for the different rates at which different people learn. Because one man makes excellent progress it is unrealistic to expect his colleagues to make identical progress and to criticise them for failing to do so. One quick learner sometimes conceals defects in a teaching system. It is possible for people to learn despite the system and not because of it. Poor performance by a number of probationers may indicate that they are not very good material. Equally, it may indicate that the training that they are receiving is inadequate.

Cadet training
General principles
The *Working Party Report on Police Cadets* (1965) contained a useful review of the considerations governing the training of police cadets. From this review, four general principles emerged. Cadets should be:

1. kept away from premature contact with police work, but should be encouraged to retain their interest in police work by being given talks on police-related subjects by police officers;
2. given full-time educational training (including social studies) with substantial opportunities for games and physical training and for developing qualities of initiative and self-reliance;

    (It was emphasised that the aim should be to provide a course of liberal education, the youngster being "taught to think rather than merely to amass information".

    Games and physical education were considered essential, particular emphasis being laid on swimming and life-saving. The need for a police officer to be able to take command of unexpected situations and to be able to think for himself and act on his own when necessary, suggested the desirability of cadets undertaking some form of adventure training such as rock-climbing, sailing and initiative races.
3. given some opportunity to gain insight into the police service;

    (It was considered important that police cadets should appreciate the role of the police in society and, at the same time, feel that they were part of the police service.

    The working party went to some lengths to distinguish between working alongside police officers and actually performing police duties. To this end, a list of suitable duties appropriate to police cadets was produced (ibid., Appendix

D) but the main emphasis was placed on older cadets working with beat-duty constables as part of normal cadet training.)

4. encouraged to participate in voluntary community work which would broaden their horizons and develop their understanding of the community which they would serve as police officers.

Training programme

The working party suggested a pattern of training that fell into two phases to take a cadet from the age of sixteen at which he or she was recruited, to joining the police force as a constable at the age of nineteen, the then minimum recruiting age.

The first phase was seen as being composed of full-time education, and vocational and physical training. The second phase would include working alongside police officers and beginning to learn the elements of police work. This phase should also contain physical training but no full-time educational training, apart from the exceptional few, who may merit being allowed to continue for advanced-level academic qualifications.

Within this skeleton framework it was envisaged that the training would be sufficiently flexible to allow for the varying capabilities of individuals, a pre-requisite of any good training system.

The operational police supervisor has a part to play in the vocational and practical police-training of cadets. All too often, police supervisors complain of the attitudes of policemen who have joined the force from the cadet service, yet they do little to guide the attitudes formed by cadets. Cadets must rely on police supervisors to ensure that they are properly deployed with police officers who are willing and able to teach them. The problem is similar to that of probationer constables. The supervisor has a responsibility to invest in the future by paying attention to the training needs of both, not only in terms of technical knowledge but also in the formation of their attitudes.

The question of forming attitudes is particularly important with teenagers, many of whom are susceptible to strong influences that can colour their whole outlook. For this reason, it is necessary to ensure that cadets are not over-exposed to police officers whose attitudes are suspect, either in relation to their work or towards the public.

There is no reason why a police cadet cannot develop an

understanding of the public equal to that of a young man or woman who spends several years in an office, factory or shop before joining the police. It is a matter of correct training. For example, if cadets are housed in police accommodation that isolates them from the outside world, then provision should be made to compensate for that isolation. The subject of cadet training needs to be approached in the same way as all other training by first defining objectives.

Specialist training

Unlike some countries in which police officers are given lengthy and very thorough training in all aspects of policing, in Britain only a minimum of training is given initially and this is supplemented by specialist training, as and when required.

Lengthy initial courses, covering all aspects of policing, tend to be wasteful in that people are taught things that they may never need or will not encounter until long after they have forgotten their initial training. On the other hand, comprehensive training does give policemen an insight into, and an understanding of, the work of all their colleagues.

In cost-effective terms, the British system is more economical, but it does mean that training tends to be given in short, sharp bursts that may not be properly related to one another unless great care is taken. Furthermore, there is a tendency not to want to "waste" training by allowing a man trained in one specialism to take up another. This can limit the range of a man's career and condemn him to one branch of the service, not because of his aptitude or motivation, but because money has been spent on training him.

The British system of short courses aimed at specific specialisms can only work properly if it is allied to a flexible personnel-management policy.

Supervisory training

Many aspects of supervisory training are of recent origin both in the police service and outside it. The earliest forms of supervisory training for police were, very largely, "technical" in nature—mainly law and procedures. For example, early Metropolitan Police courses for constables, prior to promotion to sergeant, were heavily biased towards the law needed for the various aspects of station duty. Admittedly, lectures were given on "leadership", "duties and responsibilities of rank" and "welfare", but these formed a relatively minor part of a comprehensive course on the charging of prisoners and related aspects of criminal law.

Supervisors were expected to learn their craft mainly through experience. The value of experience as a teacher cannot be denied, but as has been said of it, "experience is the name everyone gives to their mistakes" and such mistakes on the part of a supervisor can be painful for himself, his subordinates and the service. It is therefore well worth while to try to cut down their number by suitable training.

As with other forms of police training, it is not possible for supervisory training to be completed in a classroom and much of it must be carried out under real on-the-job conditions. However, preliminary classroom training can teach supervisors how to avoid some of the more obvious pitfalls and enable them to derive greater understanding from their subsequent experience.

The effectiveness of classroom training

Classroom training, even though it contains periods of simulation training, can, at best, provide only a framework upon which people can build. To be effective, the training must be clearly related to the work that the supervisor will have to do when he leaves the course, and his own supervisors must believe in the aims of the teaching he receives. It is useless to provide training based on beliefs that are not acceptable to a trainee's own supervisors when he returns to work. This has been a consistent problem with the introduction of all forms of supervisory training; it has often been introduced at the lower levels of the organisation rather than at the top and then working downwards. It is not sensible to instil into junior supervisors attitudes that are going to be opposed to those of the chief officers of their forces, for this may cause conflict and disillusionment.

On-the-job training

There is a common assumption that because a person who was a constable a few weeks ago now wears a sergeant's insignia, he is a fully competent supervisor.

Like a probationer constable, a newly-promoted sergeant has to go through a period of adjustment as he comes to terms with his new role. For some people, the strain can be as great as for some newly-appointed constables. The isolation that comes with rank, the expectations of his subordinates and those of his supervisors, the desire to succeed, all combine to create pressures upon the newly-promoted officer. He also usually finds himself at a new station where he has to learn the geography of the area and the procedures peculiar to that unit. Even if he remains at the same station when he is promoted, the difficulty of adjusting his relationships with the men who were formerly on equal terms with him usually more than cancels out the benefits of knowing the ropes, in so far as places and procedures are concerned.

The responsibility for aiding the sergeant to grow into his role is that of the inspectors and senior officers under whom he works. This is a process that continues through the ranks, since an officer at every level has responsibility for training his subordinates, but nowhere is it more important than with a man who has just become a supervisor.

The role of the sergeant
The role of the first-line supervisor is critical in any organisation and the police service is no exception. A great deal of skill is necessary to be able to maintain a balance between his responsibilities for enforcing the policies and standards of his senior officers and maintaining his approachability and day-to-day involvement in the work of the constable in his unit.

The range of qualities expected of a sergeant include the following:

1. *Technical expertise.* A sergeant is expected to be able to advise his subordinates on the action that they should take to deal with particular problems and technical knowledge is also required if the checking of reports and action by sergeants is to have any real meaning.

2. *Ability to achieve work through people.* A sergeant has to learn that the work he is given cannot all be done by himself. He must rely on the people who make up his unit and must be able to motivate them and maintain their morale.

3. *Leadership.* It is an expectation that all police supervisors will exercise leadership over their subordinates. It should be noted that leadership is not an exact science. Every supervisor has to learn to adopt a style that fits his own personality and the situation in which he finds himself. It takes time for most people to grow into a supervisory role but the length of this time can be reduced by sound training, both in the classroom and on the job.

4. *Skill in passing written and verbal orders and information.* Good communication is of importance at all levels in the service, for the police rely heavily on quick and accurate information flows, not only within a force, but between it and the community it serves. The sergeant's role here is crucial for he is in the best position to relay up through the organisation the information and impressions gained by his men who are in immediate contact with the public.

Failure to achieve the successful implementation of new policies can be due to poor communication. It is important to get the message through to the sergeants who set the standards for the constables. There is a distinct tendency for senior officers to blame sergeants when things go wrong, but to undervalue them when it comes to involving them in the creation and pursuance of policies.

5. *Skill in detecting and solving welfare problems.* It is in the interests of all organisations that welfare problems should be immediately identified before they become too serious and, perhaps, beyond solution. The sergeant is the most likely individual to be able to initiate official action in respect of a constable's welfare problem.

6. *Ability to enforce discipline.* In a service governed by a disciplinary code, every supervisor has to play his part in its enforcement. Many sergeants find it difficult to do this because of their close identification with their subordinates. The rank of sergeant needs to be given its due status and support if its holders are to be expected to play their full part in the enforcement of discipline. Equally, every sergeant needs to be aware of the limitations of discipline as a means of getting work done.

This short summary has been included not to provide an exhaustive survey of the work of a sergeant but merely to emphasise the broad range of the training needed and to indicate those areas of his work in which some understanding of the theoretical background can aid the learning process. The aim of the remaining chapters of this book is to provide some of that background, all of which is applicable not only to the rank of sergeant but to all supervisors. The scale changes from rank to rank but the basic principles remain.

The Police College
Background
The first attempt within the British police service to provide a college aimed at training potential senior officers was in 1934, when the Metropolitan Police Commissioner, Lord Trenchard, succeeded in persuading the Home Secretary to set up a police college at Hendon.

This short-lived establishment (for it was disbanded in 1939, when, at the outbreak of war, recruiting was suspended) succeeded in producing some distinguished senior officers who played an important role in the post-war police service, but it had one unfortunate side effect. Lord Trenchard had little patience with the Police Federation, which was bitterly opposed to any form of "officer class" being created within the police. The Metropolitan Police College did just this, although only in very small numbers. A number of places on each course were allotted to people who joined from outside the police service and were immediately given a specially created rank of junior station inspector. T. A. Critchley, himself a distinguished member of the Home Office Police Department wrote: "The lasting criticism of the experiment must be the suspicion, hostility, and resentment it aroused in the hearts of many thousands of ordinary, loyal policemen everywhere" (*A History of Police in England and Wales 900–1966*, Constable, 1967).

It is against the background of these feelings that the position of the present Police College must be seen. The instigators of the scheme were clear about the role that a new national Police College should fill. It should "broaden the outlook, improve the professional knowledge, and stimulate the energies of men who have reached or are reaching the middle and higher ranks of the service" (*First Report of the Police Post-War Committee*, 1946).

Thus, from its inception, the Police College, first at Ryton-on-Dunsmore, Warwickshire, from 1948 to 1960, then at Bramshill, Hampshire, concentrated its efforts on providing training for existing members of the police.

There are currently five courses held at Bramshill: the Special Course (designed to provide a measure of accelerated promotion for outstanding young police officers); the Inspectors' Course; Command Course Part I (formerly called the Intermediate Command Course); Command Course Part II (formerly the Senior Command Course) and the Overseas Command Course (a programme specially designed for senior overseas officers).

The Special Course

The effect of the Special Course on the possible promotion of a police officer will be demonstrated in Chapter 14. To qualify for admission, a constable must have passed the qualifying examination for the rank of sergeant. He must then be selected by a Force Selection Board (consisting of a chief police officer, and a member each of the Superintendents' Association and the Police Federation), to fill one of the vacancies allotted to his police force on a *per capita* basis. If he was amongst the top 200 candidates who passed the sergeants' examination, he has the right to go before that board. After attending a Central Selection Board, the successful candidate attends for Extended Interview.

The alternative method of entry to the Special Course is through the Graduate Entry Scheme, in which graduates attend for Extended Interview *before* joining the police (but after being recommended by a Chief Constable who is prepared to accept him in his force as a graduate entrant). Serving graduate officers are also eligible for this scheme, providing that they graduated before joining the service, have not previously been considered under the scheme and submit an application to their chief officer before completing twelve-months' service. In all cases, the successful entrant must serve satisfactorily as a constable for at least two years, must pass the sergeants' promotion examination and then appear for a further interview with members of the Extended Interview Panel.

Completion of the twelve-months' Special Course is not an automatic path to rapid promotion. Although each student is given the temporary rank of sergeant on joining the course, he must qualify for a pass certificate from the Commandant or Deputy Commandant of the Police College, in order to retain his rank on a permanent basis and to gain the opportunity of obtaining further accelerated promotion.

When an officer who has successfully completed the Special Course returns to his force he must perform duty as a sergeant for one year to the satisfaction of his chief constable before he is automatically promoted to the rank of inspector (even though this may temporarily be in excess of the force's establishment in this rank).

The method of selection, the insistence on practical police duty providing a sound foundation, the arduous nature of the Special Course and the co-operation of the Police Federation in the selection of candidates, have all aided the acceptability of the Special Course as a means of ensuring a good start for people with a potential for senior rank.

The Inspectors' Course

Although from the outset the Police College has concentrated on actual or potential inspectors, there has always been a problem of numbers. Selection for an Inspectors' Course has often been a matter of chance. In an attempt to give every inspector the same training, regional training centres were established to provide the first part of a course, the second part of which was held at Bramshill. Considerable emphasis has been placed on the personal skills needed by inspectors as well as the technical aspects of police work. As with all such courses that consist of officers from many police forces, much of the value of attendance at the Police College is gained from the interchange of ideas and the sense of unity within the police service which is created, despite the existence of separate police forces.

Command courses

With two courses, attendance on the second of which requires a candidate to pass the Extended Interview procedure (*see* Chapter 14), the Police College aims to provide a multi-discipline approach to the training of senior officers. Part I of the course is geared to divisional command and Part II to chief officer rank. On these courses there is a deliberate attempt to encourage the members to look beyond the horizons of the British police service at what is happening elsewhere in society and in the world at large. At this stage of his career, if at no other, a police officer must not only appreciate his role in the police, he must also be totally aware of the police role in society. He will be responsible for policy decisions that must not only take this into account but, ultimately, will also have an effect upon it.

Chapter Twelve

Personal assessment

Career planning

Each member of an organisation brings to work with him many different attributes. If his capabilities can be properly deployed, both the man and the organisation will benefit, for he will derive a sense of achievement from his work and the organisation will obtain the full commitment of the man's abilities towards its objectives. Every organisation should, therefore, have systems that will identify the attributes and skills of its members and record these in such a way that they can be taken into account when decisions are to be made. The basic requirements of such systems are as follows:

1. Personnel policies that produce a climate in which manpower planning can be undertaken with the co-operation of the people in the organisation.
2. An information-gathering service to provide the raw materials for personnel decisions.
3. A means of storing and updating the information that has been collected.
4. The facility to retrieve this information so that it is readily available when decisions are to be made.
5. A means of making decisions that has the trust of the people whose careers depend upon it.

Personnel policies

People joining the police service have different expectations and ambitions when they join and they develop further attributes and ambitions as they gain experience in the service. If no way is provided in which a man can help to direct his career in the way in which he feels it should go, he may quickly become frustrated.

An important matter like the development of people's

careers cannot be left to chance, for it is too easy for men to drift into backwaters from which they cannot escape. A common example can be seen in someone who has been selected to fill a specialist post. Having proved himself good at the job, he is left to keep doing it and, years later, when promotions are being considered, he may be passed over because he lacks general police experience. This is often through no fault of his own, but simply because it was expedient to keep him in his specialised post. Of course there is no harm in a man taking a specialist position and remaining in it so long as he is providing a useful service to the organisation and is deriving job satisfaction from his work, but there is an important proviso: both the man and the organisation should be fully aware of what is happening. Promotion is not the only path to a satisfying career and many people enjoy one aspect of police work for its own sake and have no need to become supervisory officers to achieve fulfilment. It is as well that they do so, for it is a mathematical certainty that not everyone can be promoted. People should know what they are doing and this requires policies which they can understand, so that they can make conscious decisions about their own lives. Despite a rapidly-changing police service, in which it can be difficult to maintain consistent policies because circumstances and policy-makers change, a system designed to make the best possible use of people's attributes is essential (*see* also Chapter 7, p. 162).

Ideally, a man's career should be tailored to fit his individual requirements from the moment that he joins the service, but clearly this is not possible, for the range of jobs available is limited and far more people would like to be employed on some form of duty than others. It is also necessary to balance the needs of individuals against those of the organisation. This may mean having to choose between helping someone to further his career, for example by gaining experience in different types of work, and maintaining the efficiency of his unit, which requires as few changes of staff as possible.

Collecting information
It is necessary to have information readily available upon which decisions as to people's deployment can be based. Much of it has to be collected and evaluated by supervisors, for they are

the only people in a position to appraise their subordinates' personal characteristics, job preferences, suitability for various types of employment and domestic circumstances that should be taken into account. All supervisors, at every level, should be able to provide an up-to-date objective assessment of the people under their command when it is needed for career-planning purposes. This is often thought to be of less importance, simply because it was expedient to keep him in his specialised post. Of course, there is no harm in a man doing a specialised position and remaining in it so long as he is providing

New entrants
Probation

For the first two years of his service, a police constable is on probation and, if this is to have any meaning, there must be an effective way of monitoring his progress. A probationer-report system must be aimed at two key areas. First, at the man himself: at the qualities he displays, the aptitude that he demonstrates for police work and the personal qualities that he possesses. Secondly, at monitoring the efforts of the organisation in providing the necessary support and guidance that all new recruits need.

There is no such thing as a perfect selection system that can guarantee that every man who is brought into the service will be able to become a successful police officer. As has been stated elsewhere, the only general guide as to how a man will perform in the future is what he has done in the past. The problem with recruiting people into the police is that there is usually no experience in their past which will give clear guidance as to how they will react when placed in a police situation. In a similar way, although a recruit may believe before he joins that he is fully aware of all the implications of joining the police service, it is not until he actually is a member of it under operational conditions that he can really form any judgment as to whether or not he is suitable for the life.

There are a number of factors that can disqualify a man from being a policeman and some of these are not detectable until he is in the right situation to reveal this particular factor. One example of this, which often causes surprise, is that it is possible for a man to join the police force and not to realise the full implications of arresting someone until he has to do it.

The extent to which the new entrant into any organisation needs support in the initial stages is often under-estimated. Not only does he have to learn a new job, but there are also outside factors which have a bearing on how quickly he will settle down. Many recruits are unaware of the traumatic effect that shift work, unanticipated overtime and weekend working can have on their domestic and social life. The physical effects of shift work may be significant; some people find it relatively easy to adjust from one shift to another, but others do not. The new entrant may also have other pressures from his domestic life; money can frequently be a problem, as the rate of pay of the police may mean that he receives a lower income, a situation often not helped by difficulties in adjusting his income tax and delays in paying allowances. If he has had to move house there may be pressures from his wife and family over what, to an outsider, may be quite trivial matters, but are very real to the people living them. Finally, there is the strain induced by the need to study, since, at the same time he is learning the skills of police work while doing the job, it is expected that the recruit will continue his theoretical studies. People who have come from a non-academic background frequently find that the need to study at home places a strain on them and their families.

A new entrant often fails to bring to notice things that could be easily resolved because the formality and apparent strictness of the police system inhibits people from bringing themselves to notice. This makes it all the more important that supervisors should detect any underlying problems contributing to a man's poor performance.

Many police recruits lack sufficient confidence and social skill to be able to initiate an approach to a member of the public. A lack of self-confidence can usually be overcome with practice, under supervision, but not always. Whatever the cause of any disqualifying factors for being a police officer, they must be identified in the interests of the public at large, the police service, and of course the individual himself. A sense of dread can soon develop in a probationer who fears that at any moment he is going to be called upon to do a task that he believes he is incapable of performing.

Probationer supervision
The system of monitoring the performance of probationer constables must not be confined to trying to identify their deficien-

cies. It must also monitor the training being given to them so that any defects that are identified can be clearly attributed to the right source—the man or the service.

One common problem is to provide adequate contact between a probationer and the supervisor who is responsible for training him and preparing his assessment reports. Dependent upon the type of shift system employed, it is not unknown for constables and sergeants to be on different shift systems, so that the reporting sergeant and probationer constable are on duty together for only a small proportion of the time. Under such a system it becomes very difficult for a sergeant to gain first-hand knowledge of a probationer and there is a tendency to emphasise those aspects of his performance that can be measured without actually being with him for any length of time. A probationer is often assessed on the amount of "work" that he has done, as measured by the number of process reports that he has submitted, arrests he has made, or incidents that he has dealt with as shown in the official records. Such an assessment is often backed up by comments on the quality of his paper work and the speed with which it is completed, so that at first sight there appears to be a rounded view of the man's progress. What have not been measured are the personal qualities that are necessary if the individual is to become a successful police officer.

It will always be difficult to assess accurately how a man is able to deal with a variety of situations and people. Some indications can be obtained by working alongside him, but it has to be accepted that the way in which a probationer constable deals with an incident will be conditioned, either consciously or unconsciously, by the presence of his supervisor. Such a method of assessing a probationer should not be disregarded because of this, as seeing a man's work *can* provide some useful information. In the case of a confident or over-confident trainee, it must be expected that he will be on his best behaviour and, for example, will probably try to conceal any overbearing tendencies by moderating his approach when he knows that he is being watched. Once again, however, one can learn something, for quite often situations present themselves which occupy the man's attention sufficiently to throw him off his guard and so reveal at least part of his true nature. It is the rate of progress that is one of the most critical factors in the assessment of a probationer constable. Most policemen would accept that they are learning throughout the whole of their careers and at the end of his probationary period, a constable will be only partly trained. The important decision that has to be made is whether he has made sufficient progress to justify concluding that he has the ability to become a well-conducted police officer who can be relied upon to continue to learn the skills of his profession at a reasonable rate.

Assessment reports

Most police forces have a system of periodical personal reports on the officers in the force. The sophistication of different schemes may vary but most have elements in common. Once a police constable has completed his probationary period, during which two- or three-monthly reports are common, most officers are thereafter reported upon at longer intervals, commonly of one year. The basic aims of all systems are to identify strengths and weaknesses and use this information for career development. More complex systems may have wider aims but the attainment of even the most basic aims is more difficult than at first appears.

Objectives of assessment reports

In general, the simpler the objectives that are set for a personal-report system, the more likelihood there is of success. Some organisations, by setting too many diffuse objectives, obscure the principal issues and thus bring the system into disrepute. With any assessment-report system it is necessary, from time to time, to ensure that it is fulfilling the needs of the organisation and to check that it has not become so much a matter of routine that it fails to differentiate between individuals in the organisation.

The basic objectives of a periodical personal-report system in the police service are usually:

1. to enable more accurate decisions to be made regarding the deployment of personnel;
2. to review the work of each individual, to acknowledge good work done and to recognise weaknesses so that the individual can be motivated to improve;

3. to respond to training needs by providing opportunities to gain experience, on-the-job training or formal courses;

4. to have an indication of the potential of the individual not only in relation to possible promotion or specialist deployment but also as to suitability to continue to perform ordinary police duty;

5. to high-light welfare problems, not only to ensure that immediate action is taken, but also to build into the system controls that will serve to prevent the organisation from creating welfare problems inadvertently.

The need for action

A personnel system will soon lose credibility if it is not seen to be using the information that is gathered by the personal reports. In most personal-report systems, there is the opportunity for action to be taken at various levels. If he is wise, the supervisory officer initiating a report will check its contents with the subject and when he does, indications may emerge that clearly require him to take action. If, for example, when a constable is taxed by his inspector about a particular area of his work, the constable claims that he has not been given proper instruction about that aspect of his duty, or was not made aware of the need to do it, the onus is on the inspector to get at the truth before the report goes further. If, when diagnosing the cause of a man's apparent lack of involvement in his work, an inspector comes across an urgent welfare problem, this is a matter about which action should be taken immediately. It is a safe rule that anything revealed during a personal-report procedure should be dealt with as soon as possible. In this way, the need for action is filtered out as a personal report progresses through the organisation. It ensures that when the report reaches the central collating point, the only action that needs to be taken is that which falls within the terms of reference of headquarters. Most report systems contain a review by a senior officer and an appraisal interview. This is an opportunity to identify action that should be taken and is one of the principal reasons for holding appraisal interviews.

Collecting information

In a centralised personnel-record system, the biggest problem to overcome is usually the sheer mass of information requiring storage and retrieval. In any system, whether manual or computerised, there is a need to establish just what information is going to be needed to make decisions and to ensure that this is presented to the decision-maker in an easily digestible form. In a very small police force the staff at headquarters may need very little additional information to enable them to make proper decisions. In organisations of the size of most British police forces, this is not so. What tends to happen is that within headquarters there is a general awareness of a small proportion of the force and a number of names are constantly to the fore when selections have to be made. There is a distinct possibility that people who have considerable merit do not come to the notice of headquarters staff. It is a fundamental principle of all personnel systems that the qualities of everyone are properly recognised, irrespective of where they are employed.

The nature of the information that is collected must enable decisions to be made with proper weight given to all the factors that make many personnel decisions so difficult. For example, the benefits that may be gained from transferring a man to gain additional experience have to be weighed against a number of disadvantages. As far as the service is concerned, this may just be a matter of balancing the advantages to be gained by qualifying the man for some particular form of duty in the future, against the disruption caused by moving him from his present post. In order to make a proper judgment, however, it would be necessary to know where the man lives and under what circumstances, the extent to which he and his family have commitments in the area, and details of his children's education. These are just some of the considerations that could be affected by moving a man to another post which requires that he also move house; even a transfer which does not involve a house move is more than just a matter of how far he has to travel from home to work. Many men build their lives around the social groupings that they form at work. Some men limit their ambitions because they value stability and do not wish to face the problems of making new friends and working with new colleagues on being transferred.

It will be seen that, if decisions are to be made on the best possible information available, the type of information that must be fed into the personnel system is very personal to the individual concerned. It is therefore necessary to balance carefully in each individual case the desirability of obtaining information about a man, his involvement in the community and at work, and those of his wife and family, with the individual's own desire to keep his private life to himself. Most people are willing to provide a reasonable amount of information about themselves, if it is going to be used for a constructive purpose that may be of benefit to them and/or the organisation, but they will resent supplying information if this appears to be just to satisfy someone's curiosity. We therefore come back to the credibility of the personnel system.

The extent to which a personal-report system should be linked to promotions is discussed later; it is sufficient at this point to emphasise that if the primary objective of a personal-report system is seen to be promotion, this will quickly discredit the system.

Identifying training needs
For a system of training to succeed, particularly one in which only very basic training is given initially, supplemented by a mixture of on-the-job training and short courses, it is necessary for supervisors to identify training needs in their subordinates. Such training may be needed to enable a man to be able to perform his present job more competently, or to extend his potential to do other work. A good personal-report system may also enable individuals to identify areas of training for themselves, either directed at what they would like to do in the future, or what they are doing at the moment. Such requests for training can be useful indications as to where an individual sees himself going in the future and also the extent to which he is prepared to extend himself to attain his ambitions; he may ask for a transfer or the opportunity to undertake specific tasks in order that he may gain experience. A sensitive personal-report system would not only register that the man has gained additional experience but also that he did so at his own request.

Potential
Considering a man's potential involves attempting to forecast how his career will develop in the future and this is difficult to do with any accuracy. It is common enough for a senior officer

to be able to say: "I saw that he had great potential" of someone who has since achieved success in the police service but this tends to cloud the possibility that, because such a judgment was made by senior officers, the man's chance of success was greatly enhanced. There is always the imponderable element to be considered of the people who, for a variety of reasons, were not given a spur to their career by being noticed by a senior officer and as a result have been "born to blush unseen".

Judgments of a man's potential are often made on flimsy evidence, often as a result of just one or two incidents coming to the notice of senior officers that reflect either good or ill for the person involved. This is part of a general stereotyping which tends to take place on the basis of isolated but noteworthy incidents. Fortunately, for most people, the fact that one makes a fool of oneself on one occasion does not necessarily mean that one is a fool for evermore, yet it is surprisingly difficult for individuals to overcome the results of a mistake early in their career.

The most common meaning of "potential" on an assessment form is potential for promotion. In the case of a constable it can be quite difficult even to forecast what sort of sergeant he will be when he has to try his hand at supervision. Trying to estimate the long-term career prospects of a constable is extremely hazardous, since he may not have had the opportunity to develop the characteristics required of a senior officer. In the same way that certain qualities are necessary for a man to be a success in a specialist post, so different qualities may be required to be a senior officer as against those required to be a constable. A man's future decisions in his private life will affect his potential in the police service. People's ambitions when single may change once they settle down to family life. Alternatively, a single man who lacks ambition may, when he marries, awake to the responsibilities that he has now undertaken and as a result produce the qualities to attain promotion. Despite all of these reservations, most organisations do try to identify at an early stage those people who stand a good chance of being potential leaders. It is desirable that this should be done, provided that it is acknowledged that any such identification must be tentative and there must be a willingness to take a chance and identify rather more people than will actually be needed. To single out too many people for rapid promotion may result in a number of them reaching middle rank and being unable to proceed further because of lack of opportunity. This factor must be balanced against the need of the organisation to ensure succession and provide sufficient people from whom a selection can be made, if the object is to get the best men as the future leaders of the service.

So far, as is normal in police circles, the word "potential" has tended to be equated with promotion but, as was mentioned earlier, the identification of potential should not be confined to the senior officers of tomorrow. Unless some attempt is made to try to identify the other forms of potential in people, there is a danger that needs will be overlooked or ignored. A good personal-report system can do this by giving each individual the opportunity to discuss his ambitions in appraisal interviews, due note being taken of the man's own preferences when decisions are being made concerning him and his career.

Welfare problems
The personal-assessment system should only be a "long-stop", for serious welfare problems should not have to wait for, say, an annual report before they are brought to light. Nevertheless, it is quite common for welfare problems to be high-lighted by annual reports, because there is a review of the man's performance and serious consideration is given by supervisors as to the reason behind any fall-off in performance. Most annual-report systems provide the opportunity for individuals to discuss problems in formal interviews when reports on the standard of their work over the past year are discussed in detail.

Assessment reports—the underlying thinking
The important aspect of a report system is not the form that it takes but the thinking that lies behind it and the part it plays in the overall personnel system.

Confidentiality
There is controversy as to whether or not the subject of the report should see what has been written about him. Many systems adopt what is thought of as a compromise, they do not allow the subject of the report to see what has been written, but

have it read to him by a senior officer. In practice, many senior officers give just a general impression of the contents in their own words, but this causes communication problems between the senior officer and the subject of the report. At the end of the session, each will have his own idea of what has been communicated from one to the other and it is quite likely that those two opinions will differ. In such reporting systems, the person charged with reading the report to the subject may feel entitled to do so in his own words in the belief that, if the organisation wished the subject of the report to know exactly what is thought of him, then he would be shown the report. The people who are being reported upon may conclude that they have not been told the exact contents of their report and assume that there is something in the report to their detriment which is being concealed from them.

There are a number of arguments for and against "open" as distinct from "secret" reports. Protagonists of the latter argue that to reveal the contents of a report to a subject has an adverse effect on relations between the supervisors and subordinates and criticism will be stifled. There is of course some truth in this, as can be seen from an examination of reports submitted by supervisory officers on subordinates who work closely with them. In conditions like this, reporting officers tend to avoid making critical comments. It has also been suggested that open reports encourage subordinates to compare assessments with one another, with the result that tensions are created among members of staff who find themselves differently rated. In general, this is more likely to be true when the reporting system is linked to monetary reward or some other tangible benefit. One final criticism that is often levelled at open reports is the effect that reading an adverse comment may have on a man who is incapable of making any improvement. Such an objection would have more weight were it not that even in secret report systems it is normal tradition that adverse reports should be read to the subject. In practice, the need to do this is often avoided by wording the report in terms of "damning with faint praise", so that the adverse nature of the report is concealed.

Open reports

The main arguments in favour of at least a partial openness in personal reports are related to two factors:

1. People are entitled to know where they stand and are only likely to believe that they are being told the truth if the actual report is shown. The feed-back that people receive about their work enables them to improve in those areas which are the subject of criticism.
2. Supervisors completing a report must ensure that it is accurate because the subject of the report is going to read it and therefore be in a position to correct any statements which are untrue or which are in doubt. This is a stronger benefit than might at first be thought, for it is surprisingly easy to make incorrect statements on a personal-report form, because there is no way of ensuring their accuracy without consulting the person concerned and secret reporting systems discourage this. Particularly suspect in secret reports are statements made by supervisors as to what they believe is the cause of certain patterns of behaviour. One simple example will suffice: a supervisor stated on a report form that one of his subordinates was going through a difficult patch because his wife had recently left him and he had not had time to recover from the emotional upset that this had caused. In a later interview, the subject of this report revealed that the cause of his apparent worry was the fact that his wife wished to return to him and he was not sure of his legal position in refusing to allow her back!

A common compromise between open and secret reports is a two-part report system with an appraisal interview between the completion of the two parts. One supervisor completes the first part of the form, which he has discussed with the subject of the report in order to ensure that it is as accurate as possible. This report then forms the basis of an appraisal interview with a more senior officer who may show the first part to the subject of the report or alternatively discuss the contents with him without actually showing him what has been written. The interviewing officer then completes the second part of the report, in which he applies his knowledge of the subject, the officer who completed part one and his own impressions of the subject gained during the appraisal interview. More senior officers may review both parts of the form and possibly conduct further interviews, either on an exception basis when a report is particularly good or bad or when the subject of the report asks for an interview.

A Scottish view

Of considerable interest, particularly for the succinct way in which the various arguments were mustered, is a report prepared by a committee on behalf of the Police Advisory Board for Scotland (Scottish Home Department, 1971).

The Committee identified the "main objectives underlying any system of staff appraisal" as:

(*a*) to identify the various abilities and training needs of officers in order to plan individual careers in such a way that their special skills and talents are used to increase both job satisfaction and the overall efficiency of the organisation;

(*b*) to employ officers on duties at which they are most proficient so that the contribution to the overall efficiency of a force is realised to the fullest extent;

(*c*) to identify officers suitable for promotion, including young officers worthy of early advancement; and

(*d*) to improve communication between ranks in the police service.

The system that was advocated followed fairly conventional lines in that an annual report prepared by an officer's immediate supervisor would be the subject of a counselling interview by a senior officer. Probationer constables and cadets were to be the subject of more frequent reports.

An interesting proposal was the recommendation that personnel panels be used to oversee the working of the appraisal system and to ensure that recommendations contained in individual reports were followed up. Composed of the most senior officers in the force, this panel (or, in a large force, panels) would also help to standardise assessments and make recommendations as to promotions. It was felt that the use of such a panel would obviate the general need for interviews to select people for promotion.

The issue of confidentiality, as might be expected with a working party containing representatives of the various ranks in the service as well as non-police advisers, found the members divided. The arguments may be summarised as follows:

1. *Against showing officers their reports:*
   (a) Some officers might become demoralised by the harsh truths about their ability.
   (b) The frankness of appraising officers might be inhibited.
   (c) There is little merit in a system that places emphasis on an officer's unsuitability for promotion or more responsible duties, when the officer may be perfectly content at his present level and have no aspirations beyond it.
   (d) A bad worker might make even less effort.
   (e) Misgivings about an officer's suitability on non-operational grounds might be omitted from reports unless there is evidence to substantiate them.

2. *Against* NOT *showing officers their reports:*
   (a) It prevents the system being manifestly fair and open.
   (b) Appraising officers might imply informally that they are satisfied with an officer yet criticise him on the form.
   (c) It might erect a barrier to the complete and ready acceptance of staff appraisal by many officers in the service.

The working party concluded that "we agreed on balance that meantime officers should not see their own forms but that police associations should ascertain the attitude of their members at all levels with a view to reconsidering the decision after the system had been working for a time". At the same time, the view was expressed that the counselling sessions (another term for appraisal interviews used elsewhere in this book) would cover any extreme or otherwise surprising ratings.

This conclusion, which was clearly a compromise decision, does serve to reinforce the need for any appraisal system to have the acceptance, co-operation and goodwill of everyone in the organisation, appraised and appraisors alike.

It was such a need that resulted in one force changing from the national scheme which was adopted by the eight Scottish police forces following the working party recommendations. In 1976, the Northern Constabulary opted for a local appraisal system which allowed officers to see their assessments and provided them with the opportunity to register their own level of job satisfaction.

A supervisor's report

In a periodic report, the supervisor is trying to make a judgment about a man based upon his performance during the period under consideration. It is important that he remembers this, as there is a tendency for items to be carried forward from previous periods. Whilst it is desirable to set objectives in one year and to comment the following year on the extent to which the subject of the report has fulfilled those objectives, the impression must not be given that a man is never allowed to live down a mistake that he has made or that his whole performance is assessed against a continuous background of past criticisms. The first part of the report to be completed by the supervisor should give some indication of the work that the man has been doing, should recognise what has been done well and comment upon those aspects that have been done less well.

In a form which is to be read by the subject, care must be taken not to include things which are likely to harm him by telling him that there is something wrong with him that he cannot cure. Thus, to write that the man is of limited intelligence or that he is too short to be able to make a good impression in uniform, is both unhelpful and hurtful. The report should be factual, identifying strengths and weaknesses that have been observed and which the man can do something about. If there has been some discussion between the officer writing the report and the subject of it, about some job preference of the latter, then mention can be made in the report together with any recommendations from the supervisor. The supervisor may also identify training needs and these should be communicated to the subject of the report so that he is aware of why he is being recommended for a particular form of training.

The reviewer's report

After an appraisal interview, to be discussed in the next chapter, the senior officer should add any remarks which are necessary to counter-balance the standards applied by the reporting officer, as well as assessments which will be of help in making decisions about the deployment of the individual concerned. It is normally at this stage that an attempt is made to assess the promotional, or other, potential, a judgment that can only be made on the basis of what he has done, how well he has done it, the personal qualities that he has displayed, the rate at which he has been able to learn new tasks and the flexibility with which he has been able to adapt to new situations.

Accurate assessment

It is all too easy to over-generalise and to form an opinion of an individual based on subjective likes and dislikes. To make an accurate assessment, a supervisor needs to gather as much evidence as he can, to put all that he has learnt into a proper perspective and then to decide on the weight that he can give to the various parts of the evidence at his disposal. Research into the factors which make it difficult for all of us to make a balanced judgment about an individual has identified a number of barriers that must be overcome by any assessor if he is to achieve a reasonably objective assessment.

The "halo" effect

The "halo" effect results when an individual has created a favourable impression upon his supervisor which can be based on one incident or one particular aspect of the individual's work. The result is that this favourable impression will often cause the supervisor to give a higher assessment for all the qualities upon which he reports. An unfavourable impression causes a similar phenomenon but causes lower assessments instead of higher.

To avoid this effect, a supervisor should attempt to ignore his general impression of a man and concentrate on identifying the evidence that he has about each individual characteristic upon which he is called to report. Only by doing this will he produce an objective report and identify areas where he should be giving a little extra training or supervision.

Varying standards

The familiar problem of the different standards set by different supervisors is a difficult one to counter. It causes greatest difficulty when the assessment of one supervisor has to be balanced with those of others. For example, if the officer in charge of one police station sets very high standards for his men and the officer in charge of another station sets very low standards, the men at one station may be discriminated against in comparison with the others. To some extent each senior officer completing part of a report form can balance his junior supervisors' report against one another, so removing the problem from one level and placing it higher, so that it finally becomes a matter of balancing the standards applied by individual senior officers when the reports are collated at headquarters. It should be remembered that this is not merely a matter of overall standards, but one of different values being applied to different characteristics which are being assessed. Therefore, the only thorough-going remedy that can be applied is one which attempts to provide a common standard throughout the organisation for each characteristic which is being reported upon. One approach that has been made to this problem is to use gradings on a scale and to train supervisors in the use of the normal distribution curve, to aid them in deciding on gradings.

The way in which all human attributes are distributed amongst the population falls into a standard pattern irrespective of the attribute that is being measured, for example, height, weight, intelligence or ability to perform a given task. The pattern shown in Fig. 15 is a simplified form of the normal distribution curve or bell curve.

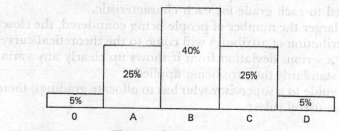

Fig. 15—Characteristic chart.

Many organisations use a five-point scale for indicating personal attributes. These may be indicated by letters or ticks in boxes or on scales, but the theory is similar: there is an "average" position, with two grades above it and two below it. Some forces use the letter B to indicate the average position, and O and A for the higher grades with C and D as the lower ones. The proportion of people in the various grades are approximately:

B = 40 per cent, A and C = 25 per cent, O and D = 5 per cent, as shown in Fig. 15. This indicates that, considering each individual characteristic for each man in the force, the distribution of grades should identify the 5 per cent of the very best, the 5 per cent of the very worst and the higher proportions of the average and just above and below average.

Whilst it does *not* follow that of the twenty men in one unit there must be one in grade D for each characteristic, it does mean that taking the large number of people in the whole force for any one characteristic, there should be about 5 per cent who are rated as grade D. To take a simple but non-measurable characteristic—smartness of appearance—there will be about 40 per cent of the force who can be described as of average appearance, there will be about 25 per cent who are somewhat below that standard and 5 per cent who are untidy. The standard of "untidiness" may not be very low, by the standards of other organisations they may be very smart: we are not talking of an absolute measure but of relative standards. This is what is so often forgotten. All reports in which there is no way of measuring a factor in absolute terms must be done by comparison—we compare the good with the less good. If supervisors are fully aware of the way in which attributes are distributed, they have some guidance as to the proportion of their men that should be allocated to each grade for each characteristic.

The larger the number of people being considered, the closer the distribution of attributes will come to the theoretical curve, so that a serious deviation from it shows up clearly any variation in standards that are being applied.

As a guide to a supervisor who has to allocate gradings, there are some useful rules:

1. Remember that each attribute, be it skill or personal quality, must be considered separately.
2. Many people believe that the best way to scale subordinates is to take the best and the worst and fit the remainder between these two extremes. This is only valid if a group is to be considered completely in isolation. Because there are relatively few really good men, it is very likely that in two similar groups of, say, ten men, the best in one group will be much better than the best in the other and so the two groups

cannot be properly evaluated against one another in this way.

3. A good method is to consider the "average" men. In any group of ten men, selected randomly, there will be four or five who *in any one respect* are difficult to distinguish from one another. If we call these "average" in that respect, the remaining members of the group of ten will take up grading on either side of "average" and it should not be too difficult to determine whether it should be one or two gradings in each case.

4. Groups, whose constituents were chosen randomly, differ mainly in the number and quality of the few exceptional people (good and bad) there are in each group and not in the inherent capacity of the bulk of the people.

Interpretation of terms

All assessment forms rely on words to try to define the particular quality that the assessor should grade. Comparison between assessors can show marked contrasts, particularly in assessing such qualities as confidence and leadership. What is seen by one assessor as being "very confident" (good), is seen by another assessor to be "over-confident" (bad). Similarly with leadership, one assessor may give a man a high grading for leadership on the grounds that he displayed a great deal of decisiveness, when another assessor may rate him very poorly on the grounds that he considered the man to be overbearing.

To overcome this sort of difficulty, some assessment forms may use "tendencies to X or Y" where X and Y are extreme forms of behaviour or extreme characteristics. This method does not eliminate the semantic problem, nor does it aid in the establishment of standards, both faults which it shares with another common type of form which provides boxes against a series of definite statements. Such forms also may require a good deal of paper to convey a small amount of information and, if not properly designed, encourage supervisors to insert ticks mechanically without adequate thought.

A further disadvantage of all systems that require a phrase to be selected from a number of alternatives is that it sometimes happens that none of them applies to that characteristic of that particular man. To overcome this, it is always necessary to

I

provide the opportunity for the assessor to qualify his assessment where necessary.

The use of assessment data

Information gathered about each member of the organisation as to his work, personal attributes, needs in terms of training and welfare and potential for promotion or specialism, must be vetted and then stored in a form in which proper use can be made of it.

The vetting process is necessary to detect:

1. reports that contain some element that needs further exploration. Hints as to welfare problems that have not been followed up, discrepancies between various parts of the report, unexplained gaps in the information provided—all require some further inquiry;
2. cases that require immediate action to solve problems that have already been identified by divisional/departmental supervisors but not resolved;
3. the need to register future steps that have to be taken such as transfers to be arranged, house moves to offer and courses booked;
4. reports that should be referred to a chief officer because they contain some abnormal feature that may require action or about which he should be informed.

Once the vetting has been done, the problem of storage and retrieval must be faced. For large organisations, a properly-prepared computer program may be necessary. A smaller force can use a less sophisticated manual index, which can be kept to record promotion and specialist potential in terms of courses and special skills. It must be designed with care, for it can be very time consuming to keep up to date; accuracy is of paramount importance in all such records.

Chapter Thirteen

Personnel interviews

The scope of personnel interviews

Most people think of personnel interviews as being formal occasions during which the interviewer and interviewee sit on opposite sides of a desk. This concept of the use of interviews and interview techniques is much too narrow. The important thing is that the interview should be conducted somewhere where it will not be overheard and will be free from interruptions. In many cases there is a good argument for not having too formal a setting. For convenience, personnel interviews can be divided into four categories dependent upon the objectives of the interviewer. In an *assessment interview*, the interviewer is trying to learn something of the man to supplement the information obtained in other ways. This is an important step in any appraisal system, for unless the officer who is completing the personal report is prepared to check his information against the man, he is likely to make some serious errors in his assessment. *Appraisal interviews* form an integral part of most personal-report systems, for they provide the opportunity for a second party to measure a personal report against the subject of that report. Not only does this provide a safeguard against bias in a supervisor, but also an opportunity for the interviewee to put forward his own doubts, beliefs, fears and ambitions, so that some notice may be taken of them. *Selection interviews*, although often criticised, still play a vital part in recruiting, in the selection of specialists and in promotion systems. The last category, *problem-solving interviews*, tend to be less formal and may arise separately or out of one of the other types of interviews. Supervisors often find themselves in a situation where a subordinate is attempting to seek help in solving a personal problem.

General principles of interviewing
A number of guidelines, some obvious, some less so, are applicable to most interview situations.

Preparation
Many interviewers start an interview on the wrong foot by not having prepared for the interview. This can take drastic forms with an interviewer who has been caught by surprise and so spends the first few minutes of the interview trying to find out who he is interviewing and why. Some interviewers fail to determine the true purpose of the interview which they are about to conduct. For example, formal appraisal interviews become such a matter of routine that senior officers conducting them are tempted merely to glance at the reports on the interviewee shortly before the interview is to take place. But unless an interviewer has analysed the contents of the reports and has set himself objectives, it is unlikely that the interview will accomplish very much. The interviewer needs to determine carefully what part of the behaviour pattern of the interviewee he wishes to explore and then structure part of the interview to achieve this aim.

Throughout this chapter on interviewing the need for *rapport* between the interviewer and the interviewee will be emphasised. It is doubtful if there is anything more calculated to damage an interview than the interviewer finding that he does not have all the necessary facts at his disposal. This is particularly important if the interviewer intends to criticise the interviewee. It is inevitable that the interviewee will wish to defend himself and, unless the interviewer has sufficient background information to be able to justify what he is saying, he may well find himself on the defensive and seeking to justify the criticism. If the interviewer wishes to give the impression, as many do, that he takes a personal interest in all his subordinates, he would also do well to make sure that he has his facts right.

Interview guide
Although it is unwise for an interviewer to stick to a set plan, it is useful to have some sort of flexible scheme that he can put into operation rather than to rely on the inspiration of the

moment. Some interviewees are notoriously uncommunicative and, in the absence of some approach, thought out before hand, the inexperienced interviewer may well find himself subjected to an embarrassing silence.

The best course for an interviewer to take, particularly when faced with an unusual or potentially difficult interview, is to prepare some form of interview guide. This may be no more than a mental approach thought out some time before the interview but, in a really difficult case, it might be a written set of headings to keep the interview on the right lines.

Notifying the interviewee

Many senior officers are unaware of the *angst* and foreboding that they can cause a subordinate by warning him of an interview without giving him some idea of why he is to be seen. There is a tendency for some people in senior positions to fail to recognise the power which they are believed to wield over the lives of other people. Human nature being what it is, most people, when warned for such an interview, as a matter of course assume the worst. It is, therefore, not surprising that they arrive for the interview in a state of nervous tension. Nor should it be assumed that a man has a guilty conscience because he takes such a pessimistic view of being summoned for an interview; most of us look at our car speedometers when we observe a police car in our mirror, even though we know we are driving within the speed limit.

Care should be taken to ensure that the timing of the interview is appropriate and adequate notice is given. To be interviewed without warning, when he has just completed a tour of duty, is not calculated to put a man in a frame of mind that will enable him to give of his best. Apart from the sheer inconvenience that such sudden requests can cause, most men like to feel that they are able to give a good account of themselves and some are ill-at-ease in an interview, simply because they feel ill-prepared, perhaps their shoes are not clean or their appearance reflects the fact that they have just completed a day's work. The fact that the interviewer is prepared to make allowances for this in judging the man is not relevant, it is how the interviewee *feels* that determines how he reacts during the interview. The timing of the interview should also be convenient for the interviewer, for one of the most inhibiting actions on his part is to look continually at his watch or at the clock, or to give the impression in any other way that he is in a hurry to get the interview over. The effect is to make the interviewee feel guilty about saying anything at all and so he may decide not to mention something of crucial interest to both parties.

The setting
No interview can succeed if it is constantly interrupted by telephone calls or knocks on the door. If the telephone rings during an interview, inevitably the interviewer will answer it and this then raises the problem for the interviewee of whether he should sit still or leave the room. In either case, the continuity of the interview has been broken and the train of thought of both participants interrupted. It is very difficult for operational police officers to insulate themselves from incoming calls in their own office and for this reason it is often better that interviews should be conducted in a neutral room.

The seating arrangements can make a lot of difference to the style of an interview. The traditional setting of a chair on its own in the middle of the room facing the desk behind which the interviewer sits, makes for a formal interview. Two chairs at angles with no table directly between them may help to create a more informal setting. This is not something that can be taken too far, since the real tone of an interview is determined by the status of the participants, the subject matter of the interview and the way in which the interview is conducted. Nevertheless, all other things being equal, the way in which people sit relative to one another can help a little. It goes without saying that common courtesies are also necessary, being interviewed with the sun shining in your eyes is distinctly reminiscent of being interrogated without benefit of Judges' Rules.

Opening the interview
Unless the interview is being conducted purely to admonish the interviewee, the interviewer should open in such a way that the interviewee is placed at sufficient ease for him to be able to think and speak naturally. Telling a man to relax is useless. It is the environment in which the interview is conducted and the attitude of the interviewer that determines whether an inter-

viewee will be able to relax or not. Some people are relatively at home in an interview—they are good self-salesmen— others are reticent and ill-at-ease and thus present a challenge to any interviewer. The difficulty of early questions should also be tailored to this introductory process. It is quite easy for an interviewer to floor an interviewee by firing a difficult question at him before he has had time to adjust himself to his surroundings and start thinking naturally. To do this accomplishes nothing other than to ensure that the interview will get off to a bad start from which it may not recover. A large number of selection interviews are marred by the way in which they are opened.

Asking questions

The style of questions is important. To ask direct questions is legitimate when seeking to verify factual information, but even here it is better not to ask questions in such a way that the interviewee can answer "yes" or "no". For example, to say: "I see that you have been a sergeant at . . .", achieves very little. When asking a more general question, the interviewer should avoid telegraphing the answer that he expects by the way in which he phrases the question. To start a question: "I have often thought . . ." and to finish it with ". . . what do you think?" seriously cuts down the options of the man who must answer it. Questions should be fairly stated and should not be too lengthy, nor should more than one question be asked at a time. A good, general rule is that the interviewee should not have to work out just what question he is being asked.

The actual rate of asking questions and their timing should be adjusted to suit each individual interviewee, but extremes of long pauses on the one hand and rapid-fire questions on the other should be avoided.

Listening

One of the most common failings in interviewers is to talk too much. In a personnel interview, the object must be to let the interviewee talk and the role of the interviewer should be to ensure that what is being said is of some value. Recordings of even experienced interviewers in action often reveal that the interviewer is using the opportunity created by an interview to put forward his own views on particular topics. Some have their own particular hobby horses that reappear at intervals throughout a series of interviews.

The purpose of the interview is to find out something about the interviewee and therefore one must listen to what he says and equally for what he does not say. Interviewers should always be alert to detect significant pauses or hesitations; these can sometimes indicate that the interview is close to some topic about which the interviewee has doubts or reservations, or which he simply does not wish to discuss. By careful probing, or by the use of non-directive techniques as described later for "problem-solving interviews", it should be possible to establish whether there are underlying feelings in the interview that should be brought into the open. A cautionary note should be sounded here: there is a limit to which an interviewer should probe into the private areas of a man's life. Care must always be taken not to intrude into private areas in which the interviewer has no business.

At some stage in the interview it is sometimes helpful to clarify the situation by summarising what has been said to ensure that the interviewer and interviewee have the same understanding of what has taken place. This may have the value of making the interviewee realise that he has been mis-understood and give him the opportunity to correct the impression that he may have made. Equally, he may realise that the interviewer *has* correctly understood what he was trying to say and this may provide reassurance and so encourage him to respond more favourably to the interviewer.

Controlling the interview

So far, most of the guidance that has been given has been directed towards the problems associated with nervous inter-viewees and it is true that the most common problem by far for police supervisors when conducting personnel interviews is to establish *rapport* with a tense and nervous interviewee. However, it must not be assumed that this is true of everyone. Some people react very well in an interview situation and may even take over the interview completely if not controlled. Such con-trol is essential if the interview is to tell the interviewer anything about the individual other than the fact that he is extremely good at being interviewed. With a nervous subject, an interviewer must apply his skills to act as an accelerator; with an over-confident one, he acts as a brake at appropriate times. Care must be taken to distinguish between a nervous man whose reaction is to talk too much and often too quickly and a truly confident one, who talks freely but with complete control.

Taking notes

In many ways it is best not to take notes at all if it can be avoided but in long interviews many interviewers find it necessary to make some form of note that will enable them to recall significant moments during interviews after they are over. The important thing to remember is not to write at a time when the interviewee is on the defensive, is being criticised, or is admitting faults or errors as this will focus his attention too much on that particular aspect of the interview and may prevent anything more constructive from emerging.

Concluding the interview

At the end of the interview, the interviewee must leave with the feeling that he has had the opportunity to say what he wishes to say and that he is being fairly treated. Unfortunately, the stock question that is often asked at the end of the interview ("Is there anything else you would like to say?") is seen by many interviewees as being something of a trap, so care must be taken not to give this impression when rounding off the interview. When the interview is over, the interviewer should quickly make notes about the important features that have emerged as memories are often not up to the task of recalling these after quite a short interval of time. Finally, he should draw his conclusions from what has transpired and bearing in mind the objectives with which he started.

Non-verbal communication

Before considering individual types of interview, there is one further subject of general application that has particular relevance to interviewing although it is also a part of normal social life. That is the range of information that people communicate to one another without the use of speech. Anyone who has ever seen a silent movie will be aware of the breadth of emotions that can be communicated in this way but the method of acting used for silent films was largely an exaggeration of the way in which people use their heads, eyes and hands in normal conversation.

In every-day life we supplement our speech with signals that amplify or qualify what we say. Thus, we frown to show displeasure; we smile to show pleasure; we shrug our shoulders to show bewilderment, and so on. The raising of an eyebrow, a twist of the mouth, a sharp exhaling of breath, can all convey a wealth of meaning to the person sitting opposite us. An interviewer must be conscious of what he is communicating silently to the interviewee sitting opposite him and the interviewee, in his turn, in communicating to the interviewer. If we wish to encourage someone, we tend to lean forward, to smile, to adopt a certain tone of voice and to look at them. If an interviewer, on the other hand, wishes to establish a more superior or dominant relationship, he leans and tilts his head back, adopts a different tone of voice and regards the interviewee with a straight face. The interviewee will quickly react to signals communicated to him; a friendly approach will tend to encourage the confident interviewee to become over-confident. To encourage an interviewee to continue speaking an occasional nod indicates to him "go on". If the interviewer looks down on to the table and possibly shuffles papers or appears to be reading, the interviewee will be discouraged from talking. Frowns meaning "Are you sure?" or "I don't understand?" are all part of an interviewer's technique. Noises like "uhuh" act in much the same way, creating either confidence or doubt in the interviewee's mind, depending on the tone of voice used.

In the same way the interviewee communicates with the interviewer. He may nod to indicate that he has understood a question or incline his head or open his eyes wide to indicate that he has not understood. All such signals whether given by the interviewer or interviewee are part of communication in every-day life and as such deserve attention in the same way as utterance of words conveying the same meaning would be listened to. Only when interviewers are shown video-tapes of themselves leaning back in their chairs staring vacantly into space, do they realise why they failed to generate any enthusiasm in an interviewee. In the same way, interviewees are often surprised to see images of themselves apparently looking sky-wards for heavenly intervention or looking past the interviewer out of the window and then realise why they have lacked success at interviews in the past.

Selection interviews

Limitations

The use of interviews to select people for jobs or promotion is very widespread but there is a good deal of evidence to suggest that selection interviews are often neither reliable nor accurate. They are not reliable in the sense that different interviewers often give widely-different assessments of the same people. There are a number of reasons for this but the most obvious are differing reactions between interviewer and interviewee and the different standards that interviewers may apply. The second of these has already been mentioned in Chapter 12, for the problem of different standards and biases being applied by assessors is not, of course, confined to selection interviews. The differing reaction between an interviewee and different inter-viewers is merely an extension of the obvious social pheno-menon that a person may hit it off with one individual but not with another. In the same way that we may, or may not, take to the person with whom we share an office, so in an interview situation the interviewer and the interviewee may find them-selves mutually antipathetic.

Selection interviews are often not accurate in that the right people are not always selected. The ability to select the right people, as shown by their subsequent performance, varies con-siderably from interviewer to interviewer. Some are very good, but some are so bad that it would be as accurate to pick people by tossing coins. Fortunately, many people can be helped to become more competent interviewers by proper training and by paying proper regard to the weakness of the interview as a selection medium. When conducting a selection interview one has to be fully conscious of how one is reacting to the inter-viewee and to give proper weight to the other evidence avail-able in relation to the interview itself.

Setting standards

If a selector is to stand any chance of choosing the right people for the right job, he must know exactly what he is looking for. Each job must be carefully analysed in order to make objective assessments of the qualities, skills, experience and qualifications required of the person who is to be selected. It is only when this has been done that the selector can set an order of priorities that will enable him to distinguish between those qualities which are essential, those that are important and those that are merely desirable in a successful candidate. Too often a selector goes into the selection procedure with the image of a stereotype in his mind against which he measures each candidate. Sometimes the stereotype is modelled on the selector, when he was at a comparable stage of his development. Equally dangerous are generalisations based on "he reminds me of so-and-so" as a basis for a judgment.

It is rare for the perfect candidate to be available; inevitably, some form of compromise is required and it is the skill with which a compromise is achieved that determines the success of the interviewer. Inevitably, all candidates will have strengths and weaknesses and in some cases the weaknesses may disqualify them. However, there is usually a possibility that the weaknesses may be counter-balanced by strengths and it becomes a matter of fine judgment as to which candidate has the better claim. Finally, a good job description helps to identify the qualities that can be assessed in an interview situation and those that cannot. For evidence of such qualities as reliability and integrity, one must supplement impressions that can be obtained from an interview. A study of the candidate's previous history will help to reveal some indication of these. Verbal ability and technical knowledge are much easier to assess, although in the case of the former, as with many other qualities that can be assessed in an interview situation, it has to be remembered that the interviewer sees these displayed in a particular and atypical situation.

Selection interview procedure
The general rules for interviewers which were itemised on p. 248 above apply to selection interviews, but because such interviews are a standard method of selecting people, there tends to be a set of expectations in both interviewer and interviewee that help to formalise the selection interview. The following

notes are not intended to act as a rigid pattern but merely to give some guidance in the way a selection interview may be conducted.

Preparation
Before the candidate enters the room, the interviewer should familiarise himself with all the previous documentary material that is available so that it is not necessary for him to refer continually to documents during the interview. It is useful at this stage to note any particular aspects of the candidate's past which are worth bringing out specifically in the interview. Some general information about the candidate should not be taken too much for granted; for example, educational qualifications should be related to the age at which they were gained and any factors such as an education interrupted by frequent moves from school to school or continuous attendance at an academically-poor school. Academic qualifications must also be scrutinised to see how much they tell the interviewer about the intellectual capacity of the candidate, as distinct from his willingness to undertake a course of study with sufficient enthusiasm to pass examinations.

Opening the interview
When the candidate and interviewer are brought together, time must be allowed for settling down. The interviewer should start by asking straightforward questions that he is sure that the candidate can answer. For example, by picking something interesting from his background upon which he can enlarge, i.e. a piece of work that he has just been engaged upon, a commendation or a feature of his schooling. At this stage of the interview, the principal object is to get him to talk and to relax enough to behave reasonably naturally.

Previous experience
Having established some form of *rapport* with the interviewee, the interviewer may now move on to more specific questions, aimed at the areas which are of principal interest, initially perhaps the person's experience. In examining a person's background, it is always important to look at the context in which things happen. For example, it is often of interest to discover

the extent to which he has determined the way that his own career should go by volunteering to widen his experience, as distinct from going where he was directed. Trying to gauge attitudes in an interview can be difficult. A few candidates can be rated as professional interviewees and are accomplished at giving the answer they think the interviewer wishes them to give. When dealing with this type of candidate, it is more important than usual that the interviewer should not communicate his own feelings to the candidate and so should ask open-ended questions that give no clue as to his own views on the matter.

Probing

Whilst an interviewer should not become hostile towards an interviewee, he should try to probe where it is necessary to ensure that he is not being misled. The line between selling oneself to the interviewer and misleading him is a fine one. To quote the old law on selling: "puffing" is permitted but lies are not. As with advertising a commercial product, the candidate is entitled to paint as good a picture of the product, that is to say himself, as he is able; but, on the other hand, he must not tell untruths in order to do so. For example, if an interviewer wishes to find out something about the general interest of the candidate he may well ask him about his reading habits, what he does with his spare time and his hobbies. It is often worth probing at least one of these in order to ensure that the candidate is not merely claiming that he does something for the sake of effect. This probing should not be unduly lengthy; it is often sufficient, if a man claims that he reads a particular type of book, to ask him how many such books he has read, when he last read one, and what he is reading now and, if possible, to ask him just a little about the book that he is currently reading.

When exploring what a candidate has done in the past, it is always worth finding out the actual part he played in any given experience which he claims to have had. In many cases people fall into the habit of using the word "we" when talking about some experience they have had. This is sometimes merely due to modesty and it is used as an alternative to "I", while other candidates may use "we" literally meaning that they had this experience as part of a team. In such a case it is useful to find out if the candidate was a leader of that team, the extent to which he contributed to the ideas that resulted in some new procedure, the actual role that he played in a joint commendation, and so on. Such questioning is legitimate and need not be carried out in hostile fashion. If a candidate is suspected of exaggeration, it is much better to ask detailed questions so that he reveals the extent of his exaggeration, rather than to say to him, in a disbelieving tone of voice, "are you trying to tell me that . . . ?"

Asking questions

The extent to which an interviewer should pursue a particular topic depends on the purpose of the questions. If he is seeking to find the extent of the candidate's knowledge on a particular topic, pursuing it at length may be necessary. In many cases such questions are merely to provide a topic about which a candidate can talk, the object of the exercise being to listen to him take a subject, analyse it, put forward arguments and finally draw some conclusions. The actual level of his knowledge about a particular subject is of secondary importance. It is all a matter of *why* the questioner takes a particular line of questioning.

General-knowledge questions

There are many reasons why one asks a candidate about a general-interest topic and not particularly related to the job he is being selected to do. One is that the interviewer may wish to obtain some measure of the intellectual capacity of the candidate. Another may be that he wishes to find out how well-read the candidate is by asking him about world or local affairs. On a controversial topic, the interviewer may wish to find out the candidate's views and so form a measure of his approach to a particular type of situation. All of these are genuine reasons for asking general questions and, provided the interviewer has clear reasons for asking such questions, he will learn a great deal about the candidate. What he should not do is to enter into an argument, the object of which is to convert the candidate to his own way of thinking on a controversial issue; otherwise much time will be wasted and the whole tenor of the interview will be upset. The hypothetical question in which the interviewer asks the candidate to imagine himself in a particular situation and then tell the interviewer what he would do about it should be avoided. In selection interviews for promotion to sergeant, for example, it is quite common to ask a candidate what he would do if he found himself in a situation which clearly called for some form of disciplinary action. The candidate can only resort to giving a stock answer which he thinks will please the interviewer. It then becomes a matter of whether the interviewer believes him or not and, as he has no evidence on which to base a judgment one way or the other, the question is unsatisfactory. The best guide as to how a man will react in a given situation is how he has reacted in similar situations in the past and, therefore, it is to what the man has done that the interviewer should direct his attention and not to what he says he might do.

Selection boards

Selection boards consisting of three or four interviewers are often used in an attempt to overcome the bias of a single interviewer and to guard against the clash of personalities that can arise in a one-to-one interview. To some extent, the use of a properly trained board of assessors may reduce some of the imperfections of selection interviews but, as with individual interviews, the interviewers must be aware of the limitations of the medium and correctly balance a man's performance before the board with all the other evidence available. A selection board often presents a formidable obstacle for an interviewee. It is extremely difficult to obtain the same affinity between interviewers and interviewees in the formal setting of a selection board and the change from member to member means that the flow is being constantly interrupted.

Allocating areas of inquiry

Prior to the interviews, the members of the board must agree amongst themselves as to what the board is looking for. Whilst this step is necessary for an individual interviewer, it is essential for a board as, unless objectives are discussed, there will be confusion when the time comes to make a decision at the end of the interview session. It is also necessary to ensure that each member of the board has a clearly defined area of inquiry to avoid asking the same questions. It is all too easy for a member of an interview board to allow his attention to be distracted for a moment and miss a question that one of his colleagues has asked; if he then repeats the question he places the interviewee in the difficult position of not knowing whether to remind the interviewer that he has already answered the question or whether he should try to answer the question in slightly different terms to the answer he gave previously. In either case it detracts from the credibility of the interviewer.

The composition of the board

No hard and fast rule can be laid down for the size of a selection board but experience suggests that three selectors provide the best balance between the requirement for a multiple view of each candidate and the need to provide each interviewer with sufficient time to go into his area of inquiry with enough depth. The division of responsibilities may vary, but a suitable scheme might be as follows:

1. *Chairman.* The chairman should open the interview in such a way that the candidate is allowed to acclimatise himself to his surroundings. Questions about his past are a good opener but they should be asked in a general way to avoid one-word answers. They should be directed only in relation to the need to clarify ambiguities or to seek an expression of opinion as to their value as experience in life.

2. *Second member.* The next questioner could concentrate on following up the previous experience of the candidate, relevant to the job for which he is being considered. In the case of a police officer, his supervisors' reports should provide some indication of his professional expertise so that it can be explored in an interview. Questions can be asked to see the extent to which he is aware of what is happening in the professional sense outside his own immediate surroundings and the extent to which he has kept himself up to date—or at any rate the extent to which he has prepared for the board! The rule as to hypothetical questions is important when testing his level of professional competence, it is better to ask him what he has done, how and why, rather than "What would you do if . . . ?"

3. *Third member.* In most cases, it is desirable to find out something about the general interests of the candidate, his involvement with other people and the extent to which he balances his working life with his domestic and social commitments. General questions may be asked to form some idea of how he sees the world about him other than in a professional sense, to form some idea of his prejudices, biases and beliefs. He could be made to discuss a topic in terms of its pros and cons to see if he is capable of a reasoned analysis, so that some indication of his intellectual capacity is revealed.

4. *Chairman.* The chairman should then round off the interview by clarifying doubtful issues and giving the man the opportunity to make any additional points that he feels would help his interests.

Rules for selection boards

The allocation of questions shown above can be no more than a general guide, but there are some basic rules that apply to most selection boards. The first is that interviewers should avoid intervening between their colleagues and the interviewee, otherwise the situation can become confused, the candidate is unsettled and may be seen to swing his head from one interviewer to the other, unsure who he is supposed to be answering.

One exception to this may be necessary should the chairman notice that a candidate is becoming unnecessarily distressed because of a lack of understanding between him and another board member. A tactful interjection may relieve tension and achieve a measure of clarity. A second rule is that the candidate must have been given the opportunity to show his qualities and this invariably means that he should have felt tested, but treated with courtesy and fairness. As has been emphasised elsewhere, there is no need to use hostile methods towards a candidate; acute but well-mannered probing will always achieve more than hectoring. The third rule applies when a person is being selected for entry into the organisation—the transaction is a two-way one. The object should be to decide whether the candidate is suitable and also to ensure that he knows enough about the organisation to be able to decide that he wishes to join it. Lastly, there is the time element. Most selection boards operate on a fixed length of time allocated for each candidate, which means that if one member of the board occupies more than his quota of his time with a given candidate, there is a tendency for his colleagues to find that they must cut their section of the interview short and thus some aspect of the candidate's make-up may not receive the attention that it should.

Weighing up the evidence

When the interview is over it is necessary for the interviewer or the board to come to a conclusion about the candidate. It is important that the candidate's performance in his interview should be properly balanced against his previous experience and the other evidence which is available. It has to be remembered that a selection interview is an artificial situation and what the interviewers have seen is not necessarily representative of the man under normal conditions. It is for this reason that many promotion selection boards have present a senior officer who knows the candidate but does not take part in the actual interviewing. He is present when the decision is made so that he can report on the performance that the man put before the interview board. It is an unfortunate fact that many people who are quite confident in normal life lose all their confidence in an interview. A good interview board will be able to encourage a nervous candidate and control an over-confident one, so that each emerges as closely as possible to his normal self but, however good the selector, he can never be wholly successful in this process and therefore it is unwise to generalise too much from what he has seen. For example, because an interviewee appeared nervous and unsure of himself on an interview, it does not follow that he has insufficient leadership ability to be able to take charge of a group of men under operational circumstances. This may be the case, of course, but equally it may be that under the conditions under which he found himself he suffered from a form of stage-fright.

First impressions

It is extremely important that assessors should avoid generalising from what they have seen and heard, and care must be taken not to be over-influenced by first impressions. Many people claim that they can assess a person as soon as they see them. Such people should not take part in selection interviews, for if they think they are able to make a decision by merely looking at a candidate, the selection interview becomes superfluous. Tests carried out at interviews indicate that interviewers who have not been properly trained tend to form a conclusion based on the initial impact that the candidate makes on them as soon as he starts to speak. The judgment that such interviewers make is based on his appearance, the way in which he walks into the room, how he sits in his chair, his speaking voice and his first observations to the interviewer. What subsequently happens is that the interviewer interprets the answers to questions in such a way that his initial judgment is backed up. The effect is that if an interviewer is asked to indicate the suitability or otherwise of a candidate after the latter has spoken his first sentence to the board, there is a very high probability that the interviewer will not change his mind and that this will still be his conclusion at the end of this interview.

This does not mean that the interviewer was right in his initial judgment. What it does mean is that the interviewer is not retaining his objectivity and is rendering the interview itself useless. The initial appearance of a candidate is of course important but care should be taken to apply the right tests when making a judgment. For example, the fact that the candidate for the police service is dressed in the latest fashion, whatever that happens to be, does not indicate frivolity of mind or that he would be unsuited to a uniformed service. It may indicate quite the contrary; for if a man is so proud of his appearance that he is prepared to buy new clothes to be fashionable, it is likely that he will be equally proud of his appearance when he dons a uniform. The appearance of a candidate must also be assessed against his background. A young man who attends an interview straight from work may be expected to have dirty fingernails if he is employed as a motor-mechanic.

When making a decision at the conclusion of a selection interview, final judgment should be based on the same sort of criteria that police officers apply when considering a difficult legal problem. The evidence is weighed against known requirements, ignoring as far as possible personal feeling, prejudices and sentiments.

Assessment interviews

What is meant by an assessment interview in this context is one that takes place between a subordinate and the supervisor who is responsible for monitoring his progress and preparing reports about him. The parties involved may be a probationer and his reporting sergeant, a constable and his inspector, or an inspector and his superintendent, the ranks involved depending on the type of personal-report system that is in use in the organisation. It is recognised that such interviews may not be formal affairs and, indeed, similar objectives may be obtained in the course of normal conversation between the two parties. However, the likelihood is that at some stage the supervisor will need to prepare a report about his subordinate and it is essential that there should be some discussion between them before the report is submitted.

Such a report is of cardinal importance to the individual who is being reported upon and it must be accurate. It is very unlikely that this condition will be fulfilled unless there is the opportunity to check the report against the individual. It is not just a matter of ensuring that factual information is correct. Most personal-report systems require the reporting officer to do more than just report the facts about an individual. He is required to make judgments about the person's work and personality, and also to identify objectives for the future, training needs and job preferences. Quite often he is also required to describe the person's involvement in social activities in and out of the service. It is extremely unlikely that any supervisor can provide such a wide range of information without an interview of some kind, however informal.

In addition to answering these questions, there are two other important requirements. First, there is the correct identification of outside factors that are affecting the individual at work. Secondly, any criticism that is going to be included in the report should already be known to its subject. No one should ever learn for the first time of criticisms of himself when he reads it, or it is read to him, at an appraisal interview. Nor should such criticisms be saved for an annual event in any case. If a man is seen to be doing wrong, he should be told at the time, so that he has the opportunity to correct what he is doing; it should not be deferred until it is time to prepare a report on him.

In addition to checking the subject matter of the report and all the factors surrounding it, a good supervisor will wish to use the opportunity to motivate his subordinate to improve his performance at work and to set himself challenging objectives that will give him a sense of purpose for the future.

Criticism

There are two basic assumptions inherent in most assessment systems. These are that people want to know where they stand and that they will improve if they are told of their weaknesses. Unfortunately, neither assumption is completely true. First, there is the small minority of people who simply do not wish to hear about themselves at all. Secondly, and by far the more numerous, there are the people who say that they want to be told where they stand but in fact want to be told of the good work that they have done and their strong points but do not want to be criticised.

There may be a number of reasons why a person does not improve his apparent weaknesses when these have been pointed out by a supervisor. One of the most common is that he does not agree that it is a weakness and so sees no reason why he should try to improve. The fact that a superior officer has told him that it is a weakness, even if this has been done in forceful terms, is no guarantee that a man will accept it. Quite often this is because the two have different standards and ideas as to what constitutes a good performance. For example, a traffic-oriented inspector may criticise one of his constables for failing to keep his eyes open for traffic offences. This criticism may not be acceptable to the constable if he sees his prime role as being to preserve good relationships with the local people in the area in which he works.

There is also a more obvious reason why a man may not improve a weakness and that is that he is unable to do so. It requires considerable skill on the part of a supervisor to know when a subordinate is at the limit of his capabilities. If this can be done, more will be achieved by encouraging him to retain this standard than by criticising him for not improving upon it when he cannot do so. In any case, such criticism tends to have an adverse effect. A man who is genuinely doing his best and who is still criticised for not doing better, may give up trying altogether.

In general, criticism is felt much more deeply than praise and if a subordinate is complimented on a number of good points but is criticised on only one, it is on the one weakness that he will concentrate in order to defend himself.

Constructive criticism
Supervisors should always try to ensure that when they do criticise a subordinate it is done in such a way that it evokes a positive response and not a negative one. Most people are willing to accept criticism if it is patently constructive, for if criticism is given in this way, the subordinate can see what he must do in order to avoid being criticised in future. Destructive criticism, given without an indication as to what positive steps should be taken by the person being criticised, is likely to evoke a negative response which may emerge as hostility or, even worse, apathy.

The relationship between the subordinate and the supervisor also affects the way in which criticism is likely to be accepted. If the person offering the criticism is known to be competent and to have the experience to be able to offer sound advice, he is likely to be listened to with respect. Few people like to be criticised by people they believe to be incompetent or uninformed.

Over-confidence
Although most people who are learning a new job are ready to accept criticism from supervisors and more experienced personnel, there are some who have such confidence in their own ability that they tend to spurn every effort to guide them. It comes back to the point mentioned earlier, that some people are not prepared to accept that they have weaknesses. If such a person can be encouraged to talk about the way in which he approaches his work, with patience and attentive listening, it may be possible to make him realise the weakness of what he himself is saying. Certainly, this is more likely to produce an improvement than to give him advice that one knows he will reject. Often the only alternative is to allow him to learn from

his own mistakes, but ensuring that his supervision is of such quality that the mistakes he makes do not cause too much harm to all concerned.

Reviewing performance
Where a man's performance is below standard, it is better to discuss it with him in terms of how he does his work rather than in terms of his personality. For example, if a man is inclined towards making naïve judgments, it is better to discuss the problem with him in terms of the need to make careful decisions rather than in terms of immaturity. Whereas he may see that he is being given good advice on decision-making, he is almost certain to defend himself against the accusation that he is immature. In any discussion about some aspect of his work, whether it be favourable or unfavourable, the subordinate can be more objective if the subject is presented as a problem to be solved rather than as a facet of his personality.

There is a general tendency to concentrate on people's weaknesses and how they can be corrected rather than to pay attention and take advantage of strengths. Provided that a weakness is not so marked as to amount to a disqualifying factor, more can often be done by way of utilising the strength of an individual than by attempting to correct his weaknesses. If a person has a particular aptitude and this can be built upon, not only will the service gain, but the man will also achieve greater job satisfaction.

Factors affecting work performance
Whenever a person is criticised in respect of his work, he should always be allowed to reply by offering an explanation. This is not just a matter of saving face, although that in itself is important. Many factors other than lack of knowledge, skill or application may contribute towards a man's poor work performance. Surprisingly, some supervisors are not prepared to allow people to defend themselves against criticism, as their defence may reflect upon the quality of supervision. A supervisor should always be prepared to accept the possibility that a person has not done a particular task well because he was inadequately briefed, or lacked the proper resources to do the job.

Whenever someone's performance at work is being discussed,

a supervising officer needs to listen for underlying factors of which he has no knowledge but of which he should be aware. Some people are only too ready to discuss their personal problems; they feel the need for sympathy and in this way may obtain it. Other people may be unwilling, or unable, to be so forthcoming, although their difficulties may be equally great. There is no hard and fast rule as to how far a supervisor should probe into the private life of his subordinate; each case must be taken on its merits. It is safe to say, however, that when a domestic problem seriously undermines a man's performance at work, a supervisor should try to be aware of its nature and extent. First, it will enable him to make due allowance when assessing the man and secondly, it may reveal a welfare problem.

A subordinate's health should also be taken into consideration when reviewing his performance. This is not just a question of physical health, although obviously this may affect the way in which work must be judged, but it must be borne in mind that it is possible for people to undergo periods of stress that can have a seriously debilitating effect upon mental health. Any abnormal behaviour or sudden change in behaviour pattern should be closely observed, as these are often the first clues to impending breakdown.

Improving work performance
There are at least four ways of improving people's work performance. It may be possible to change them through training, guidance or additional experience. Alternatively, the conditions under which they do their work may be changed so that better use is made of strengths. If it can be done, a man's work performance may be improved by transferring him to another job entirely, preferably one which takes full advantage of his abilities and will not be too seriously affected by his weaknesses. Yet another method of obtaining improvement is to change his supervisor's manner of supervision. Not all people react equally to the same style of supervision. Whereas some work well under an authoritarian leader, others react very unfavourably to such leadership. If a man who has hitherto produced a good work performance, but since a change in supervision now produces a poor one, it may be that neither the supervisor nor the man

himself is at fault—it is simply a reaction between the two that reflects adversely in the man's work.

Of the ways of improving a person's performance listed above, most supervisors aim at the first, i.e. changing the person. By taking the trouble to explore below the surface, they may find that one of the other alternatives will produce better results.

Appraisal interviews

Many modern personal-report systems consist of a report prepared by a supervisor who is in personal contact with the subject of the report, followed by an interview with a more senior officer, who uses the report as the basis for the interview. Such interviews are usually known as appraisal (or counselling) interviews and may have a number of objectives. They provide a safeguard against bias in the report which may be caused by a number of factors, including personal prejudices in the person completing it, and clashes of personality between him and the subject of the report. The interview also provides the senior officer conducting it with the opportunity to evaluate a man, to determine his attitudes and problems, to give him advice, praise and criticism and to let him know where he stands. A good interviewer may also seek to motivate the interviewee to improve his performance in the future. With such a wide variety of objectives, it is important that the interviewer should have a clear idea of how the interview is to be conducted, although it is unwise to adopt too rigid a plan of action.

Pre-interview checks

The interviewer should always check the report form that he intends to use as a basis of his interview before he starts the interview. This is particularly important if the report is to be shown to its subject. In most report systems of this nature, the type of information which should be contained in that part of the report which is read by the subject, is limited to those aspects of a man's behaviour that he can correct and should not contain hurtful comments about those aspects he cannot correct. The interviewer should also check the report to see what criticisms are being made of the subject of the interview, as it is almost certain that the interviewee will wish to take issue with at least some of them. The interviewer must be in possession of sufficient information to be able to cope with such defences by the interviewee or at least have considered how he is going to handle that aspect of the interview. In all appraisal interviews, whether part of the report is to be read by the interviewee or not, the interviewer should inform him of where he stands. This means that the interviewer must examine the reports to identify those parts which are critical and those in which the interviewee is given praise, so that due recognition can be given. Finally, the interviewer must ensure that he is clear in what he is trying to achieve in the coming interview. This may mean picking out certain aspects of the report on which he intends to concentrate in order to try to improve the man's performance. The amount of improvement that can be expected is limited and therefore it is best to concentrate on the most important aspects and try to achieve some improvement in these, rather than to try to obtain improvements on too many fronts and thus run the risk of achieving nothing.

The interview
In an appraisal interview, the interviewer is trying to check the report he has received against the person that it relates to and, as the report should be concerned with the work that the person has been doing, it is necessary that part of the interview should be devoted to that. By starting an interview with the opportunity for the interviewee to talk about things done well, a dialogue is developed out of which any weaknesses that the interviewee appears to have can be seen in perspective against his strengths. If at all possible, the interviewee should reveal his own weaknesses and recognise them as such, rather than have the interviewer identify them and put them to the interviewee. As has been said elsewhere, an individual will only correct faults if he acknowledges that he has them, so that if a senior officer tells him that he has failings, it may merely excite defence mechanisms and cause him to defend himself rather than admit that there are weaknesses which could be improved.

Not only is it desirable that the interviewee should reveal his own weaknesses, it is also best if he identifies for himself what he can do to improve them. Objectives a man sets for himself and which are acknowledged by a senior officer to be desirable, are more likely to be sought by the interviewee than those which have been pointed out and accepted reluctantly. It is helpful to try to find those parts of a person's job that he finds the most interesting and rewarding and those the least. This will help the senior officer to make recommendations as to future employment and will give some indication of potential. It may also help to identify those abilities which he feels are being under-utilised for, in general, it is in the best interests of both the individual and the organisation that the skills and abilities that a person possesses should be harnessed for their mutual benefit. The interviewee's self-evaluation should be checked against the evaluation contained in the report. If he has acknowledged that there are weaknesses that he can improve upon, the interviewer may well settle for those and remember that nothing will be gained by demoralising the interviewee, who may simply give up trying altogether.

Closing the interview

At some stage in the interview, the interviewee should be allowed to bring up any matters which are worrying him. The extent to which he reveals details of his personal life should be left to him and probing questions should not be asked about this, unless they have arisen in some way which is the direct concern of the interviewer. Most people like to keep their private lives to themselves. There is no reason why this should not be allowed and indeed encouraged, provided that a man's private life does not in some way adversely affect the service or his performance at work. There is no reason why a senior officer cannot express an interest in the man outside the context of work and, if he has established the right relationship between himself and his subordinates, he may be able to identify welfare problems which would otherwise be kept from him.

At the end of the interview, the interviewee should know where he stands and should leave feeling that he has gained from the interview. The interviewer should know more about the interviewee and be in a better position to make some judgments about him. In many report systems he is required to make an assessment of training needs, potential for promotion and possible deployment. As always in considering the results of an interview, the interviewer must make allowance for the conditions under which the interview was conducted. The same reaction cannot be expected from someone who has read a report about himself which is highly critical and someone who has read nothing but praise. As has been suggested elsewhere, criticism is only normally acceptable under certain conditions and the officer conducting the appraisal interview must ensure that those conditions were met if he is to form a proper judgment of the person's reaction. Interviewers should also remember that some people react very well to interviews and others do not. Some people enjoy the opportunity to spend an uninterrupted period with a senior officer when their work and career can be discussed in private. Others resent what they regard as an unnecessary and possibly embarrassing situation for, as was said earlier, the assumption that everyone wishes to be told how his performance at work has been assessed, is not always correct. There are people who would rather not know and these may react adversely to an interview. It is for this reason that some personal-report systems allow experienced personnel to have the option of deciding whether they will be subjected to a full appraisal or not.

Problem-solving interviews
There are a number of occasions on which the advice of supervisory officers is sought on problems outside the normal run of operational matters on which a supervisor should obviously give direct advice. Strictly speaking, personal problems are not the province of the supervisory officer at all, but he may wish to help him on welfare grounds. Often it is for the man himself to make a decision and what is really needed is someone to help him to analyse and solve his own problem. A useful method of conducting such interviews is to use the technique of listening rather than advising. This method is of particular value when dealing with subordinates who have problems they are unable to solve because their emotions have affected their objectivity. One reason why such an approach is preferable is that the senior officer may make the wrong diagnosis and give the wrong advice which, if it is followed, will cause distress to the person to whom it is given and embarrassment to the person who gave it. There is also a greater likelihood, if non-directive methods are used, of diagnosing the real problem and not just the symp-

toms. All policemen are aware when they deal with matri-
monial or domestic problems in the course of their work, that
the incident which caused the disturbance is often a trivial one
that has come at the end of a long and often bitter war of nerves.
In these circumstances, the officer listens patiently and tries to
find out what the real problem is, rather than accept the immediate causes which are offered in explanation by the parties
concerned. By making the individual think through the problem, it is often possible to get him to identify the root cause of
the trouble which may bear little relation to the original version.

Although people frequently ask for advice, they sometimes
reject it once it has been given because they want to be seen to
have an insoluble problem. Some people are merely seeking
someone to talk to for sympathy or to share the problem and
they will reject any attempt to solve it. The adoption of a
listening approach to such people usually reveals the true
nature of the problem, allows the individual the opportunity to
unburden himself and allows the listener the opportunity to
appear to be helping without actually offering advice—which
would not be taken in any case.

Active listening
The basis of non-directive interviewing is what can be termed
"active listening". The interviewer goes out of his way to
convey to the interviewee the fact that he is carefully listening
and if asked a direct question, he considers whether it is a
genuine request for information or advice based on experience.
If he is in doubt, he avoids giving a direct answer. Instead of
offering direct advice, he explores further by turning the question back on the interviewee, with a request to him that puts
him into the position of trying to answer the question himself.
The standard way of doing this is to use sentences such as
"would you like to tell me how you feel about it?", or "what do
you think?", or in some more subtle way getting him to give
his own ideas on the subject before the interviewer commits
himself. If this is done carefully, the interviewee may indicate
quite quickly by the answer that he gives that the question was
not a genuine one. He may not actually say, "well, personally,
I don't think there is an answer" but the fact that he thinks this
may emerge although expressed less explicitly. If it becomes

clear that it was a genuine request for information, then of course the interviewer may decide to answer the question directly, provided that he makes it clear that he is giving factual information and not telling the interviewee what he must do.

Acting as a reflector
Some people find it difficult to listen to what someone is saying to them without playing a normal role in the dialogue. An alternative technique to "active listening" is to reflect what is being said by restating what the interviewee is saying in such a way that he clearly indicates that he is following what the interviewee is saying and understands him. The key to this technique is that the interviewer should reflect, not the exact words, but the feelings which lie beneath the words. The idea is to make the interviewee think more deeply about what he is saying. The technique does require some skill, otherwise the interviewer may appear to mimic the interviewee. At the beginning the interviewer can start by saying, "you think that . . ." or "it seems to you that . . ." or similar prefaces until they can be dropped later in the interview, by merely seeming to reply to what the interviewee is saying. It is also important to use a statement rather than a question when reflecting what the interviewee is saying, so that one does not appear to be interrogating him. These statements should be made in a neutral tone to keep the level of the interview to as low a key as possible and also to limit the involvement of the interviewer. This is important, for if the interviewer is to be of any value he must not get emotionally involved, nor should he offer sympathy.

Some of the normal rules of interviewing do not apply when using this technique. For example, in a normal interview the interviewer tries to avoid lengthy pauses which can have the effect of unsettling the interviewee. In problem-solving situations, pauses can mean that the interviewee has something difficult to say and if the pause is broken he will merely take an easier course and react to what has been said rather than pursue his own original inclination. Another difference is the treatment of inconsistency. In a normal interview, the interviewer would probe inconsistencies to try to get at the truth. In a problem-solving interview, it is quite common for the interviewee to start to contradict himself as the interview proceeds.

This is because, in many cases, he is thinking through the problem properly for the first time and this is causing him to change his original ideas. He may also come up with useful ideas which will help him to overcome his problem. The interviewer should avoid seizing on these as soon as they are first mentioned, but should encourage the interviewee to evaluate these ideas for himself. It should be remembered that the object of the exercise is to encourage the interviewee to arrive at the solution of his own problem, first so that he can restore his own self-respect and, secondly, to obviate the objections to direct guidance that are discussed above. If a person can be helped to solve his own problems, he is being encouraged to develop his own sense of responsibility. He is also more likely to take his own advice than he is anyone else's.

The supervisor as a problem-solver

By being prepared to help subordinates to solve problems in this way, apart from fulfilling a vital welfare role, a supervisor may find reasons for poor work performance, tensions and sickness that he would not discover in any other way. The ability of people to cope with domestic and other personal worries varies greatly from individual to individual and, of course, depends on the weight and number that they carry. By being prepared to take the trouble to develop listening and "reflecting" skills, it is possible to locate real problems and get people to face up to them and in doing so relieve tensions and frustrations. The most valuable piece of advice that a supervisor can be given when facing a person who seeks his help is to assume that the real problem is *not* the one first put forward.

Chapter Fourteen

Promotion

Career development

The range of police careers

As the police in Great Britain has one point of entry, it means that all the posts within the service must be filled from the people recruited at that one point (*see* Chapter 10).

There is a tendency to think of career development in terms of promotion but, as most people who join the police do not achieve any form of promotion, clearly this is taking a much too restrictive view. Too much emphasis on promotion can be undesirable, for it creates an impression that the man who does not achieve supervisory rank is a failure and this is certainly not the case.

Numerically, the police service needs most people to carry out the work of patrolling, answering calls and dealing with the day-to-day functions of policing. If the quality of the people who are willing to do this work is to be maintained, the value placed upon this work must not be undermined by undue emphasis on promotion or specialisation.

Promotion selection systems

There can be no such thing as a "perfect" promotion selection system for a number of reasons:

1. Selection is being made of a person for a job in the future, whereas all the evidence available relates to his ability to do a different job in the past.
2. There is insufficient knowledge of the qualities needed to be an effective supervisor and as to how they can be measured.
3. It is difficult to validate any promotion system. The people it selects may be satisfactory and therefore it may be said

K

that the system has rejected people who would not have been any good. But there is no measure of those who have been rejected and might have been even better. There is a distinct tendency for "safe' candidates to be selected and this can exclude people who could contribute a great deal even though they may not be in the traditional mould.

If it is not possible to be perfect, what should be the aim of a promotion system? Above all—credibility. It would be naïve to expect everyone to concede that a system is fair, if only because the people who are not selected are very likely to take a jaundiced view of the system that rejected them. Nevertheless, any promotion system must seem to be manifestly just and free from nepotism or favouritism.

The second main aim of an effective promotion system must be to select the right people at the right time and, unfortunately, this is not quite as simple as it may seem.

The promotion pyramid

The *Report of the Joint Working Party on the Rank Structure of the Police in 1972* (Police Advisory Boards of England, Wales and Scotland), gave guidelines as to the ratios of supervisory officers to constables. For example, it suggested a ratio of 1:5 for sergeants to constables. The pyramid that this working party produced is shown in Fig. 16.

Although this is not a tall pyramid when compared with the police of some countries, it does require a steady rate of progress for someone to move from constable to chief constable. A possible route to achieve this within the span of thirty-years' service is shown by the solid line in Fig. 17. Although not drawn to represent any particular career, the steps up the rank structure are fairly realistic in that the first two steps—constable to sergeant and sergeant to inspector—may well take a third or more of the thirty years. It is for this reason that a means of accelerating promotion to the rank of inspector was introduced through the Special Course. The effect of this is shown in Fig. 17 where the dotted line illustrates the effect of promoting a person to the rank of inspector with five years in the police service. Gaining a start like this allows an exceptional person to make it to the top of the structure whilst still relatively young and also

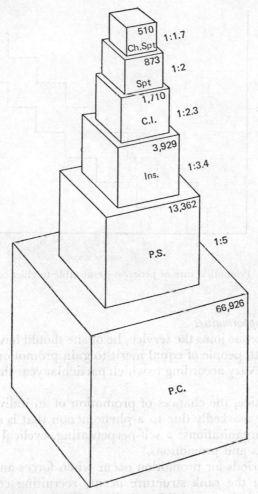

Fig. 16—Rank-structure pyramid. (Reproduced from the *Report of the Joint Working Party on the Rank Structure of the Police in 1972*, Police Advisory Boards of England, Wales and Scotland.)

provides a certain amount of leeway if later progress through the ranks is slower because of lack of opportunity.

This question of opportunity applies not only to the very few people who are going to reach the top of the pyramid but at all levels. Careful manpower planning is required to produce some measure of equality of opportunity.

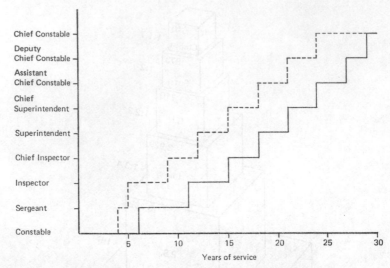

Fig. 17—Promotion rate of progress—constable to chief constable.

Promotion opportunities

When someone joins the service, he or she should have an equal chance with people of equal merit to gain promotion. Chances should not vary according to which particular year that a person joined.

In practice, the chances of promotion of an individual may vary quite markedly due to a phenomenon that is often to be found in organisations: a self-perpetuating, cyclical pattern of retirements and promotions.

Peak periods for promotion occur when forces amalgamate, changes in the rank structure occur, recruiting ceases for a lengthy period, or establishment increases are implemented. In some years, there will be a large number of vacancies for people to be promoted into, whilst in others there will be hardly any.

Such a pattern not only provides unequal chances of promotion for people within the service but acts to the detriment of the organisation itself:

1. At times of peak retirement, a considerable amount of experience is lost in a short space of time and thus the effectiveness of the organisation may be reduced.

2. Rapid turnover produces a period of continuous change which is in itself extremely unsettling for the people within the force. Even those people not directly affected by promotion or transfer will find that their supervisors and subordinates are constantly changing and proper working relationships cannot be formed.

3. At times of rapid exodus of supervisors, it is necessary to fill the vacancies with people who in other times would not be considered worthy. In years of few vacancies, good people—whose promotion would benefit the service—cannot be promoted because there are no vacancies. This in turn may discourage the very able and ambitious, who see their way ahead blocked by less-able people.

It is therefore in the interests of both the organisation and individuals within it to plan to produce a consistent promotion policy. Unfortunately, this cannot be a short-term matter, it requires the adoption of policies that will only just begin to have any real effect in a few years and may take many years to achieve a proper balance. The situation is also complicated by the retirement system within the British police service.

Promotion policies
Forecasting vacancies
In Chapter 9 the problem of forecasting future wastage amongst police officers was outlined. Clearly this makes it difficult to forecast vacancies for promotion. It is, therefore, hard to ensure an even distribution of promotions. No police officer should, therefore, be too critical of his force if it seems unable to produce a steady flow of promotions to match the career needs of its members. On the other hand, no police force should fail to make plans simply because it is so difficult.

By monitoring events, it is possible to build up a picture of what is happening. By using this as a flexible guide for the future, the worst extremes of cyclic retirements/promotions can be avoided by a judicious promotion-selection system.

Promotion and potential
Most promotion systems try to gear the promotion of individuals to their potential as supervisors. Thus an early promotion is

usually justified on the grounds of the individual's potential to reach the highest ranks of the service and early promotion is necessary to make this possible. Promotions late in a person's service are usually justified on the grounds that there is the ability to make a useful contribution in the new rank, but not beyond it.

Such considerations require a complex promotion system, linked to a comprehensive appraisal system, if it is to achieve its aims and maintain credibility within the organisation.

Selection methods

Written examinations

Police forces in most parts of the world use written examinations as a path to promotion in some way or another. Some use external examinations, for example, one police force uses a pass in the Bachelor of Law examination as a qualification for acceptance as an officer (as distinct from "other ranks"). In other countries, examinations may be set by the civil service, whilst in others the examinations may be set and marked within the police force concerned.

Whatever examination system is used, it can never stand on its own; there must be some supporting procedures for, as yet, there is no way of setting an examination that will measure all the qualities that are required in a supervisor. A good examination measures the level of people's knowledge, their ability to apply it to a given set of facts and their ability to express themselves in writing. What it does *not* do is to indicate qualities of leadership, personality, oral ability or social skill.

The big advantage of an examination is that, provided the subject-matter and format are seen to be relevant to police supervision, it can provide an objective measure of at least some human attributes. Because of this, it has an acceptability level higher than its true value as a predictor of supervisory ability. A man who fails an examination may envy the man who passed but, provided that the marking of an examination is above reproach, he will not have any grounds on which to base suspicions of favouritism or unfair treatment. Therefore, examinations are usually classed as a "fair" way of discriminating between people.

Yet people who can pass examinations do not necessarily make good supervisors and it is probable that some people who have been unable to pass an examination, would.

Some additional selection procedure is needed for reinforcement where examinations are used and to provide all the evidence where examinations are not employed at all.

Interviews

The limitations of interviews for selection purposes have already been discussed in Chapter 13, yet they remain a popular form of supplement to examinations and the reason is once again that, provided that they are conducted in a competent and professional manner, they have credibility. This is particularly true of selection boards, which are often accepted as being a "fair" way of selecting people.

As with written examinations, it is important to remember just what interviews can tell the interviewer about a candidate, for many interviewers place too much emphasis on the candidate's performance during an interview, lasting perhaps forty-five minutes, paying inadequate attention to the evidence offered by his career, which has lasted several years.

The value of an interview in a selection procedure is principally to apply a balance between different candidates who come from different areas and therefore have been assessed by supervisors with different sets of values. Beyond this, an interviewer may gain some impression of the candidate's social skills, his ability to express himself orally when under stress and, if the interviewer is skilful, some measure of the candidate's ability to reason, to conceptualise and to discuss a topic in a balanced way.

Extended interviews

In order to overcome some of the problems that organisations have with the selection of their personnel, it has become a practice for people to be sent to an assessment centre, where they can be subjected to tests of varying kinds and judged by independent assessors. The idea is not new, it was first used by the armed services in the 1940s (the War Office Selection Board, or W.O.S.B.) and later adapted by other organisations to fit their own needs.

One early variant of the W.O.S.B. procedure was used by

the Civil Service to select candidates for Administrative Class and the Foreign Service. It was from this system that the police Extended Interview procedure was developed by senior members of the Civil Service Selection Board staff (C.S.S.B.) working with senior police officers.

Extended Interview procedures are used in slightly different forms to select people for the Graduate Entry Scheme and Special Course and the Command Course Part II.

The Extended Interview procedure is notable for a number of positive features which distinguish it from most examination and selection interviews:

1. A balanced programme of tests and exercises is used to measure specific areas of interest in a potential police supervisor.
2. Candidates are marked against a standard and not against one another, for there is no competitive element in the Extended Interview system.
3. A number of the tests can be marked objectively in quantitative terms while those which provide no quantitative measure have been analysed into their component parts, which can be assessed with a fair measure of objectivity.
4. The candidates are unknown to the members of their assessment team and so biases resulting from previous contact are avoided.
5. Follow-up surveys are consistently carried out, to check the accuracy and validity of the procedures. They have been found to stand up to scrutiny of this kind.

Each Extended Interview series is conducted under a Director who is a chief police officer assisted by a senior member of the Civil Service Selection Board staff who acts as Deputy Director. Their responsibility includes the maintenance of standards between sets of assessors and from session to session. For this reason, they conduct interviews with candidates and sit in as observers on exercises.

Candidates are considered in groups of five or six and are assessed by a panel composed of two chief police officers and one non-service member who is a representative of the Civil Service Commission.

The Extended Interview assessors base their judgments on:

1. intelligence and general information tests;
2. two written exercises designed to measure a candidate's analytical ability, his capacity to put forward an argument and to express himself in writing in a clear and cogent manner. One of the tests is particularly aimed at finding out whether a candidate can express unpalatable truths in a conciliatory but honest manner;
3. two group discussions, one structured and one unstructured, test a range of abilities including the important one of being able to form a working relationship with his colleagues;
4. a minimum of two interviews, one conducted by the non-service member alone and the other by the two service members sitting as a board (a third interview may be with the Director or Deputy Director, in order to maintain comparability of overall standards of assessment);
5. a report as to what a man has done in the past, i.e. each candidate's performance at work, is available to the assessors, which is just as valuable in an Extended Interview situation as in any other selection procedure.

Even this system, comprehensive as it is, is not infallible—indeed, even its strongest supporters would not make this claim—but it does overcome many of the failings of written examinations and single or board interviews. Great care is taken not to adopt a competitive approach whereby a certain number of people are selected, but instead to set a given standard against which all candidates are assessed. This means that, in theory, it could produce many candidates one year and few the next. In practice, the numbers selected tend to be similar each year and this serves to reinforce the evidence supporting a promotion system that produces a continuous flow of able people rather than cyclic variations.

The Extended Interview system has considerable merit, including the important benefit of credibility, but it has one serious drawback: it is very expensive to run in terms of time and manpower. Its use is therefore confined to those applications which require particularly careful sifting of candidates. However, it does indicate the limitations of other commonly-employed systems and emphasises the need for care and thoroughness in their use. Nowhere is this need more apparent

than in the preparation of supervisors' reports, which form the
basis of all systems, however sophisticated they may be.

Supervisor's reports
One of the most important features of all promotion systems
is the consideration given to a man's past performance. This is
the only real guide as to how he will act in the future. Where the
jobs are essentially similar, how a man has done his work in the
past is a very good guide to how he will do it in the future.
Where they are dissimilar, it is necessary to analyse past work
for the qualities that have been demonstrated and project these
into the future.

This is particularly necessary when considering someone's
suitability for a first supervisory post, as on promotion from
constable to sergeant. It is most important that the supervisors
of all constables who aspire for promotion use every opportunity to assess their qualities and report objectively on what
they see (*see* also Chapter 12).

British promotion systems
There are two basic systems employed in Britain for selection
for the ranks of sergeant and inspector: one used by the Metropolitan Police and the other by provincial forces.

Metropolitan Police
Although the main feature of Metropolitan Police promotions
to the ranks of sergeant and inspector are competitive examinations, a number of safeguards and compromises have been
built into the system. One of the most unusual features is the
reservation of a percentage of the vacancies for each rank, for
experienced police officers who have obtained a pass mark in
the appropriate promotion examination but have not been
amongst the successful competitors.

The way in which the two methods work is as follows:

1. *Competitive examination.* Competitors must first obtain a
   "certificate of fitness" from a senior officer to show that they
   are fitted in every way for the next rank. Failure to obtain a
   certificate means that officers may not sit the promotion
   examination as competitors, although they may sit in order

to obtain a qualifying pass so as to be considered for a reserved vacancy when they have the requisite experience.

Those who have obtained a certificate of fitness and sit the competitive examination compete for a pre-determined proportion of the vacancies (decided annually) in the rank to which they aspire: constables for the rank of sergeant and sergeants for the rank of inspector. Constables are not permitted to sit the inspector's examination and the competitive examination for inspector is limited to ordinary duty station-sergeants (an obsolescent rank) or sergeants who have served at least four years with that rank.

2. *Reserved vacancies.* The remaining proportion of the vacancies for the coming year are reserved for senior constables and sergeants who have passed the annual examination at a qualifying level but have not been successful as competitors.

Officers with the right amount of service (including service in the rank of sergeant in the case of those applying for selection as inspector) may apply for consideration and are chosen by selection boards.

Included in this system is a provision for members of the criminal investigation department who wish to make the whole of their careers in that department. Under normal conditions, detectives take the competitive examinations and, if successful, spend at least one year in uniform before being able to return to the criminal investigation department in their new rank. If they are prepared to accept less rapid promotion, they may undergo selection for a reserved vacancy within the criminal investigation department and, in this way, avoid the need to enter the uniformed branch.

Provincial police forces

Two sets of written examinations are conducted by the Civil Service Commission with a Police Promotion Examination Board as advisers. One set is for the rank of sergeant, the other for inspector. A constable in a provincial force may sit the inspector's examination provided that he has already passed the examination for sergeant.

There is no competitive element in the provincial examinations and no hindrance is provided to prevent a police officer from sitting, even though the person is regarded as being unsuitable for promotion by the individual's force. Constables who have passed both examinations and so are qualified for promotion to the rank of inspector may never be promoted even to the rank of sergeant. This may be due to a lack of vacancies within the individual's police force but it may reflect a poor personal-appraisal system that fails to inform the officer as to how he is viewed by senior officers.

Promotion of officers who have qualified by passing the appropriate examination is normally by selection interview, the system used varying from force to force. Large forces tend to use multiple-level selection boards, to sift candidates who may apply each year to be considered for forthcoming vacancies. Smaller forces may use one central promotion board for all applicants, or no formal selection board procedure at all.

The Metropolitan Police system has a number of advantages and disadvantages when compared with the provincial system.

The advantages are:

1. it is simple to operate, the use of promotion boards is kept to a minimum;
2. it can be seen to be impartial;
3. constables who are patently unsuitable for supervisory positions are not permitted to sit the examination and so need not study for an examination which cannot produce an end result.

The disadvantages are:

1. it is necessary to be able to calculate the number of anticipated vacancies which, as we have seen, it is not always possible to do at all accurately;
2. considerable reliance is placed on divisional and departmental commanders to refuse to grant a certificate to unsuitable candidates. This may be a difficult decision to make on the evidence available to the senior officer concerned. His judgment will also be affected by the standards that he sets —standards vary from commander to commander;
3. as in all written examinations, the best marks are obtained by people with combinations of ability, a good examination technique, the opportunity and ability to study, and luck. It does not follow that these people will always make the best supervisors.

Chapter Fifteen

Welfare

General principles

Policemen, like other people, are subject to personal troubles and anxieties, often over family matters, in which the advice or help of some older and more experienced man would be of great benefit. Welfare in this sense was considered by the Police Post War Committee who . . . stressed the responsibility that lies upon the officers of the force and upon the Police Federation for helping the men in their personal troubles and they came to the conclusion that the appointment of welfare officers specifically to assume this function would undermine the responsibilities of the officers and Police Federation. We agree with the . . . Committee in thinking that the senior officers in each police force ought to bear the main responsibility for helping the men with their personal troubles, but we think there is a wide field in which a civilian welfare officer of the right type would be of great benefit.

> (*Report of the Committee on Police, Conditions of Service* (Oaksey Committee), Part II, Cmd. 7831, para. 319, 1949.)

In this statement can be seen confirmation of the idea of a three-part responsibility for welfare. The main burden falls on the supervisory officers, but the Police Federation have an important part to play and there should be a force welfare officer who has the expertise to provide a back-up service for the other two agencies and a confidential service to which an individual can have recourse when he prefers not to approach his supervisors or his federation colleagues.

Welfare officers

It is usual for people to be encouraged to take their personal troubles to their senior officers in the first instance, but a welfare officer can often advise a senior officer on a case, or to take it over altogether if this is necessary or desirable. Because he may not wish to take a personal problem to a supervisor, a person should have the right to take his troubles direct to the welfare officer.

The Working Party on Operational Efficiency and Management (1967) concluded that, "The policeman should feel free to tell the welfare officer things frankly and openly, on a 'solicitor and client' basis. It is important that he should be able to feel confident that nothing that is said will get back to his senior officers—although the welfare officer may well advise him that his best course would be to put the matter about which he is troubled forward through the usual channels. The appointment of such officers should in no way diminish the responsibility of senior officers for the welfare of their men. We also commend generally the practice . . . of appointing sub-committees, consisting of various ranks, who meet from time to time to deal with the welfare problems of individual officers" (para. 34).

The welfare officer has an opportunity to acquire expertise in the availability of practical methods of help outside the service that is not within the competence of the serving senior officer, e.g. in matters of civil law.

The Police Federation

The Police Federation has a statutory responsibility for "representing members of the police forces in . . . all matters affecting their welfare and efficiency . . ." (s. 44(1), Police Act 1964). Its role extends far beyond making representations to chief officers on behalf of its members and local-branch boards can make a valuable contribution towards the welfare of the personnel of a force. It is likely that information as to some welfare matters will reach a police officer's Police Federation representative before his senior officers and so liaison is necessary between supervisors and the Police Federation to be able to supplement one another's efforts in the best interests of the individual.

In addition to its ability to make representations on behalf of a member and to steer him towards sources of aid with financial problems, the Police Federation offers a unique service in that it may provide assistance for police officers needing to take legal action in respect of any injury or disease received or contracted through work. Such claims include those to the Criminal Injuries Compensation Board, and officers of the Federation have a wealth of experience in dealing with such claims.

Supervisory officers

It has always been a fundamental principle of the British police that a supervisor is responsible for the welfare of his subordinates. To some extent, of course, this is true of other organisations but the lengths to which this concern for welfare is carried is markedly greater in the police than in, say, most industrial concerns. There are a number of probable reasons for this: the nature of police work, the feeling of being in "the job" (with its strong sense of identification with the service and detachment from the rest of society), and the effects of discipline on private lives. All of these factors contribute to a long tradition of concern for the well-being of one's colleagues.

In general, perhaps it might be said that, at the very least, supervisors should have an awareness of the personal problems of their subordinates. They need this awareness if they are to carry out their normal functions of supervision, for a person's performance at work is likely to be affected by serious worries at home. The effectiveness of the supervisor is questionable if a serious, long-term welfare matter explodes dramatically without his being aware of the original problem.

The way in which people cope with their domestic problems varies from individual to individual and so does the attitude to seeking or accepting help. Some people are very often open about their affairs; they readily seek advice and are willing to accept help. They may be too dependent, in which case the supervisor must decide where to draw the line between helping them and encouraging them to fend for themselves. More difficult to deal with can be people at the other end of the scale, who do not wish their personal problems to be known outside their domestic circle, do not seek help and flatly refuse to accept any.

It is thus very difficult to make hard-and-fast rules about welfare. No two welfare problems are identical because the people involved in them are different and may react differently to similar situations. For example, people faced with debts may react in totally different ways. One may virtually starve himself and his family to try to meet his obligations. Another man will borrow money at high interest rates in the belief that, if he can postpone the day of reckoning, everything will solve itself.

A third man might give up in despair and do nothing. Thus three cases involving debt but three different welfare problems requiring an entirely different approach present themselves.

When the individual is able to cope with his affairs and maintain his work performance, there is no real justification for a supervisor to intervene in the person's private affairs. If work performance, the officer's well-being or the reputation of the service are at risk, the picture may be different.

The individual and the service
Supervisors need to be able to maintain a balance between the welfare of the individual and the good name and interests of the police. Fortunately they often coincide: for example, helping a person out of difficulties may prevent the reputation of the service from suffering. But this is not always the case and, on occasions, the problems of an individual can be attributable to conduct that conflicts with the police discipline code.

The extent to which membership of a police force places restrictions on the private lives of police officers has never been completely clear. That "a member of a police force shall abstain from any activity which is likely to interfere with the impartial discharge of his duties or which is likely to give rise to the impression amongst members of the public that it may so interfere" is laid down in Police Regulations. This is sufficiently imprecise to be capable of interpretation in many ways. The requirement that he shall not "wilfully refuse or neglect to discharge any lawful debt" is also a difficult regulation to interpret in an age when living on credit has become a way of life. A further contribution to the grey areas of police life is that part of the discipline regulations prescribing that a member of a police force commits a disciplinary offence if he "acts in a . . . manner prejudicial to discipline or reasonably likely to bring discredit on the reputation of the force or of the police service".

Although police regulations have been changed over the years, it is the interpretation of them that has changed most quickly. The concern of police forces with the private lives of members has decreased markedly. At one time adultery might be considered to be bringing "discredit on the reputation of the force". This attitude changed as the norms of society changed, albeit perhaps at a slower pace on occasions. Today, a person's private life is unlikely to excite any great reaction unless it hinges on dishonesty, or is likely to interfere with his duties.

The attentions today of senior officers are much more likely to be resented than in the days when the discipline code extended into the moral behaviour of individuals when off duty. The modern supervisory officer must use more discretion than his forebears, who could quote the discipline code if challenged.

Some general pointers for supervisors

Approachability

It is a first rule of all supervisors that they must be approachable. It is very easy to evade many of the responsibilities of rank by refusing to allow people to pose problems or by making it difficult for them to do so. This not only applies to welfare problems but, as welfare matters are often among those that people find the most difficult to discuss with a supervisor, it is here that an unapproachable supervisor can do a great deal of harm.

A supervisor needs to be a good listener and his subordinates must feel able to talk to him. A supervisor who "locks himself away" in his office or car, repulses people with sarcasm or is permanently "too busy", will not know what is happening around him until it is too late to do anything.

Awareness

Supervisors should be aware of the problems of their subordinates. They need not do anything about them—it may be the best course to do nothing—but they must have an awareness so that a decision to do nothing is a conscious one that can be changed when action is needed.

To have this awareness requires an understanding of people, the sensitivity to be able to detect changes in them, to listen to what people say and to what they do not say. The clue may be that a man has *stopped* talking about something.

Confidentiality

It is quite common for people to talk to supervisors about their problems, to obtain help, to gain sympathy, perhaps simply to be able to talk to someone so as to share the problem, but not to want anything to be done about it. The supervisor needs to be clear as to what the purpose is and whether he is supposed to take some action or whether he is merely being told.

A supervisor can never give a subordinate an absolute guarantee that what is said to him will go no further. This is an assurance that is often sought by people who have a very tricky personal problem. The answer must invariably be that the supervisor can only guarantee that he will not tell anyone else unless he considers it necessary and the subordinate must be invited to trust the supervisor to use proper judgment as to what action he takes. Some supervisory officers have found themselves in great difficulty when, after having given an undertaking not to pass on information, they have received confessions of illegal activities or have been placed in the position where to take essential action would mean breaking their promise. No subordinate has the right to extract a promise of silence; he can only demand the good faith, humanity and judgment of his supervisor.

Behaviour changes

Most people are consistent in behaviour. Their conduct tends to follow a pattern that becomes predictable, once one knows them. By their own lights, people generally behave rationally and with moderation. When people behave abnormally there is a reason, but that reason may not be clear even to the person affected by it. Indeed, on occasions, the reason for a change of behaviour may be more apparent to the people around him than to the individual concerned, whose judgment about his own situation may be clouded or lacking in objectivity.

The onset of abnormal behaviour in a subordinate serves to warn his supervisor that there is something that needs to be done. Care must be taken not to just treat the symptoms without considering the cause.

There are many causes of abnormal behaviour: difficulties at work or a sense of frustration, based on real or imagined injustices; financial or domestic worries; a sick wife or child; a marriage that is breaking up, or illness—any of these can cause a change in a man's behaviour. To minimise the effects, the supervisor needs to be able to help an individual to identify the exact nature of his problems and to advise him where he may seek help, if the problem is outside the scope of the supervisor.

Health

The demands of police work

One of the features of police work is its unpredictability. A police officer may be called upon at any time to help to restrain a prisoner, to take part in a chase, to help to control a violent crowd—all tasks requiring physical strength. It is, therefore, not a job for someone who has a serious physical disability. Police officers are also subjected to verbal abuse, are involved with emotionally-disturbed people and may have to make important decisions in seconds or minutes, under conditions that are far from conducive to quiet consideration. It follows, therefore, that as well as having physical stamina, they need also to have mental stability.

Traditionally, physical and mental illness have been treated as being totally separate subjects and to have suffered from mental illness has stigmatised the sufferer. This attitude is now changing and it is becoming more and more acknowledged that, given the causative combination of circumstances, anyone can suffer some form of breakdown in his mental capabilities and that this is no more degrading than, say, a heart attack.

Because of the importance of a police officer being able to respond to emergencies of all kinds without the fear of over-taxing himself and because of the demands which may be made of him, his supervisor has a responsibility to bring to notice anyone who is not fully fit.

People do not all react in the same way to illness. At one extreme are those who will carry on working until they drop—literally; at the other extreme, there are the people who will stay at home at the slightest excuse, or even no excuse at all. Between these extremes of stoic and malingerer come the bulk of people, who are able to continue working at widely-differing levels of effectiveness given the same complaint. In a nutshell, the supervisor's job is to ensure that the genuinely ill do not work when they should not, but also to avoid being deceived by malingerers. The force medical-officer can be of great assistance and sickness records are of great importance in this field.

Just as some people keep their private lives and problems to themselves, so they keep quiet about their physical condition. This may be just a personal characteristic or may stem from a fear of being taken off a job that they like and being given a less arduous one that they dislike. Personal pride may also come into it; many people pride themselves on not having to take time off through illness. This can mean having a less-than-fit person doing a crucial job, unless the supervisor takes care and knows his staff.

A quite different problem is posed by the people who feign illness so as to avoid work and they can cause difficulties out of all proportion to their actual numbers. Unfortunately, medicine is not an exact science. If a man tells his doctor that he has a pain, it is unlikely that the doctor can prove that he has not, however much the doctor may privately feel that he is not being told the truth. Thus malingering becomes possible.

There is no certain way of identifying a malingerer. Home visits may indicate when a person has feigned sickness so as to be able to take some time off. Work records may help, for it is unusual for very keen men suddenly to turn into malingerers.

It is also worth remembering that the human body is prone to induced illnesses caused by worry, boredom or frustration. A man with a previous good record can often be restored to perfect health by improving his motivation to work.

Finally, the fact that physical illness can be induced by psychological factors serves to emphasise that there is no hard line between physical and mental illness.

Mental strain
In addition to the physical stresses, there are pressures that can severely strain the mental balance of a police officer, particularly one who is subject to long or irregular periods of duty. Such strain can be aggravated by domestic or welfare problems that impose stress on the police officer even before he arrives for work.

The results of excessive mental strain vary considerably from individual to individual. In some, it is immediately apparent that they are unwell and they themselves are aware that they should seek medical attention. In other, much more difficult, cases the onset of some form of mental breakdown may pass unnoticed until a crisis occurs and a breakdown point is reached.

Because of the nature of his work, an undiagnosed form of

mental illness can have serious consequences and it is therefore important that police supervisors should be on the alert to detect abnormal behaviour and to ascertain the cause. If in doubt, the individual and all the facts about him should be placed in front of the police medical adviser.

The seriousness of a mental illness being undetected in a police officer, and the difficulty facing police supervisors in trying to deal with a subordinate suspected of being ill, are illustrated in the report of inquiry conducted by Mr A. E. James Q.C., *Into the circumstances in which it was possible for Detective Sergeant Challenor of the Metropolitan Police to continue on duty at a time when he appears to have been affected by the onset of mental illness* (Cmnd. 2735, 1965).

This inquiry was instigated by the Judge following a trial in which the detective sergeant had stood indicted, together with other police officers, with the offence of conspiracy to pervert the course of justice and had, by verdict of a jury, been found unfit to plead to the charge. The Judge had heard evidence from the principal medical officer of a prison, supported by a consultant psychiatrist, that the detective sergeant had been "mentally abnormal for a considerable time", whilst the head of a hospital department of psychological medicine reported that he had found him to be "very mad indeed", in the medical sense. The illness was diagnosed as paranoid schizophrenia.

The report concluded that:

[The officer] was able to continue on duty at a time when he was suffering from mental illness due to a combination of these factors:

1. the extreme difficulty in diagnosing paranoid schizophrenia in certain cases, of which this is a pre-eminent example;
2. the evidence which, at the time, would have indicated mental illness was known to [his wife] alone;
3. the existence of possible causes of abnormal behaviour other than mental illness;
4. the requirement of medical authority for removing an officer from duty on the ground of sickness, and the absence of evidence enabling such medical authority to be given until [too late]. (ibid., p. 8.)

A very necessary reminder was included against the danger of assuming that every incident of abnormal behaviour is a manifestation of mental illness and there is no suggestion that cases of this kind are common. What such a case can serve to illustrate is the need for supervisors to be aware of the causes of abnormal behaviour and to seek out those causes if they are not apparent. In many ways, the supervisor and the individual's colleagues share with his family the opportunity to detect changes in behaviour because "the onlooker judges the behaviour against the known character of the person and all the circumstances of the case in which the behaviour occurs" (ibid., p. 12).

This case also serves to highlight the need to monitor the work loads of police officers. The case load of crime per C.I.D. officer at West End Central Police Station, where the detective sergeant served up to the crucial date, was about 300. The hours worked by the detectives at that station also came in for comment, one detective sergeant averaged 12½ hours' duty for every working day in 1963, and it can be said with confidence that such hours of duty were regarded as within normal limits for a C.I.D. officer at West End Central Police Station. This was despite efforts by the senior officers at the station to make people work less hours in order to overcome strain or tiredness. The dilemma of the senior officers was: "To take a C.I.D. officer off duty or to cut down his hours of work results in his work being passed to an already fully occupied colleague, or the job does not get done—with consequential advantages to the criminal classes" (ibid., p. 18).

Since then, there has been less of a tendency to take long hours for granted and the dangers of overworking people, or of allowing them to overwork themselves, have been more widely recognised. Thanks, in part, to changes in the overtime-payment system introduced at the instigation of the Police Federation, the days when men were expected to work excessive hours as a matter of routine belong to the past. Overtime needs to be strictly controlled so that people do not work long hours and damage their health. Some people have a higher tolerance to long hours and continuous activity than others; it is quite common for them to feel that they have done it before and felt no ill effects, or that they have always done it. The only way of finding the breaking point for any given individual is when he collapses under the strain—then it is too late. Most people can produce bursts of hard work over long hours for a limited period, few can do it day-in and day-out and no one should be expected to.

In conclusion, the report contained two recommendations of general application:

1. where initiative is taken by the police to refer a police officer for medical examination, other than routine examination, by a Consultant, the fact of the examination taking place and any findings made therein should always be communicated to the officer's general medical practitioner (by the Medical Branch);
2. when a police officer is referred to the Medical Branch for medical examination on account of apparent over tiredness or mental strain, a full detailed report of all known facts should be made available for the Consultant at the earliest opportunity. (ibid., p. 9.)

Once again, there is the emphasis on being aware of people and their problems so as to be able to do everything possible to safeguard their welfare.

Shift work

The body develops a daily cycle of rhythms that cause variations in the activities of the organs and even the composition of the blood. This cycle is induced by upbringing—the way in which we work during the day, sleep at night, eat at certain times and so on.

If this rhythm is interrupted, say by a long air-flight, the body suffers from the change between its original cycle and the effects of the new hours. After some time, likely to be at least a week, the body will adopt a new cycle of rhythms geared to the new times. This process is the same whether the body is transported across the world into a new time-zone, or simply made to function against its regular cycle through working shifts.

The effects of this time-lag are similar for everyone but vary considerably in intensity from person to person and in the length of time that it takes to produce a new cycle of rhythms. The effect of the time-lag is to reduce the efficiency of the body and particularly its ability to cope with routine tasks. For example, people who have recently started night duty are at their least effective at about three o'clock in the morning. Some years ago, it used to be the custom in the Metropolitan Police for night duty Station Sergeants to have to type abstracts from accident reports for insurance companies. The abstracts had to be perfectly typed and completely accurate. The most common time for preparing them was between two and five in the morning and a more frustrating experience is hard to imagine. Most of the sergeants were untrained typists anyway but, additionally, they were trying to perform a task at just the time when they were physically and mentally least able to do it. People who work permanent night duty do not suffer in the same way. Their bodies develop a cycle that fits their work and so their problems occur when they have days off. A permanent night shift is thus less harmful to the body than rotating shifts and so we come to the ironic position that the fairest way of allocating duties, by using rotating shifts, is the least effective and causes most harm to the people working them. The harm can include digestive disorders and fatigue, the latter often being aggravated by an inability to sleep during the day. This may be in part due to social factors such as desirability of conforming with the pattern of family life.

Before dealing with shift systems in more detail, it is worth mentioning that not all countries have the same tradition of rotating shifts. In America, some forces have a tradition of working permanent shifts. The details may vary, but the broad principle is, usually, that a new recruit goes on to the night shift; this has the advantage that the least experienced police officers are on duty when they make the least contact with the public and also the least popular shift (with most people) is given to the most junior personnel.

From the night shift, people graduate to the late shift (say 4 p.m. to 12 midnight) as vacancies occur. Eventually, as they gain seniority, they may apply for vacancies on the shift they are possibly by then physically the most in need of, a regular 8 a.m. to 4 p.m. tour of duty.

The social effects of working a permanent late or night shift obviously weigh heavily against such a system, but it cannot be denied that it does fit the physical make-up of human beings better than rotating shifts.

Many shift systems have been tried, but most are aimed at minimising the social hardships that shifts cause. However, the effects of short-term night shifts on health should not be ignored and there are some ways in which their effects can be minimised:

1. Duty-rotas should be such that the periods of night duty are as long as possible, consistent with social acceptability.

Periods of one week at a time are the most likely to cause health problems.

2. If a man wishes to work continuously through an uninterrupted tour of night duty, this should be allowed if at all possible. The effect of taking one or two days off, in the middle of a three- or four-week period of night duty, unnecessarily breaks the new cycle of rhythms that people will have developed.

3. For the same reasons, quick change-overs from one shift to another should be avoided as far as possible. It is particularly difficult for someone to adjust, say, to a week of night duty, then being brought into late turn for two days and then being reverted to night duty.

4. Routine tasks calling for maintained concentration or accuracy should not be done during the early hours of the morning. It may seem a pity to waste the opportunity to get some routine work done during the night, but concentration and reliability are markedly lower.

5. Ability to adjust to time-changes varies considerably from individual to individual. Some people are able to work on shifts for thirty years with little apparent harm but others are seriously affected after a short time. Some people are almost physically incapable of coping with night duty and suffer badly from fatigue. Such a condition needs to be detected when deploying personnel on critical tasks, particularly tasks that can be dangerous if the individual loses his concentration.

Financial problems
Money matters

The position of trust that police occupy makes them particularly vulnerable to accusations of corruption. For this reason, if for no other, the private finances of some police officers are always likely to be of interest to supervisory officers. If a police officer is in serious financial difficulties, there is a common belief that he will be more susceptible to an acceptance of relief in ways that are against the public interest. These may include:

1. the acceptance of bribes for taking no action in respect of offences against the law or for supplying information about police activities;

2. obtaining money in the form of gifts or loans from such people as bookmakers and holders of liquor licences, to whom police should not be under an obligation;

3. borrowing money or cashing post-dated cheques, by using his position as a police officer to apply pressure on an otherwise unwilling lender.

From the service point of view as well as the welfare of the individual, it is desirable that aid and advice should be made available to officers who run into serious financial problems.

Most police forces have some form of provident or benevolent fund from which the payment of monetary grants can be made to members of the force in cases of hardship. There is also often a provision for making loans to members in cases of need and it is this aspect of the management of such funds that usually causes most difficulty. In some cases, the causes of a person's troubles are clearly beyond their control and there can be no objection to providing aid. Frequently, however, problems are caused by mis-management and good judgment is needed to decide on the best course of action to help, as distinct from providing money that merely postpones the evil day for a few weeks. In such cases, it has to be remembered that no one's problems can be solved so long as Mr Micawber's rule about income exceeding expenditure is broken: "Annual income twenty pounds, annual expenditure nineteen pounds nineteen and six, result happiness. Annual income twenty pounds, annual expenditure twenty pounds nought and six, result misery." A loan may pay existing bills but the repayments will add to outgoings in the future. A loan can only really be justified if it is to settle a non-repeatable account and future outgoings can be cut or income increased to meet the cost of repayments. Therefore, either the individual must cut his outgoings or he must earn more, for example, by performing voluntary overtime. A loan where neither of these courses is possible may make matters worse.

It is also sometimes necessary to bear in mind the effect that aiding one person may have on his colleagues. There is unlikely to be any resentment if a genuinely-deserving case is helped, but special treatment, loans, grants or overtime, meted out to a spendthrift can cause dissension in a unit, in which all the people basically do the same job for the same money, but one person's foolishness seems to merit preferential treatment.

Police charities

Apart from the local funds that may be applied to provide grants and/or loans, there are a number of national police charities, each with closely-prescribed terms of reference, which may be used to supplement the resources of an individual force.

The National Police Fund was set up in 1926 following an appeal organised by *The Times* in recognition of the services provided by the police to the public during the general strike of that year. The amount raised was nearly a quarter of a million pounds, a large sum even by today's standards. The fund is administered by a Board of Trustees under the chairmanship of the Home Secretary and the Board is assisted by an Advisory Council composed of members of all the police representative organisations. It provides grants to individual forces' athletic and social funds and, through an education scheme, aids the children of policemen in furthering their education. It also assists other police charities and makes compassionate grants to the widows and orphans of police officers in cases of exceptional hardship. Also providing for police orphans are two contributory funds, based originally on charitable bequests, the Gurney and the St. George's Funds, both of which provide allowances to the children of deceased or incapacitated police officers of the different forces which they cover.

Of more recent origin is the Police Dependants Trust, which was started following the shooting down of three policemen in Shepherd's Bush, London in August 1966. This incident led to an overwhelming response from the public, which resulted in donations to a trust that was to assist in cases of need the dependants of police officers and ex-police officers who die or are incapacitated as a result of injury received on duty. To be eligible, the death or incapacity must have arisen from the hazards of police duty and not be of the kind that could accidentally happen to anyone, anywhere, and the dependant's subsequent need must be related to the officer's incapacity. A small group of trustees, representing the various sectors of the police under the chairmanship of the Permanent Under Secretary of State for the Home Department, appoints a management committee which considers applications made through the local chief officer of police. Such applications are supported by detailed reports made by a local police officer experienced in welfare matters.

In addition to the various funds available, there are two notable contributors to police welfare in the shape of the Police Convalescent Homes at Hove and Harrogate. These were originally founded in 1890 and 1898 respectively, by Miss Catherine Gurney, a tireless worker for police charities. Neither establishment is a nursing home, although the people staying there are under medical care. Most police officers who are referred there are recovering from operations, although both homes also cater for police officers in need of convalescence or recuperative rest for reasons other than surgical. The homes are dependent on subscriptions for their income and upon donations and gifts from a wide range of individuals, charities and organisations, as well as from charitable funds from within the service.

Similar facilities may also be provided on a local basis through local government schemes for police officers and civilian police staff.

It will be seen that there are many different sources of aid that can be used to help people in trouble. The main problem is often not the lack of facilities to help people but, rather, a lack of awareness on the part of those in trouble of the resources that are available to them. This is where the supervisor, welfare officer and Police Federation representative can play a vital role: they can advise those who need help of the existence of possible sources of relief and can bring people in need to the notice of welfare committees who might otherwise not hear of deserving cases.

Sport and recreation

The Oaksey Committee set out a view that has influenced the police ever since: "In our view, organised games and atheletics are amenities which are good for the health and morale of policemen, which ought to do much to make the police service attractice to men of the type that it is desired to recruit" (*Report of the Committee on Police Conditions of Service*, Part II, Cmd. 7831, 1949).

The principal organisation for police sport, the Police Athletic Association, was founded in 1928 to encourage development of all forms of amateur sports in the police and to promote and control various associations, competitions and championships that form part of the police sporting and athletic activities.

Despite the generally-held view that police sport is beneficial for the reasons outlined by the Oaksey Committee and for its public-relations value, the subject of individual police officers taking part in sport can cause problems for supervisory officers. Many of the difficulties stem from having to arrange duties for people to participate in sport or athletics. A balance has to be made between providing adequate opportunities for sportsmen against the needs of the service and the inconvenience caused to non-participants, who provide cover for their absent colleagues. The effects on the manpower situation can be minimised by encouraging sporting activities on the less busy days. The inconvenience caused to non-participants is often aggravated by last-minute changes of duty that could sometimes be avoided by better planning.

As with most other aspects of life, it is a question of balance. The service provides some time for the activities that it seeks to encourage. The participants need to ensure that adequate notice is given of their commitments and be prepared to put up with a certain amount of inconvenience.

As to other aspects of police social life, there has been a tendency for many police forces to become less insular in outlook and the need for police to rely on police clubs and societies appears to have lessened. Nevertheless, social and sporting activities can form a useful way of encouraging identification with the force, division or unit. An active social programme may also have a welfare role, in that information concerning domestic problems is likely to come to light. This requires judicious handling for, while a supervisor wants to be aware of what is happening, he should not be seen to encourage gossip or spying.

The reluctance of some people to join in social activities must also be accepted. Some people prefer to live their private lives away from their work contacts and this preference should be respected. Some may not be able to attend social events because they cannot afford to, or have families that make it difficult. It is a safe rule that social activities should be encouraged but be properly controlled, to ensure that they do not assume too prominent a role in the day-to-day lives of the people in the unit.

Police housing

The whole approach to police housing has changed since the days in which policemen were compelled to live in blocks of police flats or in estates of police houses. There have been two major shifts of emphasis, the first towards integration with the rest of the community and the second towards allowing police officers to choose where they want to live.

The feature of police families living apart from the rest of the community produced a rare example of mutual agreement between the Police Federation and the National Council for Civil Liberties in their evidence given to the Royal Commission (Cmnd. 1728, 1962, p. 106). Even at that time, the practice was falling into disuse in favour of the police purchasing houses in residential areas; the general thought was that a police officer should live in the area he polices.

The Royal Commission noted that police officers were not unanimous in their desire to live in a police station in the area in which they worked because of the calls that were made upon them and their wives outside their duty hours. In another paragraph, the Commission noted the problem of moving police officers from place to place at too frequent intervals and concluded that "we should expect chief police officers to review their practice in this respect from time to time".

The situation has now changed. Relaxation in policies that sought to have police officers living in police houses has meant that more policemen and women have bought their own houses and do not wish to move. In any case, making them move house has become an expensive proposition as police allowances have improved.

The result has been a better integration of police officers into the community: police families have been able to settle and establish roots. But these things have not been accomplished without cost. The needs of the service have often meant longer journeys to work, when police officers have been transferred but have chosen not to move house. Flexibility in the deployment of personnel has diminished and career development has become more difficult.

The policy of buying police houses in residential areas has at least one drawback, unless the area has been carefully chosen. Living in a single police house, in the middle of an estate containing a proportion of people who are anti-police, is not pleasant for the family of a policeman and some have suffered harassment from the relatives of criminals who live in neighbouring streets.

On the other hand, the increasing number of police officers who have bought their own houses has caused a drift of police away from the areas where they work and concentrated them in areas where they can buy a suitable house, along with everyone else in the same income bracket. Rural houses have become unpopular as more police officers and their spouses seek the amenities of towns and the work that is available there. Thus, the voluntary presence of a police officer living in each sizeable village is difficult to secure.

Police housing and deployment is no longer a simple matter of maintaining police houses strategically distributed throughout a force area and directing police officers from house to house as the necessity arises. It now requires careful planning and the use of a flexible personnel policy to be able to safeguard the interests of the police force and those of individual police officers.

Chapter Sixteen

Decision-making

Command activities

In a small organisation, it is possible for the person at the top to make all the decisions—the members merely do as he tells them. As the concern grows larger, this becomes more difficult; there are too many people who need access to the boss for decisions to be made and so a pattern of delegation is created. Certain areas of responsibility are made over to people within the organisation, the limits of their powers to make decisions being prescribed by policies laid down by the person at the head. This will be dealt with in detail in Chapter 18.

The system of allocating responsibility for specific areas of activity, according to a hierarchy of ranks, forms a command structure. It depends for its success upon a combination of organisational features discussed in earlier chapters and the quality of the people who occupy command posts. The commander of a police unit uses resources—people, equipment and buildings—to achieve his quota of the aims of his police force. The nature of police objectives was reviewed in Chapter 4 and each police unit has some contribution to make to them on a time or territorial basis or as a specialist service. Since the principal resource of the police is manpower (it accounts for about seven-eighths of a typical police budget), a great deal of emphasis has been placed on manpower planning, personnel administration and welfare since these are clearly key activities for all police supervisors. It is now necessary to consider how a police commander directs his resources towards the aims of his unit.

Once a police system has been set up (*see* Chapters 6 and 7), it tends to run itself according to the routines that form part of the system. However, day-to-day decisions are necessary to keep the machinery running and the commander needs to take personal charge of anything requiring his authority, experience or skill. The making of decisions will be considered in this chapter and the use of personal skills to obtain the maximum effort of people in implementing decisions will be dealt with in following chapters.

Decision-making

Police officers spend their working lives dealing with a wide variety of situations and how well they deal with them depends on the skill with which they go through a series of processes in respect of each separate incident. They need to obtain enough information they can analyse to form the basis of a sensible decision. This decision must then be put into operation and its effects monitored, so that any necessary amendments can be made. Reduced to its basic essentials, the process of decision-making can be shown to consist of a repetition of a cycle of activities. These activities are as follows:

Stage 1. Receiving information.
Stage 2. Analysing the information received.
Stage 3. Making decisions.
Stage 4. Implementing those decisions.
Stage 5. Monitoring the results.

The whole process is shown diagrammatically in Fig. 18, where its continuous nature can be seen more easily. Analysing how police decisions are made and executed in this way is not meant to indicate that, every time such a decision is made, a police officer consciously goes, or should go, through these stages. What it does is to enable us to see the skills that decision-making demands of the police officer and the wide range of

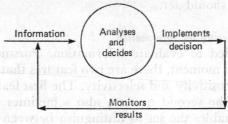

Fig. 18—Cyclic process of decision-making.

L

considerations that govern success. Clearly, most police decisions are made instinctively, these instincts becoming more reliable with experience. Similarly, once he has made a decision and starts to put it into action, the police officer, just as instinctively, watches to see whether he is doing the right thing and takes corrective action if he is not. It is at levels where instinct alone is not enough, that conscious thought about the processes of decision-making and implementation begins to bring rewards in terms of better decisions applied with greater flexibility.

Stage 1: receiving information
The range of information received by the police officer will depend to a large extent on the sensitivity of the individual. In the same way that a radio set may be only sensitive enough to receive very strong signals, so one police officer may only see and hear the most obvious features of the situation that he is facing. As a sensitive radio-receiver will be able to detect fainter signals, so a more alert individual may be able to detect underlying attitudes, minute signals that enable him to sense that there is more to an incident than meets the eye; that someone is not telling the truth or that there is a need for caution. It is the ability to be able to detect this sort of information that often distinguishes a good police officer from a less-able one.

Apart from information received direct from the incident, the police officer possesses quantities of stored intelligence he may need to be able to recall. This can include not only the obvious sorts of police information about crime, criminals and vulnerable premises, but also knowledge of the resources available to him, how he secures them and what their uses and limitations are. Finally, of course, he needs to have learned and remembered the law, procedures and policies that govern how he may and should act.

Stage 2: analysing the information
Skill is needed to evaluate information. Pursuing the radio analogy for a moment, there are two features that a good radio set needs—sensitivity and selectivity. The first feature has been dealt with, the second quality, also sometimes called discrimination, enables the set to distinguish between two or more different radio stations that on a cheaper set can interfere with

one another. This quality of selectivity is essential in a good police officer. He hears what is being said to him against a background of noise, counter allegations, protestations, conflicting interests, through which he must be able to select the relevant information and analyse it.

Text-books usually give the facts and invite the reader to make a decision. In real life, half the battle is obtaining the facts in the first place and, having obtained them, to sort out those that are relevant and those that are not. Given the circumstances under which a police officer must make many of his decisions, the ability to select the right information, upon which to base a decision, is an essential quality that requires an innate analytical ability that can be developed with experience.

Stage 3: making decisions
To be able to make a sensible decision, a police officer has to have enough information on which to base it and to be aware of the environment in which it is being made. The environment is made up of many contributory features which surround the police officer and which exercise some form of restriction or pressure upon him. Some of the most important are the law, police regulations, local policies, the practicalities of the situation and how the police officer sees his role.

The last point, the view that police officers have of their job relative to the community in which they work, is of particular importance because of the way in which it affects the attitudes and methods of police in different places. As an example, two studies have served to illustrate the way in which the environment can affect the approach of the police to their work as law enforcers. A study of some British police officers showed that they tended to use their sense of morality and fair play to guide them when to make an arrest, so that they would not arrest someone, even when the legal power was there, if it would be unfair on him to do so (*The Policeman in the Community*, M. Banton, Tavistock Publications, 1964). In contrast, the patrolmen working in a slum area of an American city, where a small incident could spark off serious violence, were much more concerned with resolving any incident as quickly as possible and made arrests according to the need to take immediate action rather than the fairness or otherwise to the individual ("The

Police on Skid Row", E. Bittner, *American Sociological Review*, 1967, cited by M. Chatterton, *The Police We Deserve*, eds. J. C. Alderson and P. J. Stead, Wolfe, 1973).

The importance of making decisions that accord with the social climate in which the police operate cannot be overstressed. If police officers move out of phase with society they start to lose their principal ally—the public: ". . . the police cannot successfully carry out their task of maintaining law and order without the support and confidence of the people" said the 1960 Royal Commission. To maintain this support and confidence means reacting in a balanced and reasonable way. To over-react brings forth an over-reaction in opposition. A police officer can only avoid over-reacting if he is aware of the limits within which he must operate, limits that change rapidly and are seldom written down.

Stage 4: implementation
Having decided what must be done, the police officer sets about doing it. Many decisions involve people—directing, arresting, questioning or helping them. To be able to do this, personal skills are required to ensure co-operation. It is at this level that some police officers have difficulty. They know what to do but they lack ability to communicate with people and so resort to force where it would have been possible to persuade.

The *way* in which a police decision is put into effect needs to accord with the acceptable standards of society. British police officers are generally expected to behave with moderation and courtesy; but these are difficult features to qualify, depending as they do on the standards of the individual passing judgment and those of the community at the time.

To be able to respond effectively to the situation facing him by implementing the action that he has decided upon, the police officer has to be wary of the limitations that he himself carries—his own pre-conceptions. As police officer/psychologist Jennifer Hilton has put it: "He too will hold stereotypes about people and events which will tend to limit the flexibility of his response to different situations. The assumptions, for instance, that 'all women are irrational' or that 'all West Indians are excitable' are well calculated to provoke irrational and excitable reactions" (*The Police We Deserve*, p. 96).

Stage 5: monitoring results
As an incident proceeds, a police officer observes the way in which things develop. For example, if he has decided to try to persuade someone to do something and that persuasion is not succeeding, he may change his decision and use his authority. Similarly, a decision to deal with something on his own may have to be changed to a rapid call for assistance as he senses that the situation is getting out of hand, or that there is some underlying danger.

The skills required here are those of stage 1; basically, sensitivity to what is happening, plus an acknowledgment that it is sometimes necessary to change one's mind. Police officers who go into a situation, make a quick evaluation, decide what should be done and then keep going irrespective of what happens are almost certain to meet with disaster at some stage of their careers. In most walks of life and particularly in the police, decisions need to be firm but flexible.

Police command
The system of decision-making described above has been related to the day-to-day work of the operational police officer but it is of more general application. If a similar exercise is carried out for police supervisors, a similar system emerges. Once again, there is the necessity to receive information, to analyse it and to make decisions but, instead of implementing these decisions themselves, much of a supervisor's work is achieved through other people. Stage 4, therefore, must reflect this aspect of a supervisor's work which is, primarily, to communicate decisions to subordinates and to exercise some control over their activities, an activity that requires leadership on the part of the supervisor and is best considered under that heading.

Leadership requires the ability to communicate with people, a fundamental skill needed by all police officers but even more vital to a supervisor who must accomplish so much of the work through the efforts of others. It should not cause any real surprise that decision-making is a similar process at all levels in the police. It is one of the singular features of the service that the most critical decisions are often those made by the most junior ranks. A parliamentary debate or High Court action may stem from a decision made by a probationer constable. Without the aid of reference books and probably even without the opportunity to be able to think quietly about the matter, the constable must make a decision that may be challenged in newspaper analysis, legal arguments and political polemics. Usually after such a decision has been implemented, more senior police officers become involved and they have to deal with a situation in which the critical decision has already been made, right or wrong.

What this means is that, from the moment that he joins the service, a police officer is having to use many of the skills and attributes that will be needed in higher ranks. Some power of command will normally be possessed by a good operational police constable, although this will clearly need to be developed.

Police command systems

The basic system described above and shown in Fig. 18 represents just one decision in a continuous process. Dealing with just one incident involves making a whole series of decisions, each of them requiring the same thought processes and linked by the flow of information that the police commander receives, analyses and converts into action.

The nature of decisions taken today is governed by decisions taken in the past that have helped to create policies, traditions, customs, law and the expectations of the public. What is decided today may affect decisions in the future; the identification of long-term effects of decisions is an essential quality of decision-making, particularly at senior officer level.

The social environment

Governing all police action there is a social environment within which the police must work. This environment varies from country to country, even from town to town and from time to time. It affects the whole style of policing and the methods used by the police. In a totalitarian country in which the police form an arm of the state, the environment within which the police operate is decided by the rulers of the state and methods may be used which do not have the agreement of the population who are being policed—quite the contrary, perhaps. In Britain, the role of the police has developed as described in Chapter 1 and so police commanders must operate according to the law and within public expectations, geared to the social climate of the day. Basically, police officers are expected to be courteous and, even when they are being firm, to use force only when necessary and then only to the minimum justifiable extent and to uphold the public's concept of fair play.

Thus the police commander does not have a free hand to make decisions based on facts alone but must operate within rules. Unfortunately, the rules are not constant, nor are all of them written down, hence the need for a police officer to be aware of the world around him and not to become too inward-looking in his approach to his work.

Police actions are subject to scrutiny and analysis by the public, the press, the courts and Parliament. At the end of the day, whether a police officer was right to take a course of action will usually depend on whether it was "reasonable". What is reasonable—did it or did it not fit the social environment at that moment for that class of incident? The rules are strict but may be relaxed if the circumstances make it essential, to save life or to capture a violent criminal, for example.

The nature and source of information

The word "information" is used in its widest sense and includes intelligence received from all sources, including the memory of the individual making the decisions, for this is an important source of information that has accumulated through experience.

Other sources of information include the following:

1. *Subordinates.* Verbal and written reports provide a major source of information for supervisors. From his subordinates, a supervisor also receives informal information, advice and suggestions. He may receive requests for additional resources or other aid, such as advice, guidance or instructions. All of this information tells the police commander something about the problems of his unit and also about his men.

It is essential that the method of leadership adopted by a senior officer should allow a free flow of such information without which much first-hand knowledge of the problems facing him would be lost.

2. *Senior officers.* Instructions and guidance help to identify a supervisor's objectives as part of those of the whole organisation and prescribe the limits of his authority. He also passes information to his senior officers, to enable them to adjust their objectives, revise strategies and institute controls. He also requests additional resources, decisions outside his authority and guidance on central policy matters in exactly the same way that *his* subordinates seek these from him.

3. *Specialists.* These supply the specialised knowledge that aids in decision-making and with specialist problems within a command. They will also be part of another system, based on their specialisation, for the police force consists of a series of inter-connected systems of which we are looking at just one, centred around one supervisor.

4. *Other police units.* Contact with other units—neighbouring territorial commands, other departments, other police force units, regional crime squads, and the like, from which information is obtained and by whom work is carried out.

5. *Non-police units.* Links with courts, other emergency services, social services departments all provide information that aids police aims or identifies police tasks. Information must flow freely into the police organisation from the public. A supervisor must play his part in monitoring the relationship between his unit and the public.

6. *Direct observation.* A police commander needs to be aware of what is happening about him for, although he can sit in an office and receive much of his information, there is some that can best be obtained at first hand. He sees the conditions in the area that he polices, the state of his own building, the work done by some members of his unit, the demeanour of his subordinates, and so on. From such information he makes judgments, a danger being a tendency to generalise too much from what he sees and so divert his attention from true objectives to insignificant ones.

7. *Books and records.* Most police forces keep many records of what happens, who did what, where and when. The supervisor needs to be able to take from this mass of writing the significant features that tell him what is happening. Too much attention to minutiae may cause important details to be overlooked.

8. *Policy*. In every organisation, there are accepted procedures and rules that help to provide a measure of consistency and order. In many organisations, some of these policies are laid down in the form of written documents. Such policies have the advantage of providing a standard response to the problems facing an organisation and reduce the time taken to make decisions. They also restrict the courses of action open to decision-makers and may unnecessarily strangle initiative unless they are periodically overhauled.

9. *History*. Previous responses from an organisation are often used as a guide for the future. They can provide a valuable source of reference provided that care is taken to ensure that they are not used to replace original thought entirely and that the conditions under which the precedent was established still obtain.

10. *Experience*. Every senior officer uses his recollection of his personal experience to guide him in his work. His memory will include details of incidents in which he has been concerned, training he has received and advice and information given in the past.

This accumulation of experience is considered as highly desirable in a police officer. It gives him credibility with his subordinates, provides a ready source of reference and usually facilitates decisions. It is worth remembering that experience can also act as an inhibitor, in that it tends to channel thoughts in one direction when it might be better to look afresh at a situation. Sometimes conscious rejection of the lessons of previous experience is advisable.

The sources of information described are shown diagrammatically in Fig. 19, where the all-pervading social environment is shown as a ring around the whole system. Three things need to be noted about this diagram. The first is that it is greatly over-simplified, for it is not possible to truly represent a multi-dimensional system by a two-dimensional drawing. Secondly, there will be a lot of inter-communication among the various sources of information that cannot be represented here. Thirdly, the communication between sources and the police commander is two-way—an imperative for all effective communication.

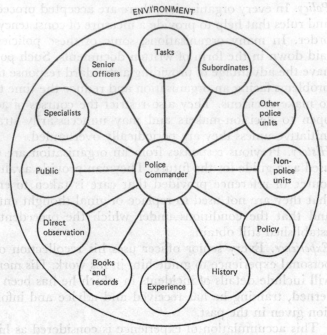

Fig. 19—Sources of information.

Analysis

If a senior officer is to be effective, he must possess the characteristics of selectivity and discrimination to be able to distinguish what, of all the information that surrounds him, can tell
him what he needs to know. A mass of material, written and
oral, besets every police commander. Simply to read all the
legislation, case law, Home Office guidance and force orders
that come his way takes up a great deal of time. Add to this the
routine reports and statistics that flow through most police
forces and it becomes clear that a senior officer must try to
learn what he *must* read and what he can glance at or read in
summary form. Many supervisors read too many routine documents that could well be dealt with at a lower level. It is here
that the principle of management by exception can be so useful.
If only those reports that contain something out of the ordinary
or require a decision outside the terms of delegated authority

are passed through the system, supervisory officers have much more time to collect the information they really need.

Once the process of selection has been applied, there comes the need to evaluate the information received. Sub-consciously, we do this all the time. When we are told something, we listen to what is said, weigh the information according to what we know of the person who is speaking and what we already know of the subject. We may conclude that what we have been told is valueless or that we should absorb it into our memories for future application, rather (but in a much more flexible way) as a computer stores information. Our memories can distort the information whereas the computer, having no imagination, just repeats what has been recorded. Whilst this process is normally a sub-conscious one, it is worth processing some information consciously when major decisions have to be taken. This is particularly true in an emergency situation, where a great deal of dubious information tends to be generated before proper communication and control channels have been established.

Finally, all the information received has to be weighed to obtain its true value. This can be difficult, because many factors can influence the value of any piece of information. This is especially true when a variety of different views have to be evaluated. Sometimes it is not facts that have to be used as the basis but opinions, which may or may not be based on facts. Often it comes down to knowing the reliance that can safely be placed, not on the opinion but on the person giving it.

Making decisions
At the heart of the system is the need for a police commander to be able to make a decision. In respect of any given information, he may decide to do nothing. That is a decision and must be distinguished from doing nothing where no conscious decision has been taken. Quite a lot of senior officers have found that problems frequently solve themselves if they decide to do nothing. In fact, in most cases, they are *not* doing nothing. What has happened is that they have considered the problem, decided that there is no solution that will help the situation and so to do nothing is as good a solution as any. Provided they have worked on adequate information and have analysed it correctly and thought deeply enough about a possible solution, this is a legi-

timate course of action—to do nothing but monitor results so that, if the situation changes, action can be taken.

The process of decision-making is a complex one but it can be simplified by applying a systematic approach. From the outset, it is worth remembering that most police problems are not simple matters requiring a "yes/no" answer. Most of the situations facing the police require a whole series of decisions all linked to a common purpose. The identification of such common purposes will be discussed later but, for the moment, let us look at the sort of questions that can be posed when a problem must be solved by a police officer:

1. *What is the problem?* Much time and effort has been poured into solving the wrong problems. Sometimes the symptoms of trouble are diagnosed as the disease; sometimes a person seeking a decision is not aware of the true nature of his own problem; sometimes only part of the problem is visible.

As an example, consider the police-vehicle maintenance programme. The problem, as posed by the head of the servicing department, is that the police cars are not being delivered to the garage on time and keep missing servicing appointments. But is that the real problem? A few inquiries reveal that the garage mechanics are paid a bonus according to the number of vehicles they service; the delay in delivering one, or a vehicle that misses an appointment, costs them money. They have protested to the garage head who presents his problem to the senior police officer as one of getting vehicles to the garage on time. But why do the police vehicles not get to the garage on time for servicing? Because they are tied up on operational work; they are needed because there are no other vehicles available. So the nature of the problem could now be, are there enough cars? But it would cost more to buy additional cars than to pay the garage mechanics their bonus irrespective of how many vehicles they serviced. And so the ramifications of the situation may go on until the full circle is completed. Any part of this problem could be seen by someone in the organisation as being the whole problem. To him, it may be. The head of the servicing department may see his objectives as the need to keep his staff fully occupied on servicing vehicles. But the reality as far as the police force as a whole is concerned is quite different; the true position can really only make sense in terms of the total objectives of the force and these are to police the area. The objectives of the servicing department should therefore be related to the need to maintain a guaranteed minimum number of usable vehicles at an economic cost—a very different concept from that of trying to produce a flow of work to justify bonuses for mechanics.

In many cases, the first difficulty with problem solving is to identify the true nature of the problem. Most police officers are faced with a set of circumstances that seem to require that they do something. Before one can decide what to do he must find out what he is dealing with and correctly identify the objectives that he must seek. Once he has done this it becomes a problem of devising the strategies that will attain those objectives.

2. *What is the time scale?* The approaches that may be made to problem-solving increase in number with the time allowed. This will be discussed in more detail in Chapter 17 when alternative decision-making methods are considered. Police officers, by tradition, are expected to be decisive and nothing is worse than a senior officer who will not, or cannot, make a decision when it is necessary. Many problems fall into a familiar class that enables a police officer to make a decision based on his experience. Where they are out of the general run, it is worth using the full amount of time available to use the most thorough method of decision-making, particularly where consultation would be of value in aiding the processes of communication and producing greater acceptability.

At a senior level, the involvement of the Police Federation, Superintendents' Association and trade unions in the making of policy decisions, either through small working parties or an advisory committee, can aid not only the acceptability of such policies but also their technical quality. At divisional/sub-divisional level, the involvement of people in decisions affecting them can achieve similar results. The process need not be a formal one; the committees need not be run on parliamentary lines to be effective. Decisions arrived at by consensus rather than by vote, although they often involve compromises, tend to be seen as committee decisions rather than those of the people with power. In matters where acceptability is vital for success, this can be very important (*see* also Chapter 17, p. 342).

3. *What are the alternatives?* It is possible to make a problem harder than it really is by artifically restricting the range of alternatives from which a course of action must be chosen. There is a tendency to assume that there are two alternative courses of action with a possible third being to do nothing. In fact, it is often not simply a case of opting for black or for white because there are many shades of grey between.

It is also necessary for senior officers to examine the extent to which decision-making is hampered by an existing policy. The object of "policy" decisions, that is to say those maintained as standards against which to measure subsequent decisions, is to ensure uniformity and consistency. For example, they may prevent one person from being treated more unfairly than his colleague in respect of the same sort of situation. They also allow decisions to be made "in accordance with policy" at a lower level in the organisation and with less effort than would be required to revert back to basic principles.

But policies are not chipped on tablets of stone and because they have existed for some years they are not immutable. At senior levels in the force, they need to be challenged or rethought at intervals to ensure change to match the situation.

Finally, decision-makers must beware of the restrictions they impose upon themselves by their own preconceptions. We are all conditioned by experience; this not only helps by giving information upon which to base decisions but it also restricts vision. It is as if we were wearing blinkers and so can only see straight ahead. When faced with any unusual problem, it is occasionally well worth while to operate a "think tank" approach, letting the imagination wander over and around the problem to see if there is some solution that has been evading our conscious level of thought, because of the "blinkers" that we are conditioned to wear.

4. *What will the effects be?* There can be few police supervisors who have not at some stage of their careers taken decisions without realising their full consequences. The higher a police

officer goes in rank, the more difficult it becomes to estimate the effects of any one decision. In part, this is so because many people are, or may be, involved, and it is difficult to calculate how a decision made at the top of an organisation will affect every single individual; it is also so because of the way in which the decision is interpreted at the various supervisory levels within the organisation.

Most decisions are made on the basis of an assumed effect. If one course of action is taken, this will happen; if another course is taken, that will happen. Careful consideration is required to estimate what the side-effects will be. A decision taken in one police force can affect others, or it may affect other organisations. Some of these effects can be seen without difficulty, while others are more subtle. Once again, the use of consultation helps, particularly as the representative organisations may be able to feed in information obtained from their own network and are also more likely to be aware of possible consequences at the grass roots of the force.

5. *What are the risks?* A lot of decision-making is concerned with uncertainty. If a course of action is taken, certain things *may* happen. What is needed is the ability to estimate the possibility of those things happening and, as most police decisions involve people, considerable understanding of people is required. It is not always possible to judge how people will react to a given course of action but the ability to be able to see their point of view certainly helps to avoid serious errors of judgment.

The risks need to be compared with the expected return; there is no point in taking unnecessary chances to obtain only a minimal advantage. The risks need to be calculated, particularly if the proposed course of action is outside the limits of normally acceptable behaviour. Risks here include that of one bad decision destroying all the goodwill that has accumulated through hundreds of good decisions.

When dealing with emotive issues, it is always tempting to use a coldly-logical approach, working on the basis that the argument is irrefutable. The trouble is that life is not always ruled by logic. A decision on overtime, shifts or rest days, may be quite logical, yet the police officers concerned will resent it if they have not been consulted. To close a country police station and replace it with mobile policing may well be logical and capable of proof (using statistics) but it is almost certain that some of the public will resent the decision unless a lot of pre-decision discussions have taken place. Even that is no guarantee of success.

6. *What resources are available?* Because police activities are difficult to quantify, it is tempting to assume that the use of police officers to do a job, at a time when they would be on duty anyway, costs nothing. This is not true, for police manpower is expensive and if it can be diverted from one job to another without good cause, it raises the question of whether the manpower was really needed in the first place.

At its simplest level, this means asking the question: "Is this the most effective way to use these men?" The same considerations apply with motor vehicles and all other resources. If they are to be used for any purpose, is this the most valuable use that can be found for them in terms of achieving the objectives of the police?

7. *Which option brings the maximum benefit with the least risk?* There is seldom one decision that provides the maximum benefit with the minimum risk. Usually there are a number of options, all of which contain some element of risk of failure and all of which bring some benefit if they succeed. So begins the process of elimination. The first to go are those in which the risk of failure is high and the rewards for success minimal. Along with these go those in which, although the prospect of failure may not be very high, the actual consequences of failure would be absolutely disastrous. Then consideration is given to the balance of the remainder, weighing benefits against risk and consequence of failure, until a "best available" solution is reached. If two courses of action seem equally safe, beneficial and economic, in theory, chance could be allowed to decide with the toss of a coin. Somehow or other this is seldom necessary, for there are few situations that cannot be evaluated by the use of further information, properly analysed. If all else fails, it may be a matter of choosing the course that leaves the maximum number of options open for the future. At least if the decision is wrong, there will be chances to correct it!

8. *Does the solution meet the needs of the situation?* This seemingly

superfluous question is inserted because at the end of a long session in which many alternatives have been considered and rejected, it is possible to lose sight of the objectives of the whole exercise. So, before committing oneself to a course of action following such a session, it is worth taking a brief but searching glance, just to make sure that, in the desire to come to a conclusion, the solution fits the true objectives.

Implementing decisions

The part that leadership plays in the practice of command will be dealt with in the next chapter but it is significant that the way in which a decision is reached will greatly affect the process of communication and control. A solution that has been reached by agreement among the parties involved will not normally require the same degree of explanation and checking of performance as one imposed without consultation. A decision to adopt methods outside the normal experience of the operators will also require careful explanation, with particular emphasis on the objectives of the scheme.

One must always beware of assuming what the reaction will be from any set of people because, although genuine efforts are made to try to see things from their point of view, it is impossible to allow for the inbuilt beliefs and biases that direct the way people think.

The involvement of members of representative organisations in decision-making is a common and useful way of helping to ensure that the final solution has a measure of acceptability and is therefore easier to implement. Care must be taken not to take too much for granted. The representatives of the Police Federation, Superintendents' Association or trade unions such as the National Association of Local Government Officers have only delegated powers and the extent of their authority varies considerably from place to place and from subject to subject. For example, a Police Federation representative on a working party dealing with an emotive or fundamental issue, may have very limited authority to commit his branch board so that it is not wise to assume that, because he agrees with a course of action, it will be acceptable to his colleagues. Individual representatives, whether of unions or police representative organisations, have their own ideas, prejudices and biases like everyone else and these can sometimes intrude into decision-making sessions. Ultimately, however, it is the contact that they have with members, their ability to understand their feelings and see their point of view, that adds a dimension to the discussion. Certainly, the aid of representative organisations in helping to communicate new schemes and procedures can be enormously helpful, whilst their opposition can mean, at the very least, that the controls needed to enforce a set of procedures will have to be multiplied several times.

The controls introduced with a new scheme should be carefully linked to the feedback that is used to monitor performance. The best controls are those which allow the maximum initiative on the part of the people putting the scheme into practice, yet ensure that their activities are properly co-ordinated.

Monitoring performance

To monitor what is happening, a stream of accurate information needs to flow quickly back to the person responsible for making decisions. An analogy might be the speed indicator on a motor vehicle: it is valueless to have one that tells you what speed you were doing some time ago; you want to know immediately, so that you can adjust the brake or accelerator accordingly.

So, every system needs feedback of information that is geared to the time scale of the situation. A long-term scheme may require monthly, quarterly or annual reports. An emergency decision may require immediate feedback to enable alternative action to be taken or adjustment or reinforcement of the original decision.

To ensure accuracy is not as easy as it sounds. Many schemes introduced into the police have been favourably reported upon when tried experimentally, but have failed when put into permanent use. There are several reasons for this. The first is that experimental groups tend to feel rather "special" and will put more effort into their work than when they are doing ordinary routine jobs. Further, any adverse comments that they may make about the experiment may not be relayed back to the person at the top, because it is filtered out by intermediate ranks who wish to prove that they can do what the boss wants. Defects will often be passed over as being due to the fact that the present set-up *is* experimental and can be overcome when the scheme becomes general. Finally, a lot of faults tend to be long term or cumulative and so do not show up clearly in a short experiment.

The author of a new scheme must be prepared to probe, to satisfy himself that he is obtaining the right information and at the right time. If he is a senior officer, there will be a reluctance on the part of his juniors to tell him that his scheme is faulty. This reluctance will vary according to the personality of the senior officer and those of his subordinates, but is, as so often, likely to be reduced by the employment of consultation when introducing schemes.

Command systems in action

From the outline above, it can be seen that the key commodity in police command is a flow of accurate information in which the police commander plays a central role. Having considered the command situation in general, it is revealing to see how these general principles apply to the command of police resources when dealing with an incident.

Different types of major police tasks—serious accidents, serious crimes, hostage situations—all have features peculiar to that type of incident but the development of the role of the man in charge contains much that is common to most emergencies. It is those elements that are of concern here rather than the details of procedure that may be adopted to deal with specific incidents.

Initial action

When an incident occurs, the first people at the scene may try to contain the situation, to save life or prevent further damage to property and, in general, deal with perceived priorities as best they can. The emergency services are called, including the police. The first police officers carry out the initial action and assess the seriousness of the situation. They radio details to headquarters, including special instructions as to means of approach and equipment requirements.

The first supervisory officer to arrive tries to ascertain the full extent of the problem and then set about establishing a system of co-ordinating the activities of the people at the scene. Soon, a system of police command is established. This will consist of a communication and control system centred on the senior police officer in charge, the identity and role of whom may change. Often a junior rank officer is the first at the scene and more senior officers arrive at later stages according to the seriousness and/or length of time that the incident lasts.

The role of the police commander
The role of the police commander can be illustrated as the centre of a communication and control system as shown in Fig. 20. As with Fig. 19, this is a simplified representation in two-dimensional form of a multi-dimensional system. The flow of information among the various units, other than through the police commander, has again been omitted although an essential ingredient in real life. Despite simplification, the diagram does give some indication of the wide range of sources from which the leader receives information, each requiring, in return, information, instructions or advice from him.

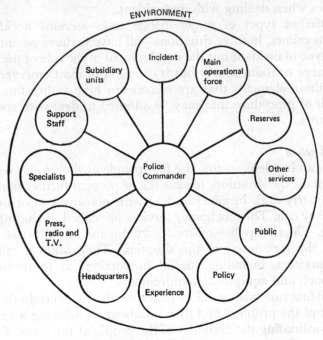

Fig. 20—Communication and control system.

The police leader may be in physical contact with the incident but quite often he will be able to form only a limited impression of what is happening directly, most of the information coming from the intelligence he obtains from other people. All information must be sifted, analysed and processed as described earlier.

Sources of communication

Of the sources of intelligence and requests for instructions and information grouped around the police commander in Fig. 20, some may not be applicable to a particular incident while others, not shown, may be required instead.

The incident itself has been included in the diagram because clearly the nature of the incident and the way in which it develops will greatly influence the system and, whilst most of the information about the way in which the incident develops will be communicated by other people, it is useful to consider the incident as an information source if only to focus attention on the objectives of the whole exercise. Some information does come direct from the incident; for example, the police leader may wish to form his own opinion of the state of mind of people holding hostages, by talking to them himself. He may make a decision about evacuation based on his own observation of the potential danger of flood-water or fire. Other sources of information include the following:

1. *The main operational force.* The main body of police dealing with the incident must be controlled to ensure that action is co-ordinated. Information will need to be fed to and from these people through an efficient communication channel, using a chain of command that ensures that every man is aware of his part in the exercise and monitors his efforts.

2. *Reserves.* In many cases, there is the need to have fresh people available to replace those who are tired, injured or hungry. This reserve must also be informed of what is happening so that, when they are required, they are ready for action and know what to do.

3. *Subsidiary units.* These may be small units deployed to seek information or to deal with problems on the fringe of the main incident, such as traffic control, public order or

search-parties for debris. Once again good communication is essential to feed information between these remote groups and the leader so that the sub-objectives of the subsidiary units can be adjusted to meet changes of strategy.

4. *Support staff*. A number of people will be required to attend to the administration needed when large numbers of people are employed. The logging of messages, records of injured people, care and listing of property, and taking of statements can all be classed as support functions as well as the more obvious feeding and watering arrangements. In order to function properly, communication will be needed to match the support facilities to the services demanded of them.

5. *Specialists*. Many incidents require a range of specialists, which may include doctors, bomb-disposal men, forensic experts, marksmen and frogmen. The police leader must know what he has at his disposal and what they can do. It is not uncommon for a police officer to be told after an incident that there was equipment or expertise that he could have used had he known of its existence. It is also possible for a leader to expect more from experts than they can supply, because he does not know enough about them. A senior officer need not be able to dive into a river wearing a frogman's suit but he should be aware of what a frogman can and cannot do or at least listen to what an expert tells him. This is particularly important when he is putting the specialist at risk: he should be fully aware of the degree of risk that he is creating, relative to the expected result.

6. *Other emergency services*. The liaison between the police leader and the leaders of other emergency organisations is of vital importance and it must be clear who is responsible for what aspect of the incident. Clearly, at a fire, the senior fire officer is in overall command, while at an accident in which there is a risk of fire, the police leader would be in overall command. In dealing with other services the comments above about dealing with specialists also apply.

7. *Press, radio and television*. Press reporters and cameramen are renowed for their ingenuity in obtaining what they want despite restrictions. It is much better to provide facilities for them so that there is proper control by police rather than have to divert resources to remove unauthorised people

from the thick of the incident (which, admittedly, may still be necessary even if facilities are supplied, but the likelihood is reduced). Once again communication is the key, for, not only should the press be informed of what is happening so that they present an accurate account, but also the media can frequently aid police by publishing inquiry telephone-numbers and directional information.

8. *The public.* There is invariably a public involvement at major incidents—spectators, witnesses, anxious relatives who will require police attention. There is also often the need to remember the interests of public at large; for example, such considerations may limit the steps that can be taken to close streets or to use tear gas or firearms.

9. *Headquarters.* The commander needs to maintain a line of communication with headquarters to enable him to obtain further resources, check the extent of his authority and receive instructions and advice.

10. *Policy.* In every organisation, there are ways of doing things that help to ensure that people follow established procedures. In exceptional cases, departure from previous policy may be necessary but care needs to be taken to ensure that other people are aware of the fact.

11. *Experience.* Every police commander relies on previous experience of similar incidents, gained for himself or acquired at second hand from other people. This is one of the values of good training; it enlarges the experience of the people who have received it.

The environment

Finally, there is the important factor that is once again shown as a circle around the whole model. In any country, at any time, there will be closely prescribed limits of behaviour beyond which the police officer goes at his peril. These limits, which include the degree to which force may be used and the attitude that the police are expected to adopt to certain types of incident, will vary from time to time, often quite rapidly.

The nature of this environmental factor and its effects on police are discussed in general terms on p. 314 above, but it is so important that it justifies further consideration. Many of the limits within which police may act are laid down by law and these may be extended or reduced according to the dangers perceived by society, for example, the additional powers given to police to curb terrorism. Other limits are less explicit and may at times be very vague. Pornography is just one example of a problem requiring the police to be alert to the need to diagnose what is, and what is not, acceptable at any given time and place.

Where the police have to contend with conflicting sections of the population, the need for clear judgment becomes vital. Consider a community composed of two different races of people. One race, A, wishes to hold a public event in the area that will seriously inconvenience members of race B and give rise to damage and crime. Race B will exert pressure on the police to stop the event. Race A will resent any police attempts to limit what they see as a legitimate activity. The senior police officer, who must decide on police action, will be conscious of the pressures upon him, not only from the local people but also from the rest of society who will judge his actions. His decisions are likely to be greatly influenced by what he thinks society expects of the police at that time. Such considerations govern all police activities and on many occasions there has been a public outcry resulting from some action taken by police which, although legal, was outside the limits of what was considered acceptable from the British police in that situation. Not even when they are carrying out their duty of law enforcement are the police safe, since they need the co-operation and support of the public and they will not receive these if they over-zealously enforce laws that lack public sympathy.

There are very few significant decisions that can be taken without considering the wider implications of proposed courses of action. Just what those implications may be requires a deep understanding of the forces at work in society. As J. C. Alderson has pointed out: "In a society where coherence is rapidly being lessened by special groups, minorities, even majorities with interests (and sometimes power) of their own, the police (who are themselves a minority) find that they are required to face in several directions simultaneously. Depending on the vested interest of groups, the police can be seen as scapegoats, fascists, beneficent guardians, interfering nuisances, father-figures or even heroes" (*The Police We Deserve*, p. 46).

Police decision-making requires a perfect sense of balance: knowing when to enforce the law and when to apply the discretion that is a feature of the British police; gauging the strength of feeling of opposing factions and steering a compromise that prevents violence; becoming involved in the community yet maintaining a degree of detachment to avoid being identified with sectional interests and, ultimately, preserving the balance between the freedom of the individual and the need to limit that freedom in the interests of society itself.

Chapter Seventeen

Leadership

The need for leadership

It is not enough for a police commander to make good decisions, he must also be able to convert them into action. The very best decisions may result in disaster unless they are acted upon by subordinates who are prepared to use skill and common sense. To gain the level of co-operation that he needs, a supervisor must use leadership, which may be defined as the ability to inspire other people towards the attainment of a common objective.

No police officer is ever likely to achieve promotion unless he can satisfy his senior officers that he possesses personal qualities of leadership but difficulty arises when an attempt is made to define just what those qualities are. From the wide variety of people who have been successful leaders, both in the police service and elsewhere, it is clear that there is no one type of personality that will guarantee leadership to the exclusion of all others.

Studies that have been made of the personal qualities of leaders have failed to identify common characteristics in successful leaders. Looking at outstanding leaders of the past, it can be seen that they range from supreme egotists to relatively mild-mannered men who, nevertheless, were able to command the allegiance of a faithful body of followers.

In many uniformed services, there has been a tendency to equate leadership with a form of extrovert behaviour calculated to secure immediate, apparent obedience in subordinates. Leadership is too often seen in terms of the stereotype of a sergeant-major on a parade ground. The result has been the general under-estimation of the leadership ability of people who are quietly spoken and reserved. Leadership also tends to be associated with the man who can lead from the front in a dynamic way and obtain instant obedience to orders, but this is only one facet of leadership. Although the ability to lead a group of men going into action in a public-order situation is obviously important, the main task for most police supervisors is to inspire their subordinates to work towards a common objective that may be no more clearly defined than to keep the crime rate under control or to provide a good service in response to calls from the public. It is one thing to lead a small group of men in pursuit of one immediate worthwhile goal; it is another to be able to obtain consistently high standards from a group of subordinates over a period of months or years.

This ability to lead people on a long-term basis is a prime requirement of a police supervisor but, in considering the ability of a man to lead, this aspect is often ignored in favour of the more obvious personality traits which may be taken to indicate leadership of the short-term dynamic variety.

In making an assessment of the leadership of a police officer, one cannot simply observe personal qualities in isolation and assume that certain combinations of traits will add up to leadership. A man may have all the apparent advantages of appearance, dynamic personality, competence and enthusiasm and yet, when placed in a position in which he is required to inspire others in trying to attain some common goal, he may be unable to do so.

Taking up a new command
Initial approach
The initial approach that a new supervisor adopts is very important. There is a proverb that suggests that a new broom will sweep clean. It is not a wise course of action until the person doing the sweeping has clearly established what needs to be swept and what can be left alone. Thus, at the beginning of any new relationship of this kind, a supervisor would be well advised to form an opinion of the work standards of the group he is now commanding and the extent to which the existing norms of the group are different from those that he would wish. He may find this difficult to do, for new supervisors are often encouraged by their senior officers to make their mark as quickly as possible and to set out as they mean to go on. Such advice is

worth following in a limited sense only. Certainly, on his arrival to take up his new position, a supervisor will be studied to assess his general qualities and it is important that a reputation for integrity, competence and fairness is established as soon as possible.

In so far as the instruction to "make his mark" refers to changing the methods of work, it should be accepted with caution; it is advisable to examine the methods being currently employed and relate them to the objectives of the unit before seeking to change them. In the early stages, most newly-arrived supervisors make changes inadvertently. To add further, deliberate, changes, until the need for them has been proved, is to court hostility and non-co-operation. The question of "involuntary decision-making" can be a tricky one for all supervisors and it is a problem that tends to increase in scope the higher the rank of the new supervisor. Involuntary decisions occur when the supervisor asks questions, comments or merely makes some gesture that can be interpreted as criticism of the way in which something is done. At sergeant or inspector level, this often occurs in relation to the method of completing reports; at chief officer level it can result in quite marked changes in force policy.

Introducing change
Many supervisors tend to change methods or practices that are different from those where they worked previously. Once again, this is most noticeable at senior officer level and it is not uncommon to find a senior officer remodelling his new command along the lines of the one he has just left. Such changes may be desirable or necessary but it is wise to ensure that there is a difference *in merit* between two systems, as distinct from just a difference. It is sometimes useful to remember that it may be easier for one senior officer to learn new practices than to insist that part of the organisation should go through a period of change in order to achieve a marginal gain.

The introduction of change in any organisation is one that must be of concern to any supervisor. Often, there will be the need for change but the method by which it is introduced is critical if it is to be made without causing harmful side-effects. This is particularly true of changes which are of great personal concern to the people who must implement them. Such matters as leave rosters, shift systems and factors influencing allowances, are particularly sensitive and any change that needs to be introduced of this type, may require great skill on the part of the supervisor. It is in this area of decision-making that the style of leadership is so important and we shall be returning to this subject in more detail later in the chapter.

Another important feature of change is that it can easily unsettle an otherwise effective working group. Many people distrust change which they may see as a threat or criticism. Once again, the way in which change is approached will affect the reaction of the people concerned.

Changing group standards
In any group of people who regularly work together, there may be just one person who exercises leadership on a long-term basis or, alternatively, a number of individuals may singly or collectively influence the attitudes and objectives of the group. When approaching a new command, in addition to carefully identifying the norms of the group before seeking to introduce change, the supervisor can learn something from observing the informal leadership pattern within the group. If the group's standards are such that they must be brought closer into line with the official rules of the organisation, then it is particularly important that the supervisor should realise that by picking on the leaders of the group who, to firmly label them as being anti-the organisation are usually called the "ring-leaders", there is always the danger of creating martyrs who will command even greater support from the rest of their colleagues. By concentrating on the followers rather than the leaders, a supervisor may find himself in direct opposition to the informal leaders and, while he may secure the outward compliance of the rules, it is possible that less overt rule-breaking may be initiated by the informal leaders. In general, by treating a working group as merely a collection of individuals and ignoring the existence of group standards and group leadership, a supervisor can create problems that could be avoided by treating the group as such. The supervisor should attempt to work with the group as a whole and seek to change its norms. If he can secure the co-operation of the informal leaders, then the rest of the group are likely to follow and his work will be made much easier.

Styles of leadership

The fact that a man is appointed as a supervisor and is given the necessary rank to place him higher in the organisational structure than his subordinates, does not make him a leader. A true leader is one who inspires his followers and, whilst in a disciplined service a supervisor may be awarded the marks of respect due to his rank, this does not mean that his subordinates will be inspired towards an objective that they and the supervisor have in common. Under supervisors who exercise no leadership, a group may pursue objectives of its own making and rely entirely on leadership from within. In other circumstances, a supervisor may find that he has a naturally well-motivated group who join him in having a common objective, but are not inspired by him, choosing to rely on their own leaders. It is thus possible for the nominal "leader" of a work group to exercise no leadership at all. This is a useful starting point from which to consider the ways in which a supervisor may exercise leadership.

Two contrasting styles

There are two opposing ways in which leadership may be exercised. A leader may act in an authoritarian manner and direct what must be done, when, how and by whom. Alternatively, he may state the problem to his subordinates, outline the limits of any action that can be taken and then allow the group to participate in making the decision as to what should be done.

It is possible to observe how these two extremes of leadership-style work in practice, their effects on followers and the quality of the action that results. In order to do this it is useful to consider individuals who operate more or less permanently at the extremes, although clearly this is unrealistic, since very few people are likely to behave in one extreme way for very long. Nevertheless, it can help to give a clear impression of the effects of these different types of leadership behaviour.

Authoritarian leadership

An authoritarian leader is characterised by a marked reluctance to consult subordinates or delegate to them. Decision-making tends to be highly centralised, and often quite minor matters have to be referred for a decision. Commonly, communication with subordinates is poor and there may be an inclination to restrict the amount of their knowledge so that the leader is the only one in full possession of all the facts as to what is going on and is, therefore, indispensable. Typically, highly-authoritarian leaders prefer weak or compliant deputies and other subordinates who are willing to accept a regime in which they are not permitted to make decisions and who are unlikely to challenge the authority of the leader.

Authoritarian leadership was the norm for most organisations —armed services, industry and the police—until the 1940s, when a reaction against it began, surfacing first in America and shortly afterwards in most democratic countries. The reason for this reaction is not completely clear but it was probably given impetus or, at the very least, the opportunity to emerge, through changes in the employee/employer balance of power. In order to succeed, authoritarianism requires one or two conditions: the people being led must accept the right of the leader to lead in that way, or the leader must have sufficient power over the followers to be able to enforce his wishes. In the period prior to the 1939–1945 war, the situation existing in most Western industrial societies provided the second of these two conditions. There was enough unemployment to ensure that the employer could use the threat of unemployment as a means of making employees accept conditions that they might otherwise have rejected.

The existence of an environment in which the second condition was fulfilled may well have masked whether the first condition was or was not also fulfilled. It seems probable, even without the pressures of mass-unemployment acting as an incentive to accept authoritarianism, that there was a greater willingness to conform to an authoritarian pattern of leadership prior to 1939 than, say, post 1950.

It should be noted that very rigid codes of conduct may not necessarily indicate the nature of an organisation: it is a question of how the rules were arrived at and how they are enforced that determines the degree of authoritarianism in an organisation. Nor is it true that people have to be forced into accepting rigid rules by the threat of unemployment outside the organisation. If rules are seen to be a necessary part of the organisation, and particularly if its status is high, there is likely to be a greater willingness to accept those rules than if they are arbitrarily made, or the status of the organisation is low. When there is a reaction against the leadership, the rules of the organisation become a battle-ground, as members challenge them and cause confrontations that can harm the organisation and the morale of the people in it.

Retreat from authoritarianism

The problem with any reaction against an existing order is that there is likely to be an over-reaction and this seems to be as true of the retreat from authoritarian leadership as anything else. From being the norm, it became unacceptable, with the inevitable result that organisations that had rigid rules and discipline codes found that a vacuum had occurred which proved difficult to fill.

Whereas, previously, orders would be accepted without question, these were now challenged and compared with the written rules. In any organisation there has to be a certain amount of give and take over the interpretation of rules. Our whole legal system is built upon the interpretation by the courts of the laws of the country. If it is necessary to test laws in this way, it is hardly surprising that the rules of an organisation should often be equally open to more than one interpretation. A number of skirmishes have taken place in different police forces over the interpretation of various rules.

Police forces are not the only organisations to be faced with the dilemma of changing attitudes to supervisory methods. In many ways, the police are insulated from some of the more dramatic effects felt in some sectors of industry. To a large extent, the strong group-identity of the police service enables it to survive many times of uncertainty, although not without problems.

The role of authoritarianism is now much clearer and the total reaction against it has eased in favour of a balance that allows that authoritarian leadership has a place in life. The nature of this place needs the understanding of leaders and led alike.

Authoritarian leadership in practice

The great advantage of authoritarian leadership is that it permits quick decision-making and there are some situations in the police service that require this. If a supervisor is in charge of a group of policemen at a violent demonstration or a sudden emergency, he is expected to give his orders quickly and decisively. In a disciplined service, it is unlikely that anyone would question either the right or need for a supervisor to give firm instructions and expect instant obedience under these circumstances.

Unfortunately, the aura of decisiveness and confidence that surrounds a supervisor who acts as though everything was a sudden emergency, and who gives his commands in this way, has deluded many supervisors into believing that this alone is true leadership. Some subordinates even prefer to work for such a man, rather than for one who gives them more responsibility to use their own initiative. The authoritarian leader largely relieves his subordinates of the need to make decisions at all and some people like this. It is also something to which subordinates can become conditioned and people who have been used to working for an authoritarian leader have some difficulty in adapting to a change in leadership style. For some, it is comforting always to be able to turn to the boss for a decision, rather than having to make up their own minds or provide their own ideas.

Although authoritarian leadership is undoubtedly needed in the police service when speed in decision-making is essential, the disadvantages of authoritarianism as a way of life should not be overlooked. If all decisions are made by the leader of a group of people without any reference to its members, only a fraction of the experience and brain power contained within that group is being deployed. Therefore, unless the leader of the group is truly outstanding, the decisions made are likely to be inferior to those which could result from making use of the total mental resources of the group. It follows from this that, if the members of the group are given no opportunity to take part in decisions, they are not being trained for future promotion themselves. There have been many classic cases of organisations in which there has been no effective succession, because the lower eche-

M

lons of the organisation have never practised decision-making for themselves.

The key factor in police work is the willingness of each policeman to use all his abilities in the cause of the service. A man who is given a beat to patrol is not merely required to carry the uniform around the streets; he is also required to use his eyes, his ears and his brain to notice what is going on, make deductions and take action. This requires that the man shall be committed to what he is doing, and such commitment is difficult to obtain under an authoritarian regime.

The limitations of an authoritarian approach to leadership are clear, but its uses in an emergency service must not be under-estimated. For the police service, it should be regarded as "rapid decision" leadership—an expression that gives an immediate impression of its value and limitations.

Participative leadership

When the reaction against authoritarianism began, it was necessary to provide an alternative means of leadership and so it was proposed that the supervisors should behave in a more democratic manner by acting as the co-ordinators of the people they led, rather than simply directing what they did. Many organisations have been concerned to try to find ways in which it is possible to give the worker the opportunity to participate in the leadership of the organisation and yet allow the leader to lead. Participation in the making of decisions has a number of advantages both for the organisation and for the people in it. Clearly, if the total intellectual capacity of a group of people is turned to a problem, the decision made is likely to be a better one than if only one man attempts to solve the problem. But there is also a by-product of this involvement: participating in a decision tends to commit the people who have been involved far more than if a decision has been made and imposed upon them. For example, if a group of policemen decide for themselves a method whereby they are going to clear up a certain type of crime, they are far more likely to be committed to what they are doing and to achieving a satisfactory result, than if they are ordered to do exactly the same thing. Being told what to do and how to do it is much less satisfying than being given an objective and allowed to devise the method of attaining it.

Clearly, working out a course of action with the participation of people who will put it into effect takes time and this is why "rapid decision" leadership is sometimes more appropriate. The use of participation also requires the use of a high order of social skills on the part of the supervisor, who must have the patience and flexibility to gain the co-operation of his subordinates yet must not abrogate his leadership role (*see* Chapter 19, p. 373, regarding the use of small groups of people for decision-making).

The extent to which democratic principles can be applied in an organisation without endangering its structure has caused speculation ever since the retreat from authoritarianism began. What can be said is that commanders must command. The responsibility for the quality of service a police force provides rests firmly with its senior officers and, however decisions are arrived at, supervisors cannot evade their responsibilities. Metropolitan Police Commissioner, David McNee, said of leadership: "Moral courage is a vital attribute, the capacity to take a decision and stand by it. Perhaps this sounds a simple matter but there are those in positions of authority today who will and do go to almost any length to avoid making a decision . . . once having made a decision you must be prepared to stand by it" (*The Police Journal*, Volume XLVII, No. 3, 1974). This is as true of a decision arrived at by consultation or participation as one made independently. In fact, it sometimes requires more moral courage to use participative methods than to make an autocratic decision and then refuse to discuss it.

The range of applications of participative decision-making was indicated in Chapter 16, p. 321. The actual mode of participation can vary from consultation with an immediate subordinate to full-scale delegation (*see* Chapter 18). According to the nature of the problem, it may or may not be appropriate to include members of representative organisations in the discussions. Where a problem is mainly technical in nature and the range of solutions falls within existing personnel policies, consultation with immediate subordinates and people in a position to provide expert advice is required. Where personnel policies are likely to be in issue, representative organisations should be invited to participate. Between the extremes of purely technical and purely personnel matters there may be a range of problems involving elements of both. It becomes a matter of judgment as to when representative organisations should be brought in but, if there is any doubt, it is usually wise to choose involvement.

The use of participation is not just a formal matter of making decisions; it is an integral part of a person's leadership. Subordinates will soon know whether their senior officer is basically authoritarian in his approach or not and this will affect the relationship between them. For example, a leader who regularly indicates that he values the ideas of his subordinates is much more likely to receive a warning when, like Homer, he nods for a moment, than one who rebuffs.

Commitment to work
It is often assumed that, because the police service has a discipline code, lawful orders will always be accepted but the basic fact is that there are varying levels of acceptance of decisions and directions. The dual concepts of acceptability and commitment need to be explored in depth.

At a lower level, a subordinate accepts the need for him to carry out a task; at a higher level, he is committed to it. The difference between the two results is a different level of effort towards work. Even acceptability cannot be guaranteed unless proper leadership is given.

If a factory manager wishes to introduce a form of method-study into his factory, he knows an autocratic decision to introduce the study will almost certainly result in a strike or "work to rule". The probability is that he will use a consultative approach to try to arrive at a means whereby he can improve the efficiency of his factory. A problem of this kind has a high "acceptability factor" and a solution must be found that will obtain the co-operation of the workers.

Such problems can occur in a police force. They may not be as obvious as where non-acceptance is indicated by a strike but it is unwise to assume that non-co-operation cannot occur in a service with a discipline code. There have been cases of police officers individually or collectively taking action on the "go-slow" principle, as a protest against a real or imagined wrong. Such action is particularly effective where the output of the police officers is directly measurable, for example, in a traffic unit where the number of offenders reported forms an index, or at a station where there are normally large numbers of arrests or summonses for routine offences.

Achieving the outward acceptance of instructions is relatively simple, as few men are willing to risk action under the discipline code for disobedience of orders. Achieving complete acceptance so that the men do the job *as well as they are capable of doing it* is less simple, for some men show ingenuity in avoiding something they do not want to do. Normally, it is only possible to achieve good results against the wishes of the people carrying out the instruction if it is feasible to supervise every man engaged on the job very closely. In the police service this is seldom possible. A man can be ordered to walk along a street but he cannot be made to see and hear what is happening unless he accepts the need for him to be in that street and to see and hear.

Even more difficult to obtain than acceptance is the commitment to objectives that require a man to use initiative or skills of a high order. In such circumstances, participation is to be advocated wherever possible. Success is partly dependent upon the personal qualities of the leader and the degree of esteem in which he is held: his personal, as distinct from his executive, authority, held by virtue of his position. There are definite limitations to the use of the latter since it is not possible to *force* people to work to the best of their ability. Nevertheless, executive authority is a subject that must be considered for it is part of the business of being a supervisor.

Executive authority

Executive authority indicates the power that an individual holds by virtue of his rank and position. It places resources at his disposal and enables him to issue orders to, and control the activities of, subordinates. Like all power, it can be used well or badly and some people try to use it as a substitute for leadership although, as we have seen, its value as a motivational force is limited.

Executive authority enables a supervisor to maintain the administrative standards of his group: time-keeping, attention to routine tasks, and conformity to the functional rules of the group. What it does *not* do is to inspire subordinates to put real effort into their work. At most, it can produce a "busy" impression from subordinates, but their level of involvement will generally remain low. Some may exert themselves to gain the recognition and favour of their supervisor and some will be committed already and need no encouragement from any outside source. Leadership is needed because merely asserting authority through rank is at best a temporary substitute that will quickly produce overt conformity but covert uninvolvement. A man cannot be forced to use his brain imaginatively or his personal qualities to order. He commits himself to the aims of the organisation voluntarily and leadership is often necessary to gain this commitment.

Rules

As has been suggested earlier, the titular leader who can obtain the support of his subordinates to the extent that the norms of the group are closely related to the rules of the organisation, is in the happy position of having help from within the group in the maintenance of standards. A work group tends to enforce the observance of its "rules" or "norms" on individual members. It is therefore in the interests of the supervisor to take advantage of this but he must accept that the norms of his group will not *exactly* fit the ideals of the organisation. There will always be ways in which the group does not quite stick to the rules, for example, in such matters as illicit breaks from duty. Provided such deviations from the rules are not harmful to the organisation (or to the group itself for that matter), discretion can be mixed with official disapproval. But—and it is a big "but"— there will be times when the norms of the group are widely at variance with the rules of the organisation or there will be individuals who defy the rules and so confront authority.

Enforcing rules

All organisations have rules and their observance is necessary for survival. Provided the rules are updated to conform to current requirements, most people are willing to accept them as being a necessary part of civilised life. The people of a country surrender part of their freedom in return for a system of law and order; at work they surrender part of their right to do as they want in the interests of the organisation of which they are part. It can then be so run as to prevent anarchy.

However, as in society at large, there are people who will not obey the law—despite social pressure on them to do so—so there will be people in the police service who will not obey the rules. Depending on the extent of their refusal to conform to the rules, they may constitute a threat to society, the organisation and/or the morale of their colleagues.

At its worst, failure to stick to the rules can cause serious damage to the whole police service; there have been several cases in which the actions of a few policemen have threatened to bring the whole service into disrepute by their conduct, whether by corruption for financial gain, or manufacturing evidence for professional glory. The results are out of all proportion to the numbers involved. Clearly, there must be a mechanism to deal with such people and supervisors must be prepared to accept their part in its workings. If there is one thing worse than a corrupt policeman, it is that corruption was ignored or covered up by supervisors. Such actions throw doubt, not just on the honesty of one man, but on the integrity and standards of the whole organisation.

Whilst it is accepted that the criminal law and/or discipline code must be available to deal with serious offences that threaten the service, it is less clear when it is necessary to resort to discipline for minor transgressions. One guide may be whether the offence was deliberate or not. This may become a matter for that time-honoured distinction that crops up for policemen elsewhere: when does carelessness become recklessness? Deliberate contraventions of the rules cannot be ignored: if they are repeated and apparently go uncorrected, it adversely affects the morale of other men. What might be termed the "why should *he* get away with it?" attitude emerges and may even develop into the more serious "if he can get away with it, so can I".

There are some points that need to be borne in mind when giving an admonition, punishment or reporting someone for a discipline offence. The first is that it must be fairly done. For example, more harm than good will stem from punishing a man without warning for actions that have hitherto been tolerated (or are still being tolerated from other people). The next is that punishment does not always work the way that it is intended.

The effects of punishment

Most people conform to the rules, not out of fear of punishment, but because they prefer to do so. Fear of detection and punishment, however, can restrict some forms of incorrect behaviour. The reason why drivers conform to a speed limit is often not because of their wish to conform to the rules, but because there may be a speed-trap and they do not want to be caught. After all, that is the basic method of enforcing such laws: the police try to make motorists think that they *might* get caught! Thus, the threat of detection and punishment can act as a disincentive to do something.

But the threat of punishment can produce forms of behaviour other than conformity to the rules. For example, it may induce a determination not to be caught. Some people will go to great lengths to avoid being caught but stop short of behaving properly! Thus, a supervisor may find that behaviour has not improved, but that the recalcitrant offender has become more crafty in breaking the rules.

Punishment, in theory, is meant to act as the opposite of reward and it often does just this. Unfortunately, if the person punished thinks that he has been unfairly treated (and it is his his perception that affects the issue, not the facts), then this may induce resentment and, if his perception is matched by that of his colleagues, morale can be lowered. It is worth going to extra trouble to ensure that, when a man is being punished (including a verbal reprimand), justice really is manifestly seen to be done.

When punishment, restriction of freedom or sanctions are applied to a group of people, it is not uncommon for the situation to become worse and for more sanctions to be necessary and so create a spiral. It is often a matter of how the actions of the supervisor are perceived rather than what has actually happened. Some supervisors have been surprised at the depth of feeling a verbal reprimand can cause the recipient. Most people should not be reprimanded in a really forceful manner; any reprimand is a blow to the pride and is usually deeply felt. Administering such a reprimand in public, particularly if it is accompanied by sarcasm, is extremely harmful for the self-respect of the individual at the receiving end and no supervisor should be surprised if he fails to secure full co-operation from a person he has subjected to such treatment.

Morale

The significance of morale

Morale is usually thought of in terms of the feelings of the individuals within a group. We talk of high morale and low morale and there is a common assumption that high morale is a good thing, whilst low morale is a bad thing. Whilst it is true to say that low morale is invariably a bad sign, the converse is not necessarily true. In order to understand why high morale in a group of people does not necessarily indicate a satisfactory state of affairs, it is necessary to look at the factors that affect morale. The main determinant of a work group's morale is the extent to which the members of the group are agreed on the desirability of achieving a common goal. The nature of that goal must be of concern to the supervisor responsible for the group. It may be one that is of value to the service, for example, when a group has the detection of a particular type of crime or the arrest of a gang of thieves as its goal. Such goals are also the objectives of the supervisor of the group and of the service as a whole. But where the common goal is extraneous to the organisation altogether, for example, in connection with some unofficial sporting or social activity, the commander must be prepared to take action.

In addition to having objectives which may be parallel to those of the organisation or outside it, a group may have high morale through the pursuit of an objective which is totally against the organisation. In industry, it is quite common for morale to be high amongst a group of men who are on strike.

From what has been said, the impression might be gained that morale is of no importance, but this is by no means the case. As was said earlier, although high morale may not necessarily indicate a satisfactory state of affairs, low morale certainly does indicate a bad one. In a group where morale is high, there is a good team-spirit and the group tend to think in terms of "we" rather than "I" and to help rather than score-off one another. Success for the individual is seen as a success for all, which clearly characterises it as a group phenomenon rather than individual.

High morale means that people will be enthusiastic; there will be interest in the job and keenness to get it done. Where morale is very high, the function of the supervisor may be to apply a brake to prevent over-enthusiasm from leading to excesses.

High morale also usually means high resilience, people will not be easily discouraged or panicked and are far more likely to think out ways round a problem, whereas a low morale group is likely to exaggerate difficulties and to give up trying.

Factors affecting morale

The nature of the job that people have to do affects their morale. Obviously, an interesting job is likely to produce higher morale than an uninteresting one but the job must also be seen to be useful. For this reason, it is important that people are told the purpose behind a task where this is not otherwise clear, so that they can see what they are doing is of value.

Work must be fairly distributed, otherwise members may feel that they are carrying an unfair load or that they are being belittled because they are not given their share of the work. It is particularly important that interesting activities should be shared as fairly as possible and one of the dangers of over-specialisation is that it tends to diminish the scope and status of the general-purpose police officer.

Despite a common assumption to the contrary, the working circumstances under which people operate appear to have relatively little effect on morale, provided that everyone shares the same conditions and there is some justification for them. The supervisors in charge of a long, arduous and extensive search of moorland in order to discover the bodies of murdered children were greatly impressed by the high morale of the men carrying out the search, despite the bad conditions of weather and terrain. The factor determining the morale here was the determination of each man in the search to succeed in accomplishing a task which everyone accepted as essential.

In general, benefits or hardships do not make or break morale but the way in which they are distributed can. The problem of being fair is a difficult one for a supervisor. Most try to be fair but usually the supervisor uses his own standards of fairness rather than those of the group and these may be quite different.

A supervisor may allocate favourable duties on what he sees as a logical basis by giving such tasks to the older and, in his eyes, more-deserving men. The group may not see it that way and might well interpret fairness as being an allocation of duties by rota rather than to single out individual members for favourable treatment.

Old or inadequate buildings do not necessarily cause low morale. Quite often such buildings seem to unite the people who work in them, combining to help one another in overcoming difficulties. However, a group may become demoralised and feel that they are being unfairly treated by being made to work in bad conditions because no one is interested in them or their job. They may also become discouraged when they feel that the equipment with which they have been supplied is not adequate and that no one cares that this is so.

Insecurity and uncertainty lower morale. For this reason, when re-organisations are taking place, full use should be made of consultation and care should be taken to ensure that all those who may be involved are accurately informed how any changes will affect them.

The ill effects of another common source of uncertainty, rapid turnover of supervisors, can be minimised if each new commander observes the guidelines indicated on p. 335 above.

Balanced leadership

In every police force, it is necessary to balance the needs of the organisation against those of its members. Such highly-desirable features as cost-effectiveness, budgetary control and strict adherence to rules have to be tempered sufficiently to provide a tolerable working environment. For example, in places where more police are needed in the late evening than during the day, to make the men and women of that area perform a high proportion of late shifts may be socially unacceptable. Therefore, in many cases, cost-effectiveness is balanced against human needs and more early shifts are allowed than strictly necessary.

In any organisation, the extent to which its members are willing to allow it to make demands of them is constantly changing. The direction of change is dictated by the changes taking place in society—we have already noted the decrease in the acceptability of authoritarianism. Over the years, the balance between what may be termed "concern for people" and "concern for the organisation" has moved consistently in favour of the former and this trend is likely to continue. It is unreasonable to expect members of the police to ignore improvements being made to working conditions outside the service and they will consequently exert pressure upon their senior officers to show more concern for them. At the same time, supervisory officers feel that they must maintain the standards of their force. There is therefore a need to exercise leadership in such a way that concern for the standards of the organisation is realistically balanced with that for the people who make up the organisation.

By virtue of his position in a hierarchy, a supervisor is expected by all members to fulfil certain standards too; for example, he is expected to have integrity and professional ability. However, in some other respects, what is expected of him by his senior officers and subordinates will differ. In general, from above, he will be judged according to his professional competence, reliability, initiative, promptness in carrying out his work and loyalty to the service and to his senior officers. His subordinates will also expect competence but they will tend to assess him according to how this is applied in terms of attitude, approachability, impartiality, his loyalty to them and his consideration of their interests.

Fortunately, for most of the time, the expectations of a supervisor from above and below are compatible. But, at times, leadership skill may be needed to avoid satisfying one set of demands by neglecting the other. Failure to achieve a proper balance can have serious results: if a supervisor neglects the legitimate interests of his subordinates, his effectiveness as a leader will be reduced and the morale of his unit will suffer; if he fails to pay proper attention to what his senior officers expect of him, he will lose their confidence and so impair his ability to support his subordinates, so that his stature as a leader is diminished.

Expectations of leaders are affected by the situations facing them. For example, when faced with an emergency, police officers expect their senior officers to concentrate on dealing with it and will accept adverse conditions as part of the job. However, when the opportunity for relief occurs, people expect

their welfare to be given proper consideration and morale
quickly sinks if this is not done. It frequently occurs that there
is a good reason why people cannot be given anticipated facilities and they need to be told why that is so, so that they can
relate their circumstances to the realities of the situation.

Morale is a good indicator of the quality of leadership that
people are receiving. It is reflected in their attitude to their
work, willingness to overcome adversity and accept difficult
working conditions. To maintain good morale, a police supervisor needs the basic qualities of integrity, competence and
decisiveness combined with the ability to maintain an effective
balance between "rapid decision" and participative leadership
on the one hand and concern for people and concern for the
organisation on the other.

Chapter Eighteen

Delegation

The nature of delegation
The need for delegation

As was made clear in Chapter 16, no police commander can do all the work or take all the decisions himself. People at different levels in the hierarchy have to be given the authority to resolve certain problems, others being passed higher up the organisation according to their seriousness, wide-ranging implications, or unusual nature. In addition to making decisions in accordance with the general delegation pattern, subordinates may have specific problems delegated to them.

There are a number of misunderstandings that can arise between supervisors and subordinates if a few basic rules are not followed but first we must be clear as to what is *not* delegation. A lot of work that is done in the police service is done by officers acting on their own behalf within the constraints of law: it is not delegation to allow them to do this, this is simply part of their job. It is also *not* delegation to allocate a subordinate a task—it entirely depends on the extent to which the task involves the making of decisions on behalf of the supervisor and the extent to which the task is part of the supervisor's job.

Definition

Delegation may be defined in this way: *delegation occurs when a supervisor allocates part of his responsibilities to a subordinate, gives him the authority to act on his behalf and holds him accountable for what is done.* To make use of this definition it is necessary to clarify some of the expressions used.

Authority

As we have already seen, authority is necessary to denote the powers within a post to take decisions, to give orders and initiate action on behalf of the organisation. This is "executive authority", gained as a result of occupying a particular post in the organisation as distinct from authority originating in strength of personality, knowledge and experience—one cannot delegate these for they are inherent in the individual, whereas executive authority comes with the job and can be delegated.

When supervisors give a subordinate the authority to make decisions or take action on their behalf, then they are bound by the decisions made and the action taken.

The extent to which delegation occurs can be measured by the authority that is given and any limitations imposed. For example, it is quite common to delegate the task of adjudicating in cases of routine traffic process to an inspector, but the authority given is often limited by the classes of offence with which he may deal; for example, dangerous-driving cases may have to be submitted to a more senior officer. Another limitation may also be in the form of a policy which prescribes certain action to be taken in certain cases, for example: "all offenders who exceed a speed limit by five miles per hour shall be summoned". Such restrictions result in some authority being removed from the inspector, who from then on merely compares the cases with standards which prescribe the appropriate action and submits for directions any case falling outside the standards. If no authority is given, then there is no delegation but, in most cases, there is an area of discretion associated with such tasks which requires that the inspector be given authority to make decisions which, although bounded by policy, are not rigidly prescribed.

Responsibility

In contrast to authority which can be delegated, responsibility cannot. When a supervisor delegates an aspect of his work, he gives the subordinate the authority to make the necessary decisions. He also gives him the responsibility for the task but at the same time he also retains his own responsibility. What happens is that its nature changes slightly. From being responsible for doing the job, the supervisor becomes responsible for seeing that it is done and the subordinate for doing it.

Accountability
The last of the terms associated with delegation is account-ability, an expression that is meant to convey the way in which an individual is under an obligation to his supervisor for the action he takes and the decisions he makes. It must be noted that this accountability is always from the subordinate to the person who actually gave him the job, not that person's super-visor—it cannot by-pass a link in the delegation chain. It is this aspect that worries many supervisors; they are accountable for what is done by their subordinates and this requires faith in subordinates.

A pattern of delegation
The relationship of these concepts to one another is illustrated in Fig. 21, in which the relationships between three members of the organisation, A, B and C are shown, A being the most senior and C the most junior of the three. The most common position in which people see themselves is the middle rank

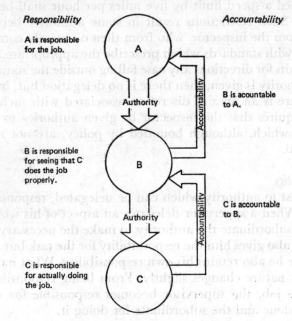

Fig. 21—Pattern of delegation.

officer (B) and it is this position that emphasises the way in which a supervisor is responsible for what his subordinates do and is accountable to the man above him for their efforts. The exact nature of this position can be seen from the following example:

A pattern of delegation: example. A large ceremonial occasion is due shortly. The Chief Constable, A, delegates the job of planning the traffic arrangements to Superintendent B who is responsible for traffic matters. He re-delegates the job to Inspector C, who deals with the planning and execution of traffic arrangements. If the plan is inadequate, Inspector C is accountable to Superintendent B who in turn, is accountable to the Chief Constable, A. Inspector C is *not* accountable to the Chief Constable; Superintendent B cannot opt out simply because he re-delegated the job.

Notice that if Inspector C was required to submit his plans to Superintendent B before they were executed, this would not be delegation. Notice too that in delegating the job it would have been possible for the Superintendent (or the Chief Constable) to place limitations on what could be done, for example by specifying the maximum number of men and vehicles that could be used. In other words, the amount of authority could have been limited—and might not have been enough to enable a successful result to be accomplished.

From this example, some of the principles can already be seen. The delegated authority must be commensurate with the responsibility and what might be thought of as delegation is not, because the authority is too restricted, the subordinate acting as an adviser only. It is for this sort of reason that some senior officers are not delegating when they think that they are.

The importance of delegation
Proper delegation is essential in any organisation and its absence can have serious short- and long-term effects on the organisation and the people in it.

Organisational effectiveness
In any organisation, or part of an organisation, in which a senior officer holds a key post, his unwillingness or inability to

N

delegate will result in an unnecessary degree of centralisation and an absence of decisions at the lower levels in the organisation. The basic rule for decision-making in any organisation is that they should be made at the lowest level possible and, provided guidelines are laid down, the decisions to be referred upwards are those which fall outside general policy. This concept of "management by exception" can only function in an organisation in which there is proper delegation. It is based on the fact that it is not possible for senior officers to absorb all the information flowing through their force, division or subdivision and, therefore, they should concentrate their time and energies on matters that require their personal intervention—in other words those that form an exception to the normal run.

In the absence of such measures, a senior officer becomes bogged down in unnecessary paperwork and lacks the time to deal with the matters that should occupy his attention. It also means that decision-making will be slow if every case must be referred to a high level in the organisation, and there are real problems when the senior officer is not available—the machinery may come to a halt.

Personnel

The results of working for a supervisor who will not delegate can be frustration and, ultimately, apathy. To be unable to take a decision is demoralising and, in the long term, damaging. People who have been consistently deprived of opportunities to make decisions may eventually become incapable of making decisions. This means that the quality of leadership falls dramatically when the head is absent but, what is worse, no training is being done for the future and a real problem is caused when the time comes for the non-delegator to move on. He leaves behind a staff untrained in decision-making, thoroughly conditioned to avoid making decisions and consequently a liability to themselves and the whole organisation.

The role of deputy

Of particular concern in the police service is the position of a deputy to a unit, sub-divisional, divisional or departmental commander, whose role is completely dependent on the extent to which his principal is willing to delegate.

The use of a deputy is primarily to provide continuity in the absence of the commander, but this cannot be achieved unless the deputy is able to make decisions in the absence of his principal. To be able to do this, he needs to be a party to the policy decisions made by the head of the unit so that he can maintain similar policies when in charge. He also needs the authority to make decisions during such periods. In a well-run organisation, things should not come to a halt due to the absence of one man, however important, and this is why the deputy system is an integral part of police organisations—but full use must be made of deputies to make the system work.

The acceptance of delegation

Although most supervisors accept the principle of delegation and claim to employ it as part of their leadership style, the fact is that many supervisors do not delegate, they merely allocate work and control it through such close supervision that they might as well be doing the job themselves.

Non-delegators

Probably the most common reason for supervisors not delegating is that they simply do not realise that they are not doing so. Most supervisors claim that they delegate and it is only by examining the way in which they work that it becomes clear they do not. Partly, this is due to a misunderstanding as to what delegation is, but also because, by continually checking on subordinates, they are, in effect, making all the decisions and initiating the action themselves without realising it. A common form is what may be termed a by-pass technique which may work like this:

Non-delegation: example.

The head of department A allocates his immediate subordinate B a task and gives him the authority to take any necessary action. B then re-delegates the task to his subordinate C. He may limit C's authority by prescribing limits of action or resources but, in theory, C is now accountable to B for what action he takes. A then periodically checks direct with C to see what he is doing and may even over-ride the limits that B has prescribed. Thus, in reality, A has not delegated at all, he has merely employed C to do the job but has allowed B to do part of his briefing for him. This situation puts B in an impossible position. There are many variations on this theme, but if A were to be approached he would assure everyone that he *was* delegating—and believe it!

Other reasons why people do not delegate are usually that:

1. they feel the need to retain total control in order to reinforce their own authority. Many people like to feel indispensable and, by not letting their subordinates know what is happening, they effectively prevent their deputies and other subordinates from taking action for lack of information; this sensitivity to what are seen as encroachments on their authority is usually entirely misplaced and, because such people seldom understand their reaction, it is difficult for them to overcome the need to deal with everything themselves. Frequently, they complain of being overworked—and indeed they often are—but will say that they have to do everything themselves because the quality of their subordinates will not allow them to delegate;
2. on occasions, the quality of subordinates is not high enough, sometimes through lack of experience. In such a case the supervisor has to weigh the long-term benefits against present inconvenience.

   A senior officer of considerable experience was always heard to complain that he had to do everything himself. He always claimed that his staff were too inexperienced or inept to do the job. The reason was that on the rare occasions that he delegated a job he gave inadequate instructions; then, as soon as a small mistake was made, he would take over. Thus, his staff were never able to learn how to work. Consequently, what he said about inexperienced staff was true but *he* had created the situation by failing to train his staff properly;
3. some people are perfectionists, who wish to ensure that everything is dealt with in a particular way and will not tolerate alternative approaches. Such people find delegation difficult because they feel that only they know how a job should be done and, as they are the best qualified to do the job, they should do it.

   Subordinates are inclined to use their own methods for dealing with problems. The test that should be applied is "what were the results of what they did?" There are usually several ways of dealing with most situations and, provided the methods adopted are effective and reputable, there is no reason why a subordinate should not ask himself the question "what is the best way to solve this problem?" rather than "how would my boss solve it?"

Over-delegation
So far, attention has been focused on supervisors who do not delegate sufficiently but mention should be made of people who over-delegate. As often as not, the question is less a matter of delegation than abdication. It is a case of non-leadership, as defined in Chapter 17 (p. 338), and such "non-leaders" often try to lay the blame for errors on their subordinates rather than accept the responsibility. A supervisor should not delegate *all* his work but should follow the guidelines laid down above in deciding just what should be delegated.

Non-acceptance of delegation
There may be a number of reasons why a subordinate may be reluctant to accept delegated work apart from the most obvious one that he is already overworked.

One of these reasons has already been suggested: people who have been brought up in an organisation where decision-making is very highly-centralised will have difficulty in adjusting to a change in leadership style. Such people are often fearful of making mistakes and would prefer to ask a senior officer than take risks. The police service is usually under critical public gaze and mistakes can result in great publicity so that there is sensitivity to error. The easiest way to avoid mistakes may seem to be to do nothing. The fear of punishment or criticism for making mistakes can be a considerable disincentive to initiative.

Another reason why people may be unwilling to take on a delegated job is that they lack the ability to do it or *feel* that they lack the ability. In either case, the answer is to delegate but to institute controls that give support but allow some opportunity to learn through doing the job.

Controlled delegation
The receiver of delegated responsibility is bound not to go outside the limits of the authority of the person who gave him the

job. In order to control delegated authority, a supervisor may place additional limits as mentioned on p. 357 above. Other possibilities include reference to other people as part of the original instruction; for example, "before you decide what to do, have a talk with your opposite number in the C.I.D. to see if he has any views", is a perfectly legitimate way to impose controls on delegation. Other ways include the provision that interim reports shall be submitted so that the time scale of the delegated authority is reduced to permit corrective action to be applied before harm is done.

The essence of sound delegation is the choice of the right man for the job, the briefing he is given and the opportunities provided to seek advice. For a straightforward job, the outcome of which is not too critical, it may be merely necessary to brief the man and let him get on with it. For more important or delicate tasks, any of the above controls may be necessary.

A guide to delegation

There are a few basic precepts that help to ensure delegation is correctly used, although clearly it is not possible to lay down absolute rules.

1. *Choose the person carefully.* Whenever possible, delegation should be to the immediate subordinate and not to his subordinate. If by-passing is necessary, the man who has been by-passed should be informed and proper lines of re-reporting and limits of responsibility made clear. The man chosen need not always be the most experienced, otherwise the rest of his colleagues will never gain the experience that they will need to develop. In a 24-hour service there must always be people available to do whatever is necessary; so, over-specialisation can cause problems.

2. *Give clear instructions.* The man who is to do the job should what his objectives are and, unless there are definite reasons to the contrary, he should know why the job is being done. In delegation, the emphasis should be on *what* has to be achieved and not *how*. That is the difference between delegation and giving working instructions.

The limits of the delegated authority should be made quite clear. There is a problem here, for the nature of the task is usually explicit while the extent of the man's authority is usually implicit. Limits need to be made clear if the job is at all complex or of far-reaching importance and instructions should include the time scale and the resources and facilities that may be used.

3. *Define the area of responsibility.* The subordinate should know to whom he is accountable and the extent of his responsibilities. These must not overlap with those of someone else, nor should more than one person be given tasks in the same area without ensuring that there are no areas of "no-man's land" between them.

4. *Provide support.* Depending on the man, the job and the possible outcome, controls and avenues for seeking advice should be created. Some people are reluctant to admit to their supervisors that they need advice; it may therefore be advisable to provide for reference to experts or specialists. If there is doubt and the job is long, progress reports (not of what is going to happen but what has been achieved) can be demanded at appropriate intervals. In some emergency situations, the report stage may be at hourly intervals while, at the other extreme, only quarterly or annual reports may be required.

Chapter Nineteen

Personal communication

Understanding and being understood

The ability to communicate with people is one of the most fundamental of all leadership skills for, without it, one cannot lead. Communication implies understanding; the speaker and the listener, the writer and the reader each having the same understanding of what has been said or written.

Communication is a process of transmission and reception, the crux of the matter being to ensure that the message that is received is the one that was intended. There are a number of aspects that are common to both oral and written methods of communication.

The importance of effective communication

The whole organisation of a police force can be looked at as a large communication system, with information flowing through it and between it and its environment. This flow of information passes upwards through the organisation enabling decisions to be made and downwards to people who execute those decisions. Information flows into the organisation bringing details of problems that must be solved and indicating changes in the environment to which the police must react. Information passes from the police organisation to the environment, reassuring members of the community, seeking help and indicating the way in which the organisation is responding to the information that it is receiving.

Diagrammatically, Fig. 22 shows a much simplified system of communication between force headquarters, one division and one department and between all of these and their environment. From this, it is easy to see why information must pass freely without distortion and why communication chains should be

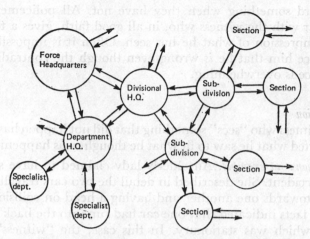

Fig. 22 Simplified communication chain between force headquarters/
division and department.

kept short by having decisions made as near the source of the
information as possible.

A parallel may be drawn between the processing of information in a police force with the method adopted in a major crime
inquiry. It is necessary in a murder hunt to obtain information,
to process it so that it can be checked for usefulness, and then
store it for retrieval on demand. The selection process must sift
out valuable information so that decisions can be made as to
what further steps are necessary. These decisions must then be
communicated to the appropriate members of the inquiry team.
At the same time, all the people on the inquiry must be kept
informed of developments so that they can adjust their own
sights. Exactly the same processes go on in a police force as a
whole.

Barriers to communication

The most obvious barrier that may be met in trying to communicate with someone else is refusal to listen or read. The
deliberate act of not listening is rare, so is the wilful act of
misinterpreting what has been said or written. The reasons for
most incorrect interpretations are more subtle. Many have their
roots in misunderstanding. People can believe they have seen

or heard something when they have not. All policemen are familiar with the witness who, in all good faith, gives a totally false impression of what he has seen. Often it is impossible to convince him that he *is* wrong even though the contradictory evidence is overwhelming.

Perception

The witness who "sees" something that did not happen has often converted what he saw to fit what he thought was happening.

Perception: an example. An elderly lady claimed to have seen a fatal accident. She described in detail the two cars travelling at speed towards one another and having a head-on collision but all the facts indicated that one car had run into the back of the other which was stationary. In this case, the "witness" had actually not seen the cars moving at all—she had heard the crash and looked out of her window. But she had been confused by the car nearest to her, which had rear-engine drive, mistaking the front of the car for the back and had formed her view of the accident accordingly.

This notion that we "see" what we expect to see is illustrated in a striking way by Dr M. L. Johnson-Abercrombie who recounts the story of an X-ray taken of a child who had a bad cough. The X-ray showed nothing abnormal but the cough persisted, so a second X-ray was taken. The second radiologist noticed that a button was wedged in the child's throat. The same button was also shown in the first X-ray but in that case the radiologist had assumed that the button was on the child's vest, for that is where one would expect to see a button—on the outside of a child, not the inside (*The Anatomy of Judgment*, Hutchinson, 1960).

A person's view is coloured also by what he wants to see—a familiar concept to the police officer. "My son is a good boy" is a common statement from a mother. A person's view of a policeman is coloured by whether he is helping the person to get his stolen property back or reporting him for speeding.

The perceptions of the speaker, and that of the hearer, of a verbal communication will be affected by the beliefs of each. The speaker knows what he is talking about (or thinks he does) and so his perception will be that he has given his instructions clearly. A hearer, whose perception is affected by the fact that he believes that he is already over-worked, may hear only the difficulties that will make life even worse for him. Similarly, an ambitious man may not "hear" the problems in his anxiety to impress his claims upon the senior officer who is outlining a job to him.

Even in written communication, perception will affect the meaning. It is not at all unusual to find that an agreement reached by two parties is subsequently interpreted quite differently by each. This is a common problem in joint agreements and occasionally results in accusations of "bad faith". It is simply a matter of the way in which each party saw what he wanted to see in the words that were agreed.

The feelings of the receiver
The way in which something is interpreted will depend on the feelings of the people who are at the receiving end. The same set of written instructions given to two different groups of people may be understood quite differently. Even when the actual effects of instructions are the same for both groups, they will react differently because of different levels of morale within the groups. A high-morale group will shrug off something that will cause a marked reaction from a low-morale group. When morale is low, anything is likely to be interpreted as an unfavourable sign, however improbable that may sometimes seem. Senior officers are often amazed to hear what they are alleged to have said when some particularly strong rumour reaches their ears.

Selective hearing and seeing
A phenomenon particularly noticeable in face-to-face situations that can extend into the interpretation of written instructions, is the selection process which goes on in the mind of a listener or reader when confronted with arguments against his own point of view.

In discussions, this amounts to a filter which tends to eliminate unwanted arguments before they reach the consciousness. Human hearing has natural filters that allow us to hear one person above a hubbub of conversation around us in a crowded room. We "tune in" on the person who is speaking to us and do not hear what is said around us. In a similar way it is possible to "tune in" on those parts of what is being said in a discussion that support our pre-conceived notions. In a heated argument, it is not at all unusual to find that the two parties are not actually listening to one another at all, they are merely repeating their own arguments. Neither makes any progress because each is too busy thinking what he is going to say next, marshalling his arguments ready for when the next opportunity comes to speak.

This is a phenomenon that police officers meet in their operational work: the irate member of the public who appears not to hear the reasoned arguments put to him. The main point to remember when this problem is encountered—whether between police and public, or police and police—is that it is not a wilful action. It is a part of normal human behaviour—we all do it to some extent—and the stronger the emotional feelings of the "non-listener" the more obvious it becomes. It is an emotional vicious circle. The speaker becomes more exasperated the longer the argument goes on and the "non-listener" becomes more emotional as he detects the exasperation of the person talking to him. This raises his emotional temperature and so he becomes even less able to "listen". The answer is to cool down the emotions and reason alone will not do this. Sometimes only an appeal to the emotions will do.

Such "non-listening" can usually be detected when a person is heard to voice arguments that ostensibly counter what has just been said by the previous speaker but bear no relation to what that previous speaker actually said.

The selective nature of perception can also apply to written material. Certain parts of a written document will register more than other parts because these are of some value or interest to the reader and this will not necessarily accord with the value placed on them by the writer.

Rejection

A factor governing the effectiveness of the written or the spoken words is the rejection of the routine and this accounts, for example, for the lack of knowledge of orders which are continually reprinted or mentioned at daily briefings. People have a mental switch that enables them to hear or read something, yet not allow it to register with them. When they hear a repetition of a familiar instruction, they switch off.

A further reason for rejection is that the subject-matter never becomes properly accepted into the behaviour pattern of the listener.

This should be familiar to all policemen: considerable publicity is aimed at making people drive slowly in fog, but pile-ups caused by excessive speed still occur. The reason why so much good advice is ignored is that it never reaches that part of an individual's sub-conscious that determines his pattern of behaviour. There is a great deal of difference between someone acknowledging that something is good advice and his accepting it as part of his mental make-up. This is exactly the same problem as was considered when discussing the problems of training someone to adopt a pattern of behaviour in Chapter 11.

Choice of words

Little need be said under this heading other than perhaps to quote a famous example:

> It cannot in the opinion of His Majesty's Government be classified as slavery in the extreme acceptance of the word without some risk of terminological inexactitude. (Winston Churchill.)

This deliberate use of several long words where one short one would have done serves as a reminder of the need to use a vocabulary that is part of the everyday language of the person who is to receive the message. If he comes up against a word outside his normal experience, he is likely to put his own interpretation on it.

Speech or writing

When deciding on the appropriate means of communicating with someone, it is useful to consider the relative advantages of the spoken and written word. The decision should be made on the basis of which will be the most effective in conveying the required information and ensuring that the correct message has been received.

The advantages of oral communication

The use of speech has the following advantages:

1. It allows adjustments of approach, depending on the reception that is being obtained. It is not usually possible to guarantee that a letter will arrive when the addressee is in a receptive frame of mind, whereas it is usually possible to pick the moment to speak to him. If what is being said is not well received, it can be adjusted by toning it down or increasing its impact by additional emphasis. Thus speech is a good way of delivering bad news, administering admonishments, sounding out proposals and so on—all matters that are affected by the personal impact they have on the person at the receiving end.

2. It permits the recipient to put his own point of view in reply. This is why weak people prefer to admonish or deliver adverse decisions in writing—they do not have to deal with the potential defence presented either as a genuine attempt to reverse the decision or to save face. The opportunity for feed-back from the recipient is one of the most valuable aspects of face-to-face communication but it is easy not to make use of it by giving peremptory comments and affording the recipient no opportunity to make a constructive reply.

3. Oral communication is immediate and simple and enables back-up information to be given to help clarify the message.

The advantages of written communication
The advantages of putting things in writing include the following:

1. A degree of permanence: but it should be noted that there are two qualifications to this. The first is that a letter, report or instruction may be still used as a source of reference long after it has ceased to have any validity. Second, the existence of a directive does not mean that people will necessarily be aware of its existence or its meaning. Written instructions are often filed and never looked at again so that only those people who can remember having read them in the first place may be aware of what they said. Despite this, new people are often expected to abide by the contents of instructions issued before they arrive on the scene.

2. Greater accuracy, brevity and clarity (the A, B, C of writing). Unfortunately, this takes time and effort. As the French

thinker, Pascal, wrote in 1656: "I have made this letter rather long only because I have not had time to make it shorter."
3. The possibility of reaching a large number of people with little effort. It should be noted that a wide circulation does not necessarily mean that all the people who receive it actually read it, much less understand it as the writer intended.
4. Ease of amendment. Once given, any attempt to amend a verbal order is likely to result in some people obeying the first command and some the second. Some check must be made that the amendment is received by all the people who received the original.

Oral communication
Creating a willingness to listen
Many personal skills are required to enable a speaker to put over his message in its intended form. Some of these skills have been indicated in Chapter 13 where one form of face-to-face personal contact, the interview, was discussed at length. In particular, non-verbal communication (*see* p. 253) has a much wider significance. A wide range of meanings can be conveyed by gestures and non-verbal noises—grunts and sighs. One senior officer in days gone by was renowed for his early morning indications of how he felt. A grunt in reply to the greetings of his subordinates meant that all would be well, a total silence indicated that it was going to be one of those days when it would be better to be elsewhere.

The whole tone of a meeting or briefing can be set by the demeanour of the speaker: nervousness will unsettle the audience, belligerence will create resentment, condescension invites hostility, and so on. The warmth or coldness of the speaker will create an openness, or the reverse, among members of a committee. In the same way that a police officer uses his social skills to handle a wide range of people in an endless variety of operational situations, a supervisor should use his social skills to aid him in being understood and gaining acceptance of what he has said. It is perfectly possible to obtain acceptance or rejection of an idea simply by adopting a particular attitude to the listener.

As was indicated in connection with personnel interviews, in a one-to-one situation, the personalities of both the interviewer and interviewee will determine the understanding that may develop between the two people. The frame of mind of the recipient of instructions or advice needs to be detected by the supervisor. Usually this is done instinctively but, under the pressures of thinking about the subject-matter, such considerations tend to be forgotten. In giving instructions, as we have already seen when talking of leadership, the object must be to secure the acceptance of the instructions by those who must carry them out, not merely so that they will do as they are told but so that they are committed to doing the job properly and using all their capabilities.

In sum, a supervisor needs to be able to create a willingness to listen to obtain a positive response from his hearers and to do this he has to be sensitive to the feelings of the people he is talking to. He must create an atmosphere which is consistent with what he is trying to achieve: a sense of urgency in an emergency situation, a sense of seriousness of purpose when giving directions or admonishments; an atmosphere of comradeship when trying to ease a tense situation. He must monitor how what he is saying is being received, for this is the "feed-back" that tells him whether he is achieving his aim.

Feed-back

In normal conversation, people are quickly able to detect when they are being misunderstood. All police control-room operators are familiar with the sort of bizarre conversations that are possible between themselves and members of the public making emergency calls:

> *Caller:* Please send a policeman as quickly as you can.
> *Operator:* Yes, where are you?
> *Caller:* I'm at home.
> *Operator:* Yes, but how do we get there?
> *Caller:* Couldn't you come in a panda car?

This sort of misunderstanding can be easily corrected because the police operator is able to detect from the replies from the caller that he is not being understood. In formal speaking such ready feed-back is rarely present and so the speaker must use more subtle means.

A good speaker watches his audience. He is looking for signs that will tell him whether he is making sense or not. From his audience he can receive messages—some consciously sent and some not, for example, raised eyebrows, puzzled frowns and people looking at their wrist-watches all convey a message.

As verbal communication is prone to inaccuracy, it is particularly necessary to obtain some form of feed-back as to the exact nature of the message that has been received when giving instructions or advice. Inaccuracies come about in any of the ways listed on p. 365 above, plus the more obvious occasions of mis-hearing or being distracted at a critical moment.

The usual way of checking that the hearer has received the message is to say something like "do you understand?" To this he may well reply "yes", either because he believes he does understand when he does not, or he realises that he has not understood and does not wish to admit this to his supervisory officer. There is no easy way of overcoming this problem when briefing large numbers of people other than carefully preparing the briefing beforehand, using adequate visual aids and providing plenty of opportunity for questions that might reveal discrepancies. The secret lies in the preparation and, to iron out many sources of potential misunderstanding, a useful technique is to use a small group of subordinates to aid in the preparation of the overall plan.

The use of small groups in decision-making
The use of small groups as a pilot for subsequent major exercises is merely one example of the way in which the abilities and viewpoints of subordinates can be used in participative decision-making. The involvement of people in the formulation of a plan they are to execute solves more than one problem. It helps to produce a decision to which they already have some commitment, it probably produces a better decision than would have been devised by one man on his own and, finally, it avoids many pitfalls that can be caused by bad communication.

The use of small groups in decision-making requires not only the use of social skills to create an atmosphere within which people will participate freely, but also an understanding as to how far the supervisor is going to allow what his subordinates say affect the decisions that are made. At one end of the scale, the super-

visor may act as the chairman of a committee with the decisions
taken either by consensus or by a vote. At the other end of the
scale, he may merely invite comments and then decide. In
practice, most sessions of this kind are concerned not just with
one decision but a series of decisions that collectively make a
plan or policy. Within the number of decisions that have to be
made, it should be possible to accept some from the group even
if others have to be against their views. Provided that the latter
are made on reasonable grounds which are explained and the
proportion is not excessive, the co-operation of the group is
likely to be maintained and communication will flow freely,
automatically throwing up doubts and misunderstandings when
they occur. Use of such a group merely as a sounding-board
may cause the members to lose any sense of involvement and so
fail to identify weaknesses.

The way in which communication takes place in a discussion
group is shown in Figs. 23 and 24. The formal committee with
everyone speaking through the chairman is shown in Fig. 23.
This type of committee tends to produce formal responses that
are suitable for set agendas where the basic decisions to be made
consist of "yes" and "no". It is much less suitable for seeking
ideas as to how problems should be tackled and is inclined to
stultify genuine discussion. More original thought is likely to
come from Fig. 24, where people may talk to one another. This
enables a quick analysis of suggestions to be made, people tend
to talk for shorter periods and are liable to interruption so that

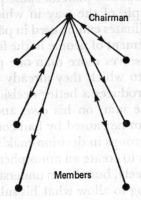

Fig. 23—Formal committee discussions.

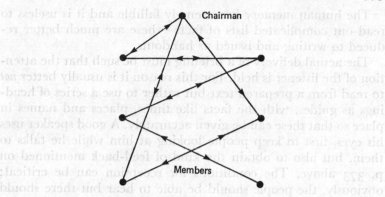

Fig. 24—General discussion group.

discrepancies in what they are saying are pounced upon by other members. Such groups tend to be rather noisy, less disciplined than Fig. 23, but much more wide-ranging in thought. They do, however, allow a chairman to sit back and listen—often a useful exercise—and, provided that he keeps the discussion to the point and summarises what has been decided at frequent intervals, more of value can often be achieved. A good leader would probably allow his subordinates a measure of both methods in a session aimed at solving complex problems, allowing free discussion to obtain the ideas and then directed discussion to shape them into a practical solution. It requires considerable skill on the part of the discussion leader, for he must keep track of the points raised, pick out the useful pieces, ensure that nothing important is overlooked and encourage free flow of ideas, while preventing fruitless discussion and personality clashes.

Briefing large groups
As has been said, the most important preliminary step in briefing a large group of people is to have thoroughly worked out the subject-matter beforehand. It is disastrous to "think out loud" in the presence of such a group because some members will go away with one idea and others with an entirely different idea. The decisions must have already been made and the vital information have been prepared in a form that can be readily understood and remembered.

The human memory is extremely fallible and it is useless to read out complicated lists of facts—these are much better reduced to writing and issued as handouts.

The actual delivery of a briefing must be such that the attention of the listener is held. For this reason it is usually better *not* to read from a prepared text but rather to use a series of headings as guides, with the facts like times, places and names in place so that these can be given accurately. A good speaker uses his eyes, first to keep people looking at him while he talks to them, but also to obtain the kind of feed-back mentioned on p. 373 above. The conditions for reception can be critical; obviously, the people should be able to hear but there should also not be confusing sounds coming from elsewhere. It is important that listeners are reasonably comfortable, so that they are concentrating on what they are being told rather than their physical discomfort.

The maximum retention is obtained if information is presented to people in a systematic and logical form, consisting of short sentences linked by a theme which begins with the objective of the exercise, then outlines the plan to be followed and concludes with the detailed instructions and administrative arrangements. Because people tend to remember the last thing that was said to them, it is sometimes a good idea to reiterate in the form of a concluding summary the most important parts of the plan.

If the instructions for different sections of the men are dissimilar, separate briefing is better than making everyone listen to it all, for someone is bound to confuse his instructions with those for someone else. For this reason, it is often advisable to brief section leaders and allow them to give the detailed briefings to their own men.

Written communication

The emphasis placed on the quality of reporting, from the moment a person joins the police, makes it unnecessary to go into great length on this topic but it is perhaps worth summarising a few basic rules of writing.

Objectives

The objective of the exercise must be clear from the outset otherwise the piece will become diffuse. Too many people pour out all they know about a topic into a report, without having considered what the object of the report is. If a decision is being requested, then obviously the reader needs all the relevant facts to make that decision, but he should not have to filter them out of a mass of irrelevant material that merely serves to confuse. Similarly, a written instruction must be viewed from the point of view of the man who is to carry it out. Will he understand what he is to do and why? Many instructions are simply expressions of the writer's disquiet or irritation because something has gone wrong, and echo his fervent wishes that it will not happen again. Such instructions as "you are to ensure that . . ." should be able to be carried out within the realms of possibility, otherwise the recipient will simply throw in his hand and do nothing; a more constructive though more limited instruction may produce some positive results.

Creating a willingness to read
Some police officers read new instructions and law out of sheer professionalism but most tend to be very selective and read only what is of direct personal interest to them and merely glance at anything else. There are a few basic rules that help to overcome this problem but do not guarantee success at having instructions or guidance read.

The way in which information is presented is as critical in writing as it is in speech. A dull presentation tends to dull the will to read. In a report, the layout, the style of writing and the length all affect the reader's reception.

A report should be composed according to a definite pattern of introduction, main body and final conclusions and recommendations. Its sentences should be quite short (about twenty words is a good average) and adequately paragraphed to break up the masses of black print.

The presentation of instructions should make quick reference possible by the use of headings and a logical layout. There is a tendency for the style of the contents to become pompous if this is not guarded against—it mainly stems from the use of a standard format in which every new item is carefully prepared along the same lines as previously. Standardisation is useful for lists, where the aim is for someone to see his own name, but it can be carried too far if it creates an overall blandness.

House magazines and news-sheets are published in good faith by many organisations but are often unread by the bulk of the people for whom they are produced. The chances of gaining a readership are enhanced if the objectives of the publication are clear; many are a cross between public-relations documents and internal social-bulletins and as such tend to fall between two audiences. An internal newsletter needs to be edited with its intended audience firmly in mind and aimed at giving information that is of genuine interest to the people concerned. Ideally, it should be a little controversial to generate real feeling but then the controversy may centre around topics that the organisational heads do not wish to advertise. Nevertheless, an "open" publication, as distinct from one which always toes the official line, is more likely to be sought than a strictly conformist one.

Control of paper

A real enemy of effectiveness is the sheer volume of paper that police forces tend to generate. The requirement that there shall always be a written record of everything that happens has the effect of burdening the police with so much written material that it is difficult to ensure that really important documents are given proper attention. A great deal can be done by adopting printed forms, books or cards to record routine data, as suggested in Chapter 8. More can be done by ensuring that the actual flow of paper through the organisation is minimised by having decisions taken at as low a level as possible and using management by exception techniques (*see* Chapter 18).

A very real danger in any organisation where accuracy and thoroughness are of prime concern, is that the maintenance of records or the submission of paper can become an end in itself and not the means of achieving an organisational objective: the filling in of gaps in books and forms, not because the information is needed but simply for completeness as though that were an important aim for its own sake; the submission of unnecessary returns; the maintenance of duplicate sets of records— often in different forms—all these are symptoms of misplaced energies that call for a review of just what paper is necessary and what can be stopped.

Bibliography

General works

Alderson, J. C. and Stead, P. J. (eds.), *The Police We Deserve*, Wolfe, 1973.

Anstey, E., Fletcher, C. A. and Walker, J., *Staff Appraisal and Development*, Allen and Unwin, 1976.

Argyle, M., *The Psychology of Interpersonal Behaviour*, Pelican, 1967.

Banton, M., *The Policeman in the Community*, Tavistock, 1964.

Banton, M., *Police Community Relations*, Collins, 1973.

Belson, W. A., *The Public and the Police*, Harper, 1975.

Brown, J. A. C., *The Social Psychology of Industry*, Penguin, 1954.

Burpo, J. H. and Irwin, J. J., *The Police Labor Movement*, Charles C. Thomas, U.S.A., 1971.

Cain, M. E., *Society and the Policeman's Role*, Routledge and Kegan Paul, 1973.

Chapman, B., *Police State*, Pall Mall Press, 1970.

Chapman, S. G. (eds.), *Police Patrol Readings*, Charles C. Thomas, U.S.A., 1970.

Cramer, J., *The World's Police*, Cassell, 1964.

Critchley, T. A., *A History of Police in England and Wales, 900–1966*, Constable, 1967.

Critchley, T. A., *The Conquest of Violence*, Constable, 1970.

Davis, E. M. and Knowles, J., "An Evaluation of the Kansas City Patrol Experiment", *The Police Chief*, U.S.A., June 1975, pp. 22–27.

English, J. and Houghton, R., *Police Training Manual*, McGraw-Hill, 1975.

Fleishmann, E. A. (ed.), *Studies in Personnel and Industrial Psychology*, Dorsey Press, U.S.A., 1967.

Fraser, J. M., *Employment Interviewing*, Macdonald and Evans, 1966.

Friedlander, C. P. and Mitchell, E., *The Police—Servants or Masters*, Hart-Davis, 1974.

Gibb, C. A. (ed.), *Leadership*, Penguin, 1969.

Gill, D., *et al.*, *Performance Appraisal in Perspective*, Institute of Personnel Management, 1973.

Glenn Stahl, O. and Staufenberger, R. A. (eds.), *Police Personnel Administration*, Police Foundation, U.S.A., 1974.

Hain, P., *Radical Regeneration*, Quartet Books, 1975.

International Computers Ltd, *Report of the ICL Merseyside Police Study Team*, 1975.

Jackson, R. M., *Enforcing the Law*, Pelican, 1972.

Johnson-Abercrombie, M. L., *The Anatomy of Judgment*, Hutchinson, 1960.

Judge, A., *A Man Apart*, Faber, 1972.

Keeling, G. L. *et al.*, *Summary Report—Kansas City Preventive Patrol Experiment*, Police Foundation, U.S.A., 1974.

Kenney, J. P., *Police Administration*, Charles C. Thomas, U.S.A., 1972.

Lambert, J., *Crime, Police and Race Relations*, Pitman, 1970.

Lewis, R., *A Force for the Future*, Temple Smith, 1976.

Mack, J. A., *The Crime Industry*, Saxon House, 1975.

Mark, Sir R., *Policing a Perplexed Society*, George Allen and Unwin, 1977.

Marshall, G., *Police and Government: The Status and Accountability of the British Constable*, Methuen, 1965.

Martin, J. P. and Wilson, G., *The Police: A Study in Manpower*, Heinemann, 1969.

Mosse, G. L. (ed.), *Police Forces in History*, Sage, U.S.A., 1975.

Purcell, W., *British Police in a Changing Society*, Mowbrays, 1974.

Radzinowitz, L. and King, J., *The Growth of Crime*, Basic Books Inc., U.S.A., 1977.

Reith, C., *A New Study of Police History*, Oliver and Boyd, 1956.

Richards, G., *The Reformed Local Government System*, George Allen and Unwin, 1973.

Sellin, T. and Wolfgang, M. E., *The Measurement of Delinquency*, Wiley, 1964.

Thurston, G., *The Clerkenwell Riot*, George Allen and Unwin, 1967.

Trevelyan, G. M., *English Social History*, Longmans, Green and Co., 1942.

Webster, J. A., *The Realities of Police Work*, Kendall/Hunt, U.S.A., 1973.
Whisenand, P. M., *Police Supervision, Theory and Practice*, Prentice-Hall, U.S.A., 1971.
Whitaker, B., *The Police*, Penguin, 1964.
Wilson, O. W. and McLaren, R. C., *Police Administration*, McGraw-Hill, U.S.A., 1972.

Official publications
(In chronological order)

United Kingdom reports, etc.
Royal Commission on Police Powers and Procedures (Cmd. 3297), H.M.S.O., 1929.
Police Post-War Committee (Home Office and Scottish Home Department), H.M.S.O., 1946 and 1947.
Committee on Police Conditions of Service (Cmds. 7674 and 7831), H.M.S.O., 1949.
Inquiry into Allegations of Assault on John Walters (Cmnd. 718), H.M.S.O., 1959.
Royal Commission on the Police, Interim Report (Cmnd. 1222), H.M.S.O., 1960.
White Paper, *Police Training in England and Wales* (Cmnd. 1450), H.M.S.O., 1962.
Royal Commission on the Police, Final Report (Cmnd. 1728), H.M.S.O., 1962.
Committee of the Police Council on Higher Police Training, 1963.
Inquiry into the circumstances in which Detective Sergeant Challenor of the Metropolitan Police continued on duty suffering from mental disorder (Cmnd. 2735), H.M.S.O., 1965.
Three Working Parties on Police Manpower, Equipment and Efficiency (Home Office), H.M.S.O., 1967.
Research and Planning Branch Report, Traffic Patrols (Home Office), 1967.
Royal Commission on Trade Unions and Employers Associations (Cmnd. 3623), H.M.S.O., 1968.
The Planning of Police Buildings (Home Office Memorandum), 1969.
Police Design Guide No. 2 (Home Office), 1970.
Committee of the Police Advisory Board for Scotland, 1971.

Joint Working Party on the Rank Structure of the Police by the Police Advisory Boards of England, Wales and Scotland, 1972.

Committee on Privacy (Cmnd. 5012), H.M.S.O., 1972.

Inquiry into the Red Lion Square Disorders of 15 June 1974 (Cmnd. 5919), H.M.S.O., 1975.

White Paper, *Computers and Privacy* (Cmnd. 6353), H.M.S.O., 1975.

White Paper, *Computers: Safeguards for Privacy* (Cmnd. 6354), H.M.S.O., 1975.

Canada

Report to the Solicitor General of Ontario—Task Force on Policing in Ontario, February 1974.

France

Organization de la Police en France, Ministère de l'Intérieur, 1973.

Germany

Polizei greist ein, Leipsig, *c.* 1934.

25 Jahre Gewerkschaft der Polizei in Berlin, 1973.

125 Jahre Schutzmannschaft Berlin, 1973.

New Zealand

The New System of Policing, New Zealand Police, 27th February 1970.

National Survey of the New Zealand Police, 1972.

Annual Report of the New Zealand Police, 1975.

United States of America

National Commission on Law Observation and Enforcement, No. 14: *Report on Police*, U.S. Government, 1931.

Task Force Report No. 16, Los Angeles Police Department, 1970.

Knapp Commission, *Report on Police Corruption*, George Braziller, New York, 1973.

Team Planning Guide, Los Angeles Police Department, 1974.

Management Principles of the Los Angeles Police Department, Los Angeles Police Department, 1975.

Index

Aberdeen system of policing, 28,
    137, 141
Acceptability factor, 344–5
Accrington system of policing, 28,
    130–1, 143–6, 154
Aircraft, 137–40
Alderson, John C., 60, 332
Amalgamations of police forces, 26,
    32
American police, 55–8
Appraisal interviews, 247, 270–3
Appraisal systems, 195, 231–46
Approachability of supervisors, 293
Assessment interviews, 247, 265–70
Assessment reports, 231–42
Association of Chief Police Officers,
    31, 47
Attitudes, learning, 210
Attitude tests, 207
Authoritarian leadership, 338–42
Authority, 345–6, 354–6

Basic car plan, 147
Basic methods of policing, 131
Beat patrols, 127
Befriending people, 96
Bow Street Runners, 4
Bramshill Police College, 26, 211,
    222–5
Brown, Charles E., 118
Building design, 182–4
Bureaucracy, 67–8
Burnside, Kenneth B., 107, 150

Cadet training, 216–18
Callaghan, L. James, 108
Career development, 227–86
Career planning, 226–8
Cars, police use of, 137

Central Planning and Instructors
    Training Unit, 212–14
Chadwick, Edwin, 13
Challenor, Detective Sergeant,
    297–8
Change, introducing, 336–7
Changes within police, 26–9
Charlies, 4
Chartist Movement, 13
Chatterton, Michael, 187, 312
Chicago, 57–8
Chief Constable, role of, 38–40
Civilianisation, 28, 174–5
Civilian police staff, 169–70
Civil Service Commission, 284, 287
Classic policing systems, 140
Clerical staff, 174–5
Clow, M. J., 112
Cold Bath Fields, 11, 12
Colquhoun, Patrick, 5
Command,
    activities, 308–9
    courses, 224, 284
    structures, 146
    systems, 314–33
    systems in action, 327–33
    taking up a new, 335–7
Commitment to work, 344–5
Committee on Privacy, 178–9
Common Police Services, 211
Communication,
    barriers to, 365–9
    importance of, 364–5
    non-verbal, 253–5
    oral, 369–70, 371–6
    sources of, 328–32
    written, 370–1, 376–8
Communists, 21
Community relations, 101
Community Relations Officers, 148

Compagnies Republicaine de Sûreté, 59
Computers, 177–9
Comrie, M. D., 112
Consultation in decision making, 321
Controlling road traffic, 95
County and Borough Police Act, 1856, 14
County Councils, 40–6
County Police Act, 1839, 13
Crime,
  patrols (New Zealand), 153
  prevention, 91
  rise in, 29
Criminal Injuries Compensation Board, 290
Criminal investigation department, 167–9
Critchley, T. A., 61, 222
Criticism, giving, 266–7
Culley, Constable Robert, 11
Cumberland and Westmorland Police, 85
Cycles,
  motor, 135
  pedal, 137

Davis, Edward M., 77, 82, 148
Decision making, 309–14, 319–33
Delegation,
  acceptance of, 359–61
  controls on, 357, 361–2
  guide to, 362–3
  importance of, 357–9
  nature of, 354–6
Deputy, role of, 358–9
Desborough Committee, 18, 23, 26, 27
Detection, 92–3
Detectives, career development, 167–9
Developing skills, 210–11
Diekman, Duane, 118
Director of Public Prosecutions, 32
Discipline, 346–9
Discretionary beats, 128
District Councils, 40
District training centres, 211–12
Duty rotas, 300–1

Educational qualifications, 197

Effects of single point entry, 198–9, 277
Electronic surveillance, 132
Enforcing rules, 343
Enquiry patrols (New Zealand), 152
Entrance tests, 197
Essex County Council, 44
Establishment records, 192
Establishments, formulae for, 106–8
Examinations, promotion, 282, 286–8
Executive authority, 345–6
Extended Interview Board, 223, 283–6
Extended responsibility supervision, 147

Fascists, 21
Federal Bureau of Investigation, 55
Feed-back, 309, 313, 326–7, 372–3
Fielding, Henry, 4
Fielding, John, 4
Financial,
  planning, 189–91
  problems, 301–4
Fires, command at, 330
Fixed points, 132
Foot beats, 126–31, 133
Forecasting manpower needs, 193–4
Forensic laboratories, 23
Forms, design of, 181
France,
  governmental system, 58
  policing system, 1800, 6
French Revolution, 6

Geheime Staatspolizei (Gestapo), 54–5
Gendarmerie Nationale, 59
General knowledge questions, 259–60
General strike, 21
Germany, 52–5
Goodhart, Dr. Arthur, 30–1, 52
Gordon Riots, 4
Göring, Hermann, 54
Graduate Entry Scheme, 223, 284
Gurney, Miss Catherine, 304

Halo effect on assessment, 242
Health, 192, 295–301
Helicopters, 137–40

Hendon,
Police College, 198, 222
Training School, 212
Highway patrols (New Zealand), 153
Hilfspolizei, 53
Hilton, Jennifer, 312
Himmler, Heinrich, 54
H.M. Inspectors of Constabulary, 14, 37–8, 183
Holt, A., 117
Home Office, 8, 23
Research and Planning Branch, 106, 143
Home Secretary, 37, 42, 46, 192, 200, 202, 212, 214, 303
powers of, 37
Horses, police, 137
Housing, police, 306–7
Hue and cry, 2, 3

Immigration, 25
Incident patrols (New Zealand), 153
Independence of police, 60–1
Inspectors' course, 224
Institute of Public Relations, 186
Interchange between departments, 167
International Computers Limited, 178
Interviewing, general principles, 248–53
Interviews,
appraisal, 247, 270–3
assessment, 247, 265–70
problem-solving, 247, 273–6
selection, 247, 255–64
In-trays, contents of, 181
Introducing change, 336

James, Mr. A. E., Q.C., 297
Job descriptions, 174–5, 193
Judge, Anthony, 108
Justices of the Peace, 2, 7–8

Kansas City Preventive Patrol Experiment, 115–20
Kelling, George L., 118
Kenny, John P., 106
Kings, E., 112
Knapp Commission, 57
Knowledge of results, 210–11

Lancashire Constabulary, 143
Law and order, 43, 88–9
Leadership,
balanced, 351–3
need for, 334–5
participative, 342–4
styles of, 338–42
Lea, M. J., 117
Learning, 209–10
Lefevre, Sir Charles Shaw, 13
Lessons of police history, 1
Listening, 251, 274–6
Liverpool, police strike in, 19
Lloyd George, D., 18
Local government, 7, 40
Local Government Act, 1972, 32–3
London,
beat system 1900, 126
growth and development, 3–5
police strike in, 19
London Government Act, 1963, 33
Los Angeles Police Department, 77–83, 147–9

McDonald, A. J., 117
McNee, Sir David, 343
Macro approach to policing systems, 157
Management,
by exception, 358
by objectives, 82
by participation, 82
Manpower planning, 163, 192
Manual personnel, 174
Mark, Sir Robert, 184–5
Mayne, Richard, 10, 82, 148
Measurement of police activity, 109–13
Measuring,
crime, 94–5
police effectiveness, 113–18
Mechanisation, 175–9
Mental strain, 296–9
Merseyside Police, 178
Metropolitan Police,
Commissioner of, 38, 61
formation of, 10
organisation, 1830, 62–4
promotion system, 286–7
Special Patrol Group, 142
Micro approach to policing system, 155
Middlesex Justices Act, 4

Modern approach to policing, 99–101
Morale, 349–51
Motor cycles, 135–6
Motorways, policing of, 165
Mullett, A. A., 112
Municipal Corporation Act, 1835, 12

National,
    Association of Local Government Officers, 325
    Council for Civil Liberties, 21, 306
    Front, 34
    police force, considerations, 51–2
    Police Fund, 303
    Socialists (Nazis), 52–5, 60
    Union of the Working Classes, 11
News, 185–6
New York Police Department, 56–8
New Zealand police, 107, 149–55
Non-verbal communication, 253–5
Normal distribution curve, 243–4

Oaksey Committee, 27, 289, 304–5
Objectives of policing, 102–4
    early, 86
    Royal Commission, 1960, 87–8
    Scottish, 87
Office of Operations, Los Angeles, 80
Ontario, policing in, 97—9
On-the-job training, 213–16
Organisational precepts, 78
Organisation charts, 75
Organisations,
    early police, 63
    modern British, 64
    nature of, 62
    relationships within, 71–6
    theory of, 70–1
Over-confidence, 267–8

Panda cars, 144
Paper flow, 180–1
Participative leadership, 342–4
Pate, Tony, 118
Patrols, foot, 127–33
Pedal cycles, 136
Peel, Robert, 10, 16, 148
Pension, qualification for, 193–4
Perception, 366–7

Personnel,
    department, 191–2
    assessment, 224–6
    assessment, a Scottish view, 239–40
    policies, 195, 226–7
    records, 192–3
    reports, 231, 242
Pickets, 34
Pitt, William, 4
Points, fixed, 132
Police,
    Advisory Boards, 31, 64, 239
    and democracy, 51
    authorities, 41–7
    cadets, 200–3, 216–18
    College,
        Metropolitan, 198, 222
        National (Bramshill), 26, 211, 222–5
    Complaints Board, 32, 46
    convalescent homes, 304
    Council, 31
    deployment, 121 et seq.
    Dependants Trust, 303
    establishments, 105, 189–91
    Federation, 19, 27, 48–9, 97, 222, 223, 290, 298, 306, 321, 325
    Foundation, 117–19
    Gazette, 4
    Nationale, 58–9
    national v. local, 51–61
    pay, 16, 18
    Post-war Committee, 128
    Promotion Examination Board, 287
    Regulations, 292
    Review, 17
    strikes, 17–19
    Union, 18
    Urbaine, 59
    War Reserve, 22
Police Act,
    1919, 19
    1946, 26
    1964, 31, 36–42, 48–9, 290
    1976, 32, 46
Policy decisions, 322, 331
Politics, police and, 49–50, 56, 60–1
Potential for promotion, 234–6
Préfets, 6, 58–9
Presidents Commission on Law Enforcement, 115

Press, *see* public media
Preventive patrol, measurement of, 112
Primary routes, policing of, 165
Priorities of policing, 97
Pro-active policing, 115, 152, 154
Probationer constables, 228–31
Problem-solving interviews, 247, 273–6
Promotion,
    potential, 234–6
    selection systems, 276–88
Propaganda, 186
Public,
    demand, 121
    media and police, 26, 184–6, 330–1
    order, 20
    relations, 184–8
Publicity, recruiting, 203–5
Punishment, effects of, 348–9

Queen's Peace, 89

Radio, *see* public media
Random patrols, impact of, 120–1
Rank structure, 64–5, 278–81
Rapid-decision leadership, 342–3
Reactive police response, 115, 152, 154
Recruiting, 196–208
    publicity, 203
Red Lion Square, 22, 137
Relating police methods to needs, 155–8
Resource allocation, 324
Retirement, 193–4
Revenue estimates, 190
Ring leaders, 337
Risk and decision making, 323–4
Road traffic, controlling, 95
Rowan, Charles, 10, 13, 82, 84, 85, 148
Royal Canadian Mounted Police, 97
Royal Commission,
    1929, 23
    1960, 27, 30–1, 44, 46–7, 87–8, 89, 90, 198, 200, 306, 312
Rule of law, 89
Rules and regulations, 75, 346–9
Rural,
    beats, 128

motor patrols, 117
policing, formula for, 107

Scarman, Lord Justice, 137, 142
Schedules of beats, 127
School liaison schemes, 100
Scotland, 1603–1800, 9–10
Scottish Home Department, 239
Selection,
    boards, 260–4
    interviews, 247, 255–64
    methods, recruits, 205–8
Self reporting cards, 112
Sergeant, role of, 220
Shift work, 299–301
Skilled civilian personnel, 175
Social,
    change, 23–6
    violence, 33–4
Spa Fields, 11
Special,
    Constabulary, 22
    Course, 223–4, 284
    patrol group, 142
Specialisation, 68–9, 162
Specialist departments, growth of, 159–62
Specialists, numbers of, 123
Specialist training, 218
Standards, change in public, 24
Statistics, use of, 114
Streamlining procedures, 179–82
Strikes by police, 17–19, 49
Superintendents Association, 19, 48, 223, 321, 325
Supervision of probationers, 228–31
Supervisors,
    welfare role, 291–4
    responsibility for training, 215
Supervisory checks, 173
Supervisory ranks, numbers of, 123
Supervisory training, 218–25
Support services, 152

Task forces, 141
Team policing, 76, 141
Television, *see* public media
Territorial imperative, 148
Terrorism, 34
Thames River Police, 5
Time, value of, 176
Trade unions, police, 48–50

Traffic,
    departments, 164–6
    duty, operational, 164–6
    growth of, 20
    management, 166
    wardens, 170
Training,
    on-the-job, 213–16
    probationer, 211–16
    specialist, 218
    steps in, 215
    supervisory, 218–25
Training by objectives, 212–13
Training needs, identifying, 234
Trenchard, Lord, 198, 222
Twentyman, G. E., 153

Uncertainty and decision making,
    323–4
Uniformed police, aims of, 132
Unit beat policing, 28, 130–1,
    143–6, 154
United States of America, 55–8
Urban foot patrols, effects of, 117
Urban policing, formula for, 106

Vans, police, 137
Village policemen, 123

War Office Selection Board, 283–4
Wastage, police, 194
Wasted effort, 171–4
Watch and ward, 1
Watch Committees, 12
Welfare, 232, 236, 273–6, 289–307
    officers, 289
Wilson, O. W., 58
Winchester, Statute of, 1
Wireless depots, 23
Work groups, 337
Working Party,
    on Manpower, 194, 198
    on Operational Efficiency and
        Management, 129–30
    on Police Cadets, 201, 216
Work load studies, 110–13
Work performance, 268–70

Younger, Sir Kenneth, 178